A LIFE OF
ARCHBISHOP PARKER

A LIFE OF
ARCHBISHOP PARKER

BY

V. J. K. BROOK

CLARENDON PRESS · OXFORD

1962

Oxford University Press, Amen House, London E.C.4

GLASGOW NEW YORK TORONTO MELBOURNE WELLINGTON
BOMBAY CALCUTTA MADRAS KARACHI LAHORE DACCA
CAPE TOWN SALISBURY NAIROBI IBADAN ACCRA
KUALA LUMPUR HONG KONG

PRINTED AND BOUND IN ENGLAND BY
HAZELL WATSON AND VINEY LTD
AYLESBURY AND SLOUGH

CONTENTS

I   Youth and Early Years at Cambridge   1

II   Cambridge and Stoke-by-Clare   13

III   Master of Corpus and Vice-Chancellor   23

IV   Parker under Edward VI and Mary   35

V   The Elizabethan Settlement   55

VI   The Archbishop and his Task   81

VII   Early Efforts for Order and Uniformity   100

VIII   Royal Intervention: Romanist Troubles   115

IX   Parliament and Convocation of 1563: The Articles   127

X   Parker in his Diocese   142

XI   Recusants and Protestants: The Universities   157

XII   The Advertisements: Their Results   183

XIII   Parliament of 1566: Growing Restlessness   206

XIV   University and Routine Business: the Bishops' Bible   229

XV   Visitation of Canterbury Cathedral; Parliament and Convocation of 1571: Articles and Canons   250

XVI   Mild Repression: the Northampton Model and the Prophesyings; Admonition to the Parliament, 1572   273

XVII   Parker Strives for Order; his Difficulties; Spread of Presbyterian views   292

XVIII   Parker and the Queen: Her Visit to Canterbury; the *De Antiquitate*; Norwich Matters and Prophesyings   314

XIX   Puritan Vigour: Unhappy closing Months   331

Index   347

CHAPTER I

YOUTH AND EARLY YEARS AT CAMBRIDGE

MATTHEW PARKER was born on 6 Aug. 1504, third son of William Parker of Norwich and his wife Alice Monins or Monings. The family was entitled to bear arms and seems to have been in comfortable circumstances. William's grandfather, Nicolas, had been Registrar to the Archbishop of Canterbury from 1450 to 1483[1] and had lived in London. It is not known when the family moved to Norwich, but by 1504 William was settled there as a worsted weaver, married to a member of a well-established Norfolk family which had provided at least one knight of the shire. He died in 1516 and his will[2] shows him to have been a man of piety as well as of substance. There were six children of the marriage—two boys who died in youth older than Matthew, and two younger. Of one of these nothing is known save that he became a cleric. The other, Thomas, rose to be sheriff of Norwich in 1558 and Mayor in 1568. The sixth child was a daughter who died unmarried. Shortly after her husband's death, Alice Parker married John Baker of Norfolk. Their son, John, was a close friend of the Archbishop during his life and was one of his executors.

The main source of information about Parker's early days and education is a parchment preserved at Corpus Christi College, Cambridge, containing his own Memoranda. It appears that the first part of it was drawn up in 1554, and that later additions were made chiefly by himself, though one or two interpolations are in

---

[1] Strype, *Parker* i, 4: all references to Strype are to the Clarendon Press Edition, 1812–24.

[2] Quoted by W. M. Kennedy, *Archbishop Parker* (London, 1908), p. 287.

another hand.[1] He was born, he writes, in the parish of Saint
Saviour, brought up in the parish of All Saints near Fye-bridge
gates, educated in the parish of St. Clement near Fye-bridge. It
is possibly a fair inference from the last statement that he was at
a grammar school in that parish. But it is not certain; he does not
himself say so, but merely gives a list of his teachers (mostly
clerics) in various subjects—reading, writing, singing and grammar (the last 'an easy and kind schoolmaster'); the first in the
list is the rector of St. Clements, which would well accord
with the view that he went to school in that parish. But the point
is obscure. The Latin life by Joscelyn[2] says that his parents
arranged for his education 'domi suae', which might mean only
that he was living at home not away, but would most naturally
suggest home-tuition. Strype explicitly says that Neve, the
master for grammar, 'was provided to teach him at home',[3]
though without giving any evidence. Possibly the implication
intended is that he attended a school for the other subjects, but
Strype does not say so, only that 'he had several masters for his
education in several faculties'. Thus though all the evidence
agrees that great care was taken for his education, it cannot be
definitely known whether it was by attendance at a grammar
school or by a number of different tutors.

At about the age of seventeen or eighteen he was sent to
Cambridge, to Corpus Christi or Benet College, at his mother's
charges.[4] He was elected to a Bible-clerkship in March 1521.

---

[1] The Latin is printed in an appendix to the *Correspondence* (Parker
Society; J. Bruce and T. T. Perowne; Cambridge, 1853), and an English
translation in the Introduction to the same volume.

[2] This life, written by his chaplain Joscelyn under Parker's instruction,
was intended to be added to the lives of the Sixty-nine Archbishops of
Canterbury included in the *De Antiquitate*, to some, though not most,
editions of which it is added. It is printed in Strype's *Parker* iii, 269 sq., and
is commonly referred to as *Matthaeus*. Strype points out that some corrections and erasures of laudatory passages were probably due to Parker's
modesty, for he presumably looked over it when complete. If there really
was such editing, the factual part of the life should be trustworthy as 'passed'
by the Archbishop himself.   [3] *Parker* i, 8.

[4] *Correspondence*, p. 481. '1522 8 Septembr. circa am aetatis meae 17 missus
Cantabrigiam'. This statement in the *Memoranda* presents difficulties, for

At first he resided in St. Mary's Hostel, some little way from Benet College, used by it as a subsidiary house. Later he was in the college itself. His instruction was in dialectics and philosophy under a tutor whom he describes as 'of small learning'. After

in September 1522 Parker would be in his nineteenth year. Strype i, 8 gives the date as 1520 when, in fact, Parker would be in his seventeenth year. Strype's statement is supported by the *Cambridge Grace Book*, B. ii, 86 (ed. Bateson; Cambridge, 1905), which at the end of the entries for 1519–20 adds: 'Memorandum quod Matthaeus Parker Archiepiscopus Cantuariensis venit Cantabrigiam in nundinis Styrbrigiensibus Anno Domini 1520 die vero Martii 20 (ut monumenta Collegii Corporis Chrisit referunt), is electus fuit alter Bibliotistarum ejusdem collegii.' It seems to be almost certain that Strype was relying on this statement, for he identifies the year as remarkable for the erection of the rood screen in St. Mary's, 'theatrum imaginis cricifixi', which is also mentioned in the same words in the same context in the Grace Book. This would suggest that Parker entered Corpus in September (the month of Styrbridge Fair) 1520 and was elected to a Bible-clerkship in the following March. Unfortunately, the college records now extant contain no reference to that election. But Mr. H. C. Porter, Fellow of the College, who has examined the evidence of the college records, has discovered that Parker's name first appears in the college accounts on Lady Day 1521, which would be entirely natural if he had, five days before, just been made a Bible-clerk. This seems to rule out September 1521 or 1522 for his matriculation, and to confirm Strype's date.

The only difficulty in accepting this dating is Parker's own statement. But there is evidence that he contradicted himself in the matter. There is a note, apparently in Parker's own hand, to a document of 1521 which reads 'Hoc anno in festo Nativitatis beatae Mariae M.P. accessit Cantabrigiam' (*Correspondence*, p. vi). Many modern authorities accept this—the Parker Society editors, Lamb, Kennedy; while Mullinger sticks to 1522. But in view of Parker's self-contradiction it looks as though he may have forgotten the exact year—a supposition which is supported by the vague statement of the *Matthaeus* that Parker was educated at home till his seventeenth or eighteenth year (Strype, *Parker* iii, 275), a statement which Joscelyn presumably drew from Parker himself. It seems safest therefore to rely on the University Grace Book and the college accounts, and to conclude that Strype is right in his dating of September 1520.

There is one small piece of corroborative evidence. The *Matthaeus* (ibid.) says that he took his B.A. more than three but less than four years after going to Cambridge. Parker himself in the *Memoranda* (*Correspondence*, p. 481) says that was 1525, and the *Athenae Cantabrigienses* accepted that date—which would make the matriculation in 1521. But the Grace Book (ut supra, 86 and 113) is quite explicit that the degree was in 1524, apparently giving an official degree list. The summer of that year would be between three and four years from September 1520.

taking his B.A. he continued, in the usual way, his course for
M.A., which he received in 1527. Meantime, he had already
been admitted to Orders. In December 1526 he was made sub-
deacon under the titles of Barnwell and the Chapel in the Fields,
Norwich.[1] The latter was a fully organized corporate institution,
with a dean, treasurer, prebendaries and lay associates who
shared a common table and collegiate life.[2] If Parker's membership of it was more than merely nominal it must have given him
an insight into the life and potentialities of such a foundation
which would be valuable later when he himself became dean of a
similar college at Stoke-by-Clare. The next year he was made
deacon in April and priest in June. In September he was elected
a Fellow of Corpus, thus joining the governing body of which he
was to remain a member for over a quarter of a century. His Arts
course over, he turned to the study of Theology, chiefly the
orthodox fathers and the Councils,[3] took his B.D. in 1535 and his
Doctorate in 1538. Already, however, he had been noticed as a
promising young man, for he was one of those invited by Wolsey
in 1525 to go to Oxford as a member of Cardinal College[4]—an
invitation he refused, like Cranmer, though several did go from
Cambridge. Parker, typically, preferred the quiet life of study in
Cambridge to what must have been the appearance of pioneering
work in Oxford. He did not even start his career as preacher so
soon as might have been expected. Though priested in 1527 it
was not until the Advent of 1533 that he 'entered on the office of
preaching'—his own words[5]—and delivered five sermons in or
near Cambridge. By then, he had a public diploma from the
King and the licence of the Archbishop:[6] but it is difficult to
suppose that had he really pressed the point he would not have
been given permission to preach until he had been six years in
the priesthood. It looks as though he was mainly concerned
to acquire the sound foundations of theological and ecclesias-

[1] *Correspondence*, p. vii.
[2] F. Blomefield, *History of Norfolk* (Norwich, 1745), ii, 607.
[3] *Matthaeus*, Strype, *Parker* iii, 275.
[4] Strype, *Parker* i, 10.   [5] *Correspondence*, p. vii.
[6] *Matthaeus*, Strype, *Parker* iii, 275.

tical learning which were to be of inestimable value later on.

Such, in bare outline, is the story of Parker's early life; it suggests a normal course of placid preparation for an ecclesiastical career. Indeed, the *Matthaeus* refers to it as a time of 'shaded leisure'. But the Cambridge of his day was agitated by arguments and passions to which a sensitive and sincere man could not remain indifferent. It was his lot, says Strype[1] 'to fall into the University in those days when learning and religion began to dawn there'. Just before his matriculation, the introduction of the study of Greek into the English universities had been violently but unsuccessfully opposed: conservative theologians had feared (not without cause) the effect on the traditional scholastic theology which might follow the study of the early Greek fathers in the original tongue. In Oxford there were serious and unseemly troubles only restrained in the end by the interposition of More, the Chancellor, and a royal letter of 1519 ordering that all students who wished to study Greek should be allowed to do so.[2] At Cambridge the opposition was not so unruly. Still, Erasmus, who was Margaret Lecturer there in 1511-14, had little popular acceptance when he offered to teach Greek, and it was not till 1519 that hostile prejudice was conquered. In that year Richard Croke of King's, who had studied both at Oxford and abroad and had won for himself a considerable reputation on the Continent, delivered an inaugural lecture in favour of the study of Greek. It was so persuasive and convincing that he was elected Public Orator for life.[3] By 1520, therefore, in both universities the battle for Greek had really been won. But the passions roused by it were almost immediately absorbed into the still more bitter struggle about religion.

How far the reform movement in Cambridge was a native growth and how far it was dependent on Lutheran teaching has been endlessly argued. But it is at least certain that Erasmus' New Testament of 1516 was a fundamental and pervasive factor.

---

[1] *Parker* i, 12.
[2] J. B. Mullinger, *History of the University of Cambridge* (3 Vols., Cambridge, 1873-1911), i, 526.   [3] Ibid., pp. 527, 539.

It was the first Greek text to be printed, and was accompanied by a new Latin translation; it won wide commendation even from men such as Fisher and Tunstall whose allegiance to Rome hardly faltered. It was to the study of Erasmus' Latin version, not to Luther, that Thomas Bilney, the admitted reforming leader in Cambridge, attributed his conversion. His own account of this is given in a letter to Tunstall,[1] the general veneration for whom he obviously shared. He had heard, he says, that the New Testament of Erasmus was eloquently done, and so, 'allured by the Latin', he bought it 'even by the providence of God as I do now well understand and perceive'. In reading it, he chanced upon the saying (1 Tim. i, 15) that Christ Jesus came to save sinners and 'immediately I felt a marvellous comfort and quietness'. From that time, the Scripture 'began to be more pleasant unto me than honey or the honey-comb'. For he learned that forgiveness depended not on fasting and watching, on masses and pardons, but that Christ alone saves from sin. So far the parallel with Luther is strikingly complete. Both were obsessed with a sense of sin which was unrelieved by the remedies, confession and absolution and mass, customarily offered by the Church. To both came peace and glorious confidence from a study of St. Paul. Both alike concentrated, perhaps too exclusively, on that part of St. Paul's teaching which was as balm to a soul stricken by consciousness of sin. Such agreement as there is in their teaching does not necessarily prove the dependence of one on the other. It may be due merely to a common grasp of what is, after all, a central part of Paulinism.

In other respects the two men were very different. There was in Bilney none of the violence, the coarseness, the robust acceptance of the good things of this world which Luther showed. He had not the strength and self-reliance which we usually associate with leadership. He was a quiet, rather timid, gentle man whose influence on his friends was due to his sheer simplicity and goodness and love. He was fitted to be an inspiring model rather

[1] *Acts and Monuments*, of John Foxe (ed. G. Townsend; 8 Vols., London, 1843), iv, 635.

than a protagonist. To the end he was an ascetic who took little food or sleep; he was sensitive and highly strung, with a dislike of music which, even in an unmusical man, amounted to abnormality. Though driven in the end by conscience to invite martyrdom, he was usually hesitant and unsure of himself. His views come out very clearly in his letter to Tunstall. He does not condemn out of hand such 'works' as pilgrimages, the buying of pardons, the offering of candles, but he is disturbed by the impression such things may produce that man must depend on his own efforts and not alone on Christ. He even pleads to be allowed to speak privately to Tunstall about his preaching, plainly regarding him as a kindly man 'who (except I be utterly deceived) will not break the reed that is bruised'. 'If I shall be found in any error (as indeed I am a man) you, as spiritual, shall restore me through the spirit of gentleness.' Throughout there is deep personal humility, a reluctance to find himself at odds with the Church of his day, combined with a conviction which will not be silenced that the Church was not really doing what it should. The clergy were ignorant of the Scriptures and were neglecting their chief duty. Their business was not merely to minister the sacraments and consecrate wood, stones and churchyards but primarily to teach and preach the free forgiveness of sin through the cross of Christ.

There is no need to suppose that such teaching could only have been derived from Luther. It might spring from simple meditation on parts of the New Testament. Certainly Bilney honestly thought that in his case it had done so. At his trial in 1527, of which there is the official account in Tunstall's register,[1] he not only agreed that Luther was a wicked and detestable heretic, but allowed many things which Luther rejected with contumely—the authority, for example, of Councils, and the duty of obedience to prelates and bishops as unto parents. He did not even explicitly reject papal pardons, which had so much enraged Luther, though he thought they had been abused and should no longer be used 'to the injury of Christ's passion'. It

[1] Quoted in Foxe, iv, 619-40.

is true that he was at the time on his trial and was probably both frightened and confused. But it is significant that even the depositions laid against him by his accusers contain no suggestion that he had seriously questioned either the central authority or the faith of the Catholic Church. He had mainly spoken against teaching and customs which even good churchmen agreed were liable to abuse—stress on the intercession of saints, on pilgrimages, on local miracles such as those at Walsingham and, of course, on human merit. Indeed the official account of his trial seems entirely to justify Foxe's verdict[1] that 'the whole sum of his preaching and doctrine' was 'chiefly against idolatry, invocation of saints, vain worship of images, false trust in men's merits and such other gross points of religion, as seemed prejudicial and derogatory to the blood of our Saviour Jesus Christ. As touching the mass and sacrament of the altar, as he never varied from himself, so likewise he never differed therein from the most gross Catholics.' Nor did he ever directly challenge the fundamental authority of Rome. Despite his insistence on free forgiveness through Christ, he even admitted[2] that 'priests alone, duly ordained by bishops, have the keys, by virtue of which they bind and loose (the key not erring); which also I do not doubt that they do even though they be sinners. For the unworthiness of ministers does not lessen much less destroy the efficacy of sacraments, so long as they are allowed by the Church.'

In fact Bilney's position seems to have been no more hostile to Rome than that, for example, of Colet with his vigorous criticism of Aquinas and his attack, before Convocation in 1511, on clerical lives. Certainly Bilney expressed himself with less venom and ridicule than Erasmus in his *Praise of Folly*. None the less he was put on trial as a heretic. Presumably, since the outbreak of Luther, the ecclesiastical authorities were much more sensitive and frightened than they had been. And, on the other hand, Bilney's criticisms were in a way more dangerous than previous attacks in England. They were contained not in addresses to Convocation nor in books which only the educated would see,

[1] Foxe, iv, 649.   [2] Ibid.

but in popular sermons to ordinary men. He just could not be allowed to go up and down the country publicly saying such things. He was found guilty and forced to recant and undergo public penance at St. Paul's Cross. He was then forgiven but condemned to imprisonment during Wolsey's pleasure. After confinement for about a year, he was set free and returned to Cambridge. But he was a broken, uneasy man, distressed by the memory of his recantation. His friends, says Latimer, were afraid to leave him by himself.[1] In 1531 he left Trinity Hall (of which he was Fellow) to 'go to Jerusalem', as he said. He returned to his native Norfolk to preach in Norwich, was arrested and burned there. His enemies said that he made a further recantation 'many days' before his death. But Foxe denies it and produces a good deal of evidence from the Mayor and aldermen of Norwich to support his view.[2]

In Cambridge Bilney became the centre of a group zealous for reform. Thomas Arthur, also a native of Norfolk, afterwards on trial with Bilney, 'imbibed Protestant opinions from his fellow-countryman Bilney'.[3] He was Principal of St. Mary's Hostel in 1518, though it is not known whether he was still so when Parker became an inmate. With them was associated George Stafford of Pembroke who, as lecturer in theology, based his instructions on the Scriptures rather than on the schoolmen, and Thixtill of Pembroke. By them 'with the assistance of Master Fooke of Benet College and Master Soud, master of the same college: to whom also were then associate Master Parker and Master Powry',[4] Richard Barnes, Prior of the Augustinian Friars, was won over to become a forceful if incautious advocate of reform. Soon afterwards Hugh Latimer was drawn into the circle. Noted for his piety—he was official cross-bearer to the University—his exercise for B.D. was an attack on Melanchthon. Bilney, says Latimer,[5] 'heard me . . . and perceived that I was

---

[1] *Sermons of Latimer* (ed. by G. E. Corrie, Parker Society, Cambridge, 1844), p. 222.   [2] Foxe, iv, 761–2.

[3] C. H and T. Cooper, *Athenae Cantabrigienses* (2 Vols., Cambridge, 1858, 1861), i, 46.   [4] Foxe, iv, 620.   [5] Latimer, *Sermons*, p. 334.

zealous without knowledge: and he came to me afterward in my study, and desired me, for God's sake, to hear his confession. I did so, and, to say the truth, by his confession I learned more than before in many years. So that from that time forward I began to smell the word of God.' His forceful and telling sermons at once became an important influence. Others too were in the group, such as John Lambert, Fellow of Queens'.[1] They met together for study and discussion at the White Horse Inn and were notable for the discipline of their lives and their practical good works. What he saved by his ascetic life Bilney gave to the needy; he and Latimer and others were assiduous in visiting the sick and the prisons. Indeed in 1529 Stafford died from plague caught on such a visit.

The growing company soon became suspect. The White Horse Inn gained the name of 'Germany', since it was common knowledge that the writings of Luther were read there. For although his works were officially condemned in England in 1521, and were publicly burned in Oxford and Cambridge as well as in London, they still circulated. It would be quite absurd to suggest that they were not studied by, and influential with, the Cambridge reformers, who would find in them much that was congenial even if they did not draw their original impulse from them. Certainly Luther does not seem to have been regarded as an infallible authority. As was shown at his trial, Bilney did not follow him blindly, nor did Parker, nor at first even Barnes, though later he became even more radical than Luther. It looks as though Luther's writings were studied keenly and sympathetically but not uncritically. But the fact that they were studied at all would be sufficient to antagonize the conservative party.

The beginnings of the movement in Cambridge may be assigned with some certainty to the years 1520-5. Bilney was not ordained priest until 1519, when his orthodoxy was presumably unquestioned; and as late as 1525 he was still sufficiently approved to receive a preaching licence from West, the conservative Bishop of Ely. But by that year the Bishop was already uneasy

---

[1] Mullinger, i, 573, where are also other names.

about Latimer, and appeared without previous notice when he was to preach from the University pulpit. On seeing him, Latimer at once abandoned his prepared sermon and delivered one which was quite unimpeachable. Invited thereupon by the Bishop to preach against Luther he parried by saying that it was not permissible to read his works (though presumably he must have studied Melanchthon before attacking him in his exercise for the B.D.[1]). The Bishop could not take drastic action, but he did shortly afterwards inhibit Latimer from preaching either in the diocese or from the University pulpit, a measure which was quickly made ineffective by Wolsey, who gave Latimer his own licence. Matters were brought to a head at the end of the year by a violent and incautious sermon by Barnes on Christmas Eve. He made the tactical mistake of attacking not only clergy and bishops but even the pomp and magnificence of Wolsey himself. Two attempts to secure his condemnation in Cambridge were foiled by noisy demonstrations of his partisans, but Wolsey was now roused to action. He sent officers to Cambridge to collect Lutheran books and arrest Barnes.[2] Warned by the President of Queens' of what was coming, the White Horse Inn party managed to conceal their books, but Barnes was arrested and taken to London. Examined first before the Cardinal and then by a group of bishops, he was forced to make a public recantation before Wolsey and a great assembly. Even after it he was kept under restraint till he managed to escape to the Continent. In his own account of his trial, Barnes insists that though he was condemned as a Lutheran he was in fact not so—a statement which, in view of his later radical development, is presumably trustworthy. His flight from England separated from the Cambridge group a difficult and outspoken member but did not remove suspicion of them. Not only were Bilney and Arthur tried in London in 1527, but in the course of their trial it emerged that even before that Bilney had been forced to take an oath not to preach any of Luther's opinions.

In so far as all this happened during Parker's early years at

[1] Mullinger, i, 583.   [2] Ibid., i, 578.

Cambridge it was inevitable that he should be affected. Despite his quiet and studious disposition, and his life-long dislike of agitators and fanatics, he was too honest and thoughtful to be able to ignore the issues which were being argued. Moreover they would be emphatically pressed on his notice by two circumstances. Many of the White Horse leaders were, like Parker, men of Norfolk. Bilney, Arthur, Thixtill, Barnes, Lambert, Sowode (Foxe's Soud), Forman of Queens' were all of the diocese of Norwich. County loyalty was strong: Parker could hardly have failed to hear what was going on. And, secondly, official influence must have tended in the same direction. Arthur was Master of St. Mary's Hostel in 1518 and may still have been so when Parker arrived; Sowode (or Soud) became Master of Corpus in 1523 and remained so till 1544 when he was succeeded by Parker. Everything would conspire to draw him to the White Horse Inn, and there is no reason to doubt that almost from the beginning he was one of the group, though it is a little hard to believe that, as an undergraduate, he had sufficient weight, as Foxe suggests, to be influential in the conversion of Barnes.[1] But he was certainly so devoted to Bilney as to journey to Norwich to be present at his martyrdom in 1531. On the other hand, he does not seem to have drawn on himself the hostile attention of the conservatives. Perhaps this was partly because he was still engaged in his theological studies and had not yet begun to preach, partly because he did not indulge in the oddities of Bilney or the indiscretions of Barnes. But his friendship was firmly with the critics of the contemporary Roman Church and it no doubt added interest and practical point to his study of the Councils and the Fathers which was to lay a solid foundation for his later approach to the problems he had to face as Archbishop.

[1] Foxe, iv, 620.

CHAPTER II

CAMBRIDGE AND STOKE-BY-CLARE

PARKER'S first sermons at the end of 1533 were delivered in ordinary parish churches in Cambridge and neighbouring villages.[1] But once he had, so to speak, emerged from his study, his rise to prominence both as preacher and administrator was quick. The reason lay more in the circumstances of the time than in any ambition of his own. Once he was licensed to preach he was eager to do it; but there is no evidence that he was desirous of great responsibility or high office. Soon after he had lost all his preferments and retired into obscurity under Queen Mary, he wrote (October 1554)[2] 'After this I lived as a private individual, so happy before God in my conscience, and so far from being either ashamed or dejected, that the delightful literary leisure to which the good providence of God recalled me yielded me much greater and more solid enjoyments than my former busy and dangerous kind of life had ever afforded me.' Nor did his life of obscurity and danger under Queen Mary change his views. When, under Queen Elizabeth, he realized that the authorities designed high office for him, he wrote to Bacon that he wished 'to be no further abled but by the revenue of some prebend (without charge of cure or of government) to occupy myself to dispense God's reverend word amongst the simple strayed sheep of God's fold, in poor destitute parishes and cures, more meet for my decayed voice, and small quality, than in theatrical and great audience'.[3] He would prefer, he said, the Mastership of Benet College at twenty nobles a year to the Deanery of Lincoln at two hundred. There is no reason to question the sincerity of such sentiments: they are typical of all we know of him.

[1] *Memoranda: Correspondence*, p. vii.   [2] Ibid., p. viii.
[3] Ibid., pp. 50–51.

But by the end of 1533 the position was such that the authorities could not afford to waste the services of so promising a young man who was known to be sympathetic to Bilney and the rest of the Cambridge reform party. King Henry had now married Anne Boleyn and the Princess Elizabeth had been born, the marriage to Katharine having been pronounced by Cranmer invalid. In reply the Pope had excommunicated Henry in July. It is almost certain that the King still hoped that the breach might be healed. As late as December there was an attempt at reconciliation. If the Pope would recognize the nullity of his marriage with Katharine and the validity of that with Anne, the King was prepared not to destroy the papal authority in England. But no agreement could be reached. Therefore, in 1534, a series of Acts of Parliament sealed the separation from Rome. The King was declared 'the only supreme head in earth of the Church in England' and equipped with full visitatorial powers. Provisions were made for the regular functioning of the Church without any regard to Rome—for the appointment of bishops, for the payment of tithes, even for the customary dispensations and so on. No change was made (nor presumably intended) either in doctrine or the services in church. Save for the elimination of papal authority and jurisdiction, things were to go on as before. All the bishops save Fisher were apparently at least content. But that did not really settle the matter. How far the laity at large were aware of what was going on it is impossible to decide. There had been disputes before this between kings and popes which had not ended in permanent estrangement: and there was a good deal of anti-clerical feeling. So most of the laity were quiescent (except More). None the less, in all probability, there was a very deep underlying general allegiance to Rome among devout laymen which was shared by the conservative clergy and felt consciously and enthusiastically by the monks. If the new arrangements were to have popular and wide-spread acceptance, the King and Cromwell and Cranmer needed all the support they could find. It is easy to see why Parker was so quickly marked out for preferment.

Parker himself gives a list of his sermons after the first parochial ones, which is curious but significant.[1] The first he mentions was in 1534 at the episcopal visitation of Balsham. The
rest, under Henry VIII, were all royal occasions—before Princess
Elizabeth (aged about two!) in 1535, before the King and Court
in Lent, before Prince Edward, and again before Elizabeth in
1540. The list is demonstrably incomplete, and one can only
suppose that those occasions stayed in his mind as memorable
(he was, after all, human). But at least they show that he had
won notice in high quarters. But there were other sermons, too.
Cromwell 'for the honest report of your learning in holy letters
and uncorrupt judgement in the same' appointed him to take his
turn as preacher at Paul's Cross in September 1537.[2] There is a
Grace of 1536 to allow him to remain covered when preaching at
Cambridge because of some head trouble:[3] evidently his sermons
were well liked there and it was desired that they should not be
prevented. When he became Dean of Stoke-by-Clare he seems to
have been a regular preacher there. Indeed, he held that 'there
can be no better service to God than sincerely to declare his will
and pleasure, no sacrifice more acceptable than to convert the
hearts of his reasonable creatures'.[4] His preaching was effective;
those who did not like the new state of things tried to silence
him by delation to the Lord Chancellor.[5] The impression one
gets is that he was, as we say, a good preacher, used on occasion
by the authorities (and duly gratified to remember the fact) but
more happy to serve in simpler congregations. About this time,
indeed, Latimer wrote to him to 'show thyself to the world . . .
what you can do is known: see to it that your will is no less than
your ability'.[6]

Apart from his preaching, Parker was also in other ways
becoming a marked man. In March 1535 he was summoned to
the court of Queen Anne Boleyn and made one of her chaplains.
It was apparently supposed that this would give him real influence

[1] *Correspondence*, p. ix.   [2] *Correspondence*, p. 5.
[3] *Cambridge Grace Book, Γ* (ed. W. G. Searle, Cambridge, 1908), p. 308.
[4] *Correspondence*, p. 10.   [5] Ibid., p. 7.   [6] Ibid., p. v.

with her, for very soon he was requested to use it to obtain financial help for a poor student at Cambridge.[1] There is clear evidence that the Queen was drawn to and trusted him. In November of the same year he was, on her nomination, appointed Dean of the College of Stoke-by-Clare and later, 'not six days before her apprehension'[2] she commended to his spiritual care the Princess Elizabeth, a charge which Parker remembered and honoured when he was summoned in her reign to be Archbishop.[3] On his side Parker not only recognized his obligation to Queen Anne, but, despite her unpopularity and final disgrace, he later on speaks gratefully of the 'great benefits' he had received of her 'whose soul I doubt not but is in blessed felicity with God'.[4] It is true that he was writing to her daughter, now Queen, when any words suggestive of disapproval would have been imprudent. But he need not have said anything had he not still felt loyalty and attachment to his early patroness. What is astonishing is that her friendliness and trust in him does not seem to have hindered his advance after her ruin in 1536. The King himself, who had already shown friendly interest in 1535,[5] made him one of his own chaplains in 1538, nominated him to a prebend at Ely in October 1541, and for the Mastership of Corpus in December 1544.[6]

The College of St. John the Baptist, Stoke-by-Clare, of which Parker was Dean for nearly twelve years (1535–47) attracted both his great affection and his vigorous interest. Originally a Benedictine house, it had been secularized in 1514 with provision[7] for a dean, six prebendaries, eight vicars, clerks, five choristers and various servants. The purpose of the foundation was to provide for the regular and full performance of the daily offices of the Church, and for special prayers for the founder and his family. Detailed regulations were laid down for the conduct of the common life—times of rising, the order of sitting at meals, the closing of the gates, the conduct of the members

---

[1] *Correspondence*, pp. 2–3.　　[2] Ibid., p. 59.　　[3] Ibid., pp. 69, 391, 400.
[4] Ibid., p. 70.　　　　　　　　[5] Ibid., p. 4.　　　[6] Ibid., p. vii.
[7] W. Dugdale, *Monasticon Anglicanum* (London, 1830), vi, iii, 1415 sqq.

when they were outside the precincts. There was, however, little direction for the employment of such waking hours as were not spent in church. The garden had, indeed, to be tended, there was fishing to be done, and similar tasks. It was also laid down that the education of the choristers in singing, grammar and morals should be provided. But such tasks would hardly employ fully so large a number of residents and there must have been long periods for which there was no prescribed occupation. To those with a gift for the life of prayer and contemplation such leisure would be a fruitful and happy freedom. For the less devout it might well often be tedious, sometimes dangerous. Even the statutes show some apprehension that free time might not be profitably employed. The visiting of taverns was prohibited, so was the keeping of hounds (except by the Dean), the carrying of arms, or going outside the college alone, because of possible scandal. Still, the visitations between 1492 and 1532[1] do not suggest that anything was seriously amiss. There were disputes about the requirements for residence, for the statutes were not clear or had been tampered with; full membership of each category was not always maintained (it was alleged that funds were inadequate); a vicar was said to be quarrelsome. But, apart from one suspected case of immorality, the records suggest that on the whole the college was well ordered and reasonably prosperous. Indeed, it even attracted the covetous eye of Wolsey, who was only prevented from taking it over to use its funds for one of his educational establishments by the quick action of the Bishop of Norwich and the protection of Queen Katharine, its patroness.

The college was only some twenty miles from Cambridge and in those days of pluralism there was no difficulty in Parker's retaining his Fellowship at Corpus while he was Dean. His new post provided him with a happy and quiet place of retirement in the country to which he became devoted—Dr. Haddon, indeed, referred to it as his 'Tusculanum'.[2] His predecessor had

---

[1] A. Jessop, *Visitations of the Diocese of Norwich* (Camden Society, London, 1888).   [2] Strype, *Parker* i, 15.

been a pluralist usually non-resident, but Parker was not the man to treat his office as a sinecure. He provided new statutes which did much to eliminate the possible risks of idleness; and he gave vent to two enthusiasms which were to be life-long— his love of building and his concern for the education of youth. By his new statutes the Dean and prebendaries were required to preach regularly not only at Stoke but in each of the parishes from which the college derived revenue. He arranged for the payment from corporate revenue of a stipend for a lecturer, either of their own body or from Cambridge or Oxford, to read a lecture on Scripture four days in the week, half an hour in English and half an hour in Latin, at which the prebendaries and vicars were bound to be present. The number of choristers was to be raised to eight, ten or more, who were to be carefully educated and the most promising of them later sent to Cambridge for six years, with financial aid from the college. He converted an old house into a newly decorated hall for the Dean, prebendaries and vicars. Most significant of all, he built in the precincts of the college a grammar school for which the college was to pay the master, and which should be open to the youth of the neighbourhood, rich or poor, the latter paying no fee.[1]

Parker himself evidently gave a lead in the matter of preaching, for he soon drew on himself the hostile attention of those who clung to the old religion. A long letter from him of November 1539 or 40[2] to Dr. Stokes, an Austin friar who had recently come from Norwich to reside at Stoke,[3] is urgent that he should not in his sermons attack or contradict the preaching of Parker. He declared himself very ready to argue points in dispute privately, but thought that public wrangles would 'learn our audiences but envy, discord and dissension . . . we should by our disagreement cause a roar and a schism in the people'. It seems that Stokes did not listen to such peaceful counsels, and was soon in trouble.[4] About the same time, too, Parker was delated to

---

[1] Strype, *Parker* i, 16–18.   [2] *Correspondence*, pp. 10 sqq.
[3] Strype says that he had actually been sent by the Bishop of Norwich to oppose Parker (*Parker* i, 23).   [4] *Correspondence*, p. 14, note 2.

Lord Chancellor Audley by certain inhabitants of Stoke. The evidence is the original draft of Parker's answer to the charges, probably in 1539.[1] The complaints and the answers are interesting as showing the sort of line that Parker was following, the ease with which it could be misrepresented and the readiness of those who did not like it so to misrepresent it either deliberately or by mistake. There were three counts against him. First, he was accused of teaching that Easter 'with the ceremonies as appertaining to the same was but a pageant or an interlude'. He answered that he had maintained that what really counted was not the external acts but their spiritual significance: the 'procession was to declare and testify openly to the world that they would henceforth follow Christ in their conversation . . . without this meditation and purpose their procession, with the solemnities thereof, was to them but a vain pageant whereof they had no profit'. Secondly, it was alleged that he taught that the cross of Christ was no holier than those on which the thieves had died. What in fact he had said, in a sermon on Relic Sunday, was that his hearers should not trust in relics of saints, about which there was often no certainty that they were what they were claimed to be. But even if the relics of the cross were genuine, to worship them in forgetfulness of the mystery of the cross was a superstitious worship. Thirdly, it was said that he had suggested that the King was buying peace with other realms with the money that he gathered from the people. His defence was simple. At the time of the rebellion (the Pilgrimage of Grace) when many folk, soldiers and others, were assembled at Clare, he had thought fit to encourage them to loyalty to their prince who had so long maintained peace with other nations, but could not do so without charges and expenses. They should therefore readily contribute to his support the little that was asked from them in return for such protection. The outcome was complete vindication for Parker. The Lord Chancellor 'blamed the promoters and sent word that I should go on and fear not such enemies'.[2] The ease with which Parker refuted the charges

---

[1] *Correspondence*, pp. 7 sqq.   [2] Ibid., p. 9, note 4.

makes it seem odd that they should ever have been brought. It may have been due to real misunderstanding: suspicion and partisanship blunt the perception of what one's opponents have really said. But it is possible that both the opposition of Dr. Stokes in the parish and the attempt to have Parker's preaching condemned by authority may really best be understood in the context of Henry's ecclesiastical policy at the moment. In 1538 the long-drawn-out negotiations with Lutherans to reach some sort of agreement between English and German reform were abruptly ended by the King's insistence on communion in one kind, clerical celibacy and propitiatory masses. In 1539 the 'catholicity' of the Anglican position was even more aggressively advertised in the Act of the Six Articles which insisted again on those three points as well as auricular confession. The King had shown his strong interest in the Act by his personal presence in parliament when it was discussed: indeed Cranmer thought its passing was due to royal pressure.[1] Probably it was no more than the re-assertion by the King of what was his fixed intention throughout, that there should, save for the abolition of papal authority and the correction of abuses, be no other significant change in traditional belief or practice. But, to those who did not know the secret workings of the royal mind, the Act, following on the dismissal of the Lutheran embassy, may well have seemed to indicate a change of course. Both Latimer and Shaxton, for example, resigned their bishoprics three days after the passing of the Act. Those who disliked Parker's preaching and feared its efficacy may have felt that the climate was now such that he could be opposed with impunity, or even condemned, on flimsy charges.

Despite his enemies, Parker's success in revitalizing the college at Stoke soon became known. In 1540, the Duke of Norfolk asked for a copy of the new statutes as a model for a college of secular priests he was intending to establish at Thetford.[2] Further, his nomination to a prebend in Ely by the King in 1541

[1] Cranmer, *Remains and Letters* (ed. by J. E. Cox, Parker Society, Cambridge, 1846), p. 168.   [2] Strype, *Parker* i, 25–26.

was presumably a testimony of the royal approval. When the existence of the college was endangered by the Act for the Dissolution of Chantries, Hospitals and Free Chapels (December 1545) Parker could confidently appeal that it should be spared on the ground of the good work it was doing. His letter was sent to the Council of Queen Katharine (Parr) its 'lady and patroness'.[1] Though he had been offered a liberal pension if he would surrender the College, he had refused to do so 'weighing my duty to God and to the Queen's Grace' (a fact worthy of note in view of charges that he was unduly fond of money). He urged that the Queen should make suit to the King for its preservation. The state of the college had been improved above the first institution at 'no small cost and charge'. Its revenues, a bare £300, would be of little use to the King but were of great value in the neighbourhood (where the Queen had estates). 'It standeth so that her grace's tenants be round about it, as well to be refreshed with alms and daily hospitality as is there kept as to be instructed with God's word of certain of her grace's orators doing the same; besides the commodity that the children of her grace's tenants and farmers fully enjoy by their teaching and bringing up, as well in grammar as in singing and playing, with other exercises and nurtures meet for their ages and capacities.' He added, with a touch of the worldly wisdom in which he was not lacking, that the survival of the college was a matter which directly touched the Queen's interest. It was the only one in the neighbourhood under her patronage, and was therefore useful to her for the lodging it gave, freely and gladly, to her representatives visiting her estates there! Parker also evidently gained the ear and support of Sir Anthony Denny, one of the King's Privy Chamber. In the event, the college was unmolested till the following reign. Denny declared[2] that Parker's 'honest and virtuous using of that college' had moved the King 'in such wise as his Majesty clearly resolved to permit the same to remain undissolved'. Of the kindly personal interest Parker took in the boys of his school there is evidence in a charming letter which

[1] *Correspondence*, p. 32.　　　　[2] Ibid., p. 33, note 2.

Strype quotes.[1] The writer expresses gratitude not only for his schooling at Stoke but for Parker's continuing care in sending him to Corpus and obtaining a Bible-clerkship for him, for sometimes taking him on visits, 'besides manifold other benefits'. It is true that when the letter was written Parker was already Archbishop and his patronage was valuable. The grateful tone of the letter, which had been long delayed, may thus owe something to self-interest. But it does show, in its mere statement of facts, how keenly Parker looked after the promising boys in his school.

[1] *Parker* i, 45–46.

CHAPTER III

MASTER OF CORPUS AND
VICE-CHANCELLOR

KNOWLEDGE of Parker's admirable work at Stoke must have come to the King's ears even before the appeal to the Queen of 1545. It is difficult to explain otherwise the terms in which Henry recommended him to the Fellows of Corpus for election to the Mastership in succession to Sowode in November 1544[1]— 'a man as well for his approved learning, wisdom, and honesty, as for his singular grace and industry in bringing up youth in virtue and learning, so apt for the exercise of the said room, as it is thought very hard to find the like for all respects and purposes'. In response, Parker was duly elected Master of Corpus on 4 Dec. 1544. For the college no less than for Parker it was a happy choice. His devotion is proved by the long list of his benefactions and by his constant care to the end of his life for the well-being of the college. Indeed, his services to the college were so substantial and lasting that he has claims to be regarded as its second founder.

His passion for careful and orderly administration at once found full scope.[2] Till now, there had been neither a proper list of the possessions and estates of the college nor official accounts. Such statements of income and expenditure as existed were kept only in the private books of the officers concerned. Parker arranged for a full inventory to be made of college property,

---

[1] *Correspondence*, pp. 16–17.
[2] For Parker's practical reforms and for his benefactions, see the *Historiola*, a history of the College drawn up by John Joscelyn under Parker's direction (Cambridge Archeological Society, ed. J. W. Clark, Cambridge, 1880) and J. Lamb, *Master's History of the College of Corpus Christi* (London, 1831) and the more modern history by H. P. Stokes (London, 1898).

to be checked triennially, and personally drew up a form for the annual accounts which should show clearly receipts, outgoings and arrears. Within a fortnight of becoming Master, 'in that reason dictates and honesty persuades that what anyone hath received from ancestors he delivers again in as good measure to posterity',[1] he and the Fellows agreed for the proper upkeep and guardianship of 'Billingford hutch', a chest in which, according to a legacy from a past Master, twenty pounds was deposited for making loans to the Fellows. The keepers of the chest were also made responsible for a collection of books left to the college by Dr. Nobis but now sadly uncared for; some needed repair, the chains of some were broken, others were actually missing. Henceforward, under the charge of the keepers of the chest, repairs were to be made at the expense of the College and none of the chained books were to be removed. Equally the College estates received his attention. He drew up a complete account of them with the rentals due from farms and tenements, and recovered for the College rents which had been lost or withheld. A particular instance of his exact carefulness was the freeing of the College from a charge for tithe which had been fraudulently passed on to it by a tenant who was himself legally responsible for its payment. The result of Parker's husbandry was that the College (like the College at Stoke) was able to put its property in repair, to build, and yet have money in hand for educational purposes. He also drew up new statutes for the College which were confirmed under Edward VI and adopted in Elizabeth's reign and remained in force until modern times.[2]

The College buildings and the comfort of its inmates were also very much his concern. He improved and added to the Master's Lodgings, enlarging and glazing the windows, and building what must have been a charming gallery, with steps down to his garden. He improved the College hall and many of the rooms while he was Master. Later on (for it is simpler to mention here his benefactions to the College in sum, though many of them were not made till he was Archbishop) when

[1] Strype, *Parker* i, 27.   [2] Stokes, p. 52.

provision was made for more scholars, he arranged what rooms they should have and paid for the furnishing of them, as well as for a new inner library. He gave a hundred pounds for a fire in hall from All Saints to Candlemas. Unlike some benefactors, he realized that some of his gifts would involve the recipients in regular annual expense and with imaginative generosity anticipated it. Five hundred pounds given to the College was to be used not only to improve the commons of Master, Fellows and scholars, but also for the repair of the books he gave to the College and the University, and for the upkeep of a road he made on land bought for the purpose and given to the University to make a better approach to the Schools. The making of the road cost him four hundred pounds, but there was practical foresight in making the College responsible for its upkeep and liable to a fine if it neglected its duty. His benefactions to the College, to the poor, and for sermons cost him two thousand pounds,[1] a very considerable sum in those days, especially in view of his other commitments. But it is not merely the total of his gifts which is impressive. It is the exact care for detail and the sympathetic appreciation of what was really needed for the wellbeing of his College and its members which is the measure of his lasting affection for it even in the midst of all his other cares as Archbishop.

Most important of all, in the long view (together with his munificent and unparalleled gift of manuscripts and books), were his efforts to build up the College as a centre of learning and education. As early as 1548, while he was still Master, the increased balances in the College accounts, augmented by what the College saved through the abolition of the costly celebration of the old Corpus Christi festival, enabled the Master and Fellows to found six new scholarships. They were for poor men's children who were, however, to be competently learned in grammar. The scholars were to reside throughout the year except for one month, were to be provided with chambers in College and facilities for reading in hall, and eight pence a week

---

[1] His son's statement. *Correspondence*, p. xii.

(later raised to twelve pence) for commons. The awards were tenable for three years for an Arts course, but were renewable for a further similar period for those who wished to pursue a course in Divinity. Later on, as Archbishop, Parker was able to do much more to help the educational work of the College financially. As supervisor of the estate of John Mere, bedel of the University who died in 1558, Parker presented a sum of eighty pounds (partly contributed by himself and others) some of the income from which was to be spent on repairs to the Schools, the rest on a scholarship at Corpus for a native of Cambridgeshire. In 1567 he bought from the Corporation of Norwich and made payable to the College an annuity of ten pounds to provide for three scholars—the Norwich scholars—to be nominated by the Mayor and Corporation out of the schools of that city and of Aylsham. The recipients were to be between fourteen and twenty years of age, instructed in grammar and able to write and sing. The College was to provide chambers and allowances for them as for other scholars, and residence was to be kept for eleven months in the year. Tenure was three years for Arts, with a further three years for Divinity if they were wanted. Apparently eight pounds a year would suffice for the three scholars; of the remainder, thirty shillings, was to be used for the payment of preachers sent by the college to deliver annual sermons at Thetford, Wymondham, and at St. Clements and in the Green Yard at Norwich; the balance of ten shillings, charmingly, was to be given to the Mayor, sheriffs and other officers who attended the sermon at St. Clements! In 1569 Parker presented to the College a further annuity of eighteen pounds (also purchased from the city of Norwich) to pay for two more scholars from Norwich, Aylsham and Wymondham, and for two Fellows who were to be appointed out of the Norwich scholars and were to undertake the instruction of those scholars free of charge. To meet this benefaction the College also provided two new Fellowships from its own revenues. It is typical of Parker's local patriotism that of the total number of Fellows, raised by his efforts to twelve, four were to be if possible Norfolk

men, besides the two Norwich Fellows who would inevitably be
so. For two of the Fellowships and five of the scholarships
Parker provided the entire emoluments, as well as contributing
to Dr. Mere's scholar, and no doubt really inspiring the other
foundations.

But his endowments for education were not confined to his
native county, and the catalogue of them (even at the risk of
wearisomeness) must be continued. In 1562 a complicated
transaction conveyed certain tenements in Westminster to the
Queen and from her to Corpus. Presumably this was a device
for avoiding the expense of a licence of mortmain; as it was all
arranged by Parker it is fair to assume that it was he who compensated the original owner. Once more, the income was to be
used to provide for three scholars at Corpus, but this time
nominated by the Dean and Chapter of Canterbury. They were
to be chosen from sons of tenants on the Chapter estates in
Norfolk, Suffolk or Lincoln who were maintained in their
school at Canterbury. If the Canterbury Chapter did not make an
election, the nomination passed to the Dean and Chapter of
Westminster. If they, too, failed to nominate, the Master and
Fellows of Corpus could choose candidates from any school in
the Province of Canterbury. (It is interesting to note here,
as in the case of the road at Cambridge and later of his books,
what elaborate precautions Parker took to see that his benefactions were fully used.) In 1569 he arranged that Eastbridge
Hospital in Canterbury should pay £6 13s. 4d. a year for two
hundred years to Corpus (this was afterwards made permanent
under Whitgift) for the maintenance there of two scholars,
natives of Kent, out of the King's School at Canterbury. Finally,
in pursuance of his will, his son presented to the College a
further annuity of ten pounds for the support of three more
scholars from the schools of Canterbury, Aylsham and Wymondham. Nor was Parker satisfied merely to provide these openings:
he personally saw to it that the scholars were provided with
suitable accommodation in college. Three further proofs of his
zeal for education, unconnected with Corpus, may be noted.

He gave money to Caius for a student in physics, and to Trinity Hall for one in law. At Rochdale, in Lancashire, of which as Archbishop he was rector or proprietary and appointed the vicar, he secured from the farmer of the rectory an annuity of seventeen pounds ten shillings, to pay a master and an usher for a free grammar school in the place, again with most careful precautions to secure that the posts were actually filled.

Once Parker was Master of Corpus the University was not slow in showing its sense of his abilities. In January 1545, within two months of becoming Master, he was elected Vice-Chancellor. The election was in the hands of the regents, that is those masters of arts who were still constrained by statute to the office of teaching. The period of regency was two years (it might be longer), dating immediately from the taking of the master's degree, so the regents were the younger and presumably more lively of the resident graduates. In 'a very great house' which recorded ninety-eight votes, Parker received seventy-nine, his nearest rival only eight, and Ridley a paltry five.[1] Such a decisive majority for one whose association with the White Horse Inn was well known must be regarded not only as an indication of the mood of at any rate the younger teaching M.A.s in the University, but also as a personal tribute to Parker himself. (So far as religion was concerned, Ridley was a much more prominent protestant.) But religion also doubtlessly played a part.

Such an inference is strongly confirmed by the only incident in his year of office of which we have any detailed knowledge. In the Lent term, members of Christ's College, including two of the Fellows, produced a play called *Pammachius*.[2] It was a bitter satire on the history and actions of the papacy which had achieved, says Mullinger, 'an almost European fame'. Before it was played at Christ's, the text was censored, and the College seems to have been satisfied with it and even contributed nearly twenty nobles to its production. But one of the Fellows, Scot, was offended and reported the matter to Stephen Gardiner,

---

[1] *Correspondence*, p. 18, note 2.
[2] Ibid., pp. 20-30. Mullinger, ii, 72-76.

Bishop of Winchester and Chancellor of the University. His reaction, immediate and strong, not only shows how much more intimately the Chancellor was concerned in the day to day running of the University than is now the case, but was also entirely typical of the character and aims of Gardiner himself. Though he had supported the rejection of papal authority in England and had written the *De Vera Obedientia* to justify his doing so, he was in all other respects conservative. He did not wish for further changes and was probably at this period both the ablest and stoutest supporter of the policy of the King in rejecting definitely protestant reforms and doctrines. He could not consistently disapprove of an attack on the papal claims, but the *Pammachius*, even when censored, attacked some ceremonies and observances to which he was still attached. He therefore wrote to Parker as Vice-Chancellor to make enquiries about the play 'a part of which tragedy is so pestiferous as were intolerable'.[1]

Gardiner was not a man whom it was safe for the University to regard as a mere figure-head. He had already shown his quality in 1542 when a new method of pronouncing Greek was introduced. To the astonishment of the University, he issued a decree imposing severe penalties on all who used the new pronunciation. Regents were to lose their place in the Senate, applicants for degrees were to be refused leave to proceed, if they offended: undergraduates were to be birched in front of their fellows![2] Probably the excessive violence of his proposals defeated his purpose; for in the next year he still had to declare 'I did it seriously and will maintain it'.[3] He was by then, however, roused by another issue—the eating of flesh in Lent by graduates. He ordered them to be fined. 'Lands have not been given nor lectures founded for any such evil purposes.' The whole letter is blustering and threatening. He means to use his authority and will see that it is not treated with contempt. Characteristically in 1545 (the first occasion, so far as we know,

---

[1] *Correspondence,* p. 21.   [2] Mullinger, ii, 60.
[3] Strype, *Ecclesiastical Memorials,* i, ii, 481–3.

on which Gardiner and Parker were at open variance) he used a similar bullying style in treating the performance of *Pammachius*. 'I know mine office there, and mind to do it as much as I may. Requiring you therefore that, in such matters of innovation and disorder, I may be diligently advertised from you from time to time.'[1] But he wished not to be precipitate and therefore sought fuller information from his Vice-Chancellor. Parker duly made enquiries. The play had been allowed by the Master and Fellows of Christ's who had ordered the omission of 'all such matter whereby offence might justly have risen'. Nor could Parker find anyone who had in fact been offended by it, though some agreed that time and labour might have been better used. But Gardiner (presumably further primed by Scot) was more suspicious than before. He had heard there was an attack on Lent fastings and on the mass, though those terms were not used. If so, it was a serious matter that 'Such as by the King's Majesty's privileges and supportation be there preserved in quiet to learn all virtue, should presumptuously mock and scorn the direction of their prince in matters of religion.' So Parker was bidden to make further enquiry, spurred on by the ominous remark that Oxford with fewer privileges lived quietly. The Heads of colleges were therefore asked by Parker to consult their colleagues and subsequently reported (so he writes) that 'none of all their companies declared unto them that they were offended with anything, that now they remember was then spoken';[2] very many of themselves had not seen the play. Parker enclosed for the Chancellor's information a copy of the play as corrected for the performance, and let him know of the resentment of Scot's colleagues who now accused him, really, of undue inclination to papal claims. When Gardiner saw what had really been performed, he was furious; 'perusing the book of the tragedy which ye sent me, I find much matter not stricken out, all which by the parties' own confession was uttered, very naught, and on the other part something not well omitted'.[3] That the University could have heard the play without grief is 'an undoubted proof

---

[1] *Correspondence*, p. 21.　　　[2] Ibid., p. 25.　　　[3] Ibid., p. 27.

of their lewdness'. 'How soon soever I forget the offence upon their reconciliation, I shall hardly of a great while forget the matter.' He added that he heard of other things out of order, and seemed particularly irritated that his orders about Greek pronunciation had not been observed. 'I will do that I can for the maintenance of virtue and good order there, and challenge again, of duty, to be regarded after the perfection not of my qualities but mine office.' The words of Mr. Scot he had referred to the Council, which in fact pronounced on the whole affair.

Though he was a member of the Council and indeed signed their letter to Parker, Gardiner can have got little pleasure from it. Here was a matter much more serious than the pronunciation of Greek. It is hard to suppose that he would not have wished for severe penalties. But, in effect, the matter was taken out of his hands by the Council and entrusted to Parker and the Heads of colleges 'to do, for reformation of those that have misused themselves in playing of the said tragedy, as to your wisdoms shall be thought requisite'.[1] The only satisfaction Gardiner got was that Scot was to some extent protected from the dislike he had attracted to himself. Parker was to call the parties together and admonish them 'so to employ their wits and studies in knowledge of that is good, true and wholesome, as all that is indeed poison, either in learning or manners, be expelled'.

The incident is interesting not only for the light it throws on Gardiner but because it shows Parker in typically cautious and moderate action. He took great trouble over what was obviously a tiresome business, obtaining full and first-hand information so far as he could. A less honest man might not have taken the risk of forwarding the acting copy of the play, for which there is no evidence that Gardiner asked. Parker was throughout quiet, methodical, straightforward and just. The outcome was really a triumph for him.

He deserved it, not only for his pains in this particular matter, but also for his general concern for the discipline of the University. Gardiner's interference seemed to suggest that the Vice-

[1] *Correspondence,* p. 29.

Chancellor was indifferent to matters needing correction. But on the back of one of Gardiner's letters there is written in Parker's own hand a list of matters which, as Strype conjectures,[1] can only have been his reaction to the Chancellor's remark that he hears 'many things to be very far out of order, both openly in the University and severally in the colleges'. It includes such things as the dress of members of the University and their personal appearance (beards should not be allowed!), attendance at divinity disputations and sermons, the pronunciation of Greek, 'revelation of secrecies' (no doubt caused by Mr. Scot's conduct). Whether in his year of office Parker was able to do anything about such matters we do not know. But obviously he was keenly aware of what needed to be reformed and was known to be so. During the next year, he was made one of a committee appointed to take measures to see that public lectures were 'more diligently read and heard', and 'likewise' for disputations in various faculties and for sermons *ad clerum*.[2] He was also allowed to be regent or non-regent *ad placitum*[3]—a device, presumably, for giving him a place and vote among the regents without forcing on him the corresponding duty of teaching.

Even after he ceased to be Vice-Chancellor, Parker continued to be much concerned in University business. The Act of 1545 which presented to the King chantries, hospitals and the like, caused alarm in Cambridge as well as at Stoke-by-Clare. It seemed as if it might result in the suppression of the colleges and the confiscation of their property by the King. The University at once took protective measures through influential friends at court—Cheke, formerly Professor of Greek and now tutor to Prince Edward, and Thomas Smith, Professor of Law when Parker became Vice-Chancellor and now Clerk to the Council of Queen Katherine Parr. The University through the Vice-Chancellor sent a letter to be presented by Smith to the Queen, to which she replied in February 1546.[4] Though she fully

[1] *Parker* i, 39, 40–41.
[2] *Cambridge Grace Book, Δ* (ed. J. Venn, Cambridge, 1910), p. 47.
[3] Ibid., p. 38.   [4] *Correspondence,* p. 36, note.

recognizes 'his Majesty's property and interest, through the consent of the high court of parliament', she re-assures them. Confident in their zeal for religion ('rather an University of divine philosophy than of natural or moral, as Athens was'), she had approached the King and assures them that his love of learning was such that he would rather advance than confound their ancient institutions. Even before that, the University must have felt its fears at least diminished. A royal commission, dated January 16, 1546, and addressed to Parker, still called Vice-Chancellor, is still preserved in Parker's papers.[1] It nominated him together with Redman, Master of Trinity, and May, Master of Queens', to be the King's agents in the matter. That in itself augured well, for it met the request of the University that it should not be put to 'great charges' through 'costly officers'—and of course secured that their case would be considered in as favourable a light as possible. Parker seems to have been the chief of the visitors and the work must have occupied him much in 1546. The outcome was thoroughly satisfactory. It is described in a memorandum by Parker still at Corpus.[2] The commissioners waited on the King and presented to him 'a brief summary . . . describing the revenues, the reprises, the allowances, and number and stipend of every college'.[3] The King 'diligently perused' it, and was surprised by the fact that most colleges (in fact all but one, according to the return) seemed to have revenues smaller than their expenses. He naturally asked 'what it meant'. Such a matter was entirely within Parker's province: he really understood college finances. The deficit, it was explained, was made good by fines for leases and their renewal and by the sale of wood. The King, genuinely concerned to promote learning, was entirely satisfied. He was favourably impressed that so many could be maintained 'by so little land and rent', and declared to the chagrin of some of his courtiers ('*lupos quosdam hiantes*' Parker calls them) that it

[1] *Correspondence*, p. 34, note.   [2] Ibid., p. 35.
[3] Printed in J. Lamb, *Letters, Statutes and other Documents from the M. S. Library of Corp. Christ. Coll. Cambridge* (London, 1838), p. 60.

would be a pity that 'these lands should be altered to make them worse'. Thus encouraged, the commissioners made request that the colleges should not be forced by royal letters to make disadvantageous exchanges of property with his courtiers. That caused the King, who at least was no fool, to smile. He explained that he must write letters asking for favours for his servants who helped the realm in wars and other matters, but would leave 'us' completely free to accede to such requests or not. In fact, he 'bade us hold our own, for after his writing, he would force us no further'. From so masterful a King more could hardly be expected: Parker and his fellows had done their work well.

With his work for Stoke College, Corpus and the University, Parker can hardly have had much time for strictly clerical work. None the less, he held at this period more than one ecclesiastical preferment. In addition to his prebend at Ely he held the rectory of Ashen in Essex, to which he was presented by Stoke College in 1542. He resigned that living in 1544, but only to accept, the next day, presentation to the rectory of Burlingham in Norfolk. To this, in 1545, was added the gift by Corpus of the college living of Landbeach[1] (where typically enough he made a careful record of the College estates and built a barn). To modern views such pluralism is surprising, but it was then so usual as to be quite unremarkable. Gardiner, for example, who became Master of Trinity Hall in 1525, retained the office until he was ejected in 1549, although he was made Bishop of Winchester in 1531 and later Chancellor of the University. Even Ridley seems to have had no scruples. When he became Bishop of Rochester in 1547 he retained the Mastership of Pembroke Hall and was given permission to keep his two vicarages and two canonries *in commendam* for five years. Similar cases could be quoted almost without limit. The remarkable thing about Parker is, indeed, the moderation of his pluralism. He did at least resign Ashen before accepting Burlingham; and he resigned Burlingham in 1550 apparently without any compensation.

[1] *Memoranda: Correspondence*, pp. vii, viii.

CHAPTER IV

PARKER UNDER EDWARD VI AND MARY

UNDER Edward VI Parker's condition was changed in two important respects: he lost the Deanery of Stoke College; and he married. In his *Memoranda* he says that he resigned the Deanery, compelled (*ex vi*) by Act of Parliament, on 1 April 1547. The date raises difficulties. Henry's power over chantries and colleges was expressly granted for his life-time only and therefore lapsed with his death in January 1547. A similar grant was made to King Edward, but by a Parliament which did not meet till November of that year. In April 1547 there would not therefore be any valid Act which enforced Parker's resignation. The commissioners under the new Act did not start their proceedings until 1548, and Strype says[1] that they ordered Parker to supply an inventory of the possessions of the college: presumably he was therefore still Dean in 1548. Moreover, in February of that year—if the letter is rightly dated in the *Correspondence*[2]—Sir Anthony Denny wrote to the commissioners urging in view of Parker's 'worthiness above the common sort' that he should have 'an honest and convenient pension' until it could be redeemed by some other spiritual preferment. From this letter it is clear that the college had not, at the time of writing, been taken over. Finally, a letter simply dated '7th of June' but assigned in the correspondence to 1548[3] from John Cheke (the ultimate possessor of the college) to Parker assures him that no pensionary will be better treated and that the matter should be settled in a week or so. It looks, therefore, as though 1548 rather than 1547 was the year in which Parker finally lost his happy

[1] *Parker* i, 44. [2] *Correspondence*, p. 33, note. [3] Ibid., p. 40.

possession of Stoke. But certainly he did lose the Deanery. He was, however, compensated with a pension of £40, a handsome allowance if he is right in saying later on that the living of Benet College was only worth twenty nobles at most.[1] In time, the pension ceased when he was given other preferment. In June 1552 he was presented by the Crown to a prebend in Lincoln, and nominated for the Deanery there a week later. He was duly installed as prebendary in July and as Dean in October, and his pension from Stoke then ceased. But he still continued to be Master of Corpus and rector of Landbeach.

On 24 June 1547, Parker was married to 'Margaret, daughter of Robert Harlston of Mattishall in the county of Norfolk, gentleman'.[2] They had become affianced seven years before, according to the *Matthaeus*, but could not be married so long as Henry VIII lived and maintained the law enjoining clerical celibacy. Though her hand was sought by other eligible suitors in the interval, Margaret remained loyal to Parker, and the marriage took place within six months of Edward's accession. So Parker says, and presumably he has not made a mistake at any rate about that date. But, if it is correct, the marriage took place while the law enforcing clerical celibacy was still unrepealed. It was not until the following December that Convocation resolved that all canons, laws and usages which forbade the marriage of priests should be declared void. The bill to effect this was discussed in Parliament at the end of 1548, but was not actually passed till February 1549, some twenty months after Parker's marriage. He was forty-two at the time, his wife twenty-seven. She died in 1570 after what seems to have been an ideal married life. The fullest picture of her we have is given in the *Matthaeus*.[3] She was both gracious and self-effacing, managing her housekeeping at first with care and taste, afterwards rising easily to the calls made on her as wife of an Archbishop. Everything was then ordered in seemly state in such a way that, untroubled by domestic cares, he could devote himself freely

---

[1] *Correspondence*, p. 51.   [2] Ibid., p. x.
[3] Strype, *Parker* iii, 285, 294.

to affairs of Church and State, despite his large household and the lavish entertainment he liked to give. Equally, in his obscurity under Queen Mary, she was his solace. To her children she was a wise and devoted mother. Such is the picture drawn by Joscelyn. It may be partly coloured by his devotion, but at least he was in a position to know what he was talking about. Moreover, the little we learn from other sources supports what he says. Before he had even met her, the austere Ridley wrote to Parker[1] to 'commend me to mistress Parker whom, although I do not know, yet for the fame of her virtue in God I do love'. Later, moved by her charm, her seriousness and her prudence, he is reported to have asked whether she had a sister,[2] as though he might himself be tempted to marriage. Even Queen Elizabeth, if the well-known story is true,[3] was moved to some sort of approval despite her dislike of clerical marriage. After being entertained at Lambeth, she took her leave with the not very gracious but, for that, the more sincere remark 'Madam I may not call you; mistress I am ashamed to call you; so I know not what to call you; but yet I thank you.' With moving simplicity Parker himself writes of her as 'my most dearly beloved and virtuous wife'.[4] Of their four sons, two died within a year of birth, the other two lived to manhood and married the one a daughter of Cox, Bishop of Ely, the other a daughter of Barlow of Chichester. So happy and quiet a domestic background was of incalculable worth to Parker in the troubles and strains he had to face as Archbishop.

The authorities under Edward continued to use Parker's services as a preacher, more often indeed than his own *Memoranda* would suggest. He himself only mentions a sermon in Lent 1548–9, and three sermons on Wednesdays in Lent 1551–2, all at Court. The first occasion throws an interesting light on his character. Cranmer notified him[5] that 'my Lord Protector's grace, having good opinion of your learned know-

---

[1] *Correspondence*, p. 45.   [2] Strype, *Parker* iii, 294.
[3] Sir John Harington, *Nugae Antiquae* (3 Vols., London, 1779), i, 4.
[4] *Correspondence*, p. x.   [5] Ibid., p. 40.

ledge and godly zeal in the advancement of God's word' had appointed him to preach on the third Sunday in Lent. The letter is dated 17 February. By March 4, Parker had apparently not even acknowledged the invitation. On that date Thirlby of Westminster wrote[1] to urge him to prepare for the sermon, and 'to advertise his grace by your letters of your determination therein'. Normally Parker was neither discourteous nor un-businesslike. The delay can hardly have been due to anything but his preference (as he later describes it) 'to dispense God's reverend word among the simple strayed sheep of God's fold, in poor destitute parishes and cures . . . than in theatrical and great audience'.[2] But he was not allowed to indulge what he called his 'natural viciosity of overmuch shamefastness'.[3] He was summoned again to preach at Court in Lent 1551.[4] He was also pressed into service at Paul's Cross, by Cranmer, in July 1548[5] and March 1551,[6] and by Ridley in the same year,[7] when once again he seems to have tried to avoid the appointment. For Ridley writes that though he has a wide choice of preachers, some lack learning, others judgement or godly conversation or sober-ness and discretion. 'He in whom all these do concur shall not do well to refuse (in my judgment) to serve God in that place.' And he offers if the date suggested is not convenient to appoint another. It is only by the chance survival of letters that we know of these sermons not listed by Parker in his *Memoranda*; there may well have been other similar occasions of which we know nothing. But it is clear that while he did not like preaching such sermons he was not allowed to avoid doing it.

On the other hand he did not hesitate to speak out if occasion seemed to require it. At the time of Kett's rebellion in 1549 he was in Norwich when the insurgents were encamped on Mouse-hold Heath. Inflamed by poverty and enraged by recent enclo-sures of common land by well-to-do property owners, the mob was not an easy one to be handled by the representatives of

---

[1] *Correspondence*, p. 41. [2] Ibid., pp. 50–51. [3] Ibid., p. 199.
[4] Ibid., p. 43. [5] Ibid., p. 39. [6] Ibid., p. ix, note.
[7] Ibid., p. 45.

order. When Parker visited the camp one evening he 'seeing the miserable common people drowned in drink and excess, thought that sober and wholesome communication would little profit drunkards over-charged with meat and drink . . . thought good to say nothing unto them that day'. But he returned next morning and, finding them at prayers (for one of the local vicars was acting as chaplain), he mounted the 'Oke of Reformation' from which their leaders were accustomed to address them, and to administer rough justice. He spoke directly, honestly, and without any sort of attempt to appease. They should not, he urged, waste the provisions they had in the camp (no doubt mindful of what he had seen the night before), nor use the occasion to settle private enmities or to shed blood. He ended with an exhortation to cease from their enterprise and submit to the King or his representatives, for that would best serve the common good. The crowd listened quietly till 'one wretch of the basest of the people' began to shout that Parker had been paid by the gentry to speak so. It was, of course, enough to turn his hearers against him: it is even said that as he stood in the tree 'he himself felt under his feet the points of the spears and javelins'. The local vicar, however, caused a diversion by setting the people to sing the *Te Deum*: the crowd was 'appeased' and Parker 'having gotten his opportunity thought it not good to tarry'. In a sense, it had all really been none of his business, and his attempt to deal with a tumultuous mob is evidence not only of physical courage but of a real anxiety to preach to poor simple folk who seemed to him to need help.

The incident had a sequel which shows Parker in a rather different light. The next morning, in one of the city churches, he returned to the attack on the 'pernicious tumults', though some of the rebels were now actually in church. Enraged, they told him after the service that three or four geldings he had with him were needed for what they called the King's service and would be fetched after dinner. With unexpected craftiness Parker sent for a smith to remove the shoes and pare to the quick the feet of some of the horses, the others were smeared over with green 'copperasse' as though they had been sick. The rebels were deceived and would not take such poor-looking animals. Parker set out on foot from Norwich, but after a few miles was rejoined, as he had arranged, by his horses and so made his way back to Cambridge without loss.[1]

But, in the main, Parker's chief work under Edward was still in Cambridge. In 1548 he was again elected Vice-Chancellor, almost unanimously.[2] In that capacity he had a letter from Dr. May, who was now Dean of St. Paul's and one of the Masters of Requests to the King as well as President of Queens' College, and who was destined to be one of the royal visitors again in 1549. The letter is to tell Parker that[3] 'we here look for your device touching the order of your University. And doubt you not but all things shall be done moderately and in due order.' In view of those words, though the actual date of the royal commission to the visitors for Cambridge was November 12, 1548, there can be little doubt that preparations for the visitation were already in hand in March when May wrote to Parker, whom he knew and with whom he had worked in a similar business in 1546, to make ready in Cambridge for it. Nor did Parker's work in connection with the visitation end with his Vice-Chancellorship. For there is a note in his own hand in the manuscript account of the visitation of Corpus in 1549 to the effect that Parker was 'supplying the room of the Vice-Chancellor in his absence for most of the visitation'.[4] For those two years at least

---

[1] The account of Parker's dealings with the rebels is drawn from R. Wood's translation (under the title *Alexander Nevill or the Furies of Norfolk*: London, 1623), of Alexander Nevill's *Kettus, sive de furoribus Norfolciensium Ketto duce*. The account is no doubt favourable to Parker since Nevill was one of his secretaries and in fact seems to have written at the Archbishop's instigation. He 'supplied the author with many instructions and remarks, while he was writing, being himself so well acquainted with the subject'. (Strype, *Parker* ii, 441.) This makes the story of the geldings even more amusing. It looks as though Parker, years later, treasured the memory of his ingenious ruse. One cannot help wondering whether he had learned such tricks in his dealings with unsatisfactory College tenants!

[2] *Correspondence*, p. 37.   [3] Ibid., p. 38.

[4] J. Lamb, *Letters, Statutes etc.*, p. 111.

he must have been busy, despite the reassuring words of May, in defending the interests of the University. And casual references in the *Grace Book* show how frequently the University turned to him for help in administrative and financial business. It has already been noted that, in the year after his first Vice-Chancellorship, he was one of the committee to provide for better attendance at lectures, disputations and sermons.[1] In 1549–50, he was one of those chosen to examine the University accounts for the year, and to check the expense account of the Vice-Chancellor on official business in London.[2] Later, with the Vice-Chancellor and one other, he was authorized to inspect and set in order the chests of the University,[3] and, in 1551–2, with others, to search the muniments to settle a matter of University patronage.[4] Plainly those among whom he lived at Cambridge had as high an estimation of his probity and administrative ability as had the Council of his loyalty and soundness as a preacher. Possibly it was the position and respect he enjoyed in the University which led to his being chosen to preach before the commission of the Bishop of Ely in Holy Trinity, Cambridge, on December 7, 1550. It was not an easy occasion, for it marked the publication of an order for the destruction of altars and the substitution for them of holy tables—a change not greatly welcomed by average churchgoers. No doubt it was thought that it might help to win their approval that the order was read 'a Sermon having first been preached and the Word of God publicly expounded in the Mother Tongue by the venerable man Mr. Matthew Parker, D.D.'.[5]

It is clear that Parker later on regarded this as a happy period in his life. Under Elizabeth he would have preferred to return to the Mastership of Corpus rather than be thrust into some more eminent sphere. But it is also notable in another respect. Sometimes it seems to be suggested that he was made Archbishop only or chiefly because he had not, like so many others, fled

---

[1] *Grace Book, Δ*, p. 47. [2] Ibid., p. 68.
[3] Ibid., p. 74. [4] Ibid., p. 82.
[5] G. C. Gorham, *Gleanings and a few Scattered Ears during the Period of the Reformation in England* (London, 1857), p. 213.

D

abroad to imbibe continental ideas; or because he had been chaplain to Elizabeth's mother and been kind to herself when she was young. It should therefore be noted that he obviously won for himself under Edward a high reputation as a man of affairs and practical efficiency, and that this must have been well known to men such as Cecil and Bacon who were familiar with what was going on in Cambridge at the time and were later on among Elizabeth's chief early advisers.

While Parker was a leading figure in the University, there arrived in Cambridge Martin Bucer, sent by the King, no doubt at the suggestion of Cranmer. The latter was hoping and working for a closer understanding with the German reformers, several of whom he had invited to England. His schemes were helped by the imposition of the Augsburg *Interim* by the Emperor in 1548. This was propounded as a temporary ruling about ecclesiastical affairs in Germany, to be valid only until a General Council could reach agreement. Despite some slight concessions, however, the *Interim* in essentials maintained the Catholic position and, in alarm, some of the German protestants were glad to escape to England. Among them were Bucer and his friend Fagius, a learned Hebraist, who arrived in April 1549. Cranmer received them gladly and for some months entertained them at Lambeth. In November they were sent on to Cambridge where Fagius had been appointed Professor of Hebrew. But he was already a sick man and died within ten days of reaching Cambridge. Even Bucer had not a long career there; he died at the end of February 1551, having held the Chair of Divinity for less than fifteen months (his appointment by the King was dated December 4, 1549). His influence on the English church, and probably on Parker, was out of all proportion to the brevity of his life in Cambridge.

Bucer was one of the most attractive of the continental reformers. By nature gentle and peaceful, he was anxious to overcome rather than exacerbate differences. His considerable learning and complete sincerity were joined with a feeling for history and tradition which saved him from the mere arid negations so frequent among protestants, while his deep sense of the underlying mystery of religion resulted in a reverence in dealing with holy things which they did not all share. He had the wisdom to see that, in such matters, sheer logic may not be the only guide, and he thus achieved a degree of sympathetic reasonableness and toleration very rare in his age, but very congenial both to Cranmer and to Parker. Before coming to England he had been for years the leading figure in Strasburg and had used his best endeavours to bring about a friendly understanding between Germans and Swiss, first at Marburg in 1529, and again at Württenberg in 1536, but without success. His teaching on the Eucharist, which was more and more coming to take central place in current arguments, followed a middle line, insisting on real presence but rejecting alike consubstantiation and transubstantiation on the one hand and on the other what is usually regarded as the Zwinglian concept of a mere memorial service. His views are not easy to determine, possibly because he really disliked the attempt to enclose so deep a mystery in logical propositions. But they seem very near to Cranmer's ideas as expressed in his *The Lord's Supper*, and to the subsequent teaching (as it seems to the present writer) of the Elizabethan Prayer Book, both in the insistence on the reality of the presence and in the reticence as to the exact mode of it; it is to Bucer intensely real, but spiritual, without involving any change in the elements. Few things are more revealing both of his views and of his tolerance than his reply to Peter Martyr when the latter sent him an account of his position after the Disputation he had in Oxford in June 1549. Bucer starts by expressing his fundamental agreement with Martyr[1]: there is no local presence in the elements, but the body and blood of Christ are so joined to them sacramentally that to them that believe 'Christ is here truly exhibited; to be seen, however, received, enjoyed, by faith, not by any sense or manner of this world.' He is sure that is the view of the 'ancient church' (an important point to him). He would like to drop all the words about which men were contending—

[1] Gorham, *Reformation Gleanings*, pp. 83–92.

substantially, carnally, really—and just insist that the believer does receive the body and blood of Christ. But he is afraid that some may understand Martyr to mean that it is an empty sign to stimulate faith (as Martyr certainly did hold, later on) and wishes, therefore, that he would add 'that Christ undoubtedly is (since we must speak with the scriptures) in His sacraments'. To him, adherence to the words of Scripture was fundamental. But, provided there is that, he would allow an astonishing range of freedom of belief. 'To require that no brother should retain his peculiar sentiments in any degree whatsoever—that would be either to tyrannize over the mind, or to expect the perfection of the saints here, which belongs to the future world.'[1] Perhaps,

[1] Such views were naturally unacceptable to the extreme continental reformers, but the more moderate respected and even liked Bucer. Luther, of course, would not accept his views, but Melanchthon was friendly. After Luther's bitter attack on Zwingli in his *Short Confession concerning the Supper*, Melanchthon wrote to Bucer (Gorham, *Reformation Gleanings*, 27, n.) to say it was 'a fierce attack in which you and I are beaten black and blue'. And, on the other hand, though he was suspected by the Zwinglians who classed Bucerians with Lutherans—one of them actually wrote to Bullinger to say that the death of Bucer would be a great piece of good fortune for England. (*Original Letters relative to the English Reformation,* ed. by Hastings Robinson for the Parker Society, 2 Vols, Cambridge, 1846–7, pages numbered continuously: p. 662.)—Calvin recognized his worth. Knowing the attitude of some of the Zurichers, he wrote to Bullinger in 1548 (Gorham, p. 51), 'We lie under some displeasure by reason of the intercourse which we have cultivated with Bucer. Let me ask you, my Bullinger, for what reason should we be alienated from Bucer, since he subscribes to this our confession which I have stated?' He regarded him as 'very profitable to England' (Ibid., 268) and actually sought his views on the six heads of the agreement which, when accepted by Zurich, formed the Consensus Tigurinus. Bucer's answer was so typical as to deserve notice (Ibid., 100 sqq.). He would like more use of the exact words of Scripture and insistence that 'we receive Christ Himself . . . so that we remain in Him and He in us'. He was distressed that such care was used in the discussions to explain what the mystery does not do rather than what it does. The presence is not 'of this world' and cannot be 'excogitated by the human mind'. None the less, he regrets the flat rejection of the Lutheran view because it will hurt the Lutheran churches 'consisting of multitudes of the most holy souls'. So he is desirous that 'the greatest scrupulosity should be shown in treating of the mysteries of Christ . . . that nothing (should be introduced) beyond the spirit and words of the Lord, nothing which may offend any one of Christ's least ones, nothing which may disgrace our conjunction in the Lord and charity'.

in those times, such a degree of tolerance was not a practical possibility. But the spirit of it seems to be very near to Cranmer's attitude till he was badgered by his opponents, and is certainly closely akin to the policy of Parker when he was Archbishop. It is small wonder if both of them were drawn to Bucer.

Before he came to England, Bucer had made a more astonishing attempt at an even wider reconciliation. Along with Melanchthon he had taken part in drawing up the so-called *Consultation* of Hermann, the Elector Bishop of Cologne. This was intended to form the basis for a reformed Catholicism such as even protestants could accept. It failed of its purpose and was rejected by the Council of Trent. But it had importance for the Church of England, even before Bucer set foot in the country. An English translation of it appeared in 1547 from which in the main was drawn the *Order of Communion* in 1548. The *Order* contained a form of exhortation, confession and prayers, to be inserted in the Latin mass after, in 1547, the communion of the laity in both kinds was enjoined. It was subsequently incorporated in the Communion Service in the Prayer Book of 1549. In that book, too, the Baptismal service was largely influenced by the scheme laid down in the *Consultation*. Thus the service for each of the two sacraments in the first English Prayer Book is indebted to the *Consultation*—and it is explicitly stated by Melanchthon that, in the *Consultation*, those two services were drawn up by Bucer.[1] Nor does that exhaust the debt of the Prayer Book to him. The first English translation of the Psalms to be printed was published at Strasburg in 1530. It was made from a Latin version for which Bucer was responsible. There is evidence[2] that the Strasburg English translation was one of the sources used by Coverdale, through whose version, by way of the Great Bible and the Book of Common Prayer, the religious life of England has been enriched ever since.

The new Prayer Book was already in use when Bucer reached

---

[1] C. Hopf, *Martin Bucer and the English Reformation* (Oxford, 1946), p. 94. This book is a most complete and authoritative account of Bucer in his relationship to the Church of England.   [2] Ibid., pp. 205 sqq.

Cambridge, and in the main he seems to have liked it.[1] But
he did draw up a long list of suggestions for changes in detail
(the so-called *Censura*), many of which seem to have been
incorporated in the Second Prayer Book.[2] He did not find much
fault with the doctrine of the first Book, but was chiefly concerned to secure an even greater simplification of ceremony.
He did not 'intend to overthrow tradition, and his constant
reference to the Church Fathers and to ancient practices are
evidence how much he valued that inheritance'.[3] All he wished to
do was to sweep away what he regarded as later accretions.
Certainly he was no Puritan in the later sense of the word.
When Hooper, appointed to a bishopric, refused to wear the
usual episcopal habits at his consecration, Bucer, rather unwill-
ingly, became involved in the controversy because Cranmer
invited his views. Obviously he did not himself like the vestments and, since they caused serious offence to some, wished
them to be abolished. But they should not be refused if legally
ordered. He even went so far as to say that, while Christ had
prescribed the substance of the sacraments, He 'has left His
church at liberty to order everything else which appertains to
the decent and useful administration of His mysteries'.[4] Thus
the vestments might be legally ordered—a view which enraged
the Puritans under Elizabeth against whom Bucer's letter was
produced later as a sort of trump card. Like that of many of the
early Elizabethan bishops, his personal preference was for the
abolition of the vestments, but quite definitely he taught that
personal preference should give way to lawful orders.

The presence of Bucer at Cambridge in 1549–51, with his
learning and great reputation combined with broad-mindedness
and charity, was important. The leading members of the Royal
Council were just about to press for (and indeed achieve)
sweeping ecclesiastical changes and innovations in a spirit harsher
than had hitherto been shown in England. Bucer firmly stood for
a tolerant and liberal way of doing things and won very wide

[1] Hopf, pp. 58–59.   [2] Ibid., pp. 69 sqq.   [3] Ibid., p. 58.
[4] Gorham, *Reformation Gleanings*, p. 205.

respect and affection in Cambridge though he was there so short a time. In particular, it appears that a close friendship grew up between him and Parker, who found in him congenial confirmation of the moderate position to which his own studies had led him. It was, suitably enough, Parker who was selected by the Vice-Chancellor to present Bucer for his degree of D.D.[1] But there are indications of real intimacy. Bucer consulted him, his 'patron in the Lord' about the arrangement of his lectures;[2] he relied on Parker (among others) for support in a dispute in which he was involved in 1550.[3] He accepted an invitation to dinner for his wife and himself on one occasion,[4] and on another had to decline because of the arrival of a German friend[5]—unless there was room for him too. In the last month of his life he wrote for the loan of ten crowns, to be repaid speedily.[6] His executors were Parker and Walter Haddon (who as Vice-Chancellor had received him) and they took considerable pains over their trust.[7] When the University wrote to the King that some provision should be made for Bucer's widow, Parker was their spokesman: at any rate Sir John Cheke's assurance that she shall be 'well and worthily considered' was addressed to Parker.[8] And, presumably, it was as Bucer's friend that Parker was invited to preach the sermon at his funeral in March 1551. The service was in Great St. Mary's and there could be no greater proof of the respect and affection he had won than the crowd of over 3,000 who together with the Vice-Chancellor and the Mayor assembled for the service.[9] After an oration by Walter Haddon, the Public Orator, Parker preached in English.[10] The sermon was not a mere panegyric but was almost prophetic in vein. A phrase here and there may be regarded as of the common courtesies of such an occasion—'in all ways perfect for the promotion of the glory of God', or, 'brave and immutable to the last breath'. But in the

---

[1] Hopf, p. 15.   [2] *Correspondence,* p. 41.
[3] Gorham, *Reformation Gleanings,* p. 166.   [4] *Correspondence,* p. 41.
[5] Ibid., p. 42.   [6] Ibid., p. 42.   [7] Ibid., pp. 46-47.
[8] Ibid., pp. 43-44.   [9] Cooper, *Ath. Cantab.,* pp. 101-2.
[10] A Latin version of the sermon is printed in Bucer's *Scripta Anglicana* (Basil, 1577 foll.).

main it is assumed that all will recognize his merits, and the
preacher devotes himself to pointing out that such a blow to the
University as Bucer's death can only be the sign of divine wrath
for their sins and a serious warning to amend their ways. To
speak so would have been farcical if Bucer's influence and
example had not been very great. The next day there was a
further service, with another sermon in Bucer's honour, and a
communion at which there were four hundred communicants.
The University further showed its regard for him by a gift of a
hundred crowns to help his widow in addition to the hundred
marks presented to her by the King. It is impossible to suppose
that the friendship of such a man and the memory of his broad
toleration (so long as central truths were not affected) did not do
much to encourage and fortify Parker in the course he tried to
pursue as Archbishop, and to strengthen him in resisting the
narrow sectarianism which later on favoured extreme Swiss
views.

Besides his work in Cambridge and his preaching, Parker was
being used in affairs of state. In January 1551 he was nominated
one of the commissioners to enquire into heresy (with explicit
reference to Anabaptists and Libertines) and to punish those who
opposed the Book of Common Prayer.[1] In December of the same
year he was called before the Council for consultation, though it is
not stated about what.[2] The next year, in February, he was made
one of the commission of thirty-two for the revision of Ecclesiastical Laws,[3] while in January he had been ordered to be admitted to visit Sir Thomas Arundel in the Tower 'for his instruction
to dye well'.[4] (Arundel seems to have been a supporter of Somerset, but details are obscure.) The impression one forms is that he
was well known, outside Cambridge, as a loyal and capable man
of affairs. The impression is confirmed by the list of those whom
Strype notes as his friends and as being anxious to see that he was
used—the Archbishop of Canterbury, Goodrich, Bishop of Ely
and Chancellor of the realm, Ridley of London (and, it might be

---

[1] Patent Rolls, Edward VI, iii, 347.   [2] *Correspondence*, p. 46.
[3] Patent Rolls, Edward VI, iv, 354.   [4] *Acts of Privy Council*, iii, 466.

added, Thirlby of Westminster). Even more striking is the list of laymen—Sir John Cheke, the King's tutor; Walter Haddon, Professor of Civil Law and Public Orator at Cambridge, successively Master of Trinity Hall and President of Magdalen, Oxford, one of Cranmer's main co-adjutors in drawing up the *Reformatio Legum Ecclesiasticarum*; Nicholas Bacon, afterwards Lord Keeper to Queen Elizabeth, who had been a contemporary at Corpus and remained a life-long friend; William Cecil, brother-in-law of Bacon and already one of the principal secretaries of the Council; William Petre, another secretary of the Council. Indeed, his friends seem to have been already pressing for preferment for him. Strype, though without giving his authority, says[1] that he was nominated both to a bishopric and to the Mastership of Trinity College. His statement seems to be supported, at least about the Mastership, by Parker himself who says[2] that Sir John Cheke had procured his nomination to the 'worship of Trinity College', but that it 'chanced not to that effect, God otherwise determining'. In the same letter, he suggests that Cheke had made this move since Parker had asked to be excused another post because he preferred work in Cambridge, which possibly confirms that he had declined nomination to a see.

With such friends and his increasing employment in public business, added to his position in Cambridge and the Deanery of Lincoln, Parker might well, at just under the age of fifty, have viewed his future (had he been an ambitious man) with complacency. But there is evidence that, even at this time, he was distressed by what was taking place. Anxious for reform rather than destruction, he was offended by the wide-spread confiscation of college and chantry property and of other ecclesiastical wealth, and its use to enrich prominent laymen. He drew up a statement about such confiscations of which Strype reproduces part and summarizes the rest.[3] It is undated, but probably belongs to this period, as it seems to assume that a king not a queen is on the throne. It is a clear and logical statement depending for its effect on cogency of argument rather than on emotional appeal. The

[1] *Parker* i, 61. [2] *Correspondence*, p. 51. [3] *Parker* iii, 12 sqq.

well-being of the Church depends on a vigorous and flourishing ministry. Church property had been accumulated so that men might the more readily enter on that ministry and, untroubled by worldly cares, give themselves wholly to the duties of their office without being burdensome to their flocks. Thus provided, they would be the more respected (Parker did not live entirely in the clouds) and would have to give to the poor. To take away clerical revenues was really to take away from Christ. Besides—and once more he comes down to earth—there was already a great dearth of pious ministers, preachers and learned men. There would be even less chance of satisfying the need for them if the hope of adequate reward were taken away. He did not object to a re-distribution of revenues so that large stipends should be divided, but to take the money away completely was simply to break the tenth commandment. 'We can produce no one honest man out of history who transferred the revenues of the Church to external men.' It had not been done in Germany. Bucer's description of it is quoted with satisfaction: 'lessening the patrimony of the crucified Christ'. Nor can it be justified by the King's need. It is for him to give to the Church, not the reverse; and anyhow 'little or nothing of the emolument came to the King'. The argument was reinforced, as was natural to Parker, by Scripture references and copious historical instances. The tract was not published in Parker's lifetime—possibly he was too timid to speak out. But it expresses a conviction, based on moral grounds as well as practical interests, which always remained strong in Parker and to which he did dare to give open expression under Elizabeth.

The death of King Edward inevitably brought a complete change in Parker's condition. It was a sign of his importance in Cambridge that Northumberland, on his way through the town on July 15 to attempt to overthrow Queen Mary, should have invited him, along with Vice-Chancellor Sandys and the Masters of Trinity (Dr. Bill) and St. John's (Lever) to supper.[1] His advice and support were evidently valuable. But neither that incident nor his previous dependence on Anne Boleyn seems to have

[1] Mullinger, ii, 147.

marked him out subsequently for serious or determined persecution by the authorities under Mary. On one occasion, it is true, he was nearly taken. 'Flying in a night, from such as sought for me to my peril, I fell off my horse so dangerously that I shall never recover it.'[1] But that seems to have been the only time he was in personal danger. On the other hand, he lost all his preferments, as he carefully notes in his *Memoranda*.[2] The Mastership of Corpus he was allowed to 'resign', in December 1553; he was even permitted to choose his successor; but it was 'necessitate quadam'. Of his other offices he was simply deprived, presumably on the ground that he was married. In April 1554, he lost his prebend in Ely and the rectory of Landbeach, though for that, too, he chose his own successor; in May, he lost the Deanery of Lincoln and his prebend there, though, oddly, if his *Memoranda* are reliable, he seems to have exercised a right of presentation to the latter which had been granted to him by the Bishop of Lincoln. If that was really so, it is but one more example of the way in which patronage was regarded as a kind of property; the Marian authorities were anxious not to seem to attack that. Parker's own *Register*, later on, gives ample evidence of the same attitude: grants of patronage by an abbey or even by Bishop Gardiner previously made were not questioned under Elizabeth.[3]

Stripped of his offices, Parker for the rest of Mary's reign lived hidden in the house of a friend, with his wife and two children. So says Joscelyn,[4] who describes his condition as poor and needy since he had no pension from any of his previous offices. But Parker himself does not seem to have felt unduly oppressed. When the time came, under Elizabeth, for his

---

[1] *Correspondence*, p. 59. [2] Ibid., p. 482.
[3] Parker's *Register* (*Registrum Matthei Parker*, ed. W. H. Frere, Oxford, 1928), pp. 204 and 205: As late as 1563, Jewel wrote to Parker to ask if one who neither had nor used priestly apparel, but went 'as a serving man' could hold a prebend in Salisbury by virtue of a 'Roman dispensation under lead'. Jewel, *Defence of Apology* (ed. J. A. Ayre for Parker Society; 2 Vols., Cambridge, 1848–50), 1262.
[4] Strype, *Parker* iii, 277–the *Matthaeus*.

promotion to be considered, he wrote to Bacon[1] 'Your lordship
knoweth with what patrimony I began the world with, and yet
have hitherto lived with enough; yea, when all my livings were
taken from me, yet God, I thank him, ministered to me sufficiently above the capacity of my understanding or foreseeing.'
Possibly that means that he was really dependent not on his
patrimony but on the generosity of friends. Certainly he did not
think of himself as wealthy for, in the same letter, he declares
that 'When I first came to London I had thirty pounds in my
purse, not ten shillings more, whereof I have wasted a good part':
he could, he says, certainly not afford to furnish a big house.
But at least, whether because of his patrimony or his friends, he
had no sense of being oppressed with penury, and his years of
obscurity were years of real happiness. 'The delightful literary
leisure to which the good providence of God recalled me yielded
me much greater and more solid enjoyments, than my former
busy and dangerous life had ever afforded me.'[2] There is a
succession of notes in his *Memoranda* under various dates, each
in turn testifying to his continuous contentment and all marked
by quite simple sincerity.

The only literary outcome of his leisure which he mentions is
'a metrical version of the Psalter into the vulgar tongue' and 'a
defence of the marriage of priests against Thomas Martin'.[3]
Though Strype says that he does not know what became of the
Psalms, it is now generally supposed to be the version printed by
John Day, without date or author's name, conjecturally dated
1567. It is a painstaking version without any great poetical merit.
The book on clerical marriage is, however, a very substantial
work. It is a reply to an attack on such marriages by 'Thomas
Martin', now usually thought to be Stephen Gardiner—Ponet,
indeed, who started to answer the book, definitely so identifies
its author. Ponet's answer was not completed and was used by
Parker as a basis for his own work. This may partly explain its
bitterness and violence. There can, of course, be no doubt that
Parker felt strongly on the point at issue, but there is nothing in

---

[1] *Correspondence*, p. 62.   [2] Ibid., p. viii.   [3] Ibid., p. ix.

his correspondence to match the sustained invective and sarcasm of the *Defence*. Maybe it was partly due to the conventional tone of religious controversy at the time—but again, Parker usually managed to keep remarkably free from that. Ponet, on the other hand, who chose Bale as one of his chaplains, rivalled even him 'in the fluent scurrility of his polemical writings'.[1] The argument in Parker's tome is confused and turgid, but there emerge two main points—that clerical celibacy is only an ecclesiastical ordinance, and that those priests who had married were being treated with extreme and unjust rigour. At the time of their marriage they had not been acting against the laws prevailing in England. The King's Supremacy and his dispensing power had been recognized by the bishops (he pointedly refers to Gardiner's *De Vera Obedientia*), and some of the clergy now being dispossessed had royal dispensations. They had only done what was publicly allowed at the time. If they were wrong, they should be dealt with gently, not with harshness. In fact they were being evicted with great cruelty—some without a chance of renouncing their wives, some when a half-year's income was almost due, and without any provision of pension from their cures. But the main argument concerns the question of clerical obligation to celibacy. Parker admits that for the clergy, celibacy is more to be wished than matrimony 'considering both states in themselves', though he does also point out that with a married clergy residence is better observed, houses are better kept, hospitality and relief are given on a larger scale. He also admits that the canons of the church are confused, and that Martin can quote some on his side. But he has little difficulty in showing that some of Martin's arguments and evidence are at least *ex parte* if not actually dishonest. 'He misconstrueth his authors, misreporteth his allegations, misnameth the persons' (105). He attributes to Luther's *Babylonish Captivity* a sentence which is not there (50). He refers for authority to a book in Magdalen College, Oxford, library, but advises the reader not to look for it as it is probably

---

[1] R. W. Dixon, *History of the Church of England* (London, 1878 foll.), iii, 274.

now not there (118). He attributes ordinances to two popes which are not to be found in their decrees (151-2), and misrepresents a Council (154). He misquotes Augustine and confuses his writings (104-5), and so on. It is all closely and convincingly argued so as to give the impression that Martin's book had been unscholarly and unreliable. On the other hand, his own arguments are supported by a great wealth of authorities—Ambrose, Augustine, Chrysostom, Bernard, Hilary, Jerome. And there are pages of extracts from papal pronouncements and conciliar decisions, mostly removing married clergy from their ministerial functions but still allowing them to keep their wives, but certainly not insisting that they lose both. Moreover, he points out that on getting married the secular clergy (unlike the monastic) did not even break their vows: there was no oath of celibacy in the English Ordinal (181-2). But his main and fundamental contention is that it is all a matter of Roman canon law—and that such was only valid in England 'upon consent' (176) (the normal point of view among the reformers of Henry's day). For 'the Church of England . . . is as well a catholic and apostolic church as Rome church, or any other, and of like and equal authority, jurisdiction and power' (233). And so 'as this particular Church by their (i.e. the clergy's) assent received that Law (about celibacy); so by dissent again hath refused that law. And therefore is no further bound.' Martin, of course, held that canon law was binding irrespective of King or Parliament.

Parker obviously devoted much care and attention to this work, and seems to have written or at least revised the preface after Queen Mary's death. For though in the body of the book she and Philip are referred to as reigning, and Calais had not fallen (131), in the preface he refers to the childlessness of the Queen and the fall of Calais among the other misfortunes which prove God's displeasure with the realm. It would therefore seem likely that he revised the book for publication by Richard Jugge (to whose edition the page references above apply) under Elizabeth, perhaps in the hope (vain as it proved) of winning her consent to the legalizing of clerical matrimony.

CHAPTER V

THE ELIZABETHAN SETTLEMENT

QUEEN MARY died on 17 Nov. 1558; without challenge, Elizabeth succeeded to the throne amidst demonstrations of enthusiasm, although hitherto the general public had had little chance of knowing much about her. She had been usually kept in obscurity in the country, when not actually in prison in the Tower, during Mary's reign. But that, apart from anything else, would have sufficed to secure for her a popular welcome. And her accession was full of hope. There might now be a change from the disastrous policy of Mary with its persecutions, its submission to Spanish influence, its unsuccessful wars, its financial failures.

As the years passed, Elizabeth was to increase rather than to lose her hold on the hearts of her people. She was, it has been said, 'English to the bone, with less foreign blood in her veins than any English sovereign since the Danish conquest.'[1] Probably her deepest emotion was love of her country. But in superficial things, too—things which much affect the relationship between a people and its sovereign—she was in natural sympathy with them, sharing their likes and dislikes. Almost parsimonious in small matters—the first pair of silk stockings she ever owned were a present to her at the first New Year of her reign[2]—she yet rejoiced in processions and splendour, tournaments and shows (even to bull-baiting), dancing and entertainments: in a word, in all the things which could bring colour into life after the drab days of Mary. Of her tastes she had already given such proofs as she was allowed to do. On the few occasions of her public appearance in London she had been careful to be sumptuously

[1] Conyers Read, *The Tudors* (Oxford, 1936), p. 149.
[2] C. Morris, *The Tudors* (London, 1955), p. 157.

dressed and magnificently escorted.[1] Such hints were not missed. Ten days after her accession it was said that the English had bought up all the cloths of silk at Antwerp so as to appear 'with very great pomp at the coronation of the new Queen'.[2] Truly, the sun was rising. The Spanish ambassador wrote that she is 'very much wedded to the people and thinks as they do'.[3]; a few days later, that she seems 'incomparably more feared than her sister, and gives her orders and has her way as absolutely as her father did'.[4]

Those who had official dealings with her were at times infuriated. Her obstinacy, her secretiveness, her tortuous policy, her evasiveness completely baffled them: she 'must have a hundred thousand devils in her body' a Spanish ambassador once remarked.[5] But the ordinary man was untouched by such things. Even when unpopular policies were enforced, really by her, she managed to escape odium. Ministers or bishops (especially the latter) had all the blame even when they were only acting under royal compulsion. Nothing, it seemed, could shake the common loyalty almost akin to adulation. It was one of Elizabeth's greatest assets.

She sorely needed it. An acute observer, Armagil Waad, who had risen from obscurity to be Secretary to the Council under Edward VI, summed up the *Distresses of the Commonwealth* as 'the poverty of the Queen, the penury of noblemen and their poverty, the wealth of the meaner sort, the dearth of things, the divisions within the realm, the wars, want of justice'.[6] There were indeed dangers from both France and Scotland. Yet he rightly saw that they were of only comparative urgency as against the need to set in order the domestic scene, sorely disarrayed by the decline of the old territorial aristocracy and the rise of a new body of wealthy merchants and smaller landowners,

[1] *Diary of Henry Machyn* (ed. J. G. Nichols for the Camden Society, London, 1848), pp. 37, 57, 120, 166.
[2] Calendar of Venetian State Papers (London, 1884), vi, 1549.
[3] Calendar of Spanish State Papers: Elizabeth (London, 1892), i, 4.
[4] Ibid., p. 7.   [5] Ibid., p. 119.
[6] Quoted by H. Gee, *The Elizabethan Prayer Book* (London, 1902), p. 207.

by the emergence of an independent-minded middle class, by
the real poverty of the very poor. As it emerged from the middle
ages, the country needed a breathing space to shake down, so to
speak, in its new social pattern. And for that, above all, some
clear and definite religious settlement was vital after the changes
and frustrations of the last five and twenty years.

That there would be alterations was universally expected: as
soon as they heard of Elizabeth's accession the Marian exiles
hastened with confidence and joy to return. But the Queen was
very cautious. Her fundamental wish and policy was to provide
a settlement which would appeal to the widest possible range of
her subjects and thus provide a bond and unifying inspiration for
the nation. Wary by nature, she had no need of Waad's warning
of the danger involved in any attempt to pour liquor 'suddenly or
violently' into 'glasses with small necks'. She wished to take
her time. Thus at first she sought only to prevent either of the
extreme parties, Roman or protestant, from establishing so dominant a position that her hand would be forced. On the second
Sunday of her reign, the Bishop of Chichester, Christopherson,
preached at Paul's Cross a violent sermon denouncing the new
views as heretical and human inventions. The sermons at the
Cross were great public, almost official, occasions, often attended
(as Machyn abundantly shows) not only by the Lord Mayor and
aldermen, but by the leading nobility as well; and by great
crowds, sometimes as many as six or seven thousand.[1] The
bishop's public and forcible exposition to such an audience of full
Romanism could not be allowed. He was summoned to the royal
presence, examined, and ordered to be imprisoned.[2] Similarly,
when White, Bishop of Winchester, in his sermon at Queen
Mary's funeral on December 14, warned of the 'wolves' who
were coming from Geneva, denounced 'infidels, rebels and
heretics', insisted that 'the church judgeth all men and is judged
of none', and warmly commended Mary for her refusal of the

[1] *Zurich Letters* (ed. for the Parker Society by Hastings Robinson; 2
Vols., Cambridge, 1842, 1845), i, 71.
[2] Ibid., i, 4.

title of Head,[1] he was confined to his house by the Council, and only set free a month later with 'a good admonition'.[2] But an eye was equally kept on the other side. Even under Mary protestants had ventured to maintain their meetings in London secretly—on business premises or at a private house, at times on shipboard on the Thames, or even in the open; two of their leaders, Scambler and Bentham, under Elizabeth became bishops.[3] They had kept in close touch with the English protestants abroad, and were now much emboldened, especially when strengthened by the returning exiles, whose arrival the Spanish ambassador already observed by December 29.[4] The result was a royal proclamation on December 28 noting that there had been assemblies of 'great number of people' resulting in 'unfruitful dispute ... contention and occasion to break common quiet'. Therefore all preaching either by ministers or others was forbidden, and also all listening to any doctrine or preaching beyond what was contained in those parts of the service authorized to be read in English—the Ten Commandments, the Epistle and Gospel for the day, the Creed and the Lord's Prayer —'without exposition or addition'.[5] The services by law established were alone to be used.

Such measures were obviously precautionary, not the final word: the proclamation itself promised consultations by Parliament, the Queen and the three estates of the realm. So, when Parliament met in January 1559, both sides girded themselves to battle. The Queen was still cautious: all she wanted at first was the recognition of the Royal Supremacy,[6] and certain financial measures, not as yet a new Prayer Book. Her original personal preference was probably for a middle course. She is credited with saying that she would not renounce the use in which she was

---

[1] The Sermon is printed in Strype's *Memorials*, III, ii, 536 sqq.
[2] *Cal. S. P. Span.* i, 18 and *Acts of the Privy Council*, vii, 45.
[3] Strype, *Memorials*, III, ii, 132-5, 147-8; Machyn, p. 160.
[4] *Cal. S. P. Span.* i, 16.
[5] The Proclamation is in Strype, *Annals* I, ii, 391.
[6] Cf. Sir J. E. Neale, *Elizabeth and Her Parliaments, 1559-81* (London, 1953), pp. 33-84; a completely convincing reconstruction of the course of events.

brought up[1] and that she wished to put religion where her father left it.[2] In fact, however, even before the Uniformity Act, she had advanced beyond that. On Christmas Day she withdrew when the celebrant disobeyed her order that there should be no elevation of the consecrated host;[3] her proclamation in December allowed certain parts of the service to be in English; in March, a further proclamation ordered communion to be ministered on Easter Day in both kinds.[4] It looks as though she would have been best satisfied by a restoration of Edward's First Prayer Book, with its retention of much traditional ritual and ornament, its insistence on real presence and its exclusion alike of papalism and protestant extremes. But she did not seek to impose any change hastily. Professor Neale argues convincingly that her first plan was to get rid of the most bigoted of the Romanist bishops on their refusal to take the Supremacy oath while hoping to retain some of the less rigid. After all, Tunstall the venerated Bishop of Durham, and the popular and respected Archbishop of York, Heath, had both been bishops under Henry and might again agree to renounce the papal claims. With a hierarchy under such leaders, supported by new and suitable bishops, there might be a chance of a service book to the Queen's liking, drawn up with the approval of Convocation—the proper authority for such a work—and thus backed so authoritatively as to be accepted by all the returning enthusiasts save the most rigid.

If there was any such plan—its existence is not proved but is an attractive conjecture, entirely suited to the Queen's subtlety and in accord with her hesitancy about the revision of the Prayer Book—it fell through. Convocation, with an alacrity which showed the alarm of its members, asserted enthusiastically the full Roman doctrine of transubstantiation, the supreme power of Peter and his successors and the exclusive right of the clergy alone to deal in matters of faith, sacrament, and doctrine. In the Lords, no single bishop would vote even for the restoration of

---

[1] *Cal. S. P. Ven.* vi, p. 1563.   [2] *Cal. S. P. Span.* i, 37.
[3] Ibid., i, 17.   [4] Gee, *Elizabethan Prayer Book*, pp. 255-7.

Royal Supremacy. In the Commons, on the other hand, there was an energetic and well-led group which showed its determination not to be satisfied with anything less than a return at least to the position at the end of Edward's reign.

Concerning the papal claims, the Queen could make no concession in view of her parentage.[1] The unyielding attitude of Convocation and bishops inevitably drove her, probably more than she would have wished, to look to the other side for support. Already, by the end of January, Jewel had heard that the return of the exiles was acceptable to her.[2] Except for Parker, all those who are mentioned by Machyn as chosen to preach before her in Lent were returned exiles, though, significantly, none of them had close associations with Geneva; they were from Germany. By March 20, Jewel knew of the arrangements for a disputation between the two sides, Roman and protestant, to be held at Westminster starting on March 31—he was himself to take part in it.[3] The mere holding of a disputation does not prove that Elizabeth was even yet thinking of immediate action. Such public arguments were common form in all countries where there were religious dissensions at the time. Anyhow, there is evidence that when she arranged it, the Queen was still intending to dissolve or prorogue Parliament within a few days, content with the restoration of the Supremacy and without any action to revise the Prayer Book. But the mere announcement of the disputation showed that, officially, the pronouncements of Convocation were regarded as arguable, not final.

Then the Queen changed her mind. Parliament was not prorogued but simply adjourned till after the disputation, which opened on March 31, with Bacon and Heath of York as moderators. Three matters were to be argued—the use in services of a

---

[1] Before Anne's execution Cranmer had ruled that her marriage with Henry was null and void. No legal step had been taken to alter that. Elizabeth was therefore illegitimate in the view of the English law. But there was little danger of that point being raised when she was on the throne. The Pope could have dispensed her illegitimacy and seems to have hinted that he might. But the line taken by English Catholics threatened trouble.

[2] *Zurich Letters*, i, 6.   [3] Ibid., pp. 10–11.

tongue unknown to the people, the power of particular churches over rites and ceremonies, the doctrine of propitiatory sacrifice in the mass. For the conservatives the outcome was disaster.[1] They did not observe the carefully pre-arranged rules of procedure; they had not properly prepared their case and tried to defend it by violent abuse of their opponents. Our accounts, it is true, are from the protestant side and may be biased. But even Heath rebuked the bishops for their disorderliness which, in the end, prevented the third point even being considered at all. Two of the bishops, White of Winchester and Watson of Lincoln, were sent to the Tower for their conduct, and the others forbidden to leave London for the time being, heavily fined, and ordered to present themselves personally to the Council whenever it met. The two prisoners were soon released.

For the protestants the outcome was as striking as would have been a victory in debate. Their opponents were discredited by conduct which suggested that they knew they could not win by argument. The sequel, if not the direct result, was a new Act of Uniformity such as the Queen before the disputation had plainly not intended for this session of Parliament. The details of its preparation are not known. Strype mentions a committee,[2] but there is no evidence at all that it ever met or was, indeed, appointed. There is some ground for suggesting that a different committee did actually draw up a new book of a type more advanced than Edward's Second Book.[3] If so, its labours bore no fruit. The only certainty is that just over a fortnight after the disputation, the new Uniformity Bill was put forward on April 18, and passed through all its stages in the Commons on three successive days. In the Lords also, despite solid episcopal opposition, it went through with remarkable rapidity, though the majority was not large. On May 8 it received the royal assent. So quick a passage by the Commons suggests, indeed, that before

---

[1] Jewel's account is in *Zurich Letters*, i, 13 sqq. Cf. Strype, *Annals* I, i, 128–38. The Venetian State Papers, vii, 64–65, though suggesting that the bishops were badly treated, yet admits that they expatiated 'on many matters which it would be tedious to narrate'!

[2] *Annals* I, i, 75, 119.   [3] Neale, op. cit., pp. 76–77.

the Bill was first read negotiations and bargaining had taken place behind the scenes. But we have no certain information about them.

The Act ordered the restoration of the Second Book of Edward VI with certain specified though apparently very limited changes —in the lessons, in the Litany, in the words of administration at communion—'and none other or otherwise'. It seems as though it was sought deliberately to minimize the alterations. At the end of the Act there was slipped in, looking almost like an afterthought, a proviso that the 'ornaments of the church and of the ministers thereof' should be 'retained and be in use' as in King Edward's First Book. In effect, however, the Act was a retreat rather than an advance from the position at the end of Edward's reign, though put in a manner as conciliatory as possible. In the Litany, the omission of the petition for deliverance from 'the tyranny of the Bishop of Rome and all his detestable enormities' showed a less bitter spirit than prevailed at the end of Edward's reign. The few changes and additions in lessons and prayers had no doctrinal significance. But other changes were important. First of all, at communion the addition of the words of administration from Edward's First Book to those in the Second, resulting in the double formula still authorized, stressed the reality of reception to the exclusion of the idea of a mere memorial, a view reinforced by the omission of the Black Rubric, intruded into the Book of 1552 without authority. Secondly, the ornaments proviso, for all its innocent appearance, was deliberately meant to secure that the traditional look of things should be maintained.

Both changes, in all likelihood, were due to the insistence of the Queen. She certainly believed in the real presence—there is no reason at all to doubt the truth of her remark, reported by the Spanish ambassador between the passing of the Bill and the royal assent to it, that she 'believed that God was in the sacrament of the eucharist'.[1] And she certainly preferred churches and services which were not bare of ornament and ceremonial. Thus personal choice, native caution against too rapid change,

[1] *Cal. S. P. Span.* i, 62.

political sense of what would be likely to make the widest appeal to her subjects, would all combine to make her insist on such changes. Nor, at first sight, would they seem serious blemishes to the protestants. So far, the returned exiles involved were not from Geneva but from Germany where they had been at least tolerated by Lutherans, and become familiar with their views of the reality of the presence. They would not be startled by the eucharistic doctrine. The matter of ornaments was, indeed, different. From the first they clearly disliked them. Strype gives a list of seven who were afterwards bishops (and two of them archbishops) who 'laboured all they could' against ceremonies and papistical habits, though without success, against Queen and Parliament.[1] But the proviso only commanded such ornaments to be used 'until other order be taken' by the Queen on the advice of her ecclesiastical commissioners or the Metropolitan. It looked like a temporary measure. Sandys consoled himself by the thought that it was not meant to enforce the use of the ornaments but only to prevent them falling into other hands before the Queen could collect them.[2] When the book actually appeared it must have been a shock to find a rubric ordering the prayers to be read in the 'accustomed place' (not 'where the people may best hear', as in 1552) and chancels to remain as 'in times past'—a further clear attempt to maintain traditional appearances of which the Act said nothing. When a few years later it became obvious that the Queen did not really mean to take further order, the trouble about ornaments became serious. But in April 1559 the protestants had no suspicion of that. Anyhow, they had no practical choice other than to accept. If they had not done so, the Queen would have refused her assent to the Act and they would have been left with the services as they had been under Mary.

It was, to say the least, a serious drawback that the new book should have been authorized in this fashion by Parliament alone. It had no proper ecclesiastical backing; on the contrary, it was against the known wishes of Convocation and the solid

[1] *Annals* I, i, 264.   [2] *Correspondence*, p. 65.

opposition of the bishops in the Lords. Moreover, the whole procedure gave the Commons the unfortunate idea that they had a right to interfere in such matters—a cause of constant trouble with the Queen for the next thirty years. But it is hard to see what else could have been done. Bishops and Convocation would not give way an inch; the eager protestants in Parliament would not wait—and the nation as a whole did probably desire the break with Rome (or at least the break with Mary's policy). The Act represented the best compromise Elizabeth could obtain; had she waited longer it is very unlikely that in any succeeding Parliament she would have obtained a settlement nearly so conservative.

The new book was ordered to be obtained by all churches before June 24, and to be in use within three weeks after. Not to use it, or even to speak against it, were made punishable offences. Another Act restored the Royal Supremacy under the title of 'Supreme Governor'; Elizabeth herself preferred this in view of the objections raised, even by protestants, to the title of Head. Under this Act the royal authority could be used to visit, reform, and amend by means of commissioners appointed as often and for so long as the Queen desired—the origin of the Elizabethan ecclesiastical commissioners.[1] Futher Acts restored to the Crown the tithes, first-fruits and impropriations Mary had alienated; conveyed to the Crown the endowments of such religious houses as Mary had re-founded; allowed the Queen, during the vacancy of a see, to take to herself such episcopal manors and lands as she wished, giving in exchange tithes or

---

[1] The Elizabethan commissioners are to be distinguished from the nineteenth-century Ecclesiastical Commission (now the Church Commissioners). Elizabeth issued a series of commissions under the Supremacy Act. The first, in 1559, authorized enquiry into the working of the Supremacy and Uniformity Acts, examination of cases of heresy and sedition, of irregularities in service, of absences from church and so on. It was centred on London (Gee, *Elizabethan Clergy*, p. 139). It was superseded in 1562 by another commission with similar purposes (Ibid., pp. 175, 178). There seems also to have been a separate commission for the North in 1561-2 (Ibid., pp. 165-6). In 1570 Parker refers to separate commissions for different dioceses—Winchester, Chichester, Canterbury. (*Correspondence*, p. 371.)

impropriations of (apparently) equal value. This last Act was to result in the serious impoverishment of many of the bishops, for what they received was usually far smaller in real value than what they lost.

So ended Elizabeth's first Parliament. Ecclesiastically it effected very nearly a return to the state of things in the early part of Edward's reign. It is true that clerical marriage was not legally allowed—Elizabeth never agreed to that, though she took no steps to stop it. It is also true that the actual services ordered were not so similar to the Roman services as those of Edward's First Book. But the earlier eucharistic doctrine was firmly maintained, the accustomed appearances were ordered to be retained in church, the monasteries disappeared and the financial interests of the Crown were restored.

It is remarkable that in all these transactions Parker seems to have played no part at all. From letters we have a fairly detailed picture of what he was doing, and of what was intended for him.[1] He was, at first, ill of a quartan ague and unwilling even to travel to London: he was suffering, too, from the accident which befell him when 'flying in a night'. He was thus driven 'sometime to be idle when I would be occupied, and also to keep my bed'. In one letter in December 1558 he seems to think—even to hope—that he has not much longer to live.[2] The authorities— the Queen, Cecil, Bacon—were determined that he should be Archbishop. He was striving by every means to avoid the office— by long letters, by self-depreciation, by not presenting himself when summoned. As early as 9 Dec. 1558, Bacon invited him to London to be told what he and Cecil planned for him. He replied with a long letter pleading ill-health and urging that he should not be given a post 'above the reach of mine ability' but a prebend without cure or the Headship of Benet College. If some such post was not available, 'without public state of living', he asked Bacon to see that 'I be quite forgotten'. Such hopes were vain. At the end of December Cecil wrote that he should 'forthwith' make his 'indelayed repair' to London to hear the Queen's

---

[1] *Correspondence*, pp. 49–71.   [2] Ibid., p. 50.

pleasure. In January, Bacon wrote to confirm the summons, in case Cecil's letter had gone astray. So far, Parker seems simply to have stayed in his country retreat. But on 10 Feb. 1559, the first Friday in Lent, he was in London preaching before the Queen.[1] By March 1 he was back in Cambridge, apparently settled there, having given up his other home as he could not afford to keep up two establishments. He wrote then to warn Cecil, the Chancellor of the University, to keep a close eye on it, since it seemed likely that, in view of the Supremacy Act, 'some masters be about to resign to their friends chosen for their purpose, peradventure to slide away with a gain'.[2] On the same day he wrote a long letter to Bacon.[3] He saw the difficulties an Archbishop would have to face, even to the possibility of the 'private quarrels' among the exiles being 'brought home' and so shivering them asunder. The new Archbishop should be neither arrogant (for such a one would 'sit in his own light' and not understand) nor faint-hearted nor covetous. So far as he himself was concerned, he was afraid that the 'over-much good will' of Bacon and Cecil might jeopard him into prison because of his unwillingness to comply. But he would rather suffer with a quiet conscience than be intruded into a position where he could not answer the charge to God nor serve the Queen's honour nor give satisfaction to the friends who had put him forward. His visit to London had upset his health, and he wished for a post in which he would not be 'occasioned to come up to any con-vocations, as having no voice in that house'. Besides, he was not well off. When he went to London he had but thirty pounds, of which he had 'wasted' a good part: he could not begin to furnish a household such as would be required. (Though he thought that the 'seniority' of the Queen's 'spiritual ministers' were 'acloyd with worldly collections, temporal commissions and worldly provisions', it never seems to have occurred to him that bishops could be rid of such things.) 'Think not', he pleaded, 'that I seek mine private gain or my idle ease. Put me where ye will else.'

[1] Machyn, p. 189.   [2] *Correspondence*, p. 54.   [3] Ibid., pp. 57–63.

The obvious sincerity of the letter is pathetic in view of the burdensome years, even worse than he guessed, which lay ahead for Parker. For the moment, however, he was left in Cambridge. At the very time when the Westminster Disputation was being arranged, Cecil wrote to him, not to summon him to take part in it, but along with the Vice-Chancellor and Dr. Leeds, to deal with a local quarrel which had arisen about the election of some Fellows at Queens' College! The outcome was that the President of the college resigned, and two young Fellows about whose election there had been trouble—described by Parker as 'well minded in the service of God'—were admitted to the College. On April 30, when the Uniformity Act was passed but had not yet the royal assent, Sandys, one of the Westminster disputants, wrote to Parker that 'ye are happy that ye are so far from these tossings and griefs, alterations and mutations: for we are made weary with them. But ye cannot long rest in your cell. Ye must be removed to a more large abbey, and therefore in the meantime take your pleasure, for after ye will find but a little.'[1]

Why, at such an important juncture, the authorities left Parker to 'rest in his cell' there is no means of knowing. The most likely guess is that they judged—very rightly—that he was not the man for the rush and tumble of acrid disputation. He was too gentle, too quiet, too moderate to stand up to the violence of the champions of the old religion. For that, the passionate partisanship of the returned exiles was needed. Besides, if the Queen wished—as she did—to pursue a middle course, it was doubtless clever tactics to oppose to each other the extremists, and then take the path between them, keeping Parker, her already chosen agent, free from involvement in the disputes. But Sandys was right in his belief that Parker's quiet time was near its end. On May 17, Bacon wrote that a resolution made in the Queen's presence put an end to any hope that he could be spared the charge. On the 19th, there was a formal letter from Cecil and Bacon saying that the Queen's pleasure was that he

---

[1] *Correspondence*, p. 66—a clear hint that there had been much bargaining about the Act of Uniformity.

should 'with such speed as you conveniently can' repair to London to hear what service was required of him. On the 28th they had to write again because their letter had been ignored! Parker now made a last effort in a letter to the Queen, probably to be dated in June, pleading for gracious consideration of his poor suit which only extreme necessity compels him to make. He beseeches that he may be discharged of that 'so high and chargeable an office which doth require a man of much more wit, learning, virtue and experience than I see and perfectly know can be performed by me, worthily to occupy it to God's pleasure, to your Grace's honour and to the wealth of your loving subjects'; he pleads also his lack of financial means and infirmity of body. Loyalty both to her and her mother alike impel him to serve her to the best of his power in some lesser office, and he is 'right sorry and do lament within myself that I am so basely qualified inwardly in knowledge and outwardly in extern sufficiencies'. It was in vain. Another letter from Bacon (undated but probably written in June) told him that the former resolution had now been confirmed by a second.[1] On July 8 the Queen sent her licence to the Dean and Chapter of Canterbury to proceed with the election of a new Archbishop. On August 1, Parker was duly elected by the Chapter—but seven canons were absent: only the Dean and four canons elected. On August 6 he formally consented. During the 'process' it is mentioned that the Queen had 'commended' him for election; he was described as 'nominated Bishop of Canterbury' in the writ for the ecclesiastical commission as early as July 19.[2] So there must have been the usual royal 'letters missive' to the Dean and Chapter indicating that they were to choose him, although there is no direct reproduction of such nomination in the formal account of the proceedings given at the beginning of his *Register*.

[1] Perhaps this is what is referred to by Machyn (p. 201) when he says that six new bishops were 'elected' on June 23. Certainly Parker's technical election was on August 1. What happened on June 23 may have been a decision of the Council as to who the new bishops should be. It was evidently public property as Machyn knew of it so quickly.

[2] H. Gee, *The Elizabethan Clergy*(Oxford, 1898), p. 147.

Parker now moved to London. On August 27 he was writing from Lambeth: though not yet consecrated he was regularly addressed by Cecil as 'your lordship' or even 'your grace'.[1] On one occasion he actually signed a letter 'Matth. C.'[2], though usually he does add 'elect' in this period. He took the leading part, presumably as chief minister of the Church, in the magnificent obsequies of Henry II of France, provided at the Queen's charges in September.[3] But he was not actually consecrated until December 17, thirteen months after Pole's death. The delay was not inexcusable: there were strong reasons for it. The Supremacy and Uniformity Acts did not miraculously produce a settled calm. Waves of Roman obstinacy and winds of reforming ebullience still had to be checked. First of all, the remaining Roman bishops—seventeen of them still at the beginning of 1559—had to be dealt with. So, on May 23, a commission of eighteen was nominated by the Queen (under the Supremacy Act) to administer the oath to all ecclesiastical persons, judges and lay officers of the Crown. The commission did not include any ecclesiastics and was practically identical with the Privy Council—doubtless to give it the weight of great authority, but also, possibly, so that its proceedings should seem a mere enforcement of the law untinged by religious bias. First to be dealt with was Bonner of London, the most hated as well as the most ruthless of the Marian persecutors. He was, besides, a real nuisance at the moment. Though the new Prayer Book was not enforceable until June 24, in many churches changes began to be made well before that date. On Easter Day, even before the Uniformity Act was passed, there were alterations in the royal chapel: before administering communion, the celebrant discarded his vestments and used only a surplice.[4] By the end of May most London churches were living 'in the Lutheran fashion'—but at St. Paul's, Bonner still kept the old services going.[5] Legally, he was within his rights—but so conspicuous an example was tiresome. He was

---

[1] *Correspondence*, passim.   [2] Ibid., p. 74.
[3] *Machyn*, pp. 209–10; Strype, *Annals* I, i, 188–91.
[4] *Cal. S. P. Ven.* vii, 57.   [5] Ibid., p. 94.

offered a liberal pension if he would resign, but refused: he could, he said, support himself by teaching or even as a gardener or by begging if need be.[1] It is very significant that he had obviously no fear that he would be treated as harshly as he had treated others. So, on May 30, he was deprived for refusing to take the oath.[2] On June 11, the old services ceased at St. Paul's.[3]

Other bishops were similarly treated, being given time to think over their position before deprivation. By the middle of August, however, there were only five who had not been deprived; Kitchin of Llandaff (who satisfied the authorities), Tunstall of Durham, and three others. At first there were real hopes of winning Tunstall's support for the new order. It would have been invaluable, for he was very deeply respected. Moreover, he had genuinely agreed with Henry's rejection of papal authority, and had not thought it right to make the doctrine of transubstantiation a test for heresy.[4] Nor, so far, had he, like the other bishops, committed himself to opposition; he had been excused from attendance in the Lords during the Parliament on the grounds of health and so had not given his views. But he was now shocked by the violence and riot which he saw in London. On August 19 he wrote to Cecil that he could not consent to the visitation of his diocese if it were to extend to pulling down altars, defacing churches and taking away crucifixes.[5] Even so, there were still hopes of him. On September 9, a commission issued from the Queen to him and five other bishops to consecrate Parker.[6] On the 23rd, the Council asked Parker to find him 'a fit chamber . . . in your house near unto you' and to have conference with him.[7] At first Parker was able to report optimistically, but it became clear by October 5 that the aged bishop would not comply. He, too, was therefore deprived. He died in November, probably still under the care of Parker,[8] who

---

[1] *Cal. S. P. Ven.*, vii, 95.   [2] Strype, *Annals* I, i, 205.   [3] Machyn, p. 200.
[4] R. W. Dixon, *History of the Church of England* (Oxford, 1902), v, 187, note.
[5] *Calendar of State Papers, Domestic, 1547–80* (London, 1856), p. 137. All references to the Calendar are to this volume, unless otherwise stated.
[6] Ibid., p. 138.   [7] Parker, *Correspondence*, pp. 77, 78.   [8] Ibid., p. 106.

saw to his burial in the parish church of Lambeth. Of the three remaining bishops two were deprived in October or November; the third—Sodor and Man—retained his see till well in the sixties, but does not seem to have had any part in church matters outside his diocese. The deprived bishops were not imprisoned: indeed, the Act did not authorize imprisonment for mere refusal of the oath, but only loss of benefice or office: loss of goods and further punishment were for those who maintained foreign authority in the country. Later on, some of the bishops were to suffer imprisonment for this, but not yet. In July, even the two who had been sent to the Tower after the Westminster Disputation were set free.

But the bishops were not the only difficulty. Many of the cathedral dignitaries were recalcitrant, and ordinary parish clergy and even laymen caused trouble. It was reported, on June 30, for example, that the Dean and canons of Winchester, the Warden and Fellows of New College and the Master of St. Cross Hospital had all left their services for conscience sake.[1] The Privy Council had constantly to issue orders for dealing with 'lewd' priests or a layman who hindered the saying of the service in English (even before it was legally enforceable).[2] On the other hand, protestant hopes of liberty were being celebrated with licence. The Lord Mayor of London had to be rebuked at the end of March for doing nothing about sacrilege at St. Mary-le-Bow—the pulling down of images and of the sacrament, the defacing of vestments and books: he was ordered to discover and punish the culprits.[3] On Ascension day at St. Paul's the procession was attacked, the cross seized and broken: but no one was punished. Already, by the middle of May, many crucifixes were down in London, altars denuded and images defaced.[4]

Both conservative obstinacy and excited lawlessness obviously called for special measures. Accordingly there went out, probably towards the end of June, orders for a Royal Visitation to survey and, so far as possible, set in order the whole ecclesiastical

[1] *Cal. S. P. Dom.*, p. 133. [2] *Privy Council Acts*, vii, 96.
[3] Ibid., p. 77. [4] *Cal. S. P. Ven.* vii, 84.

position. There were six groups of visitors for the six areas into which the whole of England and Wales was divided; each group contained leading local nobility or landed magnates, some lawyers and not more than one or two ecclesiastics—again giving the impression that they were, without religious bias, simply to enforce the laws. And, once more, though several who were destined for high office in the church—Sandys, Horne, Jewel—were included in this or that group, Parker was, significantly, omitted. The powers of the visitors were very wide. As was customary on such occasions, episcopal functions were suspended (which no doubt made the delay in filling the vacant sees less inconvenient), and the visitors were empowered to carry out many normal ecclesiastical duties, such as appointing to livings and dealing with testamentary affairs. But they were also to conduct a thorough examination of clergy and people and, particularly, to administer the Supremacy oath, punishing refusers by deprivation or other methods. Rebellious or contumacious persons might be imprisoned as well as visited with ecclesiastical censures. The visitors were to restore such of the clergy as had been deprived (for matrimony) under Mary, and were to deliver everywhere the Royal Injunctions.

The Injunctions are of prime importance. Though prepared for the visitation, they were not meant to be transitional, but to set out the permanent scheme for the Church—the scheme, in fact, which Parker would be expected to enforce. The clergy were required to take an oath that the orders and rules in them were 'according to the true word of God and agreeable to the doctrine of the primitive Church.'[1] Though based on the Edwardine Injunctions, they included changes and additions which could not be wholly agreeable to the extreme reformers. Thus, though there was a very careful and balanced statement of what was meant by the Royal Supremacy (to meet qualms as to

---

[1] Gee, *Elizabethan Clergy,* p. 78. The oath was composite, and included also recognition of the Supremacy, and of the Prayer Book. Though not one of the visitors, Parker helped in 'devising' the oath thus used in the visitation. *Correspondence,* p. 74. The Injunctions are printed in *Documents Illustrative of English Church History* (H. Gee and W. J. Hardy: London 1896), pp. 417 sqq.

whether the Crown was claiming prerogatives which were properly only ministerial—or even divine) there was less explicit rejection, by name, of Roman claims. Again, though there was great stress on regular preaching (the only time during service when a bell might be rung was before the sermon: the *sanctus* bell was forbidden), and overseers were to be appointed to report those who did not go to church, yet only those licensed to preach were to do so. If no such preacher was available, officially provided homilies were to be read. Moreover, all printing of books etc. was to be strictly controlled. By such measures, unordered eloquence and enthusiasm were to be severely curbed. Even worse, in their teaching the clergy were to uphold 'the laudable ceremonies of the church, commanded by public authority to be observed'—and there was no hint, as there had been in Edward's Injunctions, that there was to be a further abrogation of them. Further, the clergy were to wear distinctive clothes not only in church but out of doors as well—'such seemly habits, garments and such square caps' as in Edward's reign. There were to be no more riotous destructions of altars, and the holy tables substituted for them, in orderly manner, were to be decently covered and to stand normally where the altars had stood, save when moved for convenience when there was a communion. Even then, they were still to be within the chancel, not (as the rubric ordered) 'in the Body of the church or in the Chancel'. For communion, wafers were to be once more used, in form clearly distinguishable from those used in the Roman mass but still more like them than 'the best and purest wheat bread that conveniently may be gotten' of Edward's book. All this was highly distasteful to those who found the Prayer Book of the Uniformity Act too conservative: it was retrograde rather than progressive. The segregation of clergy from laity was to be emphasized out of church as well as inside; old ceremonies as well as traditional ornaments were to be continued; the customary appearance of churches was to be maintained by placing a decently covered table where the altar had stood; wafers were to recall memories of the mass. The

Injunctions were a shock to those who hoped the Prayer Book
was only a stage on the road to further changes.

The visitation started in July or August and went on intermittently till the Queen ordered that operations should be
suspended and no new matters opened, though those already
started should be concluded. This was probably in November
or December—the document is not dated.[1] Meantime, yet a
third body was set up under the Supremacy Act—the permanent
ecclesiastical commission—by two royal writs of July 19 and
October 20.[2] There were nineteen members of it, and it was
obviously expected that it would normally be centred on London.
It had, moreover, the appearance of a definitely ecclesiastical
court. It was headed (in the second writ) by the Archbishop of
Canterbury and the Bishops of London and Ely, and contained
few if any territorial magnates; as few as four (six in the first
writ) of the nineteen could form a quorum but one of the bishops
must always be there. Its business was to see that the Supremacy
and Uniformity Acts were obeyed; it could punish by fines or
imprisonment; the second writ especially notes that it is to deal
with cases left over from the visitation, and lays particular stress
on its power to require the Supremacy oath from all 'Archbishops, bishops and other ecclesiastical persons . . . of whatever
status, dignity, pre-eminence or degree'. Like the Injunctions,
this commission was intended to be a permanent part of the new
ecclesiastical pattern for enforcing uniformity. There is evidence
that it began to function in November 1559.[3]

Though Parker was not one of the royal visitors, his position
was now so publicly recognized that he was, of course, kept busy.
Special visitors were appointed for the Universities, and he was
one of those nominated for Cambridge and Eton in a writ of
June 20.[4] The main purpose of this visitation was educational
rather than ecclesiastical. It is true that the oath was to be
administered, but there was much else to be examined—the
life and learning of the University, extravagance in expense,

[1] *Cal. S. P. Dom.*, p. 145.   [2] Gee, *Elizabethan Clergy*, pp. 147, 152.
[3] Ibid., pp. 140, sq.   [4] Ibid., p. 133.

unworthy residents, neglect of academic courses. Such functions required a different kind of visitor, and of the nine nominated, headed by the Chancellor of the University, Cecil, five were of the clergy. For such a body, Parker with his intimate knowledge of Cambridge, was an obvious nominee. There is no evidence that he ever took part in the proceedings in Cambridge in August or September: he seems to have remained in London. But it was no doubt as a visitor that he joined with others in authorizing the University to appoint a preacher 'in consideration of your small number and weak state' who had not the degree qualifications required by statute.[1] Several Heads were deprived— and presumably Parker knew about it all and agreed, though he was not there.

He was also used a good deal by the Council for dealing with those who refused to take the oath before the visitors. In this he was not very successful, so far as the evidence goes—perhaps because only the more eminent or the most stubborn were sent to him. He failed with Tunstall. He was really hood-winked by Dr. Smyth, Reader of Divinity at Oxford. This man, who had been prominent in the action against Cranmer, professed himself, to Parker, convinced by argument and ready to take the Supremacy oath. He was released in order to make a public profession before the visitors in Oxford—but fled to Douay.[2] Dr. Boxall, Dean of Peterborough, Norwich and Windsor was another sent to him by the Council[3] whom Parker failed to persuade. He was deprived—but was afterwards considerately treated by the Archbishop when committed to his charge by the Council.[4] The *Correspondence* shows that at least seven others of varied importance were sent to him;[5] six of them in the end suffered deprivation, the fate of the seventh is unknown. It is very unlikely that there were not others as well—these cases are only known because letters about them happen to survive. Arguing with them must have been tiresome; their lack of compliance a

---

[1] *Correspondence*, p. 72.   [2] Ibid., pp. 72–74.
[3] Ibid., p. 104.   [4] Ibid., p. 194.
          [5] Ibid., pp. 75, 76, 96–97, 103, 105–6.

real distress to a man at once so sensitive and so conscientious as
Parker.

Besides such things, however, he was now beginning to
shoulder his responsibility as Archbishop-elect. The royal
commission of September 9 to Tunstall and others to consecrate
him remained without effect. All the same, some time in October,
probably—the letter is undated—he and four other bishops elect
(Grindal, Cox, Barlow and Scory), alarmed by the damage being
done to church property under the Act allowing exchanges of
royal for episcopal possessions during a vacancy, ventured to
write a long appeal to the Queen.[1] Basing their argument on the
danger to the church from the lack of a learned ministry, they
urged her to 'stay and remit this present alteration and exchange', offering to give her in exchange a thousand marks a
year from the province of Canterbury, for they recognized her
financial difficulties. Their offer shows how much they were
afraid the Church would suffer practically, though on paper the
exchanges were made to seem equitable. The rest of the letter
shows the sort of ways in which they feared they might be in a
worse position. If the exchanges could not be stopped, then at
least they asked that the impropriations they received in place
of lands should not have heavy charges on them for pensions or
for salaries to vicars. They asked that in assessing the value of
the manors taken over by the Crown 'perquisites of courts and
woods, sales and other casual profits' should be duly reckoned
in, together with live stock and farm implements, and that the
payments due to keepers should not be set against capital value.
They also sought to be free from such feudal obligations as went
with the lands taken from them. They asked, too, for the right

[1] Ibid., pp. 97, 138. The Act looked fair enough: the Queen was only to
take over episcopal possessions equivalent in value to impropriated parsonages
or tithes handed over to the bishops. But Parkhurst took it to mean that the
bishops were henceforward to have no palaces, estates or country seats
(*Zurich Letters*, i, 29), and a correspondent in the Venetian State Papers (p. 60)
that bishops' incomes were to be limited to £500 a year. The effect varied
from diocese to diocese, but there can be no doubt that many bishoprics
were greatly impoverished by the exchanges.

to recover by process of law, in case of refusal to pay, such tithes as were given to them—a wise precaution: for the tithes had by Parliament been allowed to the Crown: it was legally doubtful whether the exchange procedure now being followed would give the bishops a legal right to collect. (Such fears were amply justified in the event: despite apparent equivalence, the bishops were not so well off as before.) Finally they asked for certain concessions quite unconnected with the exchanges—concessions without which they 'dare not enter our functions' to which they had been nominated—that they should be freed from any arrears not paid to the Crown by their predecessors, that they should be allowed to receive such rents as had fallen due at Michaelmas, and that their first fruits should be either abated or 'distributed into more years'. Else, they could not furnish their houses or pay the legal fees.

It was a clear, business-like letter, and the Queen clearly recognized, at least in part, the justice of its claims. In a letter of October 26,[1] she ordered that the exchanges should be completed with all possible speed (she was evidently not prepared to 'remit' them) so that the arrangements for filling the sees need not be delayed any longer; but she insisted that the bishops should receive 'an equal just value' for what was taken from them. More immediately important, she allowed a half year's rent to each of the bishops. It was a considerable success for Parker and his fellows in view of the straitness of the Queen's finances.

In another matter which today seems trivial but which caused much excitement at the time, Parker and his friends were not so successful. At and after Bartholomew-tide, during the London visitation, there had been great popular excitement and much destruction of church property—'copes, crosses, censers, altar-cloths, rood-cloths, books, banners, banner-stays'.[2] The legality of such a holocaust was, at the very best, doubtful. Copes, censers, altar-cloths would seem naturally to be part of the ornaments which the Prayer Book ordered to be still used. One of the Injunctions (No. 47) ordered that 'inventories of vestments,

[1] *Correspondence*, p. 101.   [2] Machyn, pp. 207-8-9.

copes and other ornaments, plate, books' and even service books
should be delivered to the visitors, not that such things should be
destroyed. Yet the civil authorities did not interfere when they
were destroyed: one can only suppose that zeal outran discretion, and that an excuse was found in the Injunction (23) to
destroy 'all monuments . . . of superstition'. Even in the royal
chapel the crucifix and candles were removed from the altar.
No doubt it was all highly acceptable to Sandys and his friends.
But suddenly there was a change. In October, the Spanish
ambassador wrote that 'the crucifixes and vestments that were
burned a month ago publicly are now set up again in the royal
chapel'.[1] Parker protested at once not, presumably, about the
vestments (which were legally ordered) but about the lights and
crucifix (or cross; it is not certain which, for both terms are
used)—'*the offendicle*' as they were termed in writings of the day.
The evidence for Parker's protest now is not the long letter,
quoting Biblical and patristic reasons against the use of images
in church, which in the *Correspondence* is attributed to him and
other bishops and placed at this time.[2] (That letter is, in fact,
undated and unsigned. It does not really belong now—it refers to
previous efforts 'at sundry times' in the matter, and refers to
brethren who 'bear the office of bishops' of whom there were
none in 1559; nor is there any reason to connect Parker with its
authorship, though a copy of it is among his papers. Probably its
proper place is the spring of 1560; its authorship is unknown.)
None the less, it is certain that Parker did take action in October
as soon as the '*offendicle*' appeared. On October 13, Sir Francis
Knollys—a returned exile very eager for reform, married to a
first cousin of the Queen and Vice-Chamberlain of the Royal
Household—wrote to wish him 'prosperity' in his 'good enterprise
against the enormities yet in the Queen's closet retained (although without the Queen's express commandment these toys
were laid aside till now a late).'[3] And on November 6, Parker
wrote to Cecil wishing that he were 'called for again to continue

[1] *Cal. S. P. Span.* i, 105.   [2] *Correspondence*, pp. 79 sqq.
[3] Ibid., p. 97.

our humble supplication to the finishment and stay of that offendicle'.[1] Yet, on November 16, 'that little silver cross of ill-omened origin still maintains its place in the Queen's chapel' wrote Jewel to Peter Martyr.[2] By January 1560 there was real alarm about it. An undated letter from Cox, probably written about then, protested to the Queen that he 'dare not minister in your grace's chapel, the lights and cross remaining'.[3] Sampson wrote to Martyr that it was only in the royal chapel that lights and crucifix remained, but feared that the Queen was about to order all bishops and clergy either to admit them into their churches or else retire from the ministry.[4] Similarly, on February 4, Jewel wrote to Martyr, and said that he did not expect again to write to him as a bishop. For 'matters are come to that pass, that either the crosses of silver and tin, which we have every-where broken in pieces, must be restored, or our bishopricks relinquished'.[5] But he says that there is to be a disputation about it the next day, with Parker and Cox on the one side, himself and Grindal on the other. The disputation certainly took place, but our only account of it is vague. It dealt not only with altar ornaments but with cross and figures on roods which 'the Queen's majesty considered . . . not contrary to the word of God, nay, rather for the advantage of the church'. So says Sandys to Martyr on April 1,[6] adding that his own vehemence in the matter nearly led to his deposition and the Queen's displeasure. 'But God, in whose hands are the hearts of kings, gave us tranquillity instead of a tempest and delivered the Church of England from stumbling-blocks of this kind.' But the 'popish vestments' still remained. The outcome seems to have been a compromise: the rood figures were not restored, and the bishops were not ordered to restore cross and lights to the parochial altars. But the Queen retained them in the royal chapel. Both on March 6 and March 24, Machyn notes that there were cross and candle on the table 'standing altar-wise'[7]—and that bishops preaching before the

[1] *Correspondence*, p. 105.   [2] *Zurich Letters*, i, 55.
[3] Strype, *Annals* I, ii, 501.   [4] *Zurich Letters*, i, 63–64.
[5] Ibid., p. 8.   [6] Ibid., pp. 73–74.   [7] *Diary*, pp. 226, 229.

Queen wore rochet and chimere. Later on, apparently, the *'offendicle'* was destroyed—'broken in pieces and, as some one has brought word, reduced to ashes', wrote Parkhurst in August 1562.[1] But by the following April, it was back, but the candles were not now lighted![2] The cross was still on the royal altar in January 1565, and in 1571 after an interval,[3] though Parker did not like it. That is the last we hear of the matter—the reformers had by then turned their attention to other things. But it obviously caused much immediate commotion, and the alacrity with which advice was sought from leaders abroad was very significant—and ominous for the future. Martyr at first was strongly opposed,[4] but was later more cautious. He could not regard 'the image of the crucifix' as indifferent, but 'You, who are in the very midst of the contest, must not expect counsel from hence.'[5] Cassander, at Worms, consulted by Cox, admitted that he did not know whether it was a cross or a crucifix which was involved—but he rather liked the symbolism of the cross,[6] provided that superstition was excluded. Parker's immediate attack on the *offendicle* showed courage: his change over, with Cox, from suspicion to defence at the disputation deserves emphasis. The Church of England was fortunate to have among its bishops men so balanced as to be able to overcome, on calm reflection, their first instinctive feeling that everything connected with the Roman usages must be wrong. Later on, Jewel was conspicuous for the same reasonableness. It contributed as much as anything to the true comprehensiveness of the Church of England.

[1] *Zurich Letters*, i, 122.   [2] Ibid., p. 129.
[3] *Cal. S. P. Span.* i, 401; *Correspondence*, 379.   [4] *Zurich Letters*, ii, 39.
[5] Ibid., p. 47.   [6] Ibid., pp. 43–45.

CHAPTER VI

THE ARCHBISHOP AND HIS TASK

THE Supremacy Act, the Uniformity Act, the Injunctions set out the official pattern; the permanent ecclesiastical commission provided the means to enforce it upon its more tiresome and persistent opponents; the exchanges of episcopal and royal property were completed for the time being. Thus all was ready for the consecration of the bishops elect and for the handing over to them of the ordering of the Church. Thereafter the Queen tried to allow them—or to appear to allow them—to be in control. Privately and behind the scenes she urged them to activity if they seemed to be insufficiently firm or vigorous, but on the whole she sought to refrain from open interference, and constantly refused to allow Parliament to act in ecclesiastical matters over the heads of bishops and Convocation.

When it came to the point, there were difficulties about the actual consecration of Parker. There still exists a paper outlining the procedure proposed, with comments by Cecil and a reply by Parker to one of his points.[1] The statute of Henry VIII (restored in Elizabeth's Supremacy Act) laid it down that, in case of an Archbishop, the royal commission should issue either to another archbishop and two bishops, or to 'four bishops within this realm'. Cecil commented that 'there are not four bishops now to be had'. Secondly, to the suggestion in the paper that 'the order of King Edward's Book is to be observed, for that there is none other especially made in this last session of Parliament,' he objected 'This book is not established by Parliament'. If valid, his objections were serious. The first seems to assume that only diocesan bishops were qualified to act. Perhaps that was why no

---

[1] Described by Strype, *Parker* i, 80–81; a facsimile is in E. E. Estcourt, *The Question of Anglican Ordinations* (London, 1873), p. 86.

difficulty was felt about the Queen's first commission on September 9th in which, with Tunstall, three others who were also still in possession of sees (Llandaff, Peterborough, Bath and Wells) were named, along with Barlow and Scory who had been but were no longer diocesans. By December, the position was changed and the only available diocesan left in possession was Kitchin of Llandaff (and obscure Sodor and Man). Still, whatever the Act originally may have meant, it did not specify that the bishops must be diocesans in occupation of sees, but only bishops 'within this realm'.

Cecil's second point was—and is—much more difficult. In 1552 Parliament added to the Prayer Book 'a form and manner of making and consecrating Archbishops, Bishops, Priests and Deacons to be of like force authority and value as the same like foresaid book'.[1] The whole of the statute was repealed under Mary. Under Elizabeth 'the said statute of repeal and everything contained therein, only concerning the said Book and the Service Administration of Sacraments Rites and Ceremonies contained or appointed in or by the said Book, shall be void and of none effect'.[2] Parker plainly thought that the Ordinal was to be regarded as part of the Book and as therefore restored, Cecil that it was not, and that therefore the rejection of it under Mary was unrepealed—in which case there was no authorized Ordinal at all, save possibly the Roman. It is obviously a difficult legal point, and some modern authorities support Cecil.[3] But there is much to be said for Parker's view. Though the Ordinal was, no doubt, technically a separate book, with only parliamentary sanction, not ecclesiastical, added to Edward's Second Prayer Book, yet they were issued in a single volume. They *looked* like a single work. Moreover the very careful language which was used in the limiting clause in Elizabeth's repeal of Mary's Act might very well be thought not to separate the Ordinal from the Prayer Book, but to treat them as a unity to be separated from other

---

[1] 5 and 6 Edward VI, C.1, iv.   [2] 1 Eliz., C2, i—the Uniformity Act.
[3] Dixon, op. cit., v, 201–2; W. H. Frere, *English Church in the Reigns of Elizabeth and James* I (London, 1911), p. 47.

items of Mary's statute, which had repealed other legislation of Edward VI as well as the Uniformity Act of 1552—the Order for communion in both kinds, for example, and the allowance for the marriage of priests. It is not unreasonable to suppose that the strict limitation 'only', was intended to exclude such matters (of the Queen's views about clerical marriage, at least, there was no doubt: communion in both kinds had already been dealt with in the Supremacy Act), not the Ordinal so closely associated with the Prayer Book. Moreover, even those who maintain that the Ordinal was excluded when the Prayer Book was re-affirmed are agreed that this was not deliberately done: if it was done, it was due to carelessness or inadvertance. In the hurried transactions which lie behind Elizabeth's Uniformity Act, that may have happened. But it is very difficult to believe that the matter was simply forgotten. It had already engaged the attention of Parliament before the Uniformity Act was passed. On March 21 and 22 the Commons passed through all its stages a Bill that 'the Queen's Highness shall collate or appoint Bishops in Bishopricks being vacant, and without rites and ceremonies'; the Bill was read three times, and concluded in the Lords on March 22–3 only two days before the adjournment on March 24.[1] It then disappears, but the only reasonable supposition, in view of such concern in both Houses, is that others besides Parker thought that the Elizabethan Uniformity Act made it unnecessary and re-established the Ordinal of Edward VI as well as his Second Prayer Book, and that that was what was intended.[2] Cecil's point was a lawyer's point of interpretation—though of course that does not mean that he may not, strictly speaking, have been right. If so, the carelessness was simply that of not ensuring that the Uniformity Act expressed clearly all that was intended. Later on, Bonner made great play with the point, and

[1] S. D'Ewes, *A Complete Journal of the House of Lords and the House of Commons* (London, 1693), pp. 52 and 26. The *Journal of the House of Commons* (i, 58) reads 'with what' instead of 'without' ceremonies.

[2] So F. E. Brightman, *The English Rite* (2 Vols., London, 1915), i, clxx. Dixon himself seems to accept this view, vi, 149. Frere, op. cit., p. 47, says that the omission of the Ordinal in the Act was due to 'inadvertance'.

Parliament, to remove all occasion of dispute, affirmed in 1566 that Edward's Parliament did 'add and put to the said Book a very good and godly manner and form' for conferring Orders,[1] and that it was therefore really a part of the Book and so covered by the Uniformity Act.

However, in view no doubt of the difficulties Cecil had raised, the greatest possible pains were taken to secure that Parker's consecration should be valid legally. The whole process of election, confirmation and consecration is most carefully recorded at the opening of Parker's *Register*,[2] the official documents being quoted. The Queen's Letters Patent, dated Dec. 6, were issued to Kitchin of Llandaff, Barlow elect of Chichester and Scory elect of Hereford, Coverdale late of Exeter, Bale Bishop of Ossory and two suffragans, Hodgkin of Bedford and Salisbury of Thetford. They were to confirm the election and to consecrate, 'according to the form of statutes set forth and provided in that behalf'.[3] It was specially laid down that four should be a sufficient number to act (thus conforming to Henry's statute; indeed, all through the process there is constant reference to the fact that the procedure is according to statute). The Letters Patent, for extra safety, included a section not found in any similar instrument—the famous 'supplentes' clause by which the Queen formally by her Supreme Royal Authority, 'supplied' anything lacking of what was required by the statutes of the realm or laws ecclesiastical either in the things done by or in the condition or status of those who carried out these her orders. How far the Queen had any legal powers thus to 'supply' defects is, of course, doubtful: even at the time it must have been felt to be so, for trouble was taken to secure the signatures of six prominent ecclesiastics and lawyers to the effect that the Queen's commission could be lawfully carried out by those named. Clearly, everything possible was done to meet Cecil's scruples. Nor can there be any serious

---

[1] 8 Eliz., C. 1.   [2] pp. 1–38.

[3] Ibid., p. 6. The fact that it is 'statutes' not 'statute' (as Strype) suggests that not only 25 Hy. VIII C. 20 was in mind, but also 1 Eliz. CC. 1 and 2, thus confirming Parker's view.

question that it was all in accordance with the intentions of Parliament, even though, perhaps, those intentions had not been embodied without possibility of question in the Act of Uniformity.

On 9 Dec. 1959, the election of Parker was duly confirmed in the Church of St. Mary-le-Bow by four of the appointed bishops, Barlow, Scory, Coverdale and Hodgkin. The consecration was on Sunday, December 17 in the chapel at Lambeth, early in the morning. It is fully described in the *Register*,[1] which makes it clear that the furnishings and procedure were meant to be such as befitted an important solemnity. Preceded by four candle bearers, Parker, robed in scarlet gown and hood, entered the chapel accompanied by the four bishops. After matins and a sermon by Scory, Parker and the bishops withdrew, to re-enter—Parker in a linen surplice, Barlow in silk cope (as celebrant; his two assistants were similarly robed), Scory and Hodgkin in surplices, but Coverdale, typically, in a long woollen gown. After the Gospel the three other bishops presented Parker to Barlow, the official documents were produced, the oath to the Supremacy was taken. Then after interrogatories, prayers and suffrages 'according to the form of the book set forth by the authority of Parliament', the four bishops all laid their hands on the new Archbishop, and all four recited the words of consecration. Except that all four said the words instead of the presiding bishop alone, the service was clearly that of Edward's Second Book. It is specifically noted that no pastoral staff was given to the new Archbishop. At the end of the service, the bishops went out by the north door to return re-robed. Parker now wore 'episcopal surplice' (presumably rochet) and black chimere and a collar of sables; Barlow and Scory rochet and chimere; Coverdale still only a long gown, joined now by Hodgkin. At the west door Parker delivered white wands of office to those who were to be his steward, treasurer and controller, and the procession marched out.

Though so early in the morning—about five or six o'clock—there was nothing secretive about the service, as the list of those

[1] pp. 31–33.

present makes clear—Grindal, Cox, Sandys, Huse the Arch-bishop's Registrar, John Incent who was soon to succeed him as Registrar, and others. Nothing can explain the attempts (some-times very wild) which have been made to discredit the official account save the desire at any cost to snap a link so essential in the episcopal chain as is Parker. The Nag's Head story no longer needs to be discussed: it did not emerge till after 1600,[1] and is now thoroughly discredited. A recent attempt to prove that the *Register* is unreliable and that Parker was in fact consecrated before the end of October by Kitchin, with the assistance prob-ably of Barlow, Bale and Salisbury of Thetford[2] has been so effectively criticized that it may be said to have been fully dis-proved.[3] The date of the consecration is put beyond any reason-able question by the almost casual remark of Machyn[4] that 'The XVII day of December was the new bishop (of Canterbury) doctor Parker was made there at Lambeth.' Nor, unless Parker himself joined in the conspiracy to falsify his *Register*, could he have ended his personal *Memoranda* 'On the 17th of December, in the year 1559, I was consecrated Archbishop of Canterbury. Alas! alas! O Lord God, for what times has thou kept me' etc.[5] Equally unsuccessful has been the attempt to show that Barlow had never himself been consecrated as a bishop, and that there-fore the legal requirements of consecration were not fulfilled in Parker's case.[6] In fact, unless the two difficulties raised by Cecil were valid (or either of them) it is beyond serious question that Parker was duly consecrated, according to the statutes of the realm, on December 17. The validity of the proceedings can only be challenged on the grounds that they did not satisfy the requirements of the Roman Church; there was no papal approval, nor was the 'intention' completely in accord with that of the Roman Church.

---

[1] Dixon, op. cit., v, 210.
[2] *The Consecration of Matthew Parker*, J. C. Whitebrook (London, 1945).
[3] F. J. Shirley, *Elizabeth's First Archbishop* (S.P.C.K., London, 1948).
[4] *Diary*, p. 220.   [5] *Correspondence*, p. x.
[6] '*Bishop Barlow's Consecration and Archbishop Parker's Register*', Claude Jenkins (S.P.C.K., London, 1935).

Once Parker was consecrated, the filling of other sees was quickly put in hand. On December 20, the election of six bishops was confirmed—Grindal (London), Cox (Ely), Scory (Hereford), Meyrick (Bangor), Sandys (Worcester), Barlow (Chichester); on the 21st the four who were not already bishops were duly consecrated in the chapel at Lambeth. On the 27th the Council urged the Queen that 'the governance of the Church be better seen unto and established' and all things belonging to the state ecclesiastical remitted to the clergy.[1] The Queen indeed needed no pressure: on that very day she assented to the election of Jewel for Salisbury, and Bullingham had already been elected to the see of Lincoln. Their election was confirmed on January 18, together with that of Thomas Young to St. David's and Richard Davys to St. Asaph. These four were consecrated on January 21. In March, three more were confirmed and consecrated—Guest for Rochester, Bentham for Coventry and Lichfield, Berkeley for Bath and Wells; Alley was made bishop of Exeter in June, and Parkhurst Bishop of Norwich in September. Thus, in just over nine months 16 of the 21 sees which had been vacant in the Southern Province were filled. In February of the next year Horne was made bishop of Winchester (to which Pilkington had been elected previously,[2] though in fact he never held that see) and Scambler of Peterborough; in April Cheyne became bishop of Gloucester, and Bristol (described by the Queen as 'in manibus nostris disponendus') was added 'in commendam' because the poverty of the see of Gloucester prevented the bishop there from doing his duties fittingly.[3] But there was still one vacant see in the south—Oxford. It was not filled until 1567 for some unexplained reason, having been vacant, as the Royal Letter of

---

[1] Quoted by H. Gee, *The Elizabethan Clergy*, p. 156. The letter is said to be in Cecil's hand.   [2] *Cal. S. P. Dom.*, p. 147.

[3] *Register*, p. 953. The bishop was also allowed to hold a living and a prebend in Westminster for 7 years because of his poverty. (Ibid., p. 956.) Oddly, though he seems to have enjoyed the emoluments of Bristol till he died, Parker's *Register* contains a whole series of commissions to others to act as guardians of the spirituality (pp. 947-51), doubtless because of Cheyney's unsatisfactory theological views.

Consent charmingly remarks, 'per aliquod tempus'. (The previous bishop had died in 1557!) In the Northern Province, there was a good deal of delay at first. May, Dean of St. Paul's, was nominated to the Archbishopric in June 1560, but died before his consecration. In July the Lord Treasurer wrote to Parker to say that he had moved the Queen to appoint 'preachers' for the vacant dioceses—three for York, two for Durham, two for Winchester. At her direction, he asked Parker to suggest names.[1] In October, Parker wrote to Cecil to urge that bishops should be appointed for the north, suggesting that 'whatsoever is now too husbandly saved will be an occasion for further expense'.[2] He even put forward the name of Young for York, to which he was translated early in 1561 from St. David's. In March of the same year, Pilkington became Bishop of Durham and Best of Carlisle; in May, Downham was consecrated for Chester. Thus, by May 1561, all the sees were filled save Oxford and Bristol.

The task facing Parker and his fellow bishops was immense: they had to organize and vitalize the Church on the lines laid down in the legislation and Injunctions of 1559. The first requisite, plainly, was the provision of suitable clergy in sufficient numbers. It is not possible to say, within very wide limits, how many clerics there were at the beginning of the reign.[3] Strype firmly says 9,400,[4] almost certainly an overstatement.[5] Anyhow, it seems to be clear, that most of such clergy as there were, even if not actively hostile to the new arrangements, were at the best luke-warm. They had showed their pro-roman preferences in the resolutions in the Convocation of 1559; at the Royal Visitation, many of them absented themselves and so avoided the Supremacy oath. Full details for the Southern Province do not exist, but from the Northern Visitation about a quarter of the clergy were absentees. Few of these, so far as the evidence goes, were actually deprived, so that they probably

---

[1] *Correspondence*, p. 119.   [2] Ibid., p. 123.
[3] The whole topic is exhaustively treated in H. Gee's invaluable *Elizabethan Clergy*.   [4] *Annals* I, i, 106.
[5] Gee, op. cit., p. 1, note 4.

submitted in time, but it can hardly have been with enthusiasm.[1] Such reluctance, however, though widespread, was not universal,[2] at least in the Southern Province. How many were in the end actually deprived is, again, a matter of doubt. A most careful enquiry suggests that in the years 1558–64 'it is impossible to conclude that many more than 200 were deprived':[3] and of those it is at least possible that some were deprived for causes other than mere non-acceptance of the new settlement. Apart from deprivations, however, it is certain that in the early years of the reign many livings were vacant.[4] This may have been due to resignations to avoid taking the oath, but what evidence there is does not suggest that such action was common.[5] Often it seems that vacancies caused by death[6] had not been filled, even in Mary's days, and the most common explanation given for vacancies was '*propter exilitatem*'. Thus, though it is probably true that the lower ranks of the Marian clergy 'in overwhelming numbers passed over into the service of the establishment',[7] it was without enthusiasm; and there was a serious shortage of clergy, especially in the higher ranks which were much more thinned by deprivation that the lower. In July 1560 Lever wrote to Bullinger 'Many of our parishes have no clergyman, and some dioceses are without a bishop. And out of that very small number who administer the sacraments throughout this great country, there is hardly one in a hundred who is both able and willing to preach the word of God.'[8]

Parker at once set about to supply the deficiency, with more zeal than discretion as the event was to show. He does not seem often to have conducted ordinations in person, but authorized other bishops to do it—there are several such commissions in his *Register*, though the ordinations took place either at Lambeth or in one of the churches of his peculiar jurisdiction—St. Mary-le-

---

[1] Gee, op. cit., pp. 83–88.   [2] Ibid., 102, note 2.
[3] Ibid., p. 251.   [4] Ibid., p. 82, note 2.   [5] Ibid., pp. 243–5.
[6] In February 1570 Parker sequestered a living because it had been vacant twelve years, *Register*, p. 970.
[7] J. B. Black, *The Reign of Elizabeth* (2nd edition, Oxford, 1959), p. 21.
[8] *Zurich Letters*, i, 85.

Bow, or St. Pancras, or All Saints', Bread Street. There are also letters dimissory to bishops for the ordination of individuals. Thus, even when he did not himself ordain, Parker was responsible for and the driving force behind the early ordinations, which rose to astonishing proportions. The earliest recorded[1] was 22 Dec. 1559, within a week of Parker's consecration, by Scory at Lambeth of eleven deacons, one priest and ten both deacon and priest on the same day. There were more on January 8 and February 11. Then there was a 'notification'[2] that on Sunday, March 3, he proposed to 'celebrate holy orders . . . generally to all such as shall be found thereunto apt and meet for their learning and godly conversation'. They were to present themselves on the previous Thursday and Friday for the Archbishop and his officers to inspect, bringing testimonials of character covering three years. The result was the ordination at Lambeth on March 10 (not 3rd) by the Bishop of Lincoln, of no fewer than one hundred and twenty deacons, thirty-seven priests and six both priest and deacon.[3] There were frequent further ordinations in the next few months. All the ordinands were not, indeed, for service in the diocese of Canterbury alone but, as the official lists make plain, for many dioceses in the Southern Province—Winchester, London, Lincoln and so on; some were even for York. But even so it was not long before Parker realized the disadvantage of such wholesale measures. In August he was constrained to write to Grindal[4] that some of the 'multitude' which included artificers and men of base occupation had proved 'very offensive unto the people' in their light behaviour, and were doing more harm than good. In future, therefore, Grindal and the other bishops were to confine themselves to those who had been 'traded and exercised in learning, or at the least have spent their time with teaching of children' until the bishops could formulate a common policy.

An attempt was also made to use 'Readers' to help out. At the ordination in January, though not at any other, five 'Lectores'

---

[1] *Register*, p. 338.   [2] Ibid., pp. 340–1.
[3] Ibid., pp. 342–3.   [4] *Correspondence*, pp. 120–1.

are actually included in the list.[1] And there is extant an elaborate
scheme attributed to the Archbishop for the use of them.[2] For
the time being incumbents were to be allowed to hold livings in
plurality, with readers deputed for the parishes where there was
no resident priest. The readers were to be 'honest, sober, and
grave laymen'; they were not to be appointed without the 'oversight of the Bishop or his Chancellor' and could be removed on
proof of disability or disorder. Their duties were carefully laid
down; they were to read the service of the day or the litany, and
a homily; they might not preach or 'prophesy' nor baptize,
marry, or celebrate the communion. The latter functions were
reserved for the ordained incumbent to perform when he visited
the parishes under his care, to see how they fared. The readers
do not seem to have been a very satisfactory innovation. Possibly,
in their zeal, they exceeded the bounds of their duties—anyhow
in 1561 the bishops formulated carefully an oath for them to take
which defined their limited functions quite clearly. Gradually—
and before long—they faded out of the picture. But their initiation
shows how seriously Parker felt the lack of pastors at first.

The Royal Visitation and Injunctions of 1559 had set the
pattern: it was now Parker's duty to see how far it was being
followed. He therefore started a metropolitical visitation of his
province, with a view to which he inhibited the new bishops
from carrying out their own visitations individually; such
visitations were expensive to the parishes in the matter of fees
and Parker wished to spare them.[3] The earliest sign of his
intention is given by an inhibition on Mary 17[4] to Scory of
Hereford, who was probably intending a speedy visitation
because of the activities of the Romans in his diocese. This was
followed on May 27 by a general inhibition to the Bishop of
London and all the bishops.[5] Then there was an interval—
possibly to allow about a year to have elapsed since the Royal
Visitation. Parker did not personally take part, but nominated

---

[1] *Register*, p. 339.   [2] Strype, *Parker* i, 130–2. Cf. *Annals* I, i, 274 sqq.
[3] *Correspondence*, p. 116.   [4] *Register*, p. 345.
[5] *Correspondence*, p. 115.

deputies—usually the bishop of the diocese concerned, if there was one; but in such cases it was made quite clear that he was acting as the Archbishop's representative, not in his own right. The first batch of commissions was dated August 8[1]—five of them, four being to the diocesan; in each case John Incent, the Archbishop's Principal Registrar, or his deputy, was to act as scribe of the proceedings. On September 11, four visitors, three lawyers and one of the prebendaries, were nominated for the cathedrals and dioceses of Canterbury and Rochester with the same secretary—not even so near home did Parker visit in person.[2] Visitors were also appointed for Salisbury (Bishop Jewel), Gloucester and Peterborough before the end of the year, and for Exeter, Oxford, Worcester, Hereford in 1561, and for Norwich as late as 1567—still with John Incent as scribe. The proceedings opened with the visitation of the Canterbury diocese, September 19 to 28; on the 30th the visitors began their work in Rochester cathedral and diocese. The main business seems to have been over by October 3: only cases pending were dealt with after that; but in other dioceses visitations continued intermittently for some time.

Parker issued two sets of Articles of Inquiry, one for cathedrals and one for parishes,[3] which show clearly the purpose of the visitation. It was not to enforce the Supremacy, but to find out the condition of churches, clergy and people. The questions reveal what were the defects expected to be commonly found. Where the churches properly equipped with Bible, Prayer Book, Homilies and the Paraphrases of Erasmus? Was there a 'comely and decent table' for communion, a pulpit, and alms chest? Were altars and images removed? Where the accounts properly kept and money not retained in private hands? Was the divine service said without variation, according to the law, and 'sensibly and distinctly'? Of the clergy, it was sought to discover whether they resided and bestowed due amounts in charity, were peacemakers in their parish, not given to superstition or 'gamesters,

---

[1] *Register*, pp. 672–4. [2] Ibid., p. 627.
[3] Ibid., pp. 621–7, or Strype's *Parker* i, 145–8, and iii, 28.

hunters, haunters of taverns . . . or fautors of foreign powers';
whether, in fact, they were 'light either in example of life or in
unwont and unseemly apparel', whether they admitted to
communion notorious sinners who had not duly repented.
Vacancies and pluralities were to be discovered and any ministers
who had intruded 'without imposition of hands and ordinary
authority'. (It is interesting to find as early as 1560 the suspicion
that protestant enthusiasts were forcing their way into livings
without episcopal Orders, or were refusing the habits in or out of
church.) The conduct of the laity, too, was to be examined.
Were they diligent in church attendance, and were the fines
legally due for non-attendance properly exacted? Were there
any that disturbed the church services or attended common prayer
other than that legally set forth; were there any conventicles?
In particular, was the schoolmaster religious and diligent in his
teaching, were wills duly executed and legacies paid? Were
there any marriages within the prohibited degrees, or solemnized
without banns? There was a long list of 'evil doers' to be sought
out—all, in fact, who did not 'conform themselves to virtue and
true religion'.

For the cathedrals, the emphasis was rather different, but
equally simple and straightforward. Non-residence, pluralism,
failure to attend the services, simony, neglect of preaching in
due course, were all to be sought out. Very significantly, it was
to be discovered 'what orders they be in'. Private lives, too, were
to be strictly scrutinized, and the collection and administration
of corporate funds. The grammar schools were to receive
attention to see whether all the places were filled and that
bribes had not been exacted for free places. And there is a long
and interesting section about the sort of views which might be
preached but should not be—opposition to the reading of the
Scriptures, denial that it was lawful for local churches to alter
rites and ceremonies, discouragement of conformity, extolling of
superstitious practices, or of clerical celibacy, on the one hand:
on the other, repudiation of infant baptism, rejection of the
authority of civil magistrates, the claim that ministers might

function without outward calling. The articles show Parker firmly treading the *via media* in faith and practice, characteristically concerned for education and for a decent moral standard for laity as well as clergy.

The findings of the visitors no longer exist, in the main, but there are some particulars for Canterbury and Rochester in Parker's *Register*.[1] They do not suggest that things were glaringly amiss, though there was much that needed attention. At Canterbury, the prebendaries were not all resident (one of them was suspected to be not ordained) and were not regular in their attendance at the services, though they duly paid the fines prescribed for such negligence; there were only six or seven minor canons instead of the statutory twelve; the schoolmaster ('much given to ebriety') and usher were not satisfactory and the boys unruly. The Dean (who was also Dean of York) was not resident, being engaged on the Queen's affairs (he was on embassy in France). But the cathedral was properly kept and the services performed. Slackness and irregularity seem to have been the worst offences. Rochester cathedral was less satisfactory—only two of the prebendaries resided regularly, and sermons were omitted. The master of the choristers was negligent; and there was a common rumour that some of the singing men were incontinent. (These last were not, of course, in Orders, but such rumours were discreditable to the cathedral.) No evidence, however, save common report, was brought against them, and they cleared themselves by process of compurgation. The impression produced is of indiscipline and lack of zeal, rather than of gross ill-living or wide-spread scandal. Of the reports about parishes much the greatest bulk concerns the proving of wills and administration of goods. Many clergy who did not present themselves were excommunicated for contumacy—but pardoned when they duly submitted. There were one or two matrimonial cases, too. It is hard to suppose that there was much more fault to be found by the visitors than the *Register* records,

[1] pp. 634–72. More diocesan returns, are in Corpus Christi College, Cambridge, MSS. 97, 122.

unless they grievously scamped their work. The general impression is that, on the whole, the new settlement was generally though not enthusiastically accepted, and that the faults disclosed—of carelessness or immorality—were such as could not be laid to the charge of the innovations of 1559. Of the other dioceses we really know nothing, save that Strype says many papists were discovered in Bath and Wells,[1] and Scory found Hereford 'a very nursery of blasphemy, whoredom, pride, superstition and ignorance' in June 1561—which probably means little more than that there were many papists, especially among the leading men in the diocese.[2]

That Parker was, as he claimed, prevented by 'certain difficult and urgent matters' from visiting in person was no mere conventional excuse. In the spring of 1560 there was much trouble about the deprived bishops. At first they were left at liberty after deprivation, but on April 20 Bonner was sent by the ecclesiastical commissioners to the Marshalsea. Despite his modern defenders, he was undoubtedly very unpopular. At one time, fears for his personal safety led him to seek sanctuary in an abbey, and Jewel says that when he was now imprisoned, one of his fellow prisoners violently refused to have anything to do with him.[3] But it was now no personal matter: others also were imprisoned. In the next few months Watson, Pates, Heath, Thirlby, Turberville and Bourne were sent to the Tower and Scott to the Fleet. Other leading dignitaries were imprisoned too.[4] As they had at first been left at liberty and as one of the bishops—Poole—never suffered imprisonment at all, presumably they were punished for causing trouble. Jewel declared that they were 'every where declaiming and railing against that religion which we now profess'.[5] Had they kept quiet, they might have lived in peace. Of course, they had not been unprovoked. As early as November 1559, Jewel preached his Challenge sermon at St. Paul's Cross, defying his opponents to produce evidence

---

[1] *Parker* i, 154. [2] Gee, *Elizabethan Clergy*, p. 161.
[3] *Cal. S. P. Ven.* vii, 102; *Zurich Letters*, i, 82.
[4] Gee, *Elizabethan Clergy*, p. 144-6. [5] *Zurich Letters*, i, 79.

from Scripture, the Fathers, Councils or primitive Church in the
first six centuries in support of certain features (fifteen of them)
in the service of the mass—a sermon he repeated with expansions
the following Lent when he was already a bishop. Soon he was
engaged on his massive and learned *Apology*, the receipt of a
copy of which from Parker Cecil acknowledged on January 1st,
1562.[1] There seems to be no doubt that Parker knew all about
this work and encouraged it.[2]

In view of these growing troubles with the Romanists which
no doubt much concerned the ecclesiastical commission of which
he was head, Parker was wise to avoid becoming personally
involved in the minutiae of visitations. Even in imprisonment,
the bishops were a care: they were regarded as, in a sense, his
responsibility. In September the Lords of the Council wrote to
him at the suggestion of the Lieutenant of the Tower to ask that
the prisoners might be allowed to meet, in two parties, for their
meals. Parker at once agreed.[3] He was not, at heart, a persecutor.
On the other hand, he did write a very firm reply to Heath and
others when they attacked the Church of England,[4] stoutly
maintaining its independence in origin from Rome.

On the other hand, he must also have been much concerned
about the relation of the Church of England to those continental
churches which had broken with Rome. There is good evidence
that at first, whether from conviction or policy, Elizabeth allowed
the impression to get abroad that she favoured the Augsburg
Confession and might form some sort of alliance with the Germans. In February 1559, it was thought that rites and ceremonies would be reformed on the lines of Edward VI or of the
Confession.[5] In April she was reported to be thinking of joining
the League of Smalkald.[6] In July she wrote friendly letters
containing explicit approval of the Confession to some German
princes who had written to her.[7] Her agent in Germany, Mundt,

[1] *Correspondence*, p. 161.   [2] Strype, *Parker* i, 197.
[3] *Correspondence*, pp. 121–2.   [4] Ibid., pp. 109 sqq.
[5] *Zurich Letters*, ii, 17.   [6] Ibid., i, 21.
[7] Calendar of State Papers, Foreign (1558–9), pp. 352–4.

wrote to Cecil in the same month that he had advised the sending of a strong embassy to her; in August three Germans wrote
a joint letter urging her to adhere to the religion based on the
writings of the apostles and prophets and in accordance with the
Confession of Augsburg.[1] But there were difficulties about any
projected alliance. The Germans themselves did not completely
agree in doctrine. Evidently Cecil took a hand, for Mundt wrote
in August approving of his attempt to unite all who had abandoned the Pope, but pointing out the difficulties, especially
about the doctrine of the presence in the Lord's Supper.[2]
Perhaps the Queen was never really in earnest about the matter:
anyhow, nothing came of it—though it was still in the air in 1560
when Martyr (now in Zurich) wrote to say that if it was determined, as report said, to embrace the Confession of Augsburg,
then his views would carry little weight in England.[3] Calvin
also was anxious to win the Queen's friendship, and corre-
sponded with Cecil.[4]

It was natural that in all this Parker should be seriously
engaged: his position and his views—which were neither
Lutheran nor Swiss—would alike ensure that. A letter and articles
from Germany were submitted to him by the Queen to answer[5]
in July 1560. In the same year, he had a communication from
Calvin which he reported to the Privy Council. He was encouraged by the Council to try to come to terms, but to insist on
episcopacy.[6] Though neither scheme for alliance bore fruit, and
details are lost, they must have caused Parker both work and
anxiety. 'God keep us' he wrote to Cecil in November 1559
'from such visitation as Knox have attempted in Scotland: the
people to be orderers of things.'[7]

---

[1] Cal. S. P. For., pp. 361, 478.   [2] Ibid., p. 480.   [3] *Zurich Letters*, ii, 48.
[4] Ibid., ii, 34–36.   [5] *Correspondence*, p. 118.

[6] R. Ware, *Hunting of the Romish Fox* (Dublin, 1683), pp. 95–96. There
does not seem to be any other evidence of this: it might be a confusion with
the letter from Germany submitted by the Queen.

[7] *Correspondence*, p. 105. None the less, he was very anxious to promote
real understanding, as a letter to Cecil shows, at the time of the Conference
of Poissy (*Correspondence*, p. 147).

There was, too, increasing trouble at home. The party of
reform was restless and called for restraint if not, as yet, correction. The returned exiles had not been welcomed or treated
as they expected; they were querulous and critical, as the
Zurich Letters abundantly show. Even Jewel was not at ease.
In April 1559, he found the pace of reform almost maddeningly
slow; a little later, just after the Royal Visitation had been
ordered, 'We are all of us hitherto as strangers', 'We are not
consulted', 'Others are seeking after a golden or, as it rather
seems to me, a leaden mediocrity'; in November 'As to ceremonies and maskings, there is a little too much foolery'.[1]
Others were even more strenuously opposed to what was being
done by authority. Thomas Sampson was already very much
worried about clerical habits—as, indeed, he long continued to
be. Dean of Chichester under Edward VI,[2] he was on his return
from exile one of the leaders chosen to preach at Paul's Cross on
Low Sunday 1559—the first sermon there after the long interval
due to the forbidding of preaching.[3] After the Royal Injunctions,
there is a whole series of letters between him and Peter Martyr—
he quite determined not to wear clerical habits, and unper-
suaded by Martyr's more accommodating view that the special
out-door dress, at least, was unobjectionable, and that he should
even wear the habits ordered in church (though 'speaking and
teaching against the use of them'!) lest unsuitable men should be
promoted to offices which he refused.[4] But Sampson was set,
as things were, not to be a bishop but to 'undertake the office
of a preacher or none at all'.[5] He did, indeed, refuse the Bishopric
of Norwich, and became instead Dean of Christ Church, where
later on he was troublesome, firmly refusing Grindal's plaintive
and surely very modest request that he would 'now and then'
wear the square cap in public meetings of the University.[6]
Perhaps he was unusually fussy and contentious—Bullinger

---

[1] *Zurich Letters*, i, 17 23, 55.
[2] C. H. Garrett, *Marian Exiles* (Cambridge, 1938), p. 279.
[3] Machyn, pp. 192 and 372.   [4] *Zurich Letters*, ii, 32, 39.
[5] Ibid., i, 63.   [6] Strype, *Parker* i, 368.

later on says that he was very troublesome to Martyr and never wrote him a letter which was not full of grievances.[1] But there he was, and he was not alone. Thomas Lever, Master of St. John's Cambridge under King Edward, was made rector and archdeacon of Coventry in 1559: but a letter from him in 1560[2] plainly implies that he would not wear the vestments, though a great many clergy did so for the sake of obedience. He even uses language which suggests that his position in Coventry was due to something like the choice of the parishioners, to whom he is bound 'not by any law or engagement, but only by free kindness and love'. Coverdale, a gentle man and even better-known than Lever, was not restored to the Bishopric of Exeter which he had held, but was unemployed until he was given a London living in 1563. It is difficult to suppose that his scrupulosity was not the cause—even at Parker's consecration he had only worn a black gown. The government at first treated such dissidents with astonishing forbearance. Sampson was made Dean of Christ Church; Lever's non-conformity was overlooked—he was made master of a hospital in Durham and given a canonry there; Coverdale was allowed to hold his living till he, conscientiously, resigned it to become a private preacher in 1566. But with such views emerging among prominent men, Parker had to be very much on the alert, despite the temporary toleration shown.

[1] *Zurich Letters*, ii, 152.   [2] Ibid., i, 84-85.

CHAPTER VII

EARLY EFFORTS FOR ORDER AND UNIFORMITY

In the Autumn of 1560, it suddenly was made plain that the patience of authority with protestant extremists was becoming exhausted. On September 19, the Queen issued a proclamation against the breaking or defacing of images of antiquity or images in glass in churches unless they were the object of superstitious reverence. Those who had injured innocuous images were to make good the damage, or, if they could not afford to do so, to be punished; and the stealing of bells and lead from churches was to cease. Three days later, another royal proclamation ordered all Anabaptists to withdraw from the realm within twenty days, or else to be liable to imprisonment. Then Parker—whether as a result of such information as his visitors had given him or not—resolved to get a clear account of all the clergy in his province. On November 18 he wrote to the Bishop of London and other bishops[1] for an account, before February 1, of names and surnames of all deans, archdeacons and cathedral clergy, and of all parsons and vicars; whether they were resident, able to preach and, if licensed, actually did preach; given to due hospitality; and which of them be 'neither priests nor deacons'. Obviously he was planning that some sort of order should be imposed on chaos.

On January 22, 1561, the Queen acted again. She wrote to the commissioners[2] ordering them to prepare some changes in the

[1] *Correspondence*, pp. 127–8. The report sent in from Ely (Strype, *Parker* i, 143–4) can have given little comfort. Of 152 livings, only 52 were properly served: 34 were vacant, 57 had non-resident clergy. Most of the returns are in the Corpus Christi College, Cambridge, MSS. xcvii and cxxii.

[2] *Correspondence*, pp. 132 sqq.

calendar of lessons, but did not confine herself to that, adding complaints of 'such negligence and lack of convenient reverence' used towards churches, and especially chancels that 'it breedeth no small offence and slander'. There were 'open decays and ruins of coverings, walls and windows'; there were 'unseemly tables with foul cloths for the communion of the sacraments'; the churches were 'desolate of all cleanliness and of meet ornaments for such a place'. She did not specify elaborate ornaments to be supplied—only that the tables of the Commandments should be set or hung in the east end for 'comely ornament' as well as edification! But the commissioners were to see that there was reformation in other matters too ('of one sort and fashion') especially in collegiate churches for which a Latin translation of the Prayer Book was provided. Parker acted at once; indeed Strype conjectures that he had himself procured the royal letter to be written, though his evidence is not conclusive.[1] On February 15,[2] he sent on his instructions, together with the changes in the calendar, to Grindal to communicate to the rest of the bishops of the province.

Even before the Queen's letter, the bishops had been concerting measures for dealing with unsatisfactory clergy and readers. The evidence is a document 'which has wandered about in the pages of historians seeking its proper place',[3] but which has now been fully treated and convincingly dated[4]—the so-called 'Interpretations and Further Considerations'. No early printed copy of this paper is known: indeed, it may not have been printed, but merely drawn up for private use by the bishops. There are two manuscript copies in the Inner Temple library, one corrected by Parker, the other—perhaps a fair copy—endorsed 'Dr. Cox'. Between these two there are only very slight and unimportant variations. With minor verbal inaccuracies,

[1] Strype, Parker I, i, 165.
[2] Correspondence, p. 135.
[3] Gee, Elizabethan Prayer Book, p. 156.
[4] W. M. Kennedy, The Interpretations of the Bishops (Alcuin Club Tracts, 8; London, 1908), to which the account in the text is very largely indebted.

they are printed in Strype.[1] There were five Interpretations, referring specifically by number to the Royal Injunction they interpreted, and some thirty 'further considerations'. It is a revealing document about the state of affairs. Those who were able to preach were to do so at least once a month—though they were to be 'tolerated' if they provided a sermon either by themselves or by a 'learned substitute' once in three months—a striking comment on the difficulties Parker and his fellows had to face in procuring adequate clergy. This is emphasized by the permission to employ even those who had been deprived for 'wilfulness' (refusal to take the oath, possibly, or absence) to serve cures for reasonable wages. There are other hints of the poor quality of clerics available. Archdeacons were to appoint passages of the New Testament to be learned by heart by curates, and subsequently to examine them therein; there was to be a longer catechism drawn up for the erudition of 'simple curates', and further homilies were to be drawn up for them to read. Even those who knew no Latin were to be allowed as deacons if well exercised in Scripture and if their lives (and those of their wives!) were suitable: after long probation they might be even admitted to the priesthood. Open notice was to be given of those to be ordained so that objections to them, if any, might be submitted. None were to be ordained outside their own diocese, save on the testimony of their Ordinaries, unless possessed of a university degree; nor might ministers or readers remove from a diocese or cure save with the permission of the Ordinary. On the other hand, the licences to preach which the Royal Visitors had been empowered to grant were now to be withdrawn. Plainly, the bishops intended to gain control over the clergy, to raise so far as they could the standard of learning and preaching, though ready, in the straitness of the times, to use worthy men, even if not educated, to fill cures. But they already felt that the readers were over-stepping the mark, for a long oath was provided for them to take, promising not to preach or minister the sacraments, to dress soberly, to give place if a

1 *Annals* I, i, 318–22, 323–4, 514–15.

learned minister were provided, and not to demand more stipend than the Ordinary thought fit, and so on.[1] It was further agreed that 'one brief form of declaration be made, setting out the principal articles of our religion' to be read publicly by all clergy on entering their cures and twice a year thereafter, 'for avoiding all doubt and suspicion of varying from the doctrine determined in the realm'. Until that was ready, a set of Latin articles, twenty-three in number, was appended, 'prescribed to ministers'.[2] They were mostly derived from the Edwardian Articles, but much shortened and simplified, omitting the more speculative subjects such as predestination, and original sin. They steer a very clear line between Roman doctrine and the beliefs of extreme reformers. In the Lord's Supper, the communion of the body and blood of Christ is truly given and displayed: but the sacrament is not to be carried about, elevated or worshipped, nor is it to be regarded as a propitiatory sacrifice, nor can the doctrine of transubstantiation be proved from Scripture. Justification is by faith alone, but some of the continental vagaries are explicitly rejected—that there is no forgiveness for post-baptismal sin, or that one who has received the Spirit cannot sin, or that children should not be baptized. Celibacy is not by the word of God enjoined on any, even ministers, but matrimony duly contracted is indissoluble (this was not in the Edwardian articles). Christians might wage war at the prince's command; private property was lawful; the civil laws were properly applicable to Christians, nor might any man undertake any function, ecclesiastical or secular, without 'external and legitimate vocation'—these last all matters about which the more violent Anabaptists would feel strongly. In particular, the cautious Edwardian attitude to rites and ceremonies was changed. It was no longer simply asserted that they need not be the same in all churches, and that they must not contradict Scripture, but more boldly (and, to many, offensively) that 'each particular church has authority to institute, change and

---

[1] This is printed by Strype, *Annals* I, i, 514, well away from the rest of the *Interpretations*.　　　　[2] *Annals* I, i, 323.

abrogate ecclesiastical rites and ceremonies, provided that it is done for seemliness, order and edification'—the first appearance of what was to be a real bone of contention.

Certain practical matters were also dealt with. Bishops were not to grant advowsons[1] of livings till they were actually vacant, they were to be vigilant to prevent the 'spoiling' of glebe and tithes by simoniacal pacts, and they were to deal expeditiously and favourably with their clergy in the matter of tithes. Shops were to be closed on Sundays, and workmen not to go about their worldly affairs; even fairs and marts which fell on that day were not to be open before service was over—a policy which would be welcome to those who affected continental views. Not so, however, the order that churchwardens should report every month to the Ordinary those who did not readily pay their fines for non-attendance at church. There was, as in the Injunctions, insistence on clerical dress even out of doors—'apparel agreeable'—neglect of which, after two monitions, was to be punishable by deprivation or sequestration. But there were three concessions about the services in church. The old eucharistic dress was definitely abandoned—perhaps because it had been found really impossible to enforce it. Henceforward, the cope only was to be used at the Lord's Supper, and the surplice for all other services. Moreover, the table might be moved at communion time not (as in the Injunctions) in the chancel, but 'into the body of the church, before the chancel door' at the great feasts and if the choir was too small. No doubt this was merely a matter of practical convenience, but it would be appreciated by those who wished so far as they could to reproduce the setting of the Last Supper rather than that of high mass. And it was agreed that the communion bread should be 'thicker and broader than it is now commonly used'—no doubt because the wafer-bread of the Injunctions was too much like that of the Roman services.

The *Interpretations* seem to represent a private agreement among the bishops to secure a uniform policy in practical

---

[1] 'Advowsons' is the word used; probably it should have been 'rights of presentation for one turn'.

matters: they had not, so far as we know, any official sanction. They were probably agreed about the end of 1560 or very early in 1561. The next step was the drawing up of 'the brief form of declaration', suggested above, to be read openly by all ministers on taking up their charge, and twice a year afterwards. This was printed by the Queen's printer in 1561,[1] said to be 'set out by order of both archbishops metropolitans and the rest of the bishops'. Generally referred to as The *Eleven Articles*, it was probably drawn up in March 1561. For there were by then two archbishops as there had not been before, Thomas Young, elected Archbishop of York in January, having been officially confirmed (the see had been vacant since the deprivation of Heath); and there is evidence of frequent episcopal meetings at the time: 'I hear that the bishops frequently meet in the Archbishop of Canterbury's house and are drawing up a profession of their faith to send to the *concilio*' wrote the Spanish Ambassador on March 25.[2] Had he seen the profess on, he could hardly have supposed that it was intended for submission to the Council of Trent! It is uncompromisingly anti-Roman. After insisting on the doctrine of the Trinity, the sufficiency of the Scriptures and the historic Creeds, it defines 'that Church to be the spouse of Christ' in which the word is truly taught, the sacraments orderly ministered and the authority of the keys duly used. There is no hint there of any need for historic continuity or apostolic succession; and each 'particular church' has authority to change, abolish or institute rites or ceremonies. The Queen's prerogative is firmly insisted on, whereas 'the bishop of Rome' by the Scriptures and Word of God has no more authority than other bishops in their provinces or dioceses. Baptism is perfectly ministered without 'exorcism, oil, salt, spittle or hallowing of the water'. Private masses (the priest alone receiving) were not primitive; the doctrine of the mass as a propitiatory sacrifice was against Christ's ordinance and apostolic doctrine and most injurious to the redemption wrought by Him

---

[1] C. Hardwick, *A History of the Articles of Religion* (Cambridge, 1859), pp. 337 sqq. Strype, Annals 1, i, 325 sqq.   [2] *Cal. S. P. Span.* i, 190.

Reception should be in both kinds. The 'extolling of images, relics and feigned miracles' is strongly condemned, and 'all kind of expressing God invisible in the form of an old man, or the Holy Ghost in the form of a dove and all other vain worshipping of God'. But, once more, an attempt is made to keep a balance. No one may undertake any office, ecclesiastical or secular, unless lawfully called by the high authorities according to the ordinances of the realm. And 'the book of common prayer and administration of the holy sacraments, set forth by authority of parliament, is agreeable to the scriptures . . . catholic, apostolic, and most for the advancing of God's glory'. On Aug. 4, Parker sent a copy to the Archdeacon of Canterbury to see that it was read by all concerned at the due times, and insisting, as does the printed form, that the Archbishop of York had been concerned as well as himself and other bishops in setting it forth.[1]

There is a document in the library of Corpus Christi, Cambridge, headed 'Resolutions and Orders taken by common consent of the bishops for this present time, until a synod may be had, for preservation and maintenance of uniformity in matters ecclesiastical throughout all dioceses in both provinces'. Strype gives the title and the opening clauses.[2] It is later than the *Interpretations* considered above, for there is no reference to the Latin articles there provided as a temporary standard, nor any suggestion of drawing up the 'brief declaration', presumably because that had now been done in the *Eleven Articles*. A reference to the revision of the Calendar, too, shows that it was after January 1561. Almost certainly the *Resolutions* were drawn up when the bishops were meeting in March or early April, to embody official policy till a formal synod could be held. An undated letter to the Queen from Parker, Grindal and Cox[3] looks as though royal confirmation or at least approbation was sought for the *Resolutions*; but there is no evidence that it was ever forthcoming. The document therefore only expresses episcopal plans. The new opening section, after once more

---

[1] *Register*, p. 378.   [2] *Annals* I, i, 329.
[3] *Correspondence*, pp. 129 sqq.

invalidating the preaching licences granted by the royal visitors, insists on a rigorous examination in 'unity of doctrine established by public authority' of those who are to be permitted to preach. They are to be urged to 'sobriety and discretion' in their teaching, 'abstaining from busy meddling with matters of controversy' and (no doubt to counteract the unfettered enthusiasm of the unofficial preachers) 'to foresee with diligence the matter which they will speak'. They are to set out the 'reverend estimation of the sacraments', and obedience to the orders of the Prayer Book and Injunctions. They are not to demand unreasonable rewards or stipends when they go to preach for poor curates! It is further laid down that baptism is to be ministered in the font, not in basins, though in case of need it may be ministered even privately by a 'grave and sober person' if no minister is available (a source of trouble later on, when there was strong objection to baptism by women).[1] Then followed a revised and reworded statement of the original *Interpretations*, not differing in substance, save for the omission of the Latin articles and the oath for readers.[2]

The *Resolutions* were, no doubt, a formal revision by the bishops of the *Interpretations* as first sketched out in the two manuscripts in the Inner Temple library. It is highly probable (though not certain) that it is what was referred to on April 12 when the bishops (and some members of the ecclesiastical commission, according to Strype) resolved 'that the Articles agreed on at the first session be ratified, confirmed and put in execution accordingly'.[3] It was at the same meeting that it was resolved that the Declaration for Unity of Doctrine—the *Eleven Articles*—be enforced throughout the realm. Further (though the new and long oath was omitted), it was resolved that the bishops were to review the existing readers, their ability and manners, and to confirm or remove them at discretion, to fix their wages, and to enjoin both on them and on ministers

---

[1] *Annals* I, i, 329–30.   [2] Kennedy, op. cit.

[3] Strype, *Parker* i, 194. E. Cardwell, *Documentary Annals* (Oxford, 1839), i, 264.

'abstinence from mechanical sciences'—which presumably meant trade and manual labour.

At the same time, the bishops resolved once more on means to check the spoliation of ecclesiastical revenues by alienation of glebe and tithe, or by new pensions or payments (presumably simoniacally exacted); to check the migration of ministers from one diocese to another without the written approval of the Ordinary and to see that priests deprived were either by their Ordinary's discretion re-employed, or excommunicated.[1]

It was a serious, carefully meditated attempt on the part of the bishops, with Parker and Cox in the lead, to bring order and uniformity into the confused variety of practice and belief which was spreading under the influence of imperfectly conciliated clergy of the old faith and the unregulated enthusiasm of the returned exiles; and to remedy the unfortunate results of the ill-advised and hasty ordinations of the previous year. If the attempt was not—as indeed it was not—successful, at least Parker and the other bishops deserve all credit for making it. It was not their fault that the forces against order and unity were at the moment too strong to be checked by such episcopal measures —even if all the bishops had been completely of one mind, which they soon appeared not to be. In February 1562, Jewel was still anxious to get rid even of the linen surplice, though he thought that, in doctrine, everything had been pared to the quick and did not differ a nail's breadth from what Peter Martyr held.[2] Yet Jewel was a tower of strength to Parker compared with some of the other bishops, such as Parkhurst or Grindal, who did not even attempt loyally to carry out the common policy.

How urgent it was in particular that steps should be taken against 'secret compacts' in the filling of livings a glance at Parker's *Register* makes clear. It is obvious at once that a right of presentation was regarded as a valuable piece of property, which was jealously guarded. Great care was taken to record how the right of presentation had come to the actual patron of the

[1] Strype, *Parker* i, 194-5. E. Cardwell, *Documentary Annals* i, 265-7.
[2] *Zurich Letters*, i, 100.

moment. In 1569, for example, a prebend was filled in Chichester by a man who had received the right to present through two intermediaries from Richard Bishop of Chichester—i.e. Bishop Sampson (1536-42).[1] Instances of such handing on through several persons of the right to present are so numerous as to be commonplace.[2] Even if they went back to Roman Catholic donors, such rights were still valid: in two cases at least they derived from Stephen Gardiner,[3] and in several from abbeys.[4] Not even such suspected sources could invalidate the property right. Moreover, in case of doubt the issue was vigorously fought out. In 1560 Parker had to sequester a living because rival claimants to the presentation were likely to take to arms, 'not without danger of blood-shedding'.[5] And there are many instances of legal proceedings to recover a right of presentation against those who had usurped it, in several cases bishops.[6] Sometimes the desire for patronage was due to motives which, though partisan, were not unworthy. By 1567 Richard Rich had amassed thirty advowsons, mostly in Essex; in the succeeding years the patronage was used to secure there a strong Puritan nucleus. There were other similar cases.[7] But in the main there can be no doubt that financial considerations were uppermost. Hence Parker's lament in 1568 that he had heard that in Norwich '*Quid vultis mihi dare?* had so prevailed among the Simonians that now to sell and buy benefices, to fleece parsonages and vicarages (sic), that *omnia erant venalia*.'[8] Even serving men and boys were put into livings.[9] The 'consideration' demanded by the patron might not be cash down—it might be some agreement not to exact tithe, or to let glebe on favourable terms or for long leases—or even to marry a female dependent of the patron.[10]

---

[1] *Register*, p. 280.   [2] e.g. Ibid., 303, 314.   [3] Ibid., pp. 204, 682.
[4] Ibid., pp. 205, 320, 826.   [5] Ibid., p. 201.
[6] Ibid., pp. 1110, 1116, 1117, 1140 (the Queen herself against the Bishop of Bath and Wells).
[7] C. Hill, *Economic Problems of the Church* (Oxford, 1956), p. 56.
[8] *Correspondence*, p. 311.
[9] Parker refused a dispensation for a boy of 13 or 14 to hold a living in 1561. *Correspondence*, p. 136.   [10] C. Hill, op. cit., p. 68.

Obviously the abuse was notorious and wide-spread, and must have much exercised the honest Archbishop. But, despite this effort of the bishops, it was not stopped—it was too much in the spirit of the age to be recognized as the open scandal which it was. The Queen herself set the fashion of plundering by her exchanges during episcopal vacancies, and her chief statesmen aided and abetted. As late as 1595 Burghley wrote to Robert Cecil to take care that the sees of Durham and Winchester were not officially filled until large annuities to the Queen (as paid by the previous bishops) were secured![1] Lancelot Andrewes twice refused bishoprics because he could only have obtained them by payments which would have crippled the sees.[2] Other bishops, more infected by the spirit of the day, were not so scrupulous and purchased their sees by large alienations or the grant of leases. Nor did they stop there. In many cases they permanently plundered their sees, not to meet the inevitable costs of their position but to accumulate large fortunes for their families.[3] Aylmer, the butt of Marprelate, was by no means an isolated example. In such an atmosphere, it is at least to the credit of the bishops at Lambeth that they recognized the evil so early and agreed to try to put a stop to the plundering of parochial endowments through simony, even if they did not succeed—and there can be little doubt that in this attempt Parker probably deserves to be thought the leader.

Apart from such matters of large policy, Parker was involved almost at once in the sort of minor troubles which were to be the regular background of his episcopate—the unrestrained enthusiasm of innovators and the only half-hearted support of some of the bishops. As early as December 1559, with others of the commission, he had to write to the Chapter of Exeter Cathedral.[4] The royal visitors had ordered morning service to be said daily at six o'clock, but large numbers who attended it were not content to join in quietly but took upon themselves to sing a

---

[1] F. Peck, *Desiderata Curiosa* (London, 1732), vol i, bk. v, 5.
[2] Cf. C. Hill, op. cit., pp. 16–17.   [3] Ibid., pp. 18–20.
[4] *Correspondence*, p. 107.

psalm and 'all together with one voice to give praise unto God'. It sounds disorderly, nor is it surprising that the Chapter tried to put a stop to it, though clearly in a tactless way. They were rebuked by the visitors, and in December Parker and other commissioners sent orders that the instructions of the visitors were to be obeyed, and the congregation allowed to 'sing or say the godly prayers in the morning, and other times set forth, used and permitted in this Church of England'. It looks like a wise attempt to direct inconvenient zeal into regular channels instead of alienating it by sheer suppression.

More ominous is a mysterious letter from Sandys at Worcester to Parker of October 1560.[1] It is mysterious because it plainly declares that Sandys had been visiting his diocese, and claimed that he did so with Parker's consent, despite the Archbishop's inhibition of May 27 to all the bishops of his province, in view of his own intended metropolitan visitation. (Strype avoids the difficulty by dating Sandys' visitation as 1561:[2] but that will not do: the letter is plainly dated October 1560.) Parker had evidently sent a rebuke suggesting that Sandys had been over-hasty in action, and even, possibly, moved by hope of profit (for Sandys carefully explains that he was £24 out of pocket over it), and apparently criticizing him for the deprivation of two incumbents. One of them, Arden, certainly met only his deserts: a Romanist, he is described later on as lurking in Herefordshire and unable to be discovered.[3] About the other we know nothing else. But plainly, Sandys thought that Parker's good nature had been abused—'They have bragged, but I never thought they should find so much favour at your hands.' And it looks as though Parker had hinted that Sandys was trying to make a profit on that transaction too! Equally Sandys, who had been in exile at Frankfurt and Zurich, thought that Parker was unduly suspicious of foreign influence—'I think ye will not utterly condemn all Germanical natures. For Germany hath brought forth as good natures as England hath.' And he bitterly rejected

---

[1] *Correspondence*, pp. 124-7.   [2] Strype, *Parker* I, i, 156.
[3] Gee, *Elizabethan Clergy*, p. 184.

Parker's suggestion that he had been acting in concert with Grindal of London (whose laxity was later on a great trouble to Parker). In fact, he was indignant: he had stood up for Parker, and had 'offended others in defending you', and now had been put by him to 'sore pinches and danger of too great displeasure'. As we have not Parker's original letter, nor his answer to Sandys, we cannot further elucidate the incident. But it shows how easy it was for misunderstanding and strain to arise between Parker and his suffragans, and that already he was criticized as too gentle to those of the old faith and hostile to continental ideas.

Quite early, too, he had trouble about his legal officers. The range of ecclesiastical jurisdiction was immense, and had scarcely decreased with the break from Rome. 'Clerical privilege' still continued—the actual words are used.[1] A cleric accused in or imprisoned by the civil courts could be 'claimed' by the ecclesiastical authorities, imprisoned and tried by them and, when 'purged', set free.[2] The bishops had sometimes their own prisons for such[3]—the Archbishop at Westgate for example—though in 1561 he had to write to the sheriff of Oxford to allow accused clerks to be lodged in the common jail at Oxford as there was no 'convenient prison' for them.[4] Moreover 'privilege' could be claimed by many who would not now be recognized as clergy: of six 'convict clerks' purged in 1569, two are described as yeoman, two as labourers, one as carpenter, one as husbandman.[5] Besides all that, the proving of wills and their due administration, and questions of tithe and matrimony fell to the ecclesiastical courts, as well as 'blasphemy, perjury, adultery, incest and incontinence'.[6] If the accused did not appear, they were, quite regularly, excommunicated for 'contumacy' and after forty days, if still obstinate, reported to the Archbishop for him to request their arrest by the civil authorities. Later, if they gave satisfaction, there would be a request for release.[7] Often, the record

---

[1] Register, p. 424.   [2] Ibid., pp. 503, 511.   [3] Ibid., pp. 203, 247.
[4] Correspondence, p. 145.   [5] Register, pp. 513–14.   [6] Ibid., p. 424.
[7] e.g. Ibid., pp. 359, 361–2. Instances are very frequent.

only states 'contumacy'—i.e. non-appearance—as the offence, but sometimes the original charge is indicated—non-payment of tithe, immorality, defamation, non-appearance in a testamentary case, even non-attendance at church.[1]

Naturally, the Archbishop was not personally involved in such cases as a rule (though he did in 1563 conduct a matrimonial enquiry which involved the daughter of Lord Howard of Effingham[2]). Such business was usually delegated. Matters of clerical privilege were normally dealt with by a bishop's Official or Vicar-General: they were clearly regarded as very important— so much so that in case of vacancy of a see express authority was issued by the Archbishop for attending to them.[3] For other cases, there was a bewildering variety of officers and courts, some of which were duplicated for the dioceses and even arch-deaconries.[4] The courts were very unpopular, probably not without cause. They were regarded as dilatory, expensive both in matters of fines and fees, and as far too numerous: a man might easily be cited in more than one court for the same offence. A large part of the Petition of the Commons against the Ordi-naries in 1532 was directed against the conduct of the courts.[5] Whitgift, to the end of his life, was still striving to restrain their excesses. The difficulty was that, though the bishops knew that much was wrong, they could not really control or easily dismiss the legal officers. These had no doubt paid for their posts, as comes out clearly in 1582 in the bitter dispute between Overton of Lichfield and Coventry and his Chancellor.[6] They regarded themselves as holding a sort of freehold, and naturally expected to re-imburse themselves through fees and fines for what they

[1] This last is interesting (p. 451). The index to the *Register* suggests that the John Man involved was the Warden of Merton. This can hardly be correct, for he was a cleric and one of Parker's chaplains.

[2] Ibid., pp. 406 sqq.   [3] *Register*, p. 178.

[4] Summarized in the *Register*, pp. xiv–xvi, xx–xxv.

[5] H. Gee and W. J. Hardy, *Documents Illustrative of English Church History*, pp. 145 sqq.

[6] Strype, *Annals* III, i, 133. On the same page is the opinion of four eminent lawyers that the bishops could not remove the grantee if the fees attached to his office were 'casual and uncertain'.

had paid. And there was, of course, a good deal of rivalry between the courts to secure jurisdiction—and, so, profit.

In November 1560 Parker was compelled to interfere to put a stop to an abuse which illustrates the complicated difficulties of procedure. The Consistory Court of the Archbishop—the Court of Arches—was a court of appeal from diocesan Consistory Courts of the province. For some cases also the Archbishop's Court of Audience, presided over by the Chancellor, was a similar court of appeal.[1] An ingenious device resulted. Those summoned to diocesan courts appealed to the Arches or Court of Audience, but did not, once their appeals were registered, pursue them. The result was that proceedings against them in the diocesan courts were stayed—no doubt at times for very long periods if not indefinitely. The Archbishop therefore wrote to the Dean of the Arches and to his Chancellor.[2] An oath was to be taken from those presenting such appeals that they really believed that the alleged grievance was true; a 'reasonable' date was to be fixed for the appeal to be heard; if the appellant did not appear to sustain his case, it was then to be remitted to the first court 'with charges reasonable'. It was surely a very practical way, as the letter says, for 'cutting off all matters frivolous and frustratory delays, and finishing all causes with such expedition as in any wise the laws may suffer'.

In the same month, he had to deal with another trouble. Complaint was made that the Archbishop's Chancellor was granting licences to marry during the seasons by law prohibited. The complainants were the Queen's Clerk of the Faculties and the Archbishop's Clerk of the Faculties, who each urged that he alone had the right to issue such licences (plainly the real issue was who was to get the fees!). Parker summoned a meeting at which his Chancellor produced precedents for his action from the times of Warham, Cranmer and Pole, the last three archbishops. Parker therefore ordered the practice to continue till its opponents could show 'further matter to the contrary'.[3]

[1] *Register*, p. 402.   [2] *Register*, p. 359; *Correspondence*, p. 128.
[3] *Register*, pp. 360–1.

CHAPTER VIII

ROYAL INTERVENTION: ROMANIST TROUBLES

DESPITE the trouble about the *Offendicle*, Parker's relations with the Queen seem to have remained easy. In July 1560 she and the Privy Council dined with him at Lambeth, after due notice of her coming.[1] But he did not hesitate on occasion to advise her with boldness—the letter which sought her support for the Bishops' *Resolutions* in 1561 also contained a long exhortation to her to marry.[2] It was a matter about which, at any rate later on, she became very touchy, regarding it as a personal concern about which she much resented suggestions from Parliament or any one else. But there is no evidence that she was angered by the advice of Parker and his fellows. (She may have been—for we have not her reply: certainly she did not underwrite the *Resolutions*.) Anyhow, she continued to rely on him and, very typically, to use him to carry out business which she wanted done without herself incurring any odium for it. When St. Paul's Cathedral was destroyed by fire in June 1561, she appointed a commission to consider the best means of re-building the cathedral and raising funds for it, and wrote to the Lord Mayor that she had appointed some of her Council to confer with him on the matter. But on the same day, apparently without waiting to see what they decided, she wrote to Parker to collect funds at once from the clergy. It was a skilful letter.[3] She did not *order* him to do anything but, assuming his eagerness to repair the damage, in order 'to join our authority with your devotion and good will' she authorized him in consultation with the other

---

[1] Strype, *Parker* i, 171; *Correspondence*, p. 120.

[2] *Correspondence*, p. 131.

[3] *Cal. S. P. Dom.*, p. 177–8; *Correspondence*, pp. 142–3.

bishops 'to devise upon some contribution of money and relief to be levied and collected' from the clergy. However great his good will, Parker can scarcely have liked the suggestion. It is, to say the least, highly questionable whether he had legal powers to levy such a contribution; apart from that, he was very much worried about clerical poverty. But such a suggestion from the Queen could not be ignored. Within a week he wrote to the Bishop of London. The legal difficulty was avoided by putting it that he should consult with his clergy and resolve with them on a reasonable contribution, thus making it seem voluntary; and that he should write to other bishops to do the same. But he did also strengthen his request to the bishop by reporting to him the Queen's letter, and indicated that he thought a reasonable payment would be a twentieth part of his income from each man beneficed in the London diocese, a thirtieth from those in other dioceses unless they were paying first-fruits, in which case a fortieth would suffice.[1] In a later letter, he suggested a concession to London clergy in first-fruits, but also added that curates and stipendiaries, previously excused, should pay something.[2] Presumably his plan was carried out—but it seems a little hard on poor clergy that they should have to contribute, whether they wished or no. But they did not have to provide the whole of the funds; Elizabeth herself contributed handsomely, both money and wood.[3] And even before she wrote to the Lord Mayor, he and the Common Council had arranged for the payment of a tax of three-fifteenths for the re-building, and had appointed overseers to look after the work and workmen. The task was started on July 1, and by November 1 it was possible for the Lord Mayor and the Livery Companies to attend a service there with a sermon by the Bishop of London.[4] But all was not finished by then: in June 1563, the Council pressed Parker to see that such of the clergy as had not paid their share should be pressed to do so in order that the roof might be completed.[5] As late as 1567

---

[1] *Correspondence*, pp. 143-4.   [2] Ibid., p. 153.
[3] Stow, *Annals* (ed. Howes, London, 1631), p. 647 b.
[4] Machyn, pp. 260, 262, 271.   [5] *Correspondence*, pp. 178-9.

Grindal was still asking for a contribution from the officers of the Court of Wards.[1]

In August of the same year, 1561, the Queen found more work for Parker. A Provost had been appointed of 'our College of Eton next Windsor', without her assent or pleasure, 'of whom there is dispersed very evil fame'. In 1559 Parker had been one of the visitors for Cambridge and Eton, but he might well have thought that his office as such had now lapsed. The Queen conveniently assumed that it still continued. She therefore ordered him with such others of the commission as were speedily available to enquire into the election and character of the Provost and of the whole order of the College.[2] Parker, together with Horne of Winchester and Sir Anthony Cook, acted with speed: there was a two-day visitation starting on September 9. The Provost, to avoid deprivation, resigned; several of the Fellows did not present themselves and were pronounced contumacious and deprived of their places, while one who did appear but refused the Supremacy oath was also deprived.[3]

In the same month, however, August 1561, the Queen took a step which grievously distressed the Archbishop. The context of it appears in a letter from Cecil on August 12.[4] She was on progress in Essex and Suffolk (parts of the dioceses of London and Norwich respectively, each under a lax bishop, Grindal and Parkhurst) and had been angered by the slenderness of the ministers and the nakedness of religion. In particular, the Bishop of Norwich was blamed for the 'great variety in ministration'. Schismatics and anabaptists were winked at: 'a surplice may not be borne here. And the ministers follow the folly of the people, calling it charity to feed their fond humour.' Cecil writes that the Queen was daily offended, and in particular was 'evil affected to the state of matrimony in her clergy'. If, he says, he had not been 'very stiff' she would have utterly and openly condemned

---

[1] *Cal. S. P. Dom.*, p. 301.   [2] *Correspondence*, pp. 149–50.

[3] Strype, *Parker* i, 205–7, quoting from a report in the 'Paper Office' which now cannot be found (*Correspondence*, p. 150, note).

[4] *Correspondence*, p. 148.

and forbidden it. (Though never legalized under Elizabeth, it was obviously tolerated, as her Injunctions show.) In the end she had been satisfied with an Injunction which he is sending to the two Archbishops for their provinces and to the Chancellors of the two Universities 'so as it shall not be promulgated to be popular'—a vain device to avoid publicity! Machyn knew of it almost at once.[1] The Injunction[2] starkly forbade the residence of women and children in any cathedral precinct or college, without any exception even for the wife of a Dean or college Head. It was to be transcribed into the statutes of every college and reputed as part of them.

Cox of Ely, hard-headed and practical, saw the danger of such a step. He did not object so far as colleges were concerned. But there were large and separate houses provided for deans and prebendaries; even so, there were very few regularly resident—at Ely only one. 'Turn him out, doves and owls may dwell there for any continual housekeeping.'[3] In view of St. Paul's respect for marriage, he was sure that the Queen would be ready, if moved, to allow three or four to reside with their families. Anyhow, the Injunction had much discouraged ministers and given the adversaries great occasion for 'rejoicing and jeering'. Probably the Queen's action was no more than an explosive expression of her fixed dislike of clerical matrimony, provoked by the general laxity of the East Anglian ministers. But Parker, while also seeing, like Cox, the practical consequences—the loss of hospitality and of preachers in the chief cities, and the laughter of 'Queen Mary's Clergy'—was even more upset by the light which the incident threw on the Queen's attitude and her imperiousness. In a long letter to Cecil[4] he says he was 'in an horror to hear such words to come from her mild nature and christianly learned conscience' about God's holy institution of matrimony when he talked with her later. She had even threatened further Injunctions. To his old friend Cecil he poured out his heart, pathetically. He regretted that he had

[1] *Diary*, p. 265. [2] *Correspondence*, p. 146.
[3] Ibid., p. 151. [4] Ibid., pp. 156 sqq.

ever entered on his office. 'I have neither joy of house, land, or name, so abased by my natural sovreign good lady.' He had earnestly tried to serve her but 'where I have, for the execution of her laws and orders, purchased the hatred of the adversaries, and also, for moderating some things indifferent, have procured to have the foul reports of some Protestants, yet all things thus borne have never discomforted me, so I might please God and serve her Highness'. But now the Queen's talk and her threat of further Injunctions 'with conference of no ecclesiastical persons' had driven him to despair and so dulled him that he could only pray to God for removal from this earth. It was not the last occasion on which Parker was to feel deeply the lack of royal understanding and support, and that he was left to bear alone the odium of carrying out what was really Elizabeth's policy. That he should have been able to write as he did to Cecil shows how close was the understanding between them.

Two further steps were taken by the Queen in October 1561 to preserve (or restore) seemliness in worship. She sent a letter to her ecclesiastical commissioners[1] ordering that the separation of chancels from the main part of the church should be clearly marked. Rood-lofts still remaining were to lose their upper parts but to be left as screens; where they had been completely destroyed, a partition was to be erected. Chancel steps were not to be removed, nor tombs of noble or worshipful people; and chancels were to be kept clean and repaired and the Commandments painted up therein. Fonts were not to be removed, and were to be used—curates were not to use basins in their stead; and God-parents were to answer for the children baptized as was customary. Nor were any holy-days or fasting days to be observed as of duty save those ordered in the calendar or by authority. It is a rather mixed collection of which the single rationale was obviously the attempt to preserve (without any concession to image-worship) the traditional appearance and usages in church.

Later in the month appeared a royal proclamation 'for avoiding

[1] Gee, *Elizabethan Prayer Book*, pp. 273 sqq.

of divers outrageous and unseemly behaviours as well within and near the cathedral church of St. Paul in London as in divers other churches'.[1] It was chiefly concerned with St. Paul's, but other churches too were covered. Measures against fighting and quarrelling in churchyards were to be strictly enforced, with imprisonment for two months and a fine for the reparation of the church concerned. Folk were not, during sermon or service, to walk about in church or churchyard, or to conduct business arrangements, but to attend to what was going on 'quietly and reverently'. To enforce such orders, the Mayor of London was to assign two aldermen, with four or six commoners and a convenient number of sergeants and officers, to attend the Sunday services in St. Paul's, with power to arrest offenders. And all justices of peace, mayors, sheriffs were commanded to cooperate in seeing that the measures here proclaimed were duly executed. The stringency of the proposals is a sufficient indication of the seriousness of the offence.

Such royal measures must have been very welcome to the Archbishop with his love of order and continuity. But another difficult duty was shortly placed on him. In January 1562 he was appointed by the Queen, along with Grindal and others, to enquire into the relationship between Lady Catherine Grey and the Earl of Hertford who claimed to have been married.[2] The matter was important and awkward. According to Henry VIII's will, Catherine (a great-granddaughter of Henry VII) was next to the Queen in the order of succession to the throne: the Earl, son of Protector Somerset, was a near relative of Edward VI. Any child of theirs would clearly have a strong claim to the throne if Elizabeth died—and she, as was often clear, was determined to keep the question of succession as open as she could. The birth of a son in September 1561 in the Tower (where Catherine had been confined since August[3]) therefore greatly angered the Queen, and raised issues of great political significance. The task of Parker and the other commissioners ordered to examine the

---

[1] Cardwell, *Documentary Annals* i, 276 sqq.
[2] *Cal. S. P. Dom.*, p. 194. [3] *Correspondence*, p. 149.

alleged marriage, was delicate. Separately examined, both the prisoners (for Hertford, too, was put in the Tower in September) made statements which agreed in all essential particulars, but they could not produce any documentary evidence nor the officiating priest in support of their statement that they had been secretly married towards the end of 1559. There would have been nothing very unusual about such clandestine proceedings,[1] and quite obviously the general view was that they had actually taken place: Catherine was regularly termed 'Countess' and her son's claim to the throne was later thought by many to be a good one. The commissioners could quite rightly have said that, under an Act of 1536, the marriage was treasonable, but that would hardly have satisfied public opinion. On May 12, 1562, they pronounced their verdict that it was illegal;[2] possibly they regarded the absence of independent evidence as justifying them in denying the validity of any ceremony which might have taken place. The truth is, no other decision would have been acceptable to the Queen, but one wonders whether the tender conscience of Parker was not troubled. 'No question' says Strype 'the Archbishop underwent censures for his proceedings.'[3]

To add to his cares there continued to be troubles with Romanists in various parts of the country, despite (perhaps because of) the stream of protestant books—the *Geneva Bible* in 1561, Foxe's Book of Martyrs, Jewel's *Apology*, and a reprint of the *Great Bible* in 1562–3. In April 1561, a priest was arrested for saying mass secretly in Kent and Essex; those who had entertained him were convicted at Brentwood and by June they and others were in the Tower for hearing mass.[4] At Hereford, Scory had great troubles, especially in his cathedral which he described as 'a very nursery of blasphemy, whoredom, pride, superstition and ignorance'. He asked to be allowed to nominate impartial witnesses to visit his diocese, feeling, no doubt, that he was himself

---

[1] *Register*, p. 583, for example, has a dispensation validating a marriage performed in a private house without banns.

[2] *Cal. S. P. Dom.*, Addenda 1547–65 (in Vol. 1601–3, p. 535).

[3] *Parker* i, 235.　　　　　　[4] *Cal. S. P. Dom.*, pp. 173, 176, 179.

unpopular and suspected of bias.[1] This perhaps explains why Parker, though nominating him alone as his visitor for the diocese and city of Hereford in July 1561, strengthened his position by adding the Bishop of Worcester as joint visitor for the cathderal.[2] In August, Scory was still complaining that Romanist justices of peace were a difficulty, and that his diocese was infested by troublesome priests from other dioceses who were 'fested in the streets with torchlight'.[3] It was not until the following March that Parker and Grindal were able to write to Cecil that it was time that the Dean, prebendaries and ministers of the church of Hereford should again be placed under the rule and obedience of their bishop.[4] Best, writing of the condition of his diocese of Carlisle, found the priests 'wicked imps of Anti-Christ', ignorant, stubborn, false, subtle.[5] Pilkington found Durham disaffected and insubordinate; in Carlisle diocese popery greatly prevailed.[6]

In Oxford, in particular, there was disquiet, despite the removal of several Heads and Fellows in 1559.[7] In September 1561 Horne dealt with the three colleges of which, as Bishop of Winchester, he was Visitor and which demurred to acknowledge the Royal Supremacy. The President of Magdalen was deprived, the President of Corpus resigned; at New College the Warden was not actually displaced, but the College did not apparently submit,[8] and several Fellows were deprived. But new appointments did not in the end make for peace. The new President of Magdalen was Lawrence Humphrey, already Regius Professor of Divinity.[9] Just before his election, too, the vacant Deanery of Christ Church had been filled, at the request of the College, by the appointment at Michaelmas 1561 of Thomas Sampson.[10] Even before he was actually installed, on September 5, he burned 'superstitious utensils' of great value.[11] He and Humphrey, both enthusiastic reformers, at once became regular preachers in the University—almost the only ones,

[1] *Cal. S. P. Dom.*, p. 177.   [2] *Register*, p. 684.   [3] *Cal. S. P. Dom.*, p. 183.
[4] *Correspondence*, p. 165.   [5] *Cal. S. P. Dom.*, p. 180.
[6] Ibid., pp. 188, 192.   [7] Gee, *Elizabethan Clergy*, p. 136.
[8] *Cal. S. P. Dom.*, p. 186.   [9] Strype, *Parker* i, 223.
[10] Strype, *Annals* I, ii, 147.   [11] Machyn, p. 266: Strype, *Annals* I, i, 404.

according to Wood:[1] later they were to prove very troublesome to Parker.

In 1562 the Archbishop, as Visitor, had to face a distressing situation at Merton College, Oxford. The Wardenship was vacant. According to the College statutes, three persons should be nominated to the Archbishop from whom he should choose one. Though the College presentation was made in due course, it was also revealed that the Fellows were not agreed, but that five names were favoured.[2] Parker met the situation by nominating John Man, who was not a member of the College or one of those proposed; seemingly he had the right to do so in case of dissension. Not unnaturally, the College was angry, and at first refused to admit the new Warden into the College and on his second appearance locked the gate in his face. When he succeeded in having it opened, he was, it is reported, met with a box on the ear.[3] But that was not all. Under the late Warden, the custom of singing Latin hymns in hall had been changed by a resolution of the College into the singing of metrical psalms in English. During the vacancy, on All Saints' Day, one of the senior Fellows had dashed into the hall, seized the psalm book from the leader of the singing and flung it away. There was plainly a bitter feud between favourers of the old and new ways, likely to lead to blows. Moreover, the old service books had not been destroyed but concealed under the chapel floor, and 'idols and painted pieces of wood' were hidden in 'blind Corners'. The Visitor had to intervene. He appointed a strong commission—his Vicar-General, Yale, the Archdeacon of Canterbury and the Warden of All Souls; even so, his seal was cut off the citation when it was posted in the College! The whole proceedings are elaborately recorded in the *Register* by Incent.[4] The new Warden was installed; Fellows who did not appear were pronounced contumacious; the violent leader of the opposition was expelled,

---

[1] Anthony Wood's *Annals* (printed by J. Gutch, edition of *The History and Antiquities of the University of Oxford*, Oxford, 1794), ii, 152.

[2] *Register*, pp. 798–800.   [3] Wood, *Annals* ii, 149–50.

[4] *Register*, pp. 684–717.

and one of his supporters—an absentee bursar—suspended, and the offences of four other of the Fellows were reported to the Archbishop for correction, of whom three shortly ceased to be members of the College.[1] Rules were laid down, for a more strict keeping and rendering of accounts, for a stricter oversight of the studies of the junior Fellows—and for a more sober style of dress —rules which suggest that there was at least some substance in the serious accusations of immorality, slackness of discipline and financial irregularity contained in the various depositions of the Fellows.

At the same time, the Archbishop also visited his other College in Oxford, All Souls, by his Vicar-General and the Archdeacon—the Warden of the College, naturally, was not included. There does not seem to have been much wrong at the moment (though there was trouble later), perhaps because of the wisdom of Warner. Warden under Henry VIII, he resigned under Mary and was restored under Elizabeth; he was sufficiently trusted to be one of the Visitors of Merton and had, indeed, according to one list been one of the Queen's visitors of the University in 1559.[2] Only 8 out of 40 Fellows failed to answer the citation and, as no sentence of contumacy was passed on them, presumably they had adequate reason. No new rules were imposed.[3] The contrast between the two colleges emphasizes what appeared in the previous year—that as yet neither party could really be said to have gained control in the University as a whole, and that feeling ran very high.

Meantime, anxiety about Romanists in London continued. In July 1562, there was some evidence of a plot to try to restore the deposed bishops.[4] In the same month, perhaps as a result of this, the Privy Council ordered that the bishops in the Tower should be more straitly confined, so as to prevent such common conference as was possible till then.[5] In September a priest was publicly conducted through London, wearing a cope, for saying

---

[1] Wood, op. cit., ii, 150.   [2] Ibid., ii, 140.
[3] *Register*, pp. 717-19.   [4] *Cal. S. P. Dom.*, p. 203.
[5] *Privy Council Acts*, vii, 118.

mass at a private house: he was then sent to prison by the Lord Mayor.[1] The Spanish embassy was a rallying point for recusants —so much so that a watch was kept on the house and the ambassador complained that no one dared to visit him, that his courier was detained while his dispatches were opened and read, that one of his servants was seduced to give evidence against him. In January 1563, he complained that new locks had been put on his doors and the keys kept so that all his visitors could be checked, and in February that those who went to mass in the embassy on the Feast of the Purification had been arrested, thought they were all foreigners, not English.[2] On the same day others were arrested for attending Mass at St. Mary's Spital.[3] In such cases, the civil authorities seem to have acted, not the Archbishop. But he also was from time to time involved in what must have been a burdensome way—for recusants were lodged with him for 'instruction', and sometimes left for as long as five weeks; he found them both expensive and tiresome.[4] In July, too, the ecclesiastical commission was re-constituted, still with Parker at its head. But it was increased from 20 to 27 in number, and the minimum needed for a quorum was reduced to three[5]—a sure sign that it was thought there was much work for them to do. They were to search out all heresies and seditious books, enormities and misbehaviour in church, and all who obstinately absented themselves from service. Almost certainly the aim was primarily to deal with increasingly bold recusancy. Parkhurst, in August, was delighted to have from the Archbishop a letter urging him to find out secretly all those who 'do not comply with the true religion'. Parkhurst's pleasure shows

---

[1] Machyn, pp. 291–2.

[2] *Cal. S. P. Span.* i, 233, 236, 241–2, 277, 295. How well justified were the government's suspicions of the Spaniards is shown by Philip's instructions to the new Spanish Ambassador in January 1564 (*Spanish Calendar*, p. 352) to encourage English catholics 'with such secrecy, dissimulation and dexterity as to give no cause of suspicion to the Queen', and later, in August (Ibid., p. 371), to try secretly to help Dudley to turn Cecil out of office.

[3] Machyn, p. 299.   [4] *Correspondence*, pp. 154–6, 170.

[5] Gee, *Elizabethan Clergy*, pp. 174, 178.

that he thought Romanists were aimed at not sectaries. He
even believed that the imprisoned bishops were now to be
firmly tried.[1] Presumably a long list of recusants and their
whereabouts, undated but still extant, was one result of the
enquiries of the commission.[2]

The commission was also to examine the rules and statutes of
all ecclesiastical corporations founded by Henry VIII or since,
so that 'enormities' might be corrected and new orders made if
needed. This was part of the general policy of tidying up, to see
that funds were not wasted or misapplied. Already, in the
previous September, there had been a proclamation to avoid
abuses of payment of pensions to religious persons,[3] mostly
monks who had resigned under Henry VIII. Strict measures were
now taken to prove the identity of claimants—there are two
certificates of such in Parker's *Register*,[4] just after the proclamation. In February 1562, the Queen had similarly demanded from
Parker an account of all the hospitals and schools in his diocese;
his return was made with expedition in May.[5] He found one
hospital 'misused' because of a long lease made to a layman; in
another the Master was a layman who was not resident and did
not distribute relief as he should. But for the most part, he
maintained, the institutions were properly carrying out their
functions on astonishingly small endowments. Such an enquiry,
at least, the Archbishop would rejoice to make—he had already
arranged for the visitation of one hospital[6] under his patronage—
provided that it did not mean that funds were to be confiscated.
His care to point out how small were the endowments, and that
they were not liable to tithe, shows not only his interest but his
desire to protect.

---

[1] *Zurich Letters*, i, 122.   [2] Gee, *Elizabethan Clergy*, pp. 179–85.
[3] R. Steele, *Royal Proclamation of the Tudor and Stuart Period* (Oxford,
1910), i, 58.   [4] *Register*, p. 384.
[5] *Correspondence*, pp. 163, 166 sqq.   [6] *Register*, p. 380.

CHAPTER IX

PARLIAMENT AND CONVOCATION
OF 1563: THE ARTICLES

In January 1563, there were meetings both of Parliament and of
Convocation. In the former as well as in the latter consideration
of religion took a prominent place. In his opening speech to
Parliament Bacon (presumably voicing official or royal views)
dealt with it first of all. Preachers were not so diligent as they
should be; there was a lack of ministers; there was slothfulness
and 'insufficiency' even among those who were ministers; the
agreed ceremonies were conducted without the right ornaments;
few attended the services. His remarks were naturally a criticism
of the way in which the settlement had been put into practice,
not of the settlement itself. But he did not suggest that Parliament should deal in it: it was the concern of the bishops. The
House of Commons, in which there was a strong element of
returned exiles,[1] was also critical but was inclined to find
fault not so much with the bishops as with the government.
The new Speaker, commenting on education, lamented the few-
ness of schools and scholars and the decay of the Universities.
The cause was 'want of livings and preferments; for covetousness
hath gotten the livings, as by impropriations, which is a decay of
learning'. 'The poor vicar hath but only twenty pounds', and
so no preachers there. He pressed for the redress of the abuse of
impropriations. He also plainly wanted stronger measures against
'Pelagians, Libertines, Papists' who leave God's commandments to follow 'their own traditions, affections and minds'.[2]

In both complaints he was faithfully expressing the mind of

---

[1] See D'Ewes *Journal*, and Sir J. Neale's *Elizabeth and Her Parliaments
1559–81*.　　[2] D'Ewes *Journal*, pp. 64–65.

the Commons. They were genuinely alarmed that stronger measures were not being taken against Romanists and were disturbed about clerical poverty. They took great pains to present a petition to the Queen to marry, or to nominate a successor, so as to secure the protestant succession to the throne because of their fears of 'malicious papists'. They initiated the Act for the Assurance of the Queen's Power over all estates in her dominions, condemning those who extolled the authority of the Pope, and ordering the Supremacy oath to be taken by further classes of people—all university graduates, schoolmasters, and lawyers as well as clergy. Bishops were now empowered to offer the oath to all ecclesiastics in their dioceses, which made it much more formidable. Moreover, the penalties for refusal of the oath were increased; for a first refusal, to that of *premunire*, for a second, of treason; though the offering of the oath a second time was really to be confined to ecclesiastics and those employed in the ecclesiastical courts. A Bill for the maintenance of the navy roused much suspicion because of a clause ordering Wednesday to be a 'fish-day', to encourage and support sailors. It was only passed when it was made clear that the eating of fish on Wednesdays was not 'of any necessity for the saving of souls or that it is the service of God'; it was to be regarded simply as other 'politic' laws, and any who maintained otherwise were to be punished as speakers of false news. They accepted, with the addition of a proviso, a Bill from the Lords to tighten up the procedure *de excommunicato capiendo*. Their main—but considerable—zeal was to deal with papists. On the other hand, there were two separate attempts, which came to nothing, to improve the incomes of clerics by facilitating the union of small benefices: the Commons were anxious to promote adequate preaching as well as to check papistry.

The Parliament was chiefly, and properly, concerned with administration rather than doctrine or ceremonies; the outcome of their labours was a tightening of the civil procedure against excommunicates and the heavy penalty for a second refusal of the Supremacy oath by clerics. But their intentions in that matter

were, in the main, defeated. It was left to the bishops to administer the oath to clerics, and Parker instructed them not to proceed
to the second offering of the oath to any before he had himself
been told the full circumstances and given his consent.[1] No
doubt such restraint would be entirely agreeable to his patient
gentleness, but it was also plainly approved, if not actually
enjoined, by the government. His letter to instruct the bishops
was submitted for previous approval to Cecil, who actually
added a paragraph telling the bishops to keep it 'secret to yourselves'. And Parker, when sending it to Cecil, implied that,
though he had 'no warrant in writing', he was none the less
carrying out the Queen's wishes, though not mentioning her
name lest it should discourage 'honest Protestants'. He hoped
that Cecil would approve his 'device'.[2] It was not the last occasion on which Parker shouldered responsibility for what was
really the Queen's policy—though this time, at any rate, it must
have been a congenial task. By his secret directions, the attack,
aimed by the Commons at the deposed bishops and such clergy
as were not really reconciled to the new ways, was rendered
largely if not entirely ineffective.

The Convocation of 1563 was of great importance. It offered
the first chance for the Church of the new settlement to express
its true mind, as the Convocation of 1559 had been completely
dominated by the Marian clergy. Parker recognized the significance of the occasion and made careful preparations for it. That
it should lack neither impressive dignity nor customary procedure (yet one more proof of his determination to maintain
continuity rather than promote innovation) a form was drawn
up stating the traditional usage for holding a convocation, and
for the election of a Prolocutor for the Lower House of Clergy.[3]

[1] *Correspondence*, pp. 174-5.
[2] Ibid., pp. 173-4. According to the Spanish Ambassador, in April steps
to demand the oath from Bonner and others were in hand, but were stopped
because the Queen put off signing the commission to summon them, *Cal.
S. P. Span.* 322-4.
[3] These are the first documents in the *Synodalia* in Parker's MSS in
Corpus Christi, Cambridge: (No. 121) analysed in Strype, *Parker* i, 238-9.

The procedure thus outlined was meticulously followed, as is shown by the record of the Acts of the Upper House;[1] the only innovation was that the Archbishop did suggest that Nowell of St. Paul's should be elected as their Prolocutor by the Lower House—as he duly was: such a suggestion from the Archbishop was not usual.

But it was not with mere formalities that Parker was chiefly concerned. Knowing that the *Eleven Articles* did not cover the field and had only the weight of episcopal backing, he was determined that the synod should authorize a new series of articles. Instead of leaving the formulation of such to be undertaken, as it were, at the random and possibly wayward impulse of Convocation, he carefully prepared a model set of articles for discussion. It seems highly likely, though it is not proved, that in doing this he had the help of other bishops.[2] But be that as it may, it is generally agreed that a manuscript copy of the Articles in the library of Corpus Christi, Cambridge, was really Parker's working copy, containing corrections and erasures made in his own hand during the discussions with the bishops and signed by them (though in small details it varies from the earliest printed form of the Articles). As an indication of the Archbishop's views and desires this exemplar is extremely significant.[3] It is based on the *Articles* of 1553, though there are alterations, omissions and additions which are important in themselves, and are typical of Parker's middle position. Some of the extreme vagaries of protestantism are carefully excluded while at the same time the differences from Rome are more firmly expressed. It is noteworthy that often, where a protestant origin of new wording can be traced, the source is a German rather than a Swiss formula—that of Württemberg.[4] Another influence was '*A declaration of doctrine offered and exhibited by the protestants to the Queen at the first coming over of them*'. That, too, is based

---

[1] E. Cardwell, *Synodalia* (Oxford, 1842), pp. 495 sqq.

[2] So Hardwick, *History of the Articles*, p. 125; the only evidence given is note 3 on p. 130.

[3] J. Lamb has reprinted it in his *Historical Account of the Thirty-Nine Articles* (Cambridge, 1829).   [4] Hardwick, op. cit., pp. 127-8.

on the Forty-Two *Articles* of 1553, but it is verbose and argumentative, much less conciliatory than Parker's version. It is a mercy that it was never officially authorized by the Church of England. By contrast with it the merits of Parker's revision—brevity, simplicity, toleration—shine out with increased brilliance. But Parker did at times borrow from it[1]—for example, about the need for good works and insistence on real reception at communion.

Parker's article on Justification, a thorny matter, much disputed and delicately balanced, is new; it maintains that justification is by faith alone, yet deliberately stresses that this is a doctrine 'full of consolation' (as Luther had found it, in that we do not have to merit salvation). On the other hand, against those who seemed to deduce that no practical effort is therefore dedemanded from men, a re-worded article on Free Will plainly suggests that we are at least expected to co-operate with the divine grace instead of being passive; and a completely new article insists that good works, though they cannot merit justification, are yet acceptable to God, the necessary fruits of faith and the inevitable proof of it. Similarly, the article on the Old Testament is expanded to insist that its moral law is still binding, though the ceremonial is not. (Similar teaching was, indeed, included in a separate and rather isolated article in 1553: but it carries much more emphasis in its new position.) It all amounted to a wise assertion of a Christian's moral responsibility against the wild deductions sometimes drawn from sheer predestinarianism. On the other hand, against Rome, the distinction is much more strongly drawn than in 1553 between the two sacraments ordained by Christ and the other five which are not to be held as sacraments of the Gospel since they have no visible sign divinely appointed. It is explicitly added in the article on the Lord's Supper that the doctrine of transubstantiation destroys the nature of the sacrament.[2] But, as if to keep the

[1] It is in Parker's MSS 121, No. 20. A full account is in Dixon's *History*, v, 107 sqq., where Parker's debt is made clear.

[2] A point also made in the protestants' *Declaration*.

balance, the statement of 1553 that Christ's natural body is in heaven, though kept, is a little watered down, and there is determined and repeated insistence that the body is 'given, taken and eaten', though in a spiritual manner, by faith. Sheer Zwinglianism is thus rejected. But a new article insists that the faithless do not receive Christ; and another that the laity are to be communicated in both kinds. Against the Anabaptists it is asserted that Infant Baptism is according to the institution of Christ (not merely the custom of the church, as in 1553). The freedom of the clergy to marry is much more strongly put than in 1553; so is the use of the vulgar tongue in church services —now not only said to be fitting and agreeable to God's word; any other use is described as plainly repugnant to God's word and primitive custom. As to traditions and ceremonies, it is not only maintained that they may differ from place to place and that no private person may violate what public authority has instituted (provided that it does not oppugn the divine word), but there is also a firm affirmation (in article 34) that each particular or national Church has the right for edification to establish, change or abolish rites which rest only on human authority—a permissive formula which later caused trouble, but was entirely reasonable on Parker's view of the English Church. One or two of the articles show Parker as very much aware of contemporary changes of opinion. Anabaptists were no longer a serious danger—so they disappear in article 8 from their partnership with Pelagians, and an article against Millenarianism is completely dropped. The article concerning civil magistrates is considerably and carefully expanded to explain the Royal Governorship of the church in a way to quiet uneasy consciences and—in most conciliatory fashion—the 1553 article accepting the Book of Common Prayer and the Ordinal is replaced by one which only speaks of the Ordinal and insists that those ordered according to it were rightly ordered. Plainly Parker knew that there were some things in the Prayer Book which were not acceptable to the extremists. But it looks as though he anticipated the trouble Bonner was to raise a year later about the Ordinal. On the other hand, the rejected doctrine of purgatory, indulgences and the like is now plainly nailed down as being that of the Romans, not merely the scholastics.

It was one of Parker's great services to the Church of England that he had ready for discussion such a model set of articles, as conciliatory as possible yet clearly and firmly showing the differences from the Church of Rome and from other continental churches, sensibly insisting on the importance of right conduct and plainly recognizing what were the disputed points at home and trying to meet them. For there were other and much less balanced views held by some, especially of the Lower House of Convocation. After one day's formal session, Convocation was solemnly opened by Parker on January 13:[1] at the third session he invited the bishops to prepare for the next session a statement of the reforms desirable in their dioceses, and there were then private conversations, possibly about procedure, or even about the Articles. Anyhow, at the next, fourth, session (January 19) the Articles were definitely under discussion, as they were at the fifth and probably at the next three sessions also, though the *Acts* only state that private discussions were held without specifying the subjects. At the ninth session (January 29) after much discussion the Articles were signed by the Archbishop and sixteen other bishops.[2] The changes that had been made from Parker's original suggestions are indicated in his MSS, and are surprisingly few. The most important was the deletion in Article 28 (Of the Lord's Supper) of a section, roughly corresponding to the Edwardian article, which insisted strongly that the natural body of Christ is only in one place, Heaven, until the Second Coming—a statement which might well seem to favour Zwinglian views. At the end of Article 3 (Of Christ's descent into Hell) the Edwardian statement, retained by Parker, that Christ preached to the spirits in prison was omitted. At the end three of the Edwardian articles, also retained by Parker, which rejected wild Anabaptist views, were also omitted; presumably

[1] The *Acts* are printed by Cardwell in *Synodalia*, pp. 495–527.
[2] Hardwick, *Articles*, pp. 135–6.

as no longer necessary. Other changes were merely verbal.
The result was, practically, the *Thirty-Nine Articles* as we have
them today, with two notable exceptions. The present article
29 (Of the Wicked which do not eat the Body of Christ) was
omitted in all printed versions before 1571, though it was in
Parker's manuscript and probably should have been included.[1]
And Article 20 does not in some printed and manuscript
versions have at its beginning the statement that 'The Church
hath power to decree Rites or Ceremonies, and authority in
Controversies of Faith: And yet . . .' Parker's proposals also did
not include that. But it does appear in the authorized printed
version of 1563, and some others, and was probably included in
the form finally ratified by both Houses of Convocation.[2]

Besides providing the set of Articles for discussion, it is highly
probable that Parker deserves considerable credit for guiding
them through the Upper House with so little change. They were
plainly not accepted without discussion, and it is notable that the
Archbishop himself always presided at the meetings till they
were signed; quite soon afterwards he appointed deputies to
take his place, and sometimes did not appear in person. No
doubt his task was made less difficult by the fact that most of the
bishops were not extremists. Four of them, like himself, had
never visited continental churches and though the rest had been
abroad their associations had been mainly with Germany and
the Low Countries rather than Switzerland (though three of the
leading bishops, Jewel, Sandys and Parkhurst had been in
Switzerland). Such episcopal suggestions for reform as have
survived, made, no doubt, in reply to Parker's invitation—from
Sandys and from Alley of Exeter[3]—are mainly concerned with
discipline. Alley, indeed, did urge the shortening of the article
about the Descent into Hell, because there was much argument
about it. Otherwise, their suggestions barely touch the Articles
at all. Sandys wished to abolish private baptism by women and

---

[1] Hardwick, *Articles*, p. 315, n.
[2] Ibid., pp. 145-7 and 135 note 2.
[3] Strype, *Annals* I, i, 500, 506-7, 519 sqq.

crossing at baptism. He wished to put an end to alienation of church property, to secure that ordinands were suitable and learned (they should be approved by six learned ministers), that children were regularly catechized and so on: that the reformation of Canon Law authorized under Henry VIII should be carried out. Alley was much concerned that uniform rules for clerical attire should be enforced on all (though he was indifferent as to what it should be), that penance should be public and not easily commuted, and excommunicates speedily punished by the civil arm; that there should be more preaching, and decent conduct in church; that simony should be stopped. Such suggestions do not indicate a contentious spirit. None the less, shortly afterwards Parker wrote to Cecil of his 'brethren' in Convocation[1] that some of them were '*pleni rimarum, hac atque illac effluunt,* although indeed the Queen's Majesty may have good cause to be well contented with her choice of most of them' (which shows that he was thinking of the bishops, not the Lower House of clergy). He adds 'where the Queen's Highness doth note me to be too soft and easy, I think divers of my brethren will rather note me, if they were asked, too sharp and too earnest in moderation, which towards them I have used, and will still do, till mediocrity shall be received amongst us'. The inference that he had to fight for his views is inescapable; and the differences, it seems likely, were about doctrine rather than discipline.

After subscription by the bishops, the *Articles* were submitted to the Lower House of Convocation. They seem to have been generally accepted without delay, though some hesitated to sign. For on February 5 the Prolocutor brought them back with some signatures but at the same time requested that those who had not signed should be compelled to do so. The bishops asked for their names to be reported at the next meeting. By then more, but not all, had signed—and it was once more asked that the names of the refusers should be reported. That is the last reference to the matter—so presumably in the end all signed.

[1] *Correspondence*, p. 173.

But the list of signatures given by Strype[1] from Parker's *Synodalia* only contains 106 signatures while there were 144 members of the Lower House; but the list presents difficulties.[2]

The bishops were now free to turn to other matters. There is quoted by Strype a paper of 'Certain Articles in substance desired to be granted by the Queen's Majesty' which Strype attributes to a chaplain of Parker, with comments by Grindal[3] and by the Archbishop. It seems to contain what those bishops, at least, would have liked. A new catechism, nearly completed by Nowell, should be authorized; certain rubrics in the Prayer Book about rites and ceremonies should be mended; a uniform external apparel should be enjoined for the clergy. Penalties should be more strictly enforced for non-attendance at church, for unchastity, for simony. Clerical incomes should be increased, chancels repaired, and dispensations for pluralities, non-residence and marriage without banns should be reformed. Steps should be taken to see that writs for the arrests of excommunicates were speedily enforced. The latter point was dealt with by Parliament; of the rest, Convocation did not really effect any. There is no evidence that these articles were ever presented to the Queen. They may be no more than the suggestions for reform made to the bishops by Parker and Grindal.

On the day that the *Articles* were signed by the bishops they appointed a committee to deal with church discipline, and, shortly after, another to deal with the catechism. As to the latter, at the twenty-second session, Nowell, Prolocutor of the Lower House, supported by Sampson, Dean of Christ Church and Day, Provost of Eton, presented to the bishops Nowell's *Catechism* as unanimously approved by the Lower House. It seems to have been approved (with or without corrections) by the bishops also, though the Convocation records do not say so. But, shortly after this, Nowell sent a fair copy embodying the corrections of both Houses to Cecil who had first suggested the work, declaring it to be 'in the name of the clergy of the convocation, as their

[1] *Annals* I, i, 488–90.   [2] Lamb, *Historical Account*, pp. 20 sqq.
[3] *Annals* I, i, 522 sqq.

book'.[1] But it was not, as yet, authorized or printed. It was in fact only printed in 1570, and then at the request of the two Archbishops, not of Convocation.

In the matter of discipline, nothing seems to have been agreed or resolved, despite the appointment of the episcopal committee. The attitude of at least a strong minority of the Lower House made it clear that it would not be satisfied with such moderate measures of reform as the bishops contemplated. Possibly that is why the matter was dropped. For the Lower House was active and full of ideas about discipline. At the very first session after he was admitted as Prolocutor, Nowell informed the bishops that several members of the House of Clergy had presented schedules of desirable reforms which had been submitted to a committee for consideration. Strype quotes three papers of suggested reforms (though it is not clear whether these were among those referred to by the Prolocutor). A list of twenty-one *Requests and Petitions*[2] of the Lower House was signed by sixty-four members. They are not on the whole extreme: they are largely concerned with securing that there should be a Catechism and Articles which all clergy and graduates of the Universities should be forced to sign. But it was also desired that baptism should only be performed by a minister, that god-parents should not answer in the name of the baptized; that at communion there should be added to the confession a statement that the communicants do 'detest and renounce the idolatrous mass', and that no non-communicant should be allowed to stay on in church during the consecration and administration; that all images and roods should be destroyed. A much more advanced list of requests, seven in number, gained the signatures of thirty-three members[3] (some of them being of the sixty-four above). The signing with the cross in baptism was objected to, as well as non-ministerial administration; kneeling at reception of communion should be left to the discretion of the Ordinary; the psalms should be sung by all, and

---

[1] Strype, *Annals* I, i, 526.   [2] Ibid., I, i, 508–12.
[3] Ibid., I, i, 500–2.

'curious singing' and organ playing abolished; all surplices and copes should be abolished in favour of a gown, and out of door dress for clergy should not be such as 'the enemies of Christ's gospel have chosen to be the special array of their priesthood'; all Saints' days should be abrogated, and the article against those who offended against the common order of the church or the authority of the magistrate (Article 33) should be 'mitigated'. There is a plain foreshadowing here of much that was to be dear to later Puritanism. The third paper given by Strype[1] was a long programme of church reform, seemingly prepared before the synod. It urges the abolition of all vestments, copes and surplices, all organs and 'curious singing' and 'superfluous ringing of bells': the table is not to be placed 'altarwise', baptism should only be by ministers, and god-parents must not answer in the child's name; there must be no dispensations to marry without banns, but also no seasons when marriages might not take place; and the number of fasting days should be limited. Most significant of all were long sections about the discipline of clergy, limitation of pluralism, stopping of simony and so on; and at the end extensive orders for the discipline of the laity, too—to secure that youth was instructed in the catechism, that such as do not communicate thrice a year be punished (the parson was to enter in a book lists of offenders), that unchastity should be punished and irregular marriages checked. Such a scheme of control suggests the kind of discipline prevalent in Geneva. Its author is unknown and there is no evidence that it was ever submitted to Convocation: but it shows what ideas were abroad, some of them actually embodied in the lists adopted by one or other of the parties whose desires were given above.

On February 13, an attempt was made in the Lower House to carry through six articles which would have effected some of the desired reforms. All holy days, save Sundays and 'principal feasts of Christ', should be abolished; in reading the service in church the minister was to face the people and speak clearly; the sign of the cross was to be omitted in baptism; kneeling to

[1] *Annals* I, i, 473–6.

receive communion should be at the discretion of the Ordinary; a surplice should be sufficient for all services (i.e. the cope should go) but even that was not to be required—'a comely garment or habit' was suggested as a minimum; the use of organs was to be removed. Less extreme than some of the paper suggestions (there was no direct attack on images or the mass, and surplices were at least to be tolerated) the resolutions really were an attempt to get rid of customs in church which might still suggest a continuance of the old services. And the attempt only just failed—by one vote. Of those present forty-three voted for the resolutions and thirty-five against. But when proxies were included they were rejected by fifty-nine votes to fifty-eight; twenty-seven members were absent or abstained.[1] In the main the supporters were men who had been abroad, the opponents men who had already risen to posts of authority—deaneries or archdeaconries: but the division was not clear cut.

None the less, on February 26, the Prolocutor and ten others of the Lower House did present to the bishops a book of discipline which had, they asserted, the unanimous approval of their House. On March 3 they asked for it back, to make additions; on March 5 they presented it again, amended. That is the last we hear of it—though some of the 'secret' later consultations of the bishops may have concerned it. It seems likely (though not certain) that a paper in Parker's *Synodalia* (MSS. 121-27) gives the headings of its fifty-one sections (though not the details)[2]— *Articles for government and order in the church, exhibited to be admitted by authority: but not allowed.* The purpose of some of the suggestions was clearly admirable (though it is not clear whether the means proposed in detail to achieve them were equally so!)—the repair of chancels, the better payment of tithe, the proper examination of clergy and the encouragement of preaching (the better-paid livings being reserved for preachers), the unhindered functioning of the church courts. But there were other suggestions which would have caused trouble—notably that the penalty for saying mass should be death, and for hearing

[1] Strype, *Annals* I, i, 502-6.   [2] Ibid., I, ii, 562-8.

it a fine of 100 marks for each time. And there came out a few points which were to re-appear with wearisome iteration in the coming years—the table should not stand altarwise, a cup should take the place of a chalice, and bread (as ordered in the Prayer Book) that of wafers. But what would surely have proved quite impracticable, in England, were the ideas for the discipline of the laity. Churchwardens failing to detect faults were to be fined; in each church was to be a *place of penitents* where those guilty of grievous sins, even when pardoned, should stand or sit, until they showed 'unfeigned signs of true repentance'. Finally, all aged fourteen years or over were to be examined each year by the clergy as to their ability to say the Creed, the Commandments and the Lord's Prayer. A book was to be kept, to be presented to the archdeacon after Easter, of those who refused to be examined, or who failed to communicate thrice in the year, and they were to be punished with 'excommunication and open penance'. One who could not say the Lord's Prayer and the Commandments was not to be married; the parent of a child who could not, at ten years, say the Catechism was to be punished. However much such a discipline might be tolerable in Geneva, it was surely out of the question in England. Small wonder that the bishops (if it was they who disallowed them) did not find in the articles any basis for agreement between the two Houses about church order.

One other communication from the Upper to the Lower House deserves mention as illustrating the careful vigilance of the Archbishop. He feared that there might be commanded a scrutiny into the value of livings by the civil power in order to raise their assessment. A series of leading questions was therefore addressed to the Lower House[1]—if there were an enquiry, would it turn to the Queen's advantage? were not some livings already over-rated? what spoliations of livings had taken place and by whom? how many benefices were charged with pensions, or were vacant? The answers to such questions, if they were ever made, are not extant. But Parker was clearly on guard.

[1] Cardwell, *Synodalia*, pp. 518–19.

Thus the only positive outcome of the Convocation (besides a subsidy to the Queen agreed by the two Houses) was the *Articles*, substantially in the form Parker had suggested. Even the most significant change, the omission of the stress in 28 on the permanent station of Christ's human body in heaven, must have been welcome to him.[1] But the suggestions and debates about order in the Lower House were of great importance. Those who wanted further change were no doubt strengthened by association and mutual discussions, and came to a clearer notion of what changes they wanted. Despairing of getting their way in Convocation, they little by little entered on a course of frank disobedience which caused Parker immense trouble; later on, they tried to work their will through Parliament. But, strictly speaking, this Convocation did not upset the pattern laid down by Prayer Book, Injunctions and *Interpretations*.

[1] About now or shortly after was printed by Day '*A Testimony of Antiquity showing the ancient Faith of the Church of England touching the sacrament of the Body and Blood of the Lord*'. Its main feature is a long sermon in Saxon (with translation), by Aelfric, Abbot of Eynsham (fl. *c*. 1000.) with great stress on the fact that bread and wine remain, that the reception of the body and blood of Christ is 'ghostly' (the word is constantly repeated) and that the means to reception is faith. 'Ye shall not search how it is done but hold it in your belief that it is so done.' Such a view is practically identical with that of the *Articles*. It is not known who was responsible for the publication—but at the end there is a guarantee signed by Parker, the Archbishop of York and thirteen other bishops to the effect that the sermon had been printed truthfully and fully. The least that can be said is that Parker thoroughly approved of it even if he was not directly responsible for it.

CHAPTER X

PARKER IN HIS DIOCESE

AFTER Convocation was prorogued on April 14, Parker left
London for his own diocese, and took up residence at his country
manor of Bekesbourne near Canterbury. His correspondence
suggests that he remained there, in the main, till the end of the
summer of 1564; we first hear of him back in London when he
was present in October of that year at the obsequies of the
Emperor Ferdinand.[1] Doubtless the change of air and scene was
welcome after his strenuous work in London—for he was not a
strong man. But he was, as he wrote to Cecil, 'loth to be idle',[2]
and there was much for him to do in the diocese. His palace at
Canterbury was in a ruinous condition partly through age and
partly through fire. He had by now paid off his first-fruits and
furnished Lambeth, and felt able to face the expense of restoration
and furnishing at Canterbury. It was a task very congenial. He
had a real passion for building; the palace was old and had been
used on famous occasions and therefore made a strong appeal to
his sense of history; he had a lively appreciation of the dignity
of his office (however unworthy he felt himself to hold it) and
the duty of generous hospitality which it involved and for which
the palace was needed as a fitting home. It was a heavy under-
taking and cost him over fourteen hundred pounds—then a
considerable sum. He had the satisfaction of using the restored
palace for lavish entertainment in 1565. The Judges of Assize
and all their company were welcomed to a great feast, the hall
ablaze with gold and silver vessels; so numerous were the guests
that their women folk had to be provided for separately in the
private apartments of the palace. At Whitsuntide, the feasting

[1] Stow's *Memoranda*, J. Gairdner, *Three Fifteenth-Century Chronicles*
(London, 1880), p. 129.   [2] *Correspondence*, p. 186.

went on for three days when he entertained the leading citizens of Canterbury and their mayor, the leading gentry of Kent, the Dean and clergy of the cathedral. This time, women were included in the hall, but they and the men sat on different sides. At Trinity-tide there was a similar entertainment for the less distinguished citizens and clergy.[1]

In strange contrast to such magnificence is a letter to Cecil asking for the gift of a 'couple of bucks' to 'avoid the shame of my table', with the statement that he was going to ask Dudley for a similar present and a hint that the Queen, too, might help as she had taken over one of his parks.[2] Later on, the Queen through Dudley actually sent him a deer for which elaborate thanks were sent by the Archbishop.[3] Clearly, he was not feeling very rich, but he was expected by the Queen to keep great state. She plainly wished him to live impressively. In May 1563 she granted him permission to maintain in his livery forty gentlemen or yeomen, besides his household and estate servants.[4] In September 1563, writing from Bekesbourne, he reveals that he has 'not many under a hundred persons up-rising and down-lying' in his house, 'besides divers of my family which for straitness of living be other where abroad'.[5] His lavish entertainment was all of a piece with such a household. But it would be doing him less than justice to suggest that his hospitality was only due to policy. There can be no doubt that he really enjoyed giving it—though at times he found it expensive.

Nor was the Queen slow to use his services if it suited her plans. After the fall of Le Havre in July 1563 and negotiations between England and France, a treaty of peace was made in April 1564. In May therefore the arrival of a French Ambassador was expected. He was to be met at Dover by the sheriff and conducted to Greenwich, and the Queen wrote to Parker to receive him at Canterbury or at Bekesbourne and give him lodging on the way. But though he was to show the ambassador

---

[1] All this is described in the *Matthaeus*: Strype, *Parker* iii, 287-91.
[2] *Correspondence*, pp. 177-8.   [3] Ibid., pp. 190-1.
[4] Ibid., pp. 175-6.   [5] Ibid., p. 195.

all due courtesy, he was not to 'neglect the place you hold in our Church', nor to go beyond the entry of his house to meet him, nor to conduct him further than the door on his departure.[1] She was anxious to impress the new ambassador, for political reasons, with the dignity still attaching to the Church in England and to dispel any idea that it had been reduced to the status it held in some of the non-catholic countries. Parker played his (not uncongenial) part very successfully, if we may trust the account he sent to Cecil of the visit.[2] 'Part by word and partly by some little superfluity of fare and provision' he disabused the ambassador of his ideas that there were 'neither *statas preces*, nor choice of days of abstinence, as Lent etc., nor orders ecclesiastical, nor persons of our own profession in any regard or estimation, or of any ability, amongst us'. He satisfied him that the wealth of the dissolved abbeys was used to maintain canons and preachers, grammarians and beadmen 'with other distributions to the poor villages yearly'. Clergy were at liberty to marry or not, at choice, though there was 'prudent caution . . . for their sober contracting'. (As clerical marriage was not legally recognized, Parker must here have spoken with a certain reserve —as he must also have done about monastic wealth!) But in the end, the ambassador (who was 'contented to hear evil of the pope') seems to have been well satisfied. He 'delighted in our mediocrity, charging the Genevians and Scottish of going too far in extremities' and even 'professed that we were in religion very nigh to them'. Thus the Queen's policy was furthered. But Parker was sufficiently insular to be very suspicious of his foreign visitors. He took care that they should see 'a piece of mine armoury' to show that 'if a bishop hath regard of such provision, belike other had a more care there-about'— just in case they were thinking of invasion! After they had gone, an immediate search showed that they were not guilty of 'purloining the worth of one silver spoon; somewhat otherwise than I did doubt of before'!

Besides his building and hospitality Parker was anxious to see

---

[1] *Correspondence*, p. 212. 　　[2] Ibid., pp. 214–17.

for himself the condition of his diocese, and told Cecil that he hoped to visit it shortly after mid-summer (of 1563) 'to know the state thereof myself personally'.[1] Naturally, there were no commissioners in the circumstances, nor any formal report. But there is evidence that he carried out his purpose in an extant inventory of the church goods of the cathedral presented in July and August—and it is implied that it was presented to him in person.[2] The Archbishop seems to have been well content with what he found—'all in so good order that I do rejoice therein; as for my ecclesiastical persons, I deal with them indifferently, that I find also obedience in them'.[3] A few days later he sent an account of a visit to Sandwich.[4] Despite an early arrival (at seven in the morning) he was received with ceremony, and found 'their service sung in good distinct harmony and quiet devotion; the singing men, being the mayor and jurats, with the head men of the town, placed in the quire fair and decent, in so good order as I could wish'.

None the less, he thought well to issue new visitation articles in 1563—presumably they were for the diocese as they are based on the diocesan articles of 1560.[5] The additions and alterations made suggest that, either because of what he had found in Kent or because of what he had heard from other dioceses, he was already finding it necessary to check attempts by reformers, after their defeat in Convocation, to carry out in action the changes which had not won approval there. He now asks whether officiants duly wear a surplice, whether they celebrate the service in the chancel or the body of the church and 'use all rites and orders prescribed in the Book of Common Prayer etc. and none other.' Is wafer-bread used according to the Royal Injunctions, or ordinary bread? Is the rood taken down but a partition between chancel and church still kept? Is the font

---

[1] *Correspondence,* p. 177.

[2] *Inventories of Christchurch, Canterbury* (J. Wickham Legg and W. H. St. John Hope, London, 1902), p. 222.

[3] To Cecil, August 22; *Correspondence,* p. 186.   [4] Ibid., pp. 188–9.

[5] They were printed in 1563: the changes from 1560 are given by W. H. Frere, *Visitation Articles and Injunctions* (London, 1910), iii, 140.

still standing and decently kept? Is the communion table decently covered? Does any of the clergy 'go and boast himself like a layman?' Such questions were a serious omen of what was to come shortly.

An enquiry addressed to him by the Council in July was not concerned with such disciplinary matters, nor indeed contemplated any visitatorial action at all, as it required an answer 'within two or three days at the farthest'.[1] What was asked for was really statistical—how many shires or counties were within the diocese, how many archdeaconries etc., how many peculiars there were, how many churches, chapels, clergy, and how many households in each parish. Such information could no doubt be given without extensive enquiries, and Parker's return is on record.[2] As similar enquiries were sent to all bishops, it is to be presumed that the Council was simply trying to get an exact account of the ecclesiastical lay-out of the country.

Though his diocese was thus satisfactory, Parker seems to have found much to alarm him in the general condition of the country 'molested universally by war, and particularly at London by pestilence and partly here at Canterbury by famine, the people wanting their necessary provision'.[3] He had assembled the Mayor and commonalty of Canterbury and appointed Mondays, Wednesdays and Fridays as days for special prayer. He did not venture to give orders to his whole diocese—still less the whole province—because he was 'holden within certain limits by statutes' and did not know 'how it will be taken if we should give order herein'. But he asked Cecil's warrant to issue his precepts for general public prayers. Cecil had evidently been thinking on similar lines, and sent in return suggested forms of prayer he had already obtained from the Bishop of London, together with the Queen's order for their use 'in this our realm'.[4] Parker found it advisable to make some alterations in Grindal's suggestions, not 'in substance and principal meaning but in the circumstances'. Grindal had wished the whole service to be said

[1] *Correspondence*, pp. 180-1.
[2] Strype, *Parker* i, 257-8.
[3] *Correspondence*, p. 182.
[4] Ibid., pp. 183-4.

in the body of the church, to which Parker cautiously objected:
it might seem to 'abolish all chancels'. He wished the ordinary
prayers to be said in the ordinary place, but allowed the special
psalms, lessons and collects to be said, like the Litany, in the
midst of the people. He suggested no other change, but did wish
the collects and, indeed, the whole service, had been shorter!
It was 'too long for our cold devotions'.[1] Later on, in January
1564, when the pestilence was abating, he and Grindal were
considering a form of thanksgiving. Parker evidently suggested a
great communion service in St. Paul's. This time, it was Grindal
who raised difficulties: 'it will be done so tumultuously and
gazingly, by means of the infinite multitude that will resort
thither to see, that the honesty of the action will be disordered'.[2]
The difference of attitude of the two men could hardly be more
clearly exemplified. Parker did not wish the order of the Prayer
Book to be compromised, even on a special occasion, by a usage
which approximated to a congregational prayer meeting; Grindal
shrank from anything which might look in the least like an old-
fashioned mass.

One result of the pestilence was that Parker was asked by the
Council in September to receive into his house Thirlby, lately
Bishop of Ely, and Boxall, Dean of Peterborough, Norwich and
Windsor. They had appealed to the Council to be removed
from the Tower in order to escape the possibility of infection,
and this was the result (one cannot help wondering what the
result would have been if Cranmer or Hooper, in similar circumstances, had asked for a like concession under Queen
Mary). In fact, at this time, all the imprisoned bishops were
removed from the Tower and either assigned to the keeping of
bishops, or restricted to certain limitations of residence.[3] The
same consideration, however, was not extended to Bonner who
was in the Marshalsea and was kept there. Though Parker's two
guests were to pay for their keep (evidently their imprisonment
had not meant the loss of their fortune), they were none the less a
responsibility. There was a risk of infection being brought by

[1] *Correspondence*, p.185. [2] Ibid., pp. 201–2. [3] Gee, *Elizabethan Clergy*, pp. 195–6.

them. He was afraid of 'much exclamation' if they spread the plague in the district, and asked that he might isolate them in an empty house near to Bekesbourne for a fortnight till they should be 'better blown with fresh air'. But he had to explain to the Council why he was acting thus, so as to forestall blame if they escaped. None the less, he gave them a gracious welcome, allowing Thirlby to bring with him a serving boy as well as a man.[1] Though sincere Romanists, neither Thirlby nor Boxall had been bitter against the protestants in Mary's reign, and their relations with Parker were obviously very friendly. He found them 'true Englishmen, not wishing to be subject to the governance of such insolent conquerors' as the French. Indeed, he actually forwarded to the Council a request from Boxall that he might be moved to some other place (possibly for health reasons)—a request which was refused because Scott of Chester had abused such a concession and fled abroad. So they were still with him till June of 1564 when he proposed shortly to return to Lambeth ('This country is very dear to dwell in') and wrote to ask what he should do about them.[2] In the event, they were both left in his charge till they died, but do not appear to have been confined to his palace at Lambeth. Thirlby at times was allowed to lodge in London, and there is a charming letter of thanks to the Archbishop from Boxall both for the 'very good entertainment' he had received in the Archbishop's house and for his 'gentleness' at his removal to Bromley to live with a relative.[3] The whole episode illustrates not only the generosity and gentleness of Parker, but also the non-persecuting attitude of the government. The dispossessed bishops were left in peace and reasonable comfort if they were not troublesome—Heath, of York, was allowed to live as a country gentleman at his seat in Surrey.[4] It was only those who actively opposed the government, like Bonner, or who engaged in traitorous plots, like Watson,[5] who were harried and kept in prison.

[1] *Correspondence*, pp. 192–5. [2] Ibid., pp. 203, 217–18.
[3] Strype, *Parker* i, 280–1. [4] Strype, *Parker* i, 281.
[5] Gee, *Elizabethan Clergy*, p. 196.

As he went about his diocese Parker was much alarmed, before peace was made with France, by the danger of an invasion, and the lack of preparations for defence, as well as by the low spirits of the country-side. He felt it his duty to warn Cecil that 'Dover Castle, Walmer and Deal Castles, Queensborough Castle, be as forsaken and unregarded for any provision, the country destitute of the lord Warden, or of a lieutenant to whom in such straits men might resort to; the people but feeble and unarmed and commonly discomforted'. He was afraid that the wealthy folk—the natural leaders—would desert the country and others might follow. All he could do was to bid his chaplains to 'comfort' the people in their sermons.[1] Possibly his fears were exaggerated; there may not have been so great a risk of invasion as he thought. But morale was obviously low, very different from what is usually regarded as the Elizabethan spirit, and Parker was infected by it. That was why he took trouble to assure himself of the loyalty of Thirlby and Boxall, and later on to display his 'piece of mine armoury' for the benefit of the French ambassador.

Despite such alarms, Parker found time for two of his favourite pursuits—the search for antiquarian remains and the support of education. 'With spying and searching' he found out where certain of Cranmer's writings remained—but 'the parties denied having them'. Parker asked for authority from the Council, naming no names, to search for them 'by all ways as by my poor discretion shall be thought good', even to the extent of visiting and interrogating the parties on oath. He would as soon have them as restore a ruined chancel. Cecil, naturally, explained that the Council could not give such wide powers of search, and that the name of the holder of the documents must be given. Parker thereon revealed that it was, astonishingly, Dr. Nevinson, who had been Parker's Commissary-General for the diocese in 1560 and 1561, and who had just been made a canon of Canterbury! The Council therefore gave him the requisite forms of search and recovery. The result was two volumes of the Common Place

[1] *Correspondence*, pp. 203–4.

books of Cranmer, now in the British Museum.[1] A little later, he wrote to Cecil that he had been busy trying to secure 'the old antiquities of Mr. Bale', the learned but not very accurate antiquary who had been Bishop of Ossory under Edward but had under Elizabeth been satisfied with a canonry at Canterbury. He had recently died, and Parker says that he has been promised his antiquities for money 'if I be not deceived'.[2] Strype believed that Parker thus obtained a 'rare collection of MSS.', and that some of the manuscripts presented by Parker to the University and to Corpus Christi were part of Bale's collection.[3] Bale certainly had claimed to have many ancient records,[4] and Parker did, after much trouble in tracing their whereabouts, acquire a large number of Bale's books, but did not value them highly.[5] Unfortunately, he does not specify what they were. But some of the manuscripts he presented to Corpus can be identified almost certainly, others with probability, as having come from Bale's collections.[6]

As to education, Parker's visit to Sandwich, mentioned above, was largely due to Sir Roger Manwood's offer to build and endow a school there. A site had been found which belonged to the Dean and Chapter of Canterbury. Parker went to inspect the site; he persuaded the Dean and Chapter to agree to grant it, subject to the Queen's licence; and after his visit wrote strongly to Cecil to urge the Queen to grant permission for the alienation or lease of the property. The good conduct of the townsmen well deserved it—and such as Cecil and Manwood 'must lay hand to the furtherance of such public endowments, or else ye be not likely to leave to your successors which ye have received of your ancestors'.[7] Parker's intervention was successful and the school was duly built.

He was, also, in 1564, called to approve Orders for Tonbridge School. It had been founded in 1553 by Sir Andrew Judd, but

---

[1] *Correspondence*, pp. 186–7, 191, 195.   [2] Ibid., p. 198.
[3] Strype, *Parker* ii, 520.   [4] *Correspondence*, p. 140.   [5] Ibid., p. 287.
[6] M. R. James, *Catalogue of the MSS in C.C.C Library* (Cambridge, 1912), p. xvii.   [7] *Correspondence*, pp. 187–9.

when he died in 1558, leaving the Skinners Company as its governors, his will was contested and an attempt made to deprive the school of its endowments. After much litigation, the Skinners Company defeated the attempt, but they were ordered to submit to Parker and the Dean of St. Paul's for approval and confirmation the rules governing the school. Both Nowell and Parker made some alterations and additions before signing the Orders.[1] The Archbishop was really interested, not merely a rubber stamp.

Possibly in the same year, the Archbishop received a depressing letter from Pilkington of Durham to tell him that 'your cures, all except Rachedale, be as far out of order as the worst in all the country'.[2] The reference was to three rectories in Lancashire—Whalley, Blackburn and Rochdale—acquired by exchange from the Crown under Henry VIII and Edward VI. There is no

[1] Ibid., pp. 210–11.

[2] *Correspondence*, 221–3. Pilkington's letter is undated, but is described as 'probably 1564'. There are difficulties about such a date. Pilkington writes suggesting two men for possible appointment as vicar of Rochdale, and he speaks of only a 'curate' at Blackburn. (The letter shows that he distinguishes between 'vicar' and 'curate'.) Now, in 1564 there was a vicar of Rochdale and a vicar of Blackburn. In March 1561, Parker appointed a certain Huntington to be vicar of Rochdale (*Register*, pp. 778–9). It seems that he was never inducted, and at a later date (not known) in the same year R. Midgeley was appointed (Victoria County History: Lancashire, v, 198)— a man after Pilkington's own heart: he regularly refused to wear a surplice, and seems to have resigned only about 1590. Pilkington's letter would most easily fit the time when Huntington had not taken up the living and Midgeley had not yet been appointed—i.e. the latter part of 1561. Such a dating of the letter would fit in with Pilkington's reference to a 'commission for ecclesiastical matters directed to my lord of York'. This commission was issued on May 5, 1561 (Gee, *Elizabethan Clergy*, p. 167). Pilkington says he has 'heard' of it. Later in the year, he was busy seeing to the discipline of his diocese (Ibid., pp. 168–9) and that may well have been the time when he found out what was happening in the Archbishop's rectories. This would also fit in with what he says about Blackburn. There the new vicar was appointed in March 1562 to succeed a deprived man (V.C.H. vi, 241–2). It is therefore quite likely that there was only a curate there in 1561. The vicar of Whalley—'as evil a vicar as the worst' according to Pilkington—had been appointed not by Parker but by the Queen (V.C.H., vi, 358). But Pilkington might well not approve one who in 1559 had been selected by the Crown and was probably fully conformist.

evidence that Parker took any action—after all, the three parishes did not technically constitute a 'peculiar' under his jurisdiction. He was only rector; the Ordinary was the bishop of the diocese. But he did, shortly after his return from Canterbury to Lambeth, use his position as rector for the promotion of education. The farmer of the rectory of Rochdale was under agreement to pay certain sums yearly for the stipend of the vicar. This he had not done. Parker therefore sued him at law and he was in danger of losing his investment. In the end, he submitted to Parker's terms. A free grammar school was to be established in Rochdale. The farmer was to provide towards its building such arrears of payment as he still held and seventeen pounds a year for a school-master (as well, no doubt, as paying the vicar the agreed stipend). Parker wrote to some leading men in Rochdale asking their support and oversight for the scheme; he sent a plan for the school and thought that a site might be found for it in the vicar's grounds. The scheme was duly carried out. The vicar provided a site and Parker provided that, after the end of the tenure of the present farmer, the seventeen pounds a year should be payable out of the rectory. He also made elaborate provision for the appointment of suitable schoolmasters in the future. If the Archbishop of the day did not appoint within three months of a vacancy, the Master and Fellows of Corpus were to nominate; if they failed, the vicar of the parish.[1] The care which he lavished on the details of the foundation and its continuance show once more how deeply he was concerned to promote education.

The comparative calm of Canterbury afforded Parker the leisure for another congenial task. Lady Bacon had translated into English Jewel's *Apologia* and submitted her version for comment by the Archbishop. He obviously studied it carefully and wrote a charming letter of praise to form a preface for it, giving it the strongest commendation without any trace of flattery. The translation had 'singularly pleased my judgment and delighted my mind in reading it'; neither he nor Jewel had

[1] *Correspondence*, pp. 231–2; Strype, *Parker* i, 363. Lamb, *History oj Corpus*, p. 97.

found any alteration at all to be desirable. He therefore returned it to her, not as she had sent it, but already printed with his letter as preface, lest her modesty should have delayed its publication.[1] There was added an appendix on the present condition of the Church of England and the Universities, presumably by Parker: it was aimed at meeting just the sort of doubts which he found in the French ambassador. His concern that the translation should be published as soon as possible not only shows his interest but also his wise judgement: it has remained the standard translation of the most balanced defence of its day of the Anglican Church against Roman criticism.

On the other hand, Parker refused to take up the cudgels himself in verbal debate in the defence of Anglicanism. There is a letter from him to Cecil, undated and without any note of where it was written, which must, however, be put before the death of the Spanish ambassador Aquila in August 1563.[2] Fortunately, Cecil did not obey Parker's request that the letter should not be kept but burned, 'read or unread, at your pleasure'—fortunately, for it is a very revealing document. Plainly, Cecil had suggested— or probably Aquila—a meeting for disputation between the Archbishop and the ambassador. Parker shrank from such a conference. Owing to his sufferings under Mary and lack of opportunity for study, and to his 'natural viciosity of overmuch shamefastness' he felt that he could not do justice to his cause in speech so well as in writing. Moreover, he was oppressed with 'bodily and painful griefs' (presumably ill-health) and 'interpellations . . . from my brethren in the whole province'. Action now rather than disputation must be his part. He therefore asked Cecil to 'shadow my cowardice' and decline such opportunities for him. At the end, he suggested an excuse by which he might be covered. If either he or the ambassador went to the other's house, it might be taken 'sinistrally', nor would it be suitable for them to meet at Cecil's house. But he did not absolutely refuse to confer with the ambassador by letter— though it would have to be kept secret. But if that were done, he

[1] *Correspondence*, pp. 219–21.   [2] Ibid., pp. 199–201.

would be able to have his books near him and so not be at a disadvantage. The letter illustrates Parker's modesty and caution
as well as his zeal to do all he could for the Church. But nothing
further is recorded of the suggestion—perhaps because Aquila
died.

Of the administrative cares always besetting him there are
some illuminating examples about now—small matters, no doubt,
but calling for time and trouble. He was anxious to obtain the
prebend of Canterbury vacant through the death of Bale for his
chaplain Andrew Pearson. Thanks to Cecil's help, he obtained
the Queen's nomination—but when it came, the document was
faulty: the clerks had made mistakes. It was not in the customary
form, and it was dated two days before Bale's death, when there
was not a vacancy! So it had to go back for correction.[1] But
Parker amusingly—and perhaps wisely—made sure of the appointment. His letter to Cecil asking for corrections was dated Nov.
20; Pearson's presentment is duly entered in the *Register* as
Nov. 3![2] Nor was that the end of the matter. In the following
February, Parker wrote to Cecil that he had learned that the
Queen had promised her next presentation of a prebend at
Canterbury to a Mr. Tamworth, who presumably should therefore have chosen Bale's successor. All that Parker could do was
to suggest that the Queen should give him her next presentation[3]
—and in January 1565 Tamworth did duly present to a prebend,
by the Queen's permission.[4]

In the same period, we find him urging Cecil that the Bishop
of St. Asaph should be allowed to retain certain benefices as
commendams. He did not like such things, but they were better
than that 'the order of godly ministers . . . should be brought to
contempt for lack of reasonable necessaries'.[5] A kindly letter to
the Bishop of Gloucester urged him to tolerate a 'poor old
man in his possession, belike not like long to continue by his
sickly age in any of his small livings'.[6]

---

[1] *Correspondence*, pp. 197–9.   [2] *Register*, p. 803.
[3] *Correspondence*, pp. 202–3.   [4] *Register*, p. 810.
[5] Ibid., p. 208.   [6] Ibid., p. 213.

The same sort of sympathy for those in danger of being hardly treated came out in his dealings with a matrimonial case which Cecil had referred to him,[1] since it involved a relation of his. A young woman had betrothed herself to a suitor of whom her parents did not approve. They declared that there was a pre-contract with another (and wealthier) suitor whose family were prepared to fight the case along with the parents against the young woman's choice. Parker saw what severe pressure she would have to face and that, if once the matter got into the ecclesiastical courts, she and the young man would not be able to bear the charges. He therefore acted at once. He first se-questered the girl out of her parents' control, and announced that he would act 'plane et summarie', 'to spare expences'. The result was that the couple were married in Feb. 1564.[2] Doubtless, apart from his sheer kindness, Parker was also glad for once in a way to defeat the delays and abuses of the ecclesiastical courts, of which he was well aware.

Another and more difficult matrimonial case did not find him so complacent. In February 1564 certain Scottish ministers addressed a letter jointly to the Archbishops of Canterbury and York.[3] The wife of one of their ministers had left him and fled to England. The 'Assembly' therefore charged the writers 'humbly to request and pray you' to see, either through publish-ing an edict or by arresting her, that the woman presented her-self for trial on May 25 in Edinburgh. To the modern eye the letter is not very humble! Along with the request to see a copy of the resultant edict or summons there is a good deal of sancti-monious presumption and a rather hectoring tone. Parker was very wary. Not for a couple of months did he do anything. He then wrote to Cecil to point out the difficulties.[4] What authority had the Assembly to make such a request? Would the wife be under any obligation to obey an edict of the Archbishops to return to Scotland? What would the Queen's reaction be if they were to order a person resident in her dominions to appear

[1] Correspondence, p. 198.　　　[2] See D.N.B. on Barnaby Googe.
[3] Correspondence, pp. 205-7.　　[4] Ibid., p. 209.

before a foreign power? It was a wise and cautious summary of the practical points involved, and though Parker expressed himself willing to be guided by Cecil if he thought that 'gratification of such neighbourhood as is now betwixt us' (i.e. England and Scotland) required him to change his mind, it is not surprising that we hear no more of the matter.

CHAPTER XI

RECUSANTS AND PROTESTANTS:
THE UNIVERSITIES

WHEN the Roman Catholic prisoners in the Tower were removed in September 1563 to less close confinement Bonner was retained at the Marshalsea in Southwark. In 1564, he was singled out for further exceptional treatment. On April 26th he was taken out of prison to take the Supremacy oath before Horne, Bishop of Winchester (in whose diocese Southwark lay). On his refusal, he was sent back to prison 'accompanied by a large crowd of heretics and boys who kept shouting insults at him'.[1] He was then duly reported, in accordance with the Act of 1563, to the Court of King's Bench. From a letter of Grindal to Cecil,[2] it is quite clear that the initiative came from Grindal and Horne, a stout protestant. Parker's leave was, indeed, sought and received, but Grindal had not 'troubled' Cecil about it so that Cecil could disclaim all knowledge if there were any objections. Horne was obviously trying to effect the purpose in the mind of those who passed the Act, and he regarded Bonner as a test case, the more suitable because of his unpopularity. If some such case were not brought, the Act would be a dead letter, and 'no more meet man to begin with than that person'. Doubtless it was such arguments which had won Parker's consent.

The result, from Horne's point of view, was disastrous. Bonner was not a conscientious simpleton, but very contentious and really able. He raised many objections to the case brought against him, some being technical legal points but one of great importance—that Horne was not lawfully Bishop of Winchester, 'according to the laws of the Catholic Church and the statutes

---

[1] *Cal. S. P. Span.* i, 360.   [2] Given by Dixon, vi, 29, note.

and ordinances of this realm'.[1] Though his minor objections were over-ruled, it was resolved that this vital point should be put to trial.[2] Bonner had, in effect, raised the whole question of the legality of the early Elizabethan consecrations. Authority, however, did not allow the case to come to trial in the courts. Bonner wrote a submissive letter to the Queen on October 26th explaining that he could not in conscience take the oath.[3] In November, the case against him was ordered to be suspended,[4] and was never re-opened. The point at issue was left to be dealt with by Parliament in 1566, and Bonner remained in prison until his death in 1569. In March 1566, his confinement was made more rigorous, and the governor of his prison was arrested for allowing him to see too many visitors.[5] He was clearly suspected—probably with justice—of intrigues against the government. Similarly, in January 1565, the violent and irreconcilable Watson was ordered to be sent back to the Tower by the Bishop of Ely with whom he was lodging.[6] He, too, was a constant intriguer who could not safely be given his liberty. On the other hand, in the same month Turberville was ordered to be released by the Bishop of London (at the latter's request) and Pate by the Bishop of Salisbury, on condition that they lived in London.[7] There was no desire to persecute: leniency was preferred if it was safe. But in some cases, such as those of Bonner and Watson, it was not regarded as safe.

Such a tolerant policy did not make Parker's pursuit of mediocrity more easy; it roused the deepest suspicion among the extreme protestants.[8] The legal point raised by Bonner was subtle and obscure, but the fact that he was protected from the

[1] Strype, *Annals* I, ii, 5.   [2] Dixon, op cit., vi, 35–36.
[3] Strype, *Grindal*, pp. 487 sqq.   [4] *Cal. S. P. Span*. i, 392.
[5] *Cal. S. P. Span*. i, 533.   [6] *Acts of Privy Council*, vii, 183.   [7] Ibid., p. 190.
[8] When the bishops were first removed from the Tower to more salubrious quarters, a preacher at Paul's Cross had wished for a gallows to be set up in Smithfield and the 'old bishops and other papists to be hanged thereon'. In the same place, Cole, Archdeacon of Essex, attributed the plague to the favour shown by the citizens to the 'superstitious religion of Rome'. (Stow's *Memoranda* (in *Three Fifteenth-Century Chronicles*, ed. J. Gairdner, London, 1880), 126 and 128.)

fate which his enemies thought he deserved was obvious and alarming. Anyhow, they were restive after their defeat in the Convocation of 1563. As early as July, Sampson, Dean of Christ Church, wrote to Bullinger at Zurich that 'the affairs of England are in a most unhappy state; I apprehend yet worse evils, not to say the worst'.[1] In August, Humphrey, President of Magdalen, wrote, also to Bullinger, about the habits—and not for the first time, as the letter makes clear.[2] Were the 'round cap and the popish surplice' indifferent despite their associations with superstition, and might they be worn when commanded 'by the just and legitmate authority of the Queen'? It was ominous that the two outstanding preachers in Oxford should so early have taken such a line. Nor can there be any doubt that they had sympathy from some of the leading bishops who, while asserting that the law about the habits should be observed while it stood, none the less wished it to be changed. Horne in July 1565 and even Jewel in February 1566 expressed themselves in that sense, and, of course, Grindal. Sandys, too, regarded the garments as 'popish'.[3] For the time being such men conformed lest by resigning they should be succeeded by others who were less worthy (i.e. less protestant) than themselves. But they can have had little enthusiasm for enforcing the use of the cap and the surplice around which, at this stage, protestant fury seems chiefly to have raged. In such a climate of opinion it is not surprising that, during 1564, there was a growing tendency for the dissatisfied clergy not to wear the lawful garb. By October, the matter was notorious; the Spanish ambassador reported that Cecil had charged the bishops to see to their clergy as the Queen was determined to reform them in their customs and their dress as the existing diversity was intolerable.[4] The Spanish ambassador was not, indeed, always correctly informed nor a very good judge of the state of affairs, and we have no other reference to such action on Cecil's part; but it is not intrinsically unlikely, nor inconsistent with what was going on. Certainly in that month

---

[1] *Zurich Letters*, i, 130. [2] *Zurich Letters*, i, 134.
[3] Ibid., pp. 143, 149, 169, 146. [4] *Cal. S. P. Span.* i, 387.

Pilkington of Durham—a protestant—wrote to Leicester that 'by common report' great offence was taken against some who did not use the garments; he pleaded strongly that no enforcing action should be taken, lest good men should desert the ministry.[1] Probably about the same time (the letter is not dated, save for the year, 1564) the Dean of Durham, Whittingham, also wrote that he had heard that a decree of enforcement was either passed or at hand,[2] and arguing against it on the ground of Christian liberty. In fact, there is no evidence of such a decree, as yet, but it was evidently thought that the authorities would soon be likely to act.

Parker was not a persecutor. He preferred to resort to reasoning rather than to coercive action; but he evidently felt that something must be done. In December 1564, he addressed to Sampson and Humphrey, the ablest and most prominent of the open dissidents, ten quite plain questions[3] to elucidate their attitude. Was the surplice evil or indifferent, and if not indifferent, why not? Might a bishop 'detesting of Papistry' enjoin the surplice and enforce its use, and ought ministers to obey his orders? Could not anything that was indifferent be 'enjoined godly' to the use of Common Prayer or Sacrament? Was it not lawful for a distinctive external dress to be ordered for the clergy? Should ministers who wore the apparel be condemned for doing so by any preacher? And were preachers who made such criticisms to be reformed or restrained? Finally, could it 'stand with a good conscience' for a man to abandon the ministry (and so open the way for less worthy men) rather than wear at the services, or outside church, the customary and lawful clothes?

Framed in a form calculated to invite the answers Parker wanted, the questions did none the less indicate what were the matters really in dispute. Sampson and Humphrey sent in their reasoned answers, quoted by Strype along with the questions. They made certain points, fundamental in the protestant position, quite clear. Though 'in substance' the surplice is indifferent,

[1] Strype, *Parker* iii, 69 sqq.   [2] Ibid., pp. 76 sqq.   [3] Ibid., i, 329 sqq.

yet it is now not so 'by circumstances', for it has been 'consecrated to idolatry'. That is their first and main contention.
But a second emerges. If things really are indifferent, they may
be ordered, but only if 'there may be brought a ground out of the
Scripture'—an argument which plainly goes against the view that
local churches may freely ordain rites and ceremonies if these
are not *against* Scriptures. At present only applied to clerical
dress, it was a principle which was soon to have much wider
and more disturbing application. Thus right at the beginning of
the troubles there emerge two of the chief puritan arguments:
that any rite or custom adopted by the Roman Church was
ipso facto defiled, and that there must be Scripture warrant for
rites and ceremonies. For the rest, Sampson and Humphrey
regarded it as inconceivable that any Ordinary should order or
enforce the use of garments so contaminated, nor could they find
any New Testament authority for a distinctive clerical dress
out of doors. They were not prepared to condemn preachers
who spoke against the habits—'to judge, disprove, or condemn
another man's servant is not our part' (a very different attitude
from that of later Puritans!)—but pleaded for tolerance, 'a
charitable permission of diversity, as on both parts there is
unitas operantium'. On two questions they were tactfully silent—
whether a minister should obey his Ordinary if he is lawfully
ordered by him to wear the habits, and whether a man might
with a good conscience resign rather than obey. At this stage, the
dispute was quiet and seemly, marked by brevity rather than
the wearisome prolixity which was soon to develop.

Other bishops besides Parker were soon involved; Guest of
Rochester (who, like Parker, had not been in exile) wrote a long
answer to those who said the apparel should not be worn, argued
with much logic and common sense.[1] Then a formula for
signature was agreed on by Parker, Grindal, Horne and Cox,
the Dean of Westminster and others.[2] Ministers of the Church
of England in which pure Christian doctrine and preaching
flourish and which publicly professes the detestation of 'Anti-

[1] Strype, *Parker* iii, 98 sqq.   [2] Ibid., i, 344.

christianism', may use distinctive dress, ordered by public authority, both in the administration of the sacraments and externally, provided that there is no idea of its necessity to worship.[1] Short of complete surrender to the critics, a more conciliatory form of words could hardly have been found. The dress had no religious significance, but was to be regarded simply as uniform ordered by authority. Even Humphrey and Sampson were induced to sign—but added to their signatures St. Paul's warning that all things lawful were not expedient or edifying! Nowell of St. Paul's, however, was only prepared to sign with the addition that the distinctive dress ought to be abolished for fear of abuse, to show detestation of corrupt religion, to profess the liberty of Christ and to remove dissension among the brethren![2] The dissidents, if pressed, might admit in theory that the garments might be worn, but wanted them abolished and, at least Sampson and Humphrey, were not prepared themselves to use them.

Cecil had been kept well posted by Parker as to what was going on. In January 1565 a new move was made. On the 15th Cecil sent to the Archbishop the draft of a letter which he thought 'should have been meet for to have procured from the Queen's Majesty to your grace'.[3] He fears it is too long and asks Parker to alter or abridge it. He is also afraid that the Queen may be angry that there is so much that calls for reformation, and may add to the letter more than he wishes. From the letter it looks as though, in this instance, at least, the initiative did not rest with the Queen but with Cecil. He seems to be sure that Parker would welcome such a letter, which would strengthen his hand.

Ten days later, the letter was duly sent from the Queen to the Archbishop.[4] It was long and was sharply phrased. Knowing the need for unity, quietness, and concord, the Queen stigmatized 'diversity, variety, contention and vain love of singularity' as not only displeasing to God, but heavy and troublesome to herself

[1] 'Modo omnis cultus et necessitatis opinio amoveatur.'
[2] Strype, Parker i, pp. 344-5. [3] Correspondence, p. 223. [4] Ibid., pp. 223 sqq.

who had the burden of government, and dangerous to the nation. She had tried to provide laws and ordinances agreeable to truth, justice and good order under which all might live 'without diversities of opinions or novelties of rites and manners'. She now found that 'for lack of regard given thereto in due time, by such superior and principal officers as you are, being the primate and other the bishops of your province' there have crept in 'varieties and novelties not only in opinions but in external rites and ceremonies', which 'impair, deface and disturb Christian charity, unity and concord'. Reports of such things had long reached her; she had hoped they were exaggerated but is now certain that troubles are increasing. She will not endure such evils to grow; they are to be repressed; there must be 'one manner of uniformity through our whole realm'. Parker was therefore required, enjoined and straitly charged with other bishops in the ecclesiastical commission to make full enquiries as to such varieties in places exempt as well as not exempt (the Universities were specifically mentioned) and to correct them 'by order, injunction or censure according to the order and appointment of such laws and ordinances as are provided by act of Parliament'. In future none were to be admitted to any ecclesiastical office who were not found to be well disposed and who did not 'orderly and formally promise' to observe and keep 'order and uniformity in all external rites and ceremonies'. Any 'superior officers' who would not co-operate were to be reported to her. A final paragraph commanded 'all due expedition', so that there may not have to be 'such further remedy, by some other sharp proceedings as shall percase not be easy to be borne by such as shall be disordered; and therewith also we shall impute to you the cause thereof'.

It is important to note that the letter was not an 'order' such as the Act of Uniformity explicitly allowed the Queen to make, under the Great Seal and with the advice of the commissioners or the Metropolitan, touching the ornaments of the church and ministers. It did not bear the Queen's signature and was not sealed. It therefore conferred no new powers on the Archbishop or the commission: they were simply to use the powers already given to them by Parliament. It was, in fact, typical of the Queen's custom of trying to keep in the background while urging the bishops to carry out her policies by their own authority, and blaming them if there was failure. But it was heavy with threats of what would happen if they did not act! In particular, the last paragraph was much stronger than one which exists in Cecil's draft to Parker.[1] In that, the Archbishop was urged to 'use all good discretion' so that no trouble should grow in the Church. In the final form expedition is urged rather than discretion. Further measures were foreshadowed if there was no improvement—and the Archbishop personally would be held to blame. Whether these changes from Cecil's draft were due to the Archbishop's own suggestion, to strengthen his hand, or to the Queen's indignation, is a matter for conjecture. But it is clear that the Archbishop was anxious to have the backing of some such letter.

He acted at once. On January 30 he wrote to the Bishop of London conveying a full summary of the Queen's letter in which, he said, she had discoursed 'very seriously and at great length'.[2] In performance of his duty to God, in obedience to the Queen and 'to avoid her heavy indignation' he then charged Grindal to carry out the terms of the Queen's letter and to enjoin the other bishops of the province to do the same. Offenders were to be punished by ecclesiastical censure, the incorrigible to be reported. After consultation with 'the most apt and grave men', the bishops were to report to the Archbishop 'what varieties and disorders there be, either in doctrine or ceremonies of the Church and behaviour of the clergy themselves'. The reports were to reach the Archbishop before the last day of February.

If the diocesan reports were ever made, they no longer exist. A letter from the Vice-Chancellor of Cambridge, dated February 27, probably contains the official reply for that University.[3] Except for a few papists, he knew of no one who impugned the

---

[1] Strype, *Parker* iii, 69.   [2] *Correspondence*, pp. 227 sqq.
[3] Ibid., p. 226, note.

substance of religion generally agreed, save that one in Christ's College and sundry at St. John's objected to wearing a surplice. Similarly a certificate from the Dean and canons of Canterbury, though undated, is assumed by Strype to belong to this time, but it may be earlier.[1] It is interesting, whatever its exact date, as showing the usage customary in a church which fully conformed. No doctrine was taught save what was set forth by public authority. The communion table stood, normally, North—South where the High Altar had stood, and prayers were sung (if there was no communion) by a minister wearing a surplice (but no hood) and standing East of the Table, facing the people. On the first Sunday of the month, when there was a communion service, the table was set East and West, the celebrant, gospeller and epistoler wore copes, and non-communicants were not allowed to tarry in the church. The bread used was that ordered by the Royal Injunctions. In attendance at the daily evening prayer, the Dean and prebendaries were duly 'apparelled'; the petty canons, lay-clerks and choristers also wore surplices. Preachers wore surplice and hood. That all seems to have been exemplary. But in the Cecil papers there is a catalogue of '*Varieties in the service and administration used*' which gives a very different picture.[2] What is its authority or source is not known, but it is dated 14 Feb. 1564 (i.e. 1565). It may be a summary of diocesan returns, though its date (a fortnight before they were due to Parker) is a little early for that; or it may have been a return for the London diocese. But at least it was submitted, evidently, to Cecil, and gives an account of non-conformist confusion which is *a priori* convincing, and which explains why Parker and Cecil felt strong measures to be necessary. Services and prayers, it alleged, were said by some in the chancel, by others in the body of the church, or from the pulpit. The order of the Prayer Book was kept precisely by some, others

---

[1] Strype, *Parker* i, 364; from C.C.C. MSS. 122, where its position suggests a date earlier than 1565.

[2] Strype, *Parker* i, 302. Strype claims to give it '*verbatim*', and nearly does so, save that he puts 'cap' for 'copes' in writing of the dress for communion.

inserted metrical psalms. Some wore a surplice, others did not. The table was variously set in the body of the church or in the chancel, altarwise, either a yard from the wall or in the midst of the chancel. There was great variety about the communion service. Some ministers wore surplice and cope; some surplice only; some neither. A chalice might be used, or a special communion cup, or a common cup. Some used leavened bread, others wafers. Some received kneeling, others standing, others seated. At baptism some used a font, others a basin; some ministers omitted the sign of the cross and were not surpliced. In outdoor apparel, some ministers wore a 'scholar's' cloak, others not; as to head gear, some had a square cap (as ordered) others a round cap, or a button cap, or a hat. Clearly there was much need for some sort of order to be imposed.

Accordingly, on 3 March 1565, Parker sent to Cecil 'a book of articles, partly of old agreed on amongst us, and partly of late these three or four days considered, which be either in papers fastened on, as ye see, or new written by secretary hand'.[1] It had been devised by himself, the Bishops of London and Ely (fellow members of the ecclesiastical commission), Winchester and Lincoln. He asked for Cecil's judgement on it so that it might be 'fair written and presented' (presumably to the Queen). Cecil must have acted promptly, for on March 8 Parker was able to send him 'our book which is subscribed to by the bishops conferrers'.[2] He asked him to present it to the Queen for approval (so as to avoid 'offences that might grow by mine imprudent talk'). If she will not authorize it, 'the most part be like to lie in the dust for execution of our parties, laws be so much against our private doings. "The Queen's Majesty with consent etc." I trust shall be obeyed.'

It is clear that Parker did not underestimate the task ahead. Fearful of over-stepping the limits laid by law on episcopal powers, he and the others had drawn up the 'book' in such a form that, if the Queen authorized it, it fulfilled the requirements of 'taking other order' under the Uniformity Act, and

---

[1] *Correspondence*, p. 233.   [2] Ibid., p. 234.

therefore would have had full legal authority. Strype gives the text from a manuscript in his possession.[1] It starts 'The Queen's Majesty . . . hath, by the assent of the Metropolitan, and with certain other her Commissioners in causes ecclesiastical, decreed certain rules and orders to be used as hereafter followeth'. It was emphatically made plain that the rules were not regarded as 'laws equivalent with the eternal word of God and as of necessity to bind the consciences' of the Queen's subjects, but 'as constitutions mere ecclesiastical . . . as positive laws in discipline, concerning decency, distinction and order for the time'. But in the form so suggested, they would have had statutory authority, had the Queen authorized them.

A great deal of what followed was taken, verbatim or with slight alteration, from the *Interpretations* and *Resolutions*. The most important additions were two, one insisting on the recently passed *Thirty-Nine Articles* which were to be publicly read twice a year in church (as well as the *Eleven Articles*), and one that if any preacher put out matter tending to dissension or the derogation of religion and doctrine as received, he was to be denounced to the Ordinary but not to be openly argued with lest there 'grow offence and disquiet of the people'. Moreover all licences to preach granted before 1 March 1564 (1565) were now declared void, not merely those granted by the Royal Visitors, as in the *Interpretations*. The rules for church services were more explicit, and especially so were those for clerical dress. Common prayer was to be said in such place as the Ordinary directed; there was to be no unlicensed preaching. In cathedral and collegiate churches there was to be a celebration on the first or second Sunday of the month, and a cope was to be worn by the officiants; at other services, surplices alone. For parish churches the cope was no longer required for any service, but only a surplice. It was clearly laid down that communion should be received kneeling, not sitting or standing. There was, too, a long section about clerical dress out of doors—for deans and all dignitaries as well as for the ordinary clergy, long gowns;

[1] *Parker* iii, 84 sqq.

and the cap ordered by the Injunctions was always to be worn, except on journeys or 'for urgent cause' with 'the Prince's toleration'. But at home, the clergy were allowed 'their own liberty of comely apparel'. Poor clergy were to provide themselves with regulation gowns so soon as they could afford; if they had not the 'ability' (but the bishop of the diocese was to be the judge of that!) then a short gown would suffice. On the other hand, such clergy as no longer served the ministry or had not taken the Supremacy oath were strictly forbidden to wear clerical dress: they were to go as laymen. The bishops were to punish offenders by suspension or even sequestration. There was, too, insistence on observing the prohibited degrees in marriage as recently laid down by the Archbishop.

Practically everything else was taken from the *Interpretations* and *Resolutions*: even the Protestation now ordered to be made by those admitted to any office was that previously laid down for readers (who are not mentioned) with suitable slight alterations and an added promise not to intermeddle with any 'artificers occupations' if the annual income of the office to be held was twenty nobles or more. Such dependence on previous episcopal orders explains why Parker described the articles to Cecil as 'partly of old agreed upon amongst us'. It was, in a way, a second attempt to get the Queen's authorization for what the bishops had agreed before, the additions being concerned with points which had recently become prominent. As before, the royal authorization was withheld.

The Queen, indeed, was in most provoking mood. Having written her violent letter she seemed to be almost deliberately holding back. Parker asked Cecil to get from her a private letter to the Bishop of London 'to execute laws and injunctions'. Grindal had agreed that if he were so charged, he would act: Parker added that 'there (i.e. in London) is the most disorder, and then is the matter almost won thorough the realm'[1] if London were reformed. A few days later he had to write that 'I marvel that not six words were spoken from the Queen's Majesty to my

[1] *Correspondence*, pp. 233-4.

lord of London, for uniformity of his London, as himself told me'.[1] Only the day before Parker had 'for pure pity' taken home to dinner Nowell, Dean of St. Paul's, who was 'utterly dismayed'[2] by the Queen's conduct. It was Ash Wednesday, and the Dean in his sermon before her had attacked a papistical book which had been dedicated to her, and had spoken against images. Once and again the Queen had angrily interrupted him and told him to drop the matter as it had nothing to do with his subject and was now threadbare.[3] No wonder the Dean was crestfallen and the Spanish ambassador exultant. A month later, a cleric appeared at court, unrebuked, in hat and short cloak.[4]

Parker had thus every ground for the querulousness and hesitations which appear in his letters about now—'I will no more strive against the stream, fume or chide who will'; 'they cease to impute it to her Majesty, for they say, but for my calling on, she is indifferent ... My Lord of London is their own, say they, and is but brought in against his will. I only am the stirrer and the incenser'. They thought Leicester and the Bishop of Durham were on their side (as indeed they were), and would not attach any blame to Cecil,[5] who like the Queen seems to have avoided taking sides publicly. It is true that in March, if the Spanish ambassador is to be trusted—there is no other record of the incident—Cecil did by invitation attend a meeting of some of the new bishops who were agreed that the habits were papistical and disagreeable to them personally. Cecil certainly showed no sympathy; he was very curt and told them that they had 'studied but little' and that worse would befall them if they did not obey the 'Queen's orders'.[6] But even if it took place, this was only a private meeting—and Cecil contented himself with telling them to obey the laws. Anyhow, it seems odd that, according to the ambassador's account, both sides spoke of the Queen's 'Order'; yet she had most carefully refrained from giving one, since the Injunctions!

[1] *Correspondence*, p. 235.   [2] Ibid.   [3] *Cal. S. P. Span*. i, 405.
[4] *Correspondence*, p. 237.   [5] Ibid., pp. 235, 237.
[6] *Cal. S. P. Span*. i, 406.

M

None the less, despite his depression and his feeling that he was playing a lone hand, Parker went steadily on to deal with Sampson and Humphrey. On March 3, he told Cecil that 'we' (presumably he and the other bishops of the commission) had resolved to see them 'to understand their reasons', and invited Cecil 'to step over to us'.[1] On the 8th the meeting took place—but Cecil was not present.[2] The two brought back copies of letters by Bucer and Martyr which had been lent to them—presumably those written to persuade Hooper to wear the vestments at his consecration—but were unconvinced. Parker felt that he could do no good with them, and hoped that the Queen or the Council or Leicester, Chancellor of Oxford, would deal with them. 'Better not to have begun, except more be done. All the realm is in expectation. . . . Your honour principally hath begun, *tua interest ut aliquid fiat*. If this ball shall be tossed unto us, and then have no authority by the Queen's Majesty's hand, we well set still.' But he had refused their request to be allowed to return to Oxford. A fortnight later he wrote to Cecil[3] 'I would ye had not have stirred *istam camarinam* or else to have set on it to some order at the beginning'. He suggested that if Cecil and Leicester and the Lord Keeper were to consult together about the matter 'ye shall spend a piece of your afternoon well', and offered to be present at their discussion, with Grindal, if it were wished. Nothing came of his suggestion. Then to his astonishment, he learned that Sampson and Humphrey had been nominated to preach at Paul's Cross[4]—'they abuse their friends' lenity on whom they trust'. Finally, on April 29th, Parker brought matters to a head[5] 'I did peremptorily will them to agree or else to depart their places'. They were 'to wear the cap appointed by Injunction, to wear no hats in their long gowns, to wear a surplice with a non-regent hood in their quires at their Colleges . . . to communicate kneeling in wafer-bread'. (It is to be noticed that, so far, the only points in dispute were the habits, wafer-bread and kneeling at communion.) Possibly this was the time

---

[1] *Correspondence*, p. 233. [2] Ibid., p. 234. [3] Ibid., p. 236.
[4] Ibid., p. 239. [5] Ibid., p. 240.

when Grindal 'prayed Sampson even with tears that he would but now and then, in the public meetings of the University, put on the square cap'.[1]

Sampson and Humphrey firmly said their consciences would not allow them to obey, and plainly expected to lose their posts, for they asked for some 'respite to remove their stuff'. Sampson pleaded that there was urgent College business for him to see to, Humphrey that he had 'divers noblemen's sons' under his charge! He even pleaded to be spared the extremity of losing his living.[2] Paker was, in fact, in a difficulty, which he explained to Cecil. He did not think they meant to resign, yet doubted his power to remove them. The Deanery of Christ Church was in the Queen's gift: he might 'after long pleading' dispossess Sampson. But the Presidency of Magdalen was the concern of the College, and he thought that only the Visitor (the Bishop of Winchester) could act there. He therefore asked Cecil to put the matter to the Queen, so that he might act according to her pleasure.

The Spanish ambassador was delighted. 'The disorders and irregularity of these ministers have done us much good' he wrote in April,[3] though he did not specifically name Sampson and Humphrey. But they were obviously the outstanding cases. Still, the dispute with them was conducted in a seemly manner and without ill temper. Nor was their non-compliance visited with very severe penalties. Humphrey, indeed, withdrew from Oxford for a short time, but was soon back. He lost neither the Presidency of Magdalen nor the Regius Professorship of Divinity, both which offices he retained till his death in 1589. He was actually Vice-Chancellor of Oxford in 1571-5. The most he seems to have suffered was when, this very year, Horne of Winchester presented him, surprisingly, to a living in the diocese of Salisbury and Jewel, the Bishop, refused his consent because of his nonconformity.[4] But again, there was no breach of friend-

[1] Strype, *Parker* i, 368. But Parker does not in his letter say that Grindal was present on this occasion.

[2] *Correspondence*, pp. 240-1. [3] *Cal. S. P. Span.* i, 418.

[4] *Works of Jewel* (ed. J. Ayre, Cambridge, 1850), iv, 1265.

ship. When Jewel died, it was Humphrey who was sought for to preach the funeral sermon, and was commissioned by Parker to write the life of Jewel.[1] Later on, when the Puritans became violent, he conformed, and became Dean of Gloucester and of Winchester. Obviously, he was much liked, and his conscientious scruples were respected.

Sampson was more difficult and contentious. Later on, Bullinger, who had known him at Zurich, said that he had 'always looked with suspicion upon the statements made by master Sampson . . . he never ceased to be troublesome to master Peter Martyr . . . the man is never satisfied; he has always some doubt or other to busy himself with . . . I used to get rid of him in a friendly way, as well knowing him to be a man of captious and unquiet disposition'.[2] Unlike Humphrey, he now lost his Oxford position; there is no record of how this was effected, but there was a new Dean by June 1565. Even so, Sampson was not, apparently, imprisoned, though for a time he was limited in his place of residence.[3] Parker did all he could to help him— wrote to Christ Church on his behalf, and to Cecil and the Earl of Huntingdon, at Sampson's request, urging that he should be set at full liberty.[4] He was provided for by being made Master of Wigston's Hospital at Leicester, and later by a prebend in St. Paul's. The kindliness of Parker could hardly be more clearly made manifest. He had to take action against such eminent nonconformists, but there was no vengefulness in what he did, and a real concern to see that they did not suffer great hardship.

Meantime, there was disquiet at Cambridge also. In January the University authorized the removal of painted windows in college chapels and elsewhere, because they seemed to sanction prayers for the dead and could therefore be regarded as superstitious. The expense involved was defrayed by a certain George Withers, who then delivered a sermon in the University Church urging a more general destruction of all superstitious windows.[5]

[1] Strype, *Parker* ii, 49–50.   [2] *Zurich Letters*, ii, 152.
[3] *Correspondence*, p. 243.   [4] Ibid., pp. 243–4–5.
[5] Mullinger, *History of Cambridge University*, ii, 196–7.

The authorities took no action against him, but the matter was reported privately to Parker who sent for Withers[1]—it is a little difficult to see on what legal grounds, for the preaching licence possessed by Withers was granted by the University, not by Parker. But naturally Parker was much concerned by anything which affected the reputation of Cambridge, and particularly of Corpus of which College Withers was a member; that no doubt explains Parker's interference. Withers arrived in March, full of confidence; Parker was correspondingly depressed. He felt that when such 'disordered men' came to London and saw 'how the game goweth' they went away with their obstinacy confirmed. He also told Cecil—and it is one of the earliest hints that he gives —that he thought that the danger now was not only concerning vestments but all ritual, and that great prudence was needed.[2] Perhaps Withers had opened his eyes to the fact that the Vice-Chancellor's report of the previous month did not fully represent the state of opinion in Cambridge.

With Withers himself the Archbishop was able to deal. He found that the form of licence to preach granted by the University was defective as it was not in the traditional form. It was issued without the Chancellor's authority, without any limitation of time, and with the express statement that the agreement of the diocesan bishops should not be required[3]—in all these points disagreeing with a similar licence issued by Bishop Fisher under papal bull, which Strype gives.[4] Parker suggested to Cecil that in future University licences should conform to the ordinary form, and that irregular ones should be annulled. He also found that Withers was refusing to wear the clerical dress ordered by the Injunctions, and therefore inhibited him from preaching, when, at his interview, he refused to enter into bonds for wearing the square cap. In May, however, Withers wrote to say that the townsmen of Bury St. Edmunds (where he was a popular preacher) had pressed him to conform rather than deprive them of his

---

[1] *Correspondence*, p. 234. [2] Ibid., p. 236.
[3] Ibid., pp. 238-9, and Strype, *Parker* iii, 122-3.
[4] Strype, *Parker* iii, 121-2.

preaching, and that he was now therefore 'content to wear the cornered cap at Bury'[1] so that he might have from the Archbishop the office of preaching.

The incident must have confirmed Parker in his view, already made clear in the articles submitted to Cecil, that it was urgent to deal with licences to preach; and it seems that, on this matter at least, the Queen was persuaded to act. Strype prints[2] a royal grant to Cambridge University to appoint preachers. It is carefully worded—the grant is to the Chancellor, Masters and Scholars (the proper description of the University, as Parker pointed out to Cecil) and licences are to be in accord with the customary usage save that the bishop's consent is not needed. Though it is undated, the grant looks as though it was meant to deal with just such irregularities as existed in the licence to Withers. Further, in May, Parker wrote to Grindal that the Queen had commanded that 'we should take for hereafter a more diligent choice of such as shall sue for such licences',[3] and that henceforward the bishops were to order that no curate should be allowed to serve, coming out of another diocese, unless he brought with him letters testimonial from the bishop of that diocese. Parker himself ordered that all licences granted by him before April 1 should be regarded as invalid, though their holders, if meet, should receive new licences at small charge if they handed in their old ones. He hoped other bishops would follow the same course. Such measures were not, indeed, immediately effective, but they show Parker's anxiety to deal with 'undiscreet preachers' and the Queen's readiness to support him at least in that respect.

Discontent at Cambridge about the wearing of the surplice, mentioned by the Vice-Chancellor, continued to grow, especially at St. John's (Cecil's own college)—so much so that on November 26 the Vice-Chancellor and four others sent to Cecil a formal letter.[4] They had heard—as doubtless he had—a strong rumour that there was to be an edict about apparel by which all members

---

[1] Strype, *Parker* i, 375.   [2] Strype, *Parker* iii, 124–5.
[3] *Correspondence*, p. 242.   [4] Strype, *Parker* iii, 125–6.

of the University were to be compelled to wear the prescribed garb. There was in Cambridge a large number (*multitudo*) of learned and pious men whose conscience would not allow them to do so. There was a great danger, if the decree were enforced, that they would leave the University 'bereft'. The writers urged Cecil to use his influence to see that such an edict should not be published. Such a concession would be neither inconvenient nor dangerous, but the enforcement of the order would be a great hindrance both to Gospel preaching and to scholarship. The letter was signed by the Vice-Chancellor, three Heads of Houses (including Hutton, later Archbishop of York), and Whitgift, Margaret Professor of Divinity, soon to be a favourite of the Queen and Archbishop of Canterbury. Cecil must have reacted forcibly, for on December 6 the Vice-Chancellor wrote to say that their letter had been sent in order to prevent the sending of two much more violent letters that had been drawn up.[1] The correspondence was, seemingly, sent by Cecil to Parker who returned it on December 8, noting that there were in Cambridge 'of the best sort and of the most part' ready to carry out orders, but also 'a few Catilines, who by sufferance will affect the whole'.[2] He urged that 'Execution of laws and orders must be the first and the last part of good government'. Let there be no more stir or alteration unless it is determined to enforce it, 'else we shall hold us in no certainty, but be ridiculous to our adversaries, contemned of our own, and give the adventure of more dangers'.

Parker had good reason for taking so firm a line. Already the dangers had come to a head at St. John's. There a young Fellow, William Fulke, a friend of Cartwright and soon to be one of the more extreme Puritan leaders, had preached in College chapel against surplices, against ecclesiastical vestments, against wafer-bread and kneeling to receive communion. On one occasion, nearly three hundred of the College had, under his impulse, attended service in chapel without surplices. The Master ignored such things and, indeed, seemed to favour Fulke.[3] Early in

[1] Dixon, op. cit., vi, 68 note, and *Cal. S. P. Dom.*, p. 262.
[2] *Correspondence*, pp. 245–6.   [3] Dixon, op. cit., vi, 69–75.

December complaint was made to Cecil about all this—just about the time when he was dealing with the Vice-Chancellor's letter. Parker, too, seems to have heard about it, though he was not directly concerned—he actually refers to 'a bragging brainless head or two' in his letter to Cecil. Cecil made the Master of St. John's read in College a recantation (though in doing it he watered down the form of words given him to read[1]), and Fulke was deprived of his Fellowship. On December 18, the Master reported that he had prevailed on most members of the College to wear surplices—but asked if he need really do so himself when preaching in College and whether they might use common bread at communion![2] His conformity was evidently not from the heart, and there were still troubles in the College as late as the following June.[3] Fulke was soon restored to his Fellowship because of popular pressure.

At about the same time, troubles at Gonville and Caius came to a head. The Master, Dr. Caius, who had most liberally enriched the College, yet treated the Fellows with astonishing brutality, so it was said, reducing some of them to penury by law suits, even putting some in the stocks.[4] The College, over a year before this, had appealed to Parker and Grindal to settle their affairs, for the Master had expelled two Fellows. (He was actually alleged, over a period, to have expelled no fewer than twenty.) Parker thought neither side free from blame, but decided that the two should not be restored, as there would never be peace in the College while they were there.[5] The Fellows had now appealed to Cecil as Chancellor. Parker, again consulted, regretted such procedure. He did not like such appeals from a College to the authority of the Chancellor: it was a bad precedent. And it would waste the Chancellor's time! 'Scholars' controversies be now many and troublous: and their delight is to come before men of authority to show their wits'. He obviously found them tiresome, and wished to support Dr. Caius (despite his tyrannical behaviour) both in the interests of

---

[1] Strype, *Parker* iii, 131-3.   [2] *Cal. S. P. Dom.*, pp. 262-3.   [3] Ibid., p. 274.
[4] Mullinger, op. cit., ii, 200-2.   [5] *Correspondence*, pp. 248-50, 251-3.

order and so as not to discourage benefactors who 'be very rare at these days'. He would himself have seen that the expelled Fellows were provided for—indeed he provided lodging for one of them—but they appealed to Cecil for restoration. He, advised by Parker, in January refused to restore them, but did order the Master to be more regular in his administration. Now Dr. Caius undoubtedly had strong leanings towards Romanism: later on it was discovered that he had hidden away old books, vestments, and ornaments in the hope that they might be brought back into use. Some of the articles now charged by the College against him, according to Parker, were 'not only sounding and savouring atheism, but plainly expressing the same, with further show of a perverse stomach to the professors of the gospel'. If they were proved, he thought the Master should be suspended. In the end such charges were not maintained, and it would be wrong to suggest that they formed the main accusation against Caius: that was his tyrannical conduct. But it is not unreasonable to suppose that the strain in the College was aggravated by the suspicion of Fellows, eager for reform, of the Master's religious inclinations.

Thus, though as yet there were not in Cambridge such eminent leaders as Sampson and Humphrey, there was much wider discontent among the younger men than showed itself in Oxford. The Universities, in fact, offered little encouragement to Parker in his desire for stronger measures to enforce discipline. But, at least, Cecil did show himself willing to insist that the law should be kept, whatever his private sympathies.

On the other hand, some of the bishops who did not even belong to the left wing, were becoming uneasy. In July 1565 Horne of Winchester, following the example of Sampson and Humphrey, sought advice from Zurich. The cap and surplice had been ordered by law before he and his follows were in authority, and 'without any superstitious conceit, which was expressly guarded against by the terms of the Act'. They had conformed lest their enemies (i.e. papists) should take their places if they deserted. But now great strife had arisen. He hoped that the clause in the Act would be repealed soon, but thought that in the meantime they should continue to conform—but he asked 'whether we can do, what we are thus doing, with a safe conscience'.[1] In November 1565 Bullinger replied: it was a very cautious letter—he plainly did not wish to be deeply involved. He did not fully know the circumstances; he was reluctant to raise the question of the authority of kings and magistrates in Church affairs. He would like the Church to be rid of 'all the dregs of popery'. But as all 'conceit of superstition' had been removed by the proclamation, he thought the bishops should carry on, lest their places should fall to 'papists or else Lutheran doctors and presidents, who are not very much unlike them'. Then all sorts of absurd ceremonies would follow, images be restored, 'artolatry' in the communion, private confession, absolution and so on. They should therefore not consider only their own feelings and reputations, but the good of the Church at large.[2] For a foreigner who disclaimed intimate knowledge of affairs in England, it was an impressively prudent letter. The extremists at home saw in the cap and surplice a danger that Romanism would spread in the church. Bullinger saw the real danger—that, if they were rejected, Elizabeth might well move in the opposite direction to that which the zealots desired.

It was a delicate situation. Parker has sometimes been accused of pusillanimity for delaying to act on his own authority until March 1566. But with some of the best of the bishops lukewarm in the cause of discipline, the Universities turbulent, and no open backing from the Queen whose favourite, Leicester, was well known to be favourable to the dissidents, the wonder is not that Parker delayed so long but that he ever screwed up sufficient determination to act. He may even have hoped at first that the firm treatment of Sampson might bring others to heel. Be that as it may, for the time being, he took no decisive action. In June of 1565 his letters show that he was in Canterbury, where he was celebrating with great hospitality the restoration of his palace. For the rest, until March of 1566, save for his dealings

[1] *Zurich Letters*, i, 142–3.   [2] Ibid., i, 341–4.

with Cambridge troubles, he seems to have been occupied with
the routine duties of his office and his own special interests.
Prominent among the latter was the production of a new English
Bible.

It is usually said that he began to plan this in 1563-4, but there
is no evidence of so early a start. Indeed, in May 1564 Cox
wrote to Cecil proposing such a revision of the Bible, so that a
single translation might be used,[1] which does not look as though
he had then heard of Parker having any such project, though he
was one of those who was soon to be engaged in it. Certainly the
Bishop of St. David's did not receive the part assigned to him
until March 1566,[2] though it was probably sent to him the
previous December. In that same month of December, Parkhurst
promised to do his part as quickly as he could.[3] In the following February, Sandys submitted his contribution, emphasiz-
ing how important it was that the whole should be 'diligently
surveyed by some well learned before it be put to print'.[4] It is
hard, in view of all this, not to suppose that it was towards the
end of 1565 that Parker really started the scheme by allocating
portions to the translators he chose, though as late as November
1566 it would seem that all the books were not yet allocated.
For Parker then expressed the desire to have 'one Epistle of St.
Paul or Peter or John' of Cecil's perusing, 'to the intent that ye
may be one of the builders of this good work in Christ's Church'.[5]
Still, in March 1566, he and Grindal informed Cecil of their
plan to produce it 'as convenient time and leisure hereafter will
permit',[6] but urged that, in the meantime, licence should be
given for twelve years to John Bodley to print in England the
Geneva version. He had already taken part in the printing at
Geneva in 1560, and had a licence for seven years to print in
England. The extension of time was suggested because of the
expense he and his associates had already had. It is doubtful if
the extension was granted, nor does Bodley ever seem to have
printed the Geneva version in England. But Parker's support of

---

[1] *Cal. S. P. Dom.*, p. 239.   [2] *Correspondence*, p. 265.
[3] Ibid., p. 248.   [4] Ibid., p. 256.   [5] Ibid., p. 290.   [6] Ibid., p. 262.

what must have appeared as a rival to the work he was planning shows not only a generous spirit, but his eagerness that an English Bible should be widely available as soon as possible— though he and Grindal do add that 'no impression shall pass but by our direction, consent and advice'. Ultimately, the *Bishops' Bible* as it is called, appeared in 1568.

The Archbishop had time to spare, too, to indulge his zeal for antiquities. Cecil submitted to him for his views a manu- script Old Testament with Saxon interpretation.[1] Parker thought it 'much worth keeping', especially as its Latin text was unusual. Parts of the beginning of the Psalter, indeed, were missing. He had thought of causing one of his copyists to counterfeit the missing portion 'in antiquity', and of moving a leaf 'having David with his harp or psaltery' from before the 19th psalm, so as to form a beginning of the work, with the forged first psalm on the reverse. He did not do so because he remembered that Cecil himself had a 'singular artificer to adorn the same'! Evidently from the point of view of a modern antiquary, Parker was a dangerous collector, for all his enthusiasm. About the same time his enquiry about 'old monuments' at St. David's elicited the information that Cecil had had them all, while the bishop and an antiquary there could make nothing of a manuscript 'of strange charects' which Parker had submitted for their views.[2] But he was able in his turn to help them with the information that some of their records were written in 'the speech of the old Saxon'[3] in which he had divers works, and those in his household who understood them.

In February 1566, Parker was much exercised about two Welsh dioceses. Llandaff had been without a bishop since the death of Kitchin in October 1563, which Parker regarded as a 'long tarriance'. Bangor had fallen vacant the previous month. In the second case, he wrote within a week to demand the customary mortuaries due to him as Primate on the Bishop's death—his palfrey with harness, his rain-proof cloak and cape,

---

[1] *Correspondence*, p. 253.   [2] Ibid., pp. 265–6.
[3] Ibid., p. 271.

his second best ring and his seals.[1] Later on, he wrote to Cecil about both dioceses.[2] For Llandaff, he had a satisfactory candidate, but needed to make arrangements about *commendams* to enable him to accept: five days later, he had all in train—a quick decision after so long delay. Bangor was more difficult. There, too, *commendams* were needed, and the Earl of Pembroke was pressing an unsuitable candidate—a man 'aforetime sheriff of the Shire, neither being priest nor having any priestly disposition'! The diocese was in a bad way: 'no preaching there, and pensionary concubinary openly continued, notwithstanding liberty of marriage granted'. He had been urged that the new Bishop should not be a Welshman: 'they band so much together in kindred, that the bishop can do not as he would for his alliance sake'. It had been suggested that Parker should hold a visitation so as to set things in order. In the event, that was the course he followed. In May he appointed two visitors for the diocese, an advocate of the Court of Arches and Nicholas Robinson, Archdeacon of Merioneth, who was appointed subsequently Bishop of Bangor in September and consecrated in October.[3] Cecil, evidently, had suggested him as Bishop.[4]

There was further difficulty, too, also with the Earl of Pembroke in the diocese of St. David's. The Earl, backed apparently by Leicester and Arundel, presented to a living by virtue of a grant of advowson which, the Bishop was sure, was a forgery.[5] All Parker could do when referred to was to urge the Bishop 'to follow right and equity'. But it is clear that Parker had much cause of concern about conditions in Wales.

Further, the protestant refugees from the Spanish Netherlands were beginning to be tiresome (as the English had been at Frankfort). Some of them had been allowed to settle at Sandwich, where Parker had deputed their minister to deal with 'disorders reformable by ecclesiastical laws'.[6] The Bishop of Norwich now complained that some of them, excommunicated at Sand-

---

[1] *Register*, p. 235.
[3] *Register*, pp. 234, 122–4.
[5] Ibid., pp. 266, 271.

[2] *Correspondence*, pp. 257, 259.
[4] *Correspondence*, p. 261.
[6] Ibid., p. 189.

wich, had gone to Norwich; he asked for power to absolve them. Parker dealt with the situation and seems to have brought about a reconciliation between them and their fellows at Sandwich.[1] But soon, on the petition of the Duke of Norfolk and at the suggestion of the Bishop, Parker caused a church to be set aside for refugees in Norwich.[2]

Amid such major worries, it is odd to find from his correspondence with what seemingly unimportant details the Archbishop had also to concern himself. He personally arranged about the Lenten preachers before the Queen. He enquired whether, after what had happened the previous year, it would be safe to invite Nowell to preach before her![3] (Nowell later excused himself on the ground that he was too busy.[4]) He had to exclude some suggested for the Spital sermons, for they were not 'conformable'; and had trouble about suitable preachers for Paul's Cross.[5] Even smaller matters, too, came to him—a letter from Foxe asking for a licence to eat meat in Lent 1565 because of his infirmities; and an order from the Queen in the same year to grant a licence to Winchester College, such as the Universities had received, to exempt the scholars from observance of 'Wednesday made a fish-day by politic constitution'.[6] But even such trifles cease to be unimportant when carelessness or a false step might result in royal thunder or sectarian explosion.

[1] *Correspondence*, p. 247, and note. [2] Ibid., pp. 255–6.
[3] Ibid., p. 254. [4] Ibid., p. 260.
[5] Ibid., pp. 264, 275. [6] Ibid., pp. 230, 235.

CHAPTER XII

THE ADVERTISEMENTS:
THEIR RESULTS

STRYPE says that 'now at last' (the end of 1565 or early in 1566), in consequence of an address by the Archbishop, the Queen issued a proclamation requiring uniformity.[1] By it, he says, 'the wearing of the apparel and obedience to the usages of the Church became absolutely enjoined'. He regards it as confirming and ratifying at least so much of the book of articles, lately submitted to Cecil, as related to apparel. But there is no other evidence extant that the Queen issued any such proclamation; in fact on March 12 Parker complained to Cecil exactly on this point. In February there had been a proclamation against excess in lay apparel:[2] his comment was 'they who think that disorder of our state were as soon reformed if we had like helps, seem to me to speak reasonably.[3] But, proclamation or no, it is certain that the Queen did bestir herself. Parker had written to her about the difficulties likely to arise if the habits were enforced. In an interview he had told her that 'these precise folk would offer their goods and bodies to prison, rather than they would relent. And her Highness willed me to imprison them.'[4] This was on March 10, two days before, and probably the cause of, his letter to Cecil just quoted. He also refers elsewhere to the Queen having called him and Grindal to her presence to charge them expressly to see her laws executed: he even appears to suggest that she had ordered them to summon the clergy to be interviewed.[5] Whether this was the same as or different from his interview with her on March 10 is not clear. But what does

[1] Strype, *Parker* i, 427.   [2] Strype, *Annals* I, ii, 194, 533 sqq.
[3] *Correspondence*, p. 263.   [4] Ibid., p. 278.
[5] Ibid., pp. 273–4.

emerge is that the Queen, without publicly expressing her views
by a proclamation, was in March urging Parker and Grindal to
severe action—even to imprisonment—against disobedient clergy.

Parker acted at last—though not without hesitation and complaint. He had tried to carry out the Queen's orders, but had been
hindered by various considerations, among them the dislike of
discouraging some 'good protestants', who were helped by
'secret aiding and comforting'. Actually, he had just heard that
some preachers before the Queen had not worn the regulation
tippet and were not rebuked! 'If I draw forward, and others draw
backwards, what shall it avail, but raise exclamations and privy
mutterings against your honour (Cecil) and against me, by whom
they think these matters be stirred?'[1] Further, he had no power
'to set out any constitutions without licence obtained of the
prince'. So once more he sent to Cecil the articles disallowed the
previous year (he did not know why), 'humbly praying that if not
all yet so many as be thought good, may be returned with some
authority, at the least way for particular apparel'. It is clear that the
articles so submitted were as yet in the original form. For Parker
explicitly refers to the suggestion that offenders should be punished by sequestration—a provision which disappeared from them
when later published as *Advertisements*. This was on March 12.

Eight days later, the Archbishop and Grindal wrote to Cecil
to tell him of their plans. They had consulted lawyers about
their action, and now were going to summon the clergy of
London to appear at Lambeth. They were to be asked to promise
conformity in ministration and apparel. Those who refused were
to be suspended, their livings sequestrated. If they did not submit
within three months, they were to be deprived—a normal
proceeding after sequestration. The bishops feared that there
would be trouble and that many would desert their livings
rather than obey. They therefore hoped that the Queen would
send 'some honourable to join with us two, to authorize the
rather her commandment and pleasure'.[2] Parker was still hoping
for public support from the Queen—in vain, as the event proved.

[1] *Correspondence*, pp. 263-4.   [2] Ibid., pp. 267-8.

The meeting of the London clergy took place on March 26th. The day before, Cecil was told of it in the hope that he, Bacon and the Marquess of Northampton might be there to support the bishops.[1] But even that amount of help was withheld, for on the very day of the meeting it was necessary for Parker to write to Cecil after it was over to tell him what had happened.[2] Sixty-one of the clergy promised obedience, nine or ten were absent, but thirty-seven refused, of whom some were 'the best and some preachers', though 'divers of them but zealous, and of little learning and judgment'. (Two days later, he wrote to Cecil that he would wish the most part of the recusants 'out of the ministry, as mere ignorant and vain heads'.)[3] The refusers were suspended, their fruits sequestered, and they were to be deprived in three months if they did not submit. When some of them asked to be dispensed from first-fruits which they owed, Parker replied that he had no power to do it. But he was surprised at their 'reasonable quietness and modesty', and 'laboured by some advertisements' to pacify those who had conscientious scruples. He evidently respected them. Others who held out 'but in a spiced fancy' he thought would soon fall into line when they felt the pinch. That, he said, was all there was 'worth the writing'. He concluded with a strong request that Cecil would 'move my lord of London to execute order'. He had just received a letter from Cox of Ely who said that 'if London were reformed, all the realm would soon follow, as I believe the same'.

Parker's brief account scarcely does justice to the occasion. It was no longer a learned disputation as with Sampson and Humphrey, nor an attempt to deal with a single dissident such as Withers. It was a public demonstration that henceforward disobedience was to be met with immediate punishment. A contemporary but hostile account given by a diarist who was there adds details[4]—a Mr. Cole, duly arrayed in clerical attire,

---

[1] *Correspondence*, p. 269.   [2] Ibid., pp. 269–70.   [3] Ibid., p. 272.

[4] *Earl's Diary* (Cambridge University Library), used by Strype, *Grindal* pp. 144–5; and Frere, *History of the English Church*, p. 119. In 1567 Withers said that the 'question was not confined to habits', but there is no further light on this point. (*Zurich Letters*, ii, 148.)

was produced as a model, and the Bishop's Chancellor used a hectoring tone, and allowed no argument. They were simply to sign or refuse—'Be brief: make no words'; when some attempted to speak, 'the answer was Peace, Peace'. Parker certainly gives the impression that he did try to reason with the conscientious—perhaps before the Chancellor impatiently took charge; it may indeed have been the latter's firmness which produced the quietness which surprised Parker at the end.

Even after it was over Parker's letter shows that he felt that he could not rely on Grindal's whole-hearted support, despite his collaboration at the meeting. This may have been due to a suspicion that Grindal had recently shown himself willing to compromise. According to the same diarist,[1] in January he had summoned his clergy to St. Sepulchre's and suggested for outdoor wear a round cap and a gown with a cape. This would no doubt have marked out the clergy from the laity—and would not have looked Roman. Only 8 out of 109 refused. Nowadays, it does not seem an unreasonable compromise. But Parker was determined on full obedience to the law and the Royal Injunctions (though even he himself no longer insisted on the cope and eucharistic vestments). As he was to put it in the last letter printed in his correspondence[2] (11 April 1575) he did not personally mind about cap, tippet, surplice or wafer-bread. But he did esteem them as established by law, and feared to what end contempt of law and authority might lead. Nor were his suspicions of Grindal unjustified. In May, according to the Spanish ambassador,[3] the Queen herself rated Grindal soundly for not carrying out the orders about apparel, and 'threatened to punish him as an Anabaptist'.

But she still refused to give her public support to the articles, and bade Parker to 'assay with mine own authority what I can do for order'. Two days after the meeting at Lambeth, he wrote

---

[1] Frere, op. cit., p. 117. Strype (*Grindal*, pp. 143–4) puts this in January 1564 (i.e. 1565); but that is surely wrong—on his own showing, it was the January immediately preceding the March of 1566.
[2] *Correspondence*, p. 478.   [3] *Cal. S. P. Span.* i, 553.

to Cecil that he was resolved to delay no longer and sent him the *Book of Advertisements* for his advice thereon. This was, in fact, a revised form of the articles of the previous year from which he had 'weeded' all articles on doctrine, which perhaps were what had prevented the Queen's approbation, leaving 'but things avouchable and, as I take them, against no law of the realm'.[1] But the book was already actually in print, so that he was not really waiting for Cecil's comment. On the same day—March 28 —that he sent it to Cecil he sent it also to the Bishop of London with a covering letter ordering him (according to custom) to transmit it to the other bishops of the Province;[2] on the same day, too, he sent it to those in charge of his peculiars[3] which were not subject to ordinary episcopal oversight. (Whether it was the '*Advertisements*' he had used to try to pacify conscientious objectors two days before must remain a matter of conjecture, but it does not seem improbable.) In sending out the *Advertisements*, Parker claimed that he was attempting to carry out the Queen's wishes; but he carefully did not claim her authority for them as he had done in the previous draft; they are 'these our convenient orders' (to Grindal) or 'orders agreed upon by me and other of my brethren of my province of Canterbury and hitherto not published' (to his peculiars). They were signed by himself, the Bishops of London, Ely, Rochester (all of the ecclesiastical commission), Winchester and Lincoln 'with others'. Thus they had the authority not only of Parker but of the leading bishops of the Province, and of the ecclesiastical commission—but definitely not of the Queen, despite claims made for them later on.[4]

As setting out the model to which Parker and the bishops demanded conformity, the *Advertisements* are of critical significance. They consist of a preface, four sections of articles (for doctrine and preaching, for administration of prayer and sacraments, for orders in ecclesiastical policy, for outward apparel)

---

[1] *Correspondence*, p. 272.   [2] Ibid., p. 273–4.
[3] *Register*, pp. 454–5.
[4] Cf. Aubrey Moore, *History of the Reformation* (London, 1890), p. 266; Dixon, *History* vi, 104–6.

and 'protestations' to be made by those admitted to any office in any church or other place ecclesiastical.[1] The most notable change from the form originally submitted in 1565 was that in the preface; it was no longer claimed that the Queen, by the assent of the Metropolitan and certain other of her commissioners in causes ecclesiastical had decreed the rules following. Great stress was still laid on the fact that she had ordered the Archbishop, in consultation with other bishops in the commission, to take orders to abolish diversity, but the 'orders and rules ensuing' were only put out as being what the bishops had agreed on. Other alterations, though much slighter, are not without significance. There is now no insistence on (or reference to) the *Thirty-Nine* or the *Eleven Articles*—perhaps to avoid the suggestion that the bishops were interfering in matters of doctrine. There is no longer any mention of sequestration as a penalty for those clergy who, allowed to be away from their parishes for study at a university, were wasting their time, or for those who offended in matters of apparel. Perhaps, in the absence of royal authority, it was thought inappropriate to mention exact penalties. The rules about how bishops should deal with advowsons and leases were omitted: they would have been suitable in royal orders, but were not so in the altered circumstances. Other changes seem to be matters of convenience, not of principle. A quarterly, not a monthly, sermon was required of those able to preach. In cathedral and collegiate churches, communion was to be celebrated 'at least' on the first or second Sunday of each month, so that dean, prebendaries, priests and clerks should receive; but others, 'of discretion of the foundation' need only receive four times in the year at least. This was clearly a drawing back from the rubric in the Prayer Book, which required all priests and deacons of cathedral and collegiate churches to receive each Sunday. New incumbents were relieved of the necessity of producing, after six months, a certificate of good behaviour from the 'honest' of the parish, and church-wardens were to report quarterly instead of monthly

[1] The *Advertisements* are printed in Gee & Hardy, *Documents*, pp. 467 sqq.

those who did not pay their fines for non-attendance at church. There was no suggestion now that the square cap might be discarded in case of urgent cause or necessity, with the prince's permission. Nor was there, as there had been, insistence that the curate should receive the value of the chrisom or customary fees at marriages and burials.

Comparison of the *Advertisements* with the *Interpretations* and *Resolutions* shows clearly that Parker and his colleagues were now taking a firmer line to control the clergy and to force uniformity. Not only the Royal Visitors' licences to preach were invalidated, but all episcopal licences dated before 1 March 1564 (i.e. 1565), though re-admission was not to involve heavy fees (the cost of parchment, writing and wax, 'four pence and no more'). Those without licence to preach might only read the homilies; and contentious sermons were to be reported. There was no longer any suggestion of employing those who were ignorant of Latin or those who had been deprived for 'wilfulness'. Together with the insistence on the examination of ordinands and the stopping of unlicensed preaching, all this was a real attempt to check non-conforming enthusiasm, and to raise clerical standards.

The rules for uniformity were made much more exact. There was, it is true, a concession about the cope: it was now required only at communion in cathedrals and collegiate churches. But the rest of the rules about apparel were made much more explicit: surplices were to be worn at all services, and hoods by the dignitaries in cathedrals and collegiate churches. The suggestion that the table be brought before the chancel door for communion was dropped: services were to be said or sung 'decently and distinctly' in the place appointed by the Ordinary. The parish was to provide a 'decent table standing on a frame', covered with 'carpet, silk or other decent covering' and a 'fair linen cloth' at the time of ministration. All were to receive kneeling, and the ordering of thicker bread than was laid down by the Injunctions was dropped. Such alterations from the *Interpretations* all tended to insist on greater reverence—but would all seem to the radicals to be steps backward towards the old services and away from the idea of a supper or common meal. There was also stronger insistence that fonts must be used for public baptism, not basins, and that no other form than that already prescribed might be used. (This is the first official hint of the difficulties, soon to be prominent, about the baptism service.) The *Interpretations* had expressed doubts about the necessity of banns before marriage, and of the power of bishops to allow marriages in prohibited seasons; there was now nothing about these. All in all, the changes show a strong attempt to impose uniformity in celebrating the sacraments, and increased reverence.

But the most offensive part to the protestants, apart from the surplices, was the ruling about apparel out of church. The *Interpretations* had only ordered that 'all ministers,[1] and others, having any living ecclesiastical, shall go in apparel agreeable' or, after two monitions, be deposed or sequestered. The *Advertisements* contained instructions which could not be misunderstood. Archbishops and bishops were to wear their accustomed apparel. Deans and all cathedral dignitaries, Heads of colleges, doctors and bachelors of divinity or law, or any other doctors with an ecclesiastical income of over a hundred marks, and prebendaries of twenty pounds or over were to wear a 'side gown with sleeves straight at the hand' and without a cape, and tippets of sarcenet. In journeying they were to wear a cloak of like fashion. Inferior clergy were to wear long gowns of the same fashion—and all alike the cap ordered by the Injunctions. Only on a journey was a hat allowed. In the privacy of home life, clergy might dress as they would. The use of clerical apparel was forbidden to persons who had been ecclesiastical but no longer served the ministry. The determination to mark off the clergy as a class apart from the laity could hardly have been more clearly expressed. Of readers there was no mention at all; there was evidently no desire to continue them.

When he sent the *Advertisements* to Cecil, Parker was seem-

[1] It is 'ministers' in the MSS., not 'bishops', as Strype *Annals* I, i, 319.

ingly in a hopeful mood. Some of the 'silly recusants' had begun
to repent their attitude at the meeting two days before; they had
not expected that, in the 'scarcity of ministers', such firm action
would be taken; Parker had actually felt strong enough to repel
one of them until two good securities out of his parish were
forthcoming. He expected other submissions would follow. 'The
sooner . . . this determination be known abroad, the sooner shall
the speech cease, and the offence assuage, and more peace and
order to follow.'[1] A few days later he was able to tell Cecil
that though some were peevish, some froward, some fearful,
yet there were some who would 'slip in with honesty'. To them
he showed 'such affability as we may' but without any sign of
fear, urging them to obedience to the law for the people's quiet.[2]

But already there was evidence that his earlier fears had not
been exaggerated. On April 2, Dr. Crowley, Vicar of St. Giles,
Cripplegate, had refused to admit into his church for a funeral
service some 'clerks' (seemingly choristers) because they were
surpliced. To avoid a tumult, all the clerks withdrew.[3] Interviewed
by Parker two days later, Crowley was violently contentious.
He would not have such 'porters' coats' in his church, but would
resist 'the wolf', meaning the surplice men, and would continue
to preach in his church unless he were actually deprived. Thereon, Parker promptly 'discharged' him of his flock and parish.
Not unreasonably Crowley insisted that he could only be deprived by due process of law. So Parker, for the time being,
'charged him to keep his house'. The following Sunday, Parker
sent a preacher to the church to whom the congregation listened
quietly, and they also received a minister with surplice.[4]

Apparently, at St. Giles the trouble came from Crowley, the
vicar, not from the congregation. But it was not always so. On
Palm Sunday (April 7) when one of Parker's chaplains was taking
a communion service at St. Mary Magdalene, Milk Street,[5]
while he 'came down' to read the epistle and gospel, a man of the
parish took away both cup and bread from the altar because the

[1] *Correspondence*, p. 272.   [2] Ibid., pp. 275-6.   [3] Ibid.
[4] Ibid., p. 278.   [5] Ibid., pp. 277-9.

bread was not common, and so 'the minister derided, and the people disappointed'—for they had asked for the service. Here, again, the general congregation does not seem to have been antagonistic, but only an individual layman. Presumably something similar lay behind a complaint to Cecil that six hundred persons had gone to church to receive communion and had been disappointed because they found the doors shut. It looks as though, during a suspension, it had not been possible to provide an alternative minister to take the service, though the congregation wanted it. On the other hand, according to Parker, at some churches the clergy he sent to take services could only preach because neither surplice nor wafer-bread was provided (presumably by the churchwardens) and 'these precise men . . . do profess openly, that they will neither communicate nor come in the church where either the surplice or the cap is, and so I know it is practised'. Thus, once more on Palm Sunday, there was practically a riot at Little All Hallows, Thomas Street. A Scot there preached violently against the apparel, even venturing to attack the Queen. The vicar of the parish, who had accepted the surplice, smiled at the vehemence of the preacher, and was afterwards rebuked by two of the congregation. Some took his side, some the preacher's—and it ended in blows. By Easter, matters were no better, so that some parish churches were closed because of contention between parishioners and ministers. Stow gives a picture of wide-spread confusion. 'In most parishes the sexton of the church did all such service as was done, and that in his coat or gown as he commonly went about other business.' In some places, he adds, the ministers did carry on, but without surplices, wearing gowns as before.

The main burden of dealing with the troubles seems to have fallen on Parker, though Grindal, as Bishop of London, would surely have been the proper authority to handle them. He did, indeed, join with Parker to interview Crowley, but thereafter seems to have stood aside, busy with a sermon for Good Friday, April 12. On that day, Parker wrote a sad letter to Cecil. He with other commissioners, had spent a whole week over 'brabbling matters'. He was now fully tired, his health had failed and he was compelled to keep his bed. 'I can do no more, nor promise any more; my age will not suffer me to peruse all the parishes . . . must I do still all things alone?' He had reduced to obedience two incumbents in his own peculiar, and had sent out such of his chaplains as he could to serve the vacant churches. Now he was appealing for help to Grindal who was younger than he, and had more spare priests available for duty.

There is no evidence of such tumultuous doings outside London,[1] and even there they gradually died down, but not all at once. How far there was any really spontaneous movement among the general laity is doubtful; they were violent only when roused by some popular and vigorous minister or some extreme layman. Even so, congregations were often divided—which no doubt explained why some churches had to be closed. For example, on Low Sunday, at St. Mildred, Bread Street, 'the worshipful of the parish' brought a minister to officiate in a surplice and, though opposed by the vicar and some of the parish, insisted on his donning a surplice, the 'chief of the parish and the alderman's deputy' standing on guard beside him as he took the service. But by Whitsuntide, the Scot who had caused the trouble at All Hallows was wearing a surplice! Others, who were obstinate, were removed. Two readers at St. Antholin's (of which Crowley was also a reader) 'on whom the greatest number of other ministers did depend' were sent to Horne, Bishop of Winchester, for three weeks, to be 'persuaded' by him. Their journey was almost like a royal progress. They were escorted by two or three hundred women, who gave them 'bags and bottles to banquet' and 'gold, silver, sugar, spice or otherwise such as they had' and urged them to stand fast by their views. But, despite all this, they were got out of the way. Crowley, too, was sent away, to Cox at Ely, for on October 27 the Privy Council wrote to Parker and Grindal to say that Cox wished to be rid

[1] The Spanish Ambassador mentioned troubles in Essex in August—but they were, he admits, chiefly due to the discontent of clothworkers: dislike of habits and surplices were only secondary. (*Cal. S. P. Span.* i, 571.) Anyhow Essex was in the diocese of London.

of him and that his case was more fit to be tried by the bishops
than by the Council.[1] As the discontented leaders were removed[2]
or conformed, the troubles gradually died down, though as late
as the following January Grindal was 'unreverently hooted at . . .
with many opprobrious words', especially by the women of the
congregation, at St. Margaret's, Old Fish Street.[3] For Grindal
was now taking his share of the burden. In May he wrote to
Cecil to say how he had been beset by sixty women for removing
a Divinity Lecturer at St. Giles; in the same month he ordered
the Dean and Chapter of St. Paul's to use such apparel as, by the
Queen's authority, was ordered in the *Advertisements*.[4] According to the Spanish ambassador he was severely rated by the
Queen in that month for not enforcing the orders,[5] which may
partly account for his activity, if the report is true.

The chief causes of offence seem to have been the surplice and
the square cap—though wafer-bread also was disliked. But it is
clear that, at this stage, the leaders of the malcontents were not,
at any rate all of them, agitating for the sweeping reforms which
the Puritans were soon to be pressing. Crowley, for example,
can have had little objection to pluralism, for he had two London
livings as well as a prebend in St. Paul's and the Archdeaconry
of Hereford. The two other readers of St. Antholin's associated
with him were both also beneficed in Winchester diocese, which
was the reason why Horne had to deal with them. Moreover,
once such hotheads were removed from the storm centre in
London, they seem to have been treated with a generous toleration which may well have helped to smooth out the troubles.
Though Crowley was deprived of the living of St. Giles and
resigned his Archdeaconry, later on he was made vicar of St.
Lawrence, Jewry. One of the other readers of St. Antholin's
subsequently had a living in Kent where he served without

[1] *Acts of Privy Council*, vii, 315.
[2] At least five in all—*Zurich Letters*, ii, 119.
[3] The above details come from Parker's *Correspondence* and Stow's
Memoranda (*Three Fifteenth-Century Chronicles*, ed. J. Gairdner, Camden
Society, London, 1880), pp. 135, 138–40.
[4] *Cal. S. P. Dom.*, pp. 271, 272.   [5] *Cal. S. P. Span.* i, 553.

surplice. Indeed, in June 1566, it was said that there was no need to 'put on a surplice when preaching, as indeed nobody is commanded to do, except in the administration of infant baptism and of the Lord's Supper'.[1] And, in 1567, certain venerated stalwarts—Lawrence, Sampson, Lever—still had official leave to preach in London without wearing the habits.[2] Such leniency, doubtless, was wise within limits; it did at least prevent the action taken by the authorities from having the appearance of persecution—as did also the fact that the Queen excused from payment of first-fruits those who were deprived 'for refusing to wear such distinct and decent apparel as by public order is commanded'.[3] None the less, at the height of the trouble, Parker wrote as though he were at the end of his tether—'Can it be thought that I alone, having sun and moon against me, can compass this difficulty? . . . If I die in the cause (malice so far prevailing) I shall commit my soul to God in a good conscience.'[4]

Besides disorders in London, the *Advertisements* provoked a further reaction which was to last much longer and ultimately to express a wider discontent than dislike of mere apparel. Many of the returned exiles were far from satisfied when reform in England halted so far short of continental standards. Even those at Frankfort who had quarrelled with Knox and remained substantially loyal to the Edwardian settlement had yet introduced changes even in that. They had given up 'private baptisms, confirmation of children, saints' days, kneeling at Holy Communion, the linen surplice of ministers, crosses and other things of like character'.[5] They, and still more those who had been drawn to Swiss usages, were hoping for still further changes. The *Advertisements* were therefore a bitter blow. They showed

---

[1] *Zurich Letters*, ii, 118. The writer, John Abel, was a merchant much used for forwarding communications between England and Switzerland. His statement is clearly wrong, so far as strict legal requirements were concerned, but it does bear witness to a wide-spread tolerance in administration that he could have written as he did.

[2] Strype, *Grindal*, p. 171; *Parte of a Register* (no date or place: probably Edinburgh, 1593), p. 27.

[3] Strype, *Parker* iii, 153–4.   [4] *Correspondence*, pp. 280–1.

[5] *Tudor Puritanism* (M. M. Knappen, Chicago, 1939), p. 148.

that, so far as Parker and the Bishops were concerned, there was
to be no further change. The result was the rapid emergence of a
definitely Puritan party—the name was in use by the winter of
1567–8[1]—which expressed its views in a long series of pamphlets.
At first it was still only the habits which were attacked, but before
long bitter criticism was directed to almost every point in which
the 'best reformed churches' had not been copied. In the end,
a completely presbyterian system was advocated by some, though
others, while still favouring simplicity in services, would have tolerated episcopacy provided that many so-called abuses were removed.

Before his ordination by Ridley, Crowley had been a printer.
Now, 'The whole multitude of London ministers, every one of
them giving their advice in writing unto Robert Crowley',[2] he
compiled and printed '*A brief Discourse against the Outward
Apparel and Ministring Garments of the Popish Church*'.
Though it opened with the rather ominous desire that ministries
should be 'erected according to His institution so far as possible
. . . utterly removing and forsaking all those unprofitable ceremonies and rites which men have devised without sure ground in
God's holy word', it yet thereafter confined itself to the matter
of apparel. While admitting that, in themselves, the garments
were indifferent, it yet urged that now, because of their associations, they were destructive. Therefore, as St. Paul said all
things should be done for edifying, they should be abolished.
The 'simple Christians' were shocked by them, 'obstinate
papists' encouraged; as they were a stumbling block they should
be removed; their imposition by the Prince was the denial of
Christian liberty and suggested that religion was merely a matter
at the disposal of royalty. Strype gives a long analysis of the
pamphlet,[3] which is fair but does not fully represent its force-
fulness and zeal. It is full of Scriptural references which, even
if they do not prove the points in question, yet give the impression that the Bible was definitely against the use of surplices.
There was, too, throughout, a high note of willingness to face

---

[1] Stow's *Memoranda*, p. 143.   [2] Ibid., p. 139.
[3] *Annals*, i, ii, 163 sq.

martyrdom for the cause—'Our goods, our bodies, our lives we
do with all humble submission yield to God's officers upon earth;
but our conscience we keep unspotted in the sight of him that
shall judge all men.'

An answer to the pamphlet quickly appeared—*A brief examination for the time of a certain Declaration,* etc. It is usually said
that Parker either composed, or at least was the inspirer of, this
reply. Despite the lack of certain proof, it is not reasonable to
doubt his responsibility for it. It was issued by the Queen's
Printer, Richard Jugge, and thus had a sort of official character.
Moreover, on May 3, Cox wrote 'Your grace's last I received by
Jugg, one of the Queen's Majesty's printers, wherein I perceive
your travail and zeal'.[1] It is difficult not to suppose that the
reference is to the *Brief Examination*. And the argument throughout is such as would have been congenial to Parker. It is longer
but less impassioned than the *Discourse*, and does, it must be
admitted, contain a good many rather niggling logical points.
But there is also much quiet wisdom and common sense. If every
minister is to be allowed to decide for himself what does or does
not edify, that is to give 'to every man in his parish an absolute
authority.' The argument that it is the 'simple' who are grieved
seems to suggest that it is the simple who are to judge of all men
and all doctrine. 'You will have everyman to understand as much
as the Prince and Council knoweth and understandeth.' 'Here
is perilous authority granted to every subject, to determine
the Prince's laws.' The fear of that sort of popular indiscipline
was very deeply implanted in Parker. Again, that surplices
confirmed the obstinate papist was much more often asserted
than proved; it might well be that surplices helped to conciliate
those who liked the old ways—a view which Parker certainly
held. In fact, the simple only objected because they were led to
do so by the discontented ministers who should now teach them
better. If there were abuses, they could wait until reform could
be made quietly and without loss of unity. Anyhow, Christ's
'little ones' had no right to be offended at what was lawfully

[1] *Correspondence*, p. 281.

ordered. It might be that the garments had been abused in the past, but it was possible 'rightly to use rites and fashions abused, all the abuses being clearly condemned'—after all, they did still use the bells, the churches, and the pulpits which had been 'horribly abused' of old. It is more than once insisted that the garments are not 'enforced as the service of God' but only for 'decency and order'. That they were not commanded in Scripture was beside the point, for many things were left open by Scripture 'to the disposition of Christ's Church from time to time'—when to fast, the services of baptism and communion, besides much else. Christian liberty was not concerned with such things, but was 'altogether spiritual and pertaineth only to the conscience'. The tract ends with a strong exhortation to the ministers not to distract their flocks by disputation, nor to neglect them by deserting their posts.

As an appendix were added certain letters which might have been expected to appeal to the dissidents, from the time of Hooper's resistance to wearing the habits. There was Cranmer's letter to Bucer and the latter's reply that such habits might be used 'with God's pleasure' provided that they were lawfully ordered and it was made clear that there was no desire to establish any 'wicked devices' of Anti-Christ. Bucer thought that, so used, the garments might well have a useful significance. There was, too, Peter Martyr's letter to Hooper. He shared the latter's wish to get rid of all superfluities in favour of 'chaste and simple purity'—and so would have preferred to be rid of 'diversity of apparel'. But that was a preference, and he was not persuaded by Hooper's arguments to affirm 'the use of such vestures to be pernicious, or of their own nature contrary to God's word; for I do utterly think it to be a thing indifferent'. It was therefore better to submit than to strive so bitterly as to hinder the Gospel. He was certainly not prepared to say that nothing ever used by popery could be used to good purpose. A letter of the extremist à Lasco was also printed, to the same effect.

Even if not actually composed by Parker, the *Brief Examination* was undoubtedly the expression on his point of view, put out with his approval. Its reasonableness and moderation might well have carried conviction, if there had been any desire on the other side for compromise. But there was not. The very speed with which the *Brief Discourse* appeared after the *Advertisements* showed that its writers were spoiling for a fight. It must have come out well within a month, if Cox's letter on May 3 already applied to the *Brief Examination* which answered it. It was, too, apparently already known abroad by the end of May.[1] The result of the *Examination* was not therefore peace, but a long *Answer for the time to the Examination*, and a wearying series of other pamphlets. Parker was, naturally, worried, and complained to Cecil early in June. It was true that Grindal, having now felt 'the marks and bounds of those good sprights' who could have been suppressed five or six years ago but for his toleration, was now roused. But Parker wanted 'personages of reputation'—presumably the Council—to take stronger action.[2] Perhaps it was as a result of his complaint that the Council did at the end of June confirm certain orders submitted for their approval by the ecclesiastical commission. No one was to print or cause to be printed, nor to import into the realm, any book against the force and meaning of any 'ordinance, prohibition or commandment, contained or to be contained in any of the statutes or laws of this realm, or in any injunctions, letters patent or ordinances passed or set forth, or to be passed or set forth, by the Queen's grant, commission or authority'. Any such books were to be forfeited, and their printers to be imprisoned and to lose the privilege of printing. Any who offered such books for sale were to be fined, and the Stationers' Company was to be empowered to make search in warehouses and shops, and even in ships' cargoes ('to open and view all packs, dry fats, maunds, and other things, wherein books or papers shall be contained'). Half of the fines imposed were to go to the informer.[3] The order was severe and comprehensive—but quite ineffective.

[1] *Correspondence*, p. 282.   [2] Ibid., p. 284.
[3] Strype, *Parker* i, 442, is the authority for this. The Register of the Privy Council is a blank for this period.

More fuel was shortly added to the fire. In February, Humphrey and Sampson, possibly sensing what was to come, had written separately to Bullinger to ask his opinion about the habits, Sampson breaking down his general discontent into a number of explicit—and leading—questions. Should 'Churchmen' be distinguished from the laity by clothes? Was it right to have anything of habits or rites in common with papists? Should even a royal edict be obeyed? Was it not better to resign?[1] Bullinger replied to both in May[2]—very patiently and reasonably, and much in the spirit of Martyr's letter to Hooper which he quotes with approval as really settling the matter. He plainly disliked the scrupulosity and contentiousness of his correspondents—'the subject being divided into so many questions and entangled in such complicated knots'. As the habits were ordered for decency only, there was no fear of superstition—and it was absurd to say that they could not use anything which the papists used. He regarded clothes as really a matter of indifference, and 'could wish that pious ministers would not make the whole advancement of religion to depend on this matter, as if it were all in all; but that they would yield somewhat to the present time, and not dispute offensively about a matter of indifference'. 'We must take care . . . lest we cloke our own feelings under the pretext of offence.' 'We shall do the church a greater injury by deserting it than by wearing the habits.' He finally warned them against concealing 'a contentious spirit under the name of conscience.'

It was not the sort of answer which was either desired or expected. What made it worse was that Bullinger, wishing to play fair, sent a copy of it to Horne, Bishop of Winchester, because 'we would not have any private communication with the brethren, without the knowledge of you, the principal ministers'.[3] Horne was asked to communicate it to Parkhurst, Jewel, Sandys and Pilkington: they had all been at Zurich and were personally known to Bullinger. In a postscript, Bullinger asked that it should also be shown to Grindal, even though he was not

---

[1] *Zurich Letters*, i, 151–5.   [2] Ibid., i, 345 sqq.   [3] Ibid., i, 356.

personally known to him, because he was an 'illustrious person-
age' whose good will Bullinger desired. As there was thus
nothing to suggest that the letter to Sampson and Humphrey was
confidential, it was quickly published by Grindal.[1] Later on it
re-appeared (still in 1566) as part of a pamphlet entitled '*Whether
it be mortal sin to transgress civil laws which be the commandments of civil magistrates*'. This was printed by Richard Jugge,
printer to the Queen, and therefore was in a sense official. Its
contents suggest that Parker now was behind it. The pamphlet
contained an introduction pressing for obedience to the laws in
matters indifferent, else 'barbarousness and destruction' would
ensue. There is a passage from Melanchthon on Romans xii,
drawing out the Christian's duty to the state; then Bullinger's
letter to Sampson and Humphrey and the covering letter to
Horne; Cranmer's letter to Bucer and the latter's reply, Hooper
to Bucer and Martyr's reply. It was an impressive compendium
which might well be expected to carry weight with those who
were constantly urging the example of 'the best reformed
churches'.

But they were not to be convinced. Dissatisfied with Bullinger's
letter (even, apparently, before it was broadcast) Sampson and
Humphrey, joined now by Coverdale, addressed their complaints
to Farel and Beza at Geneva in June.[2] Very significantly they
did not now confine themselves to the matter of the habits
but grumbled about other things too—the unleavened bread at
communion, and kneeling to receive, the obtrusion of ceremonies
on the church by the Sovereign. They asked for the views of
Geneva and besought the intervention of that church with the
bishops. Then, in July, they returned to the attack with a joint
reply to Bullinger.[3] It was long and contentious, for they had
found Bullinger's letter 'not entirely to our satisfaction', and
complained that it had been published 'without our knowledge
or consent'. They argued their case with ingenuity and scholarship, and, touched by the suggestion that they were contentious,

---

[1] *Zurich Letters*, i, 168. It was already published by July—*Zurich Letters*,
ii, 124.   [2] Ibid., ii, 121 sqq.   [3] Ibid., i, 157 sqq.

indignantly denied that they were too scrupulous. 'We make no vexatious opposition; we always avoid any bitterness of con- tention', 'far be it from us either to make our own feelings the pretence of abuse, or under the name of conscience to conceal a fondness for dispute'. At the end, as in the letter to Beza, they insist that the controversy is 'of no light or trifling character but of great importance'. It is not merely about a cap or a surplice, but of 'straws and chips of the popish religion', of which they gave a list, in an appendix, which really included all the main points of the early Puritan platform. There is a kind of 'popish superstition' in the conduct of the services; the singing is too elaborate and organs are increasingly used; in baptism, the infant is addressed, the sponsors reply, there is the signing with the cross, and women are allowed to baptize; there is the cope, kneeling to receive the wafer-bread at communion; the habits are to be worn out of doors. As to 'discipline, the sinews of religion' 'there is none at all, neither has our church its rod, or any exercise of superintendence'. The giving of the ring at betrothal is popish, and women continue to wear a veil for churching. 'Almost all things are saleable in the court of the metropolitan; pluralities of benefices, licences of non-residence, for not entering into orders, for eating meat on days forbidden and in Lent.' 'Free liberty of preaching' is taken away, and the Article of Edward VI which 'took away the real presence' is now mutilated and imperfect.

It is an odd mixture of very serious and rather trifling com- plaints; of matters of real principle with points of personal preference. But there is nothing to suggest that the writers objected to episcopacy as such ('we have always thought well of the bishops', they say) or that they regarded the calling and ordination of ministers as inadequate, or that they wished for a presbyterian form of government. It is, in fact, the expression of that Puritanism which accepted the existing polity of the Church of England but wished for further reform. Though it was the insistence on clerical dress which had provoked this summing up of 'blemishes' in the church, henceforward the habits take their

place as only one of the matters of complaint—and little by little
the list was increased by the most tedious and trifling additions.
Parker's fears had been justified, and for the rest of his life he was
to be harried by these 'precisians' as he was soon to term them.
None the less, it is difficult not to respect them despite their
perhaps over-scrupulosity. They were conscientious and, in the
main, loyal members of the Church of England who firmly
rejected anabaptism, separatism and even the Presbyterian
movement soon to develop, as well as Romanism.

Some of their grievances were surely justified—pluralism, non-
residence, the sale of livings, the conduct of the ecclesiastical
courts. Certainly they had a good many sympathizers in their
day even in court circles—Cecil himself, though he openly
backed Parker in insistence that the law should be obeyed,
yet was anxious so far as he could to protect them against any
excessive penalties: they regarded him as their friend. But they
did not get from abroad the support they desired and expected—
possibly their position was too faithfully Anglican for that.
Beza, as a result of their letter, wrote to Bullinger[1] to urge him
to try to interfere by sending someone officially to England to
solicit the Queen and bishops for a remedy. (It was useless for
the Church of Geneva to do so because it was 'hateful to that
Queen'.) But his letter shows that he was far ahead of Sampson and
Humphrey and would not have been satisfied by the changes they
wanted. He desired nothing short of Geneva, as his criticisms
show. The ministers were not called by 'a congregation of the
brethren', but ordained at the pleasure of the bishops, and that
without specific cures; there was no 'discipline', and in place of a
'lawfully appointed presbytery' they had 'deans, chancellors
and archdeacons' who administered the old canon law. As
clerical marriage was not legally allowed, there was little removal
from the law of celibacy. (He ignored the obvious fact that, in
practice, there was no bar to the marriage of clergy.) Papists
were still left in possession of their benefices. Only after all
that did he come in his letter to such abuses as dispensations,

[1] *Zurich Letters*, ii, 127 sq.

the silencing of 'teachers of the pure Gospel' and clerical dress.
In fact, 'the papacy was never abolished in that country, but
rather transferred to the Sovereign . . . nothing else is now aimed
at, than the gradual restoration of what had been in any measure
altered'. He plainly would not be content with anything less
than the full presbyterian model, and his support for moderate
reform was therefore likely to be suspect rather than useful.
Nor would Bullinger do much to help him. He was indeed
annoyed that his letter to Sampson and Humphrey had been
published without his consent, and was at pains to write to
several people in England to point out that it was concerned
solely with the habits and must not be thought to support the
blemishes (of which Sampson and Humphrey had not told him)
of which he did not know when he wrote and of which he did
not approve.[1] But he refused to send any such official representa-
tion as Beza had suggested, and replied to Sampson and Humphrey that he hoped his letter would not be distorted to represent
him as favouring 'the restoration of things that every pious person
. . . has long known us to disapprove of'.[2] He ended his letter
with a reminder that ministers were required 'by every possible
means (to) preserve peace in the church; and not by their too
great vehemence, unreasonableness, and caprice, desiring indeed
what is good, but not with prudence, (to) throw an obstacle in the
way of religion'. By August 1567, he was writing to Beza that he
could not 'withdraw our entire confidence in the bishops'. The
trouble started from 'too much rigour' on the part of the objectors,
but the feelings had been so exasperated on both sides, that
'each party was now to blame'. And so they in Zurich were
'determined among ourselves to have nothing more to do with
any one in this controversy . . . and this is now our decided
resolution. And if any other parties think of coming hither, let
them know that they will come to no purpose'.[3] Thus neither
from Geneva nor Zurich did Sampson and Humphrey and those
who thought like them get any effective support. Zurich came

---

[1] *Zurich Letters*, i, 357 sqq., ii, 136, 138.   [2] Ibid., i, 361 sq.
[3] Ibid., ii, 154–5.

down on the side of the bishops, Geneva dared not intervene. Indeed Grindal was able to tell Bullinger that, thanks to his letter, few had left the ministry, and of the few deprived Sampson was the only man of real learning[1]—a serious understatement.[2]

[1] *Zurich Letters*, i, 168, 175-6.   [2] Ibid., ii, 147.

CHAPTER XIII

PARLIAMENT OF 1566: GROWING RESTLESSNESS

AT the end of September 1566 the Parliament of 1563 was recalled for a second session: the Queen badly needed a subsidy. Though in the end she got it, Parliament was not so much concerned about that as about her marriage or at the least the nomination of a successor to the throne if she were to die childless. On such questions the Queen firmly refused to be controlled or advised, and relations between her and the Commons were seriously strained. She was very angry with them, and on one occasion is reported to have said that 'she did not know what these devils wanted'.[1] Her irritation may have some bearing on her treatment of the attempts by Parliament to deal with religion.

Early in the session the difficulties raised by Bonner concerning episcopal consecration were dealt with, in response, says the Spanish ambassador, to a petition from the bishops.[2] A Bill was rapidly passed through all its stages in the Commons in October to avoid 'slanderous speech' about the 'making of Archbishops and Bishops within this realm'. A long introduction explained what had happened under Henry VIII and Edward VI. It asserted that the Ordinal of Edward VI was in 'full force and effect' as an addition to the Prayer Book authorized by Parliament under Edward; and all things done in accordance with it were 'declared, judged and decreed at and from every of the several times of the doing thereof good and perfect to all respects and purposes'. So far as there was any legal (as distinct from ecclesiastical) doubt of the consecration of the bishops, the Bill was completely satisfactory.

---

[1] Cal. S. P. Span. i, 590.   [2] Ibid., p. 588.

When it came before the Lords, however, there was opposition and even when a proviso had been added there were still eleven dissentients. The proviso limited the confirmation of the bishops' actions to 'only those acts which they had done in discharge of their office . . . excepting, however, all matters relating to life and property'.[1] The first exception would rule out the proceedings against Bonner, the second might lead to great confusion and distress if all the bishops' dealings in property were liable to be called in question. When the Bill was returned to the Commons with the proviso there was delay. The bishops were alarmed and met together to try to devise a means for its passing.[2] In the end, the Commons did pass the Bill, but with a different proviso substituted for that of the Lords—that no one was to be impeached or molested because of any episcopal certificate heretofore made concerning the refusal of the Supremacy oath, and that all tendering of the oath by the bishops up to the end of the current session was void and of none effect. With that proviso, the Lords passed the Bill in December and with the Queen's assent it became law.[3] The whole procedure throws an interesting light on the mood of the two Houses. No doubt the original proviso was suggested to propitiate some members of the Lords who were attached to Bonner and the old religion. It is not easy to see why the Commons, with its very active and forceful group of protestants, would not accept it. It can hardly have been due to a passion to attack Bonner, for their own proviso protected him; and they were not, on the whole, favourably disposed to the new bishops. But, as later bills in the session were to prove, the extremist leaders were concerned at the moment not to upset the whole episcopal polity of the church, but to secure further reform in it without destroying episcopacy: they were, as yet, protestant but not presbyterian. They were content therefore to reach a compromise, agreeing to the proviso which protected Bonner in return for the confirmation of the bishops and all they had done up to date, save the administration of the Supremacy oath. But the right to administer that did not

---

[1] *Cal. S. P. Span.* i, 596.   [2] Ibid., p. 600.   [3] 8. Eliz. c.1, proviso.

depend on the validity or otherwise of the consecration; the 'Assurance of Supremacy Act' of 1563 had definitely allowed them to tender the oath to ecclesiastics in their dioceses, and that power significantly was not taken away from them for the future: it could be regarded as not affected by the validity of their consecration.

It is inconceivable that Parker was not much concerned about such proceedings, though there is no evidence either in the Journal of the Lords or in his correspondence that he took any part at all. The explanation can only be that he was not well. On the 1st of November he appointed proxies for himself in the Lords, because of indisposition, and Convocation, which was meeting concurrently, was moved to Lambeth for his convenience.[1] But further action over religious matters in the Commons soon caused trouble which he could not escape. On December 5 and 6 various Bills (referred to as A, B, C, etc.) were introduced and read in the Commons. The first (A) was for confirmation of 'a little book printed in the year 1562 . . . for the sound Christian religion'.[2] It had three readings in the Commons and one in the Lords before the Queen peremptorally ordered that it should be no further proceeded with. Its purpose was to give statutory authority to the articles passed by Convocation in 1563. It is sometimes said that it ordered also clerical subscription to the Articles (no doubt because later the Act of 1571 did so), but that is not stated in the Journal either of the Commons or the Lords; and later on Parker and the bishops refer to the Bill simply as giving 'confirmation' or 'approbation' to the Articles.[3] If that was all that was involved, it is difficult to see why Elizabeth was furious—after all, Parliament had been allowed to pass the Uniformity Act, a much more serious matter than merely confirming the articles approved by Convocation. Possibly her irritation with the Commons over the succession question was partly to blame—but certainly she was very angry. She sent for Parker and other bishops on December 20 and evidently berated

[1] Strype, *Parker* i, 478.   [2] D'Ewes, p. 132.
[3] *Correspondence*, pp. 293–4.

them that a bill of religion had been promoted in Parliament without her knowledge or assent.[1] The Spanish ambassador remarks that the bishops came away from the interview 'crest-fallen'.[2] In a letter to Cecil, Parker explained his position. Possibly the Queen had not full information, for Cecil, too, had been ill: but he himself knew nothing of the Bill's introduction in the Commons and had not been present when it was read in the Lords. He understood that the Queen objected not to the contents of the book but to the manner of its putting forth.[3] There followed a letter to the Queen from Parker, the Archbishop of York and thirteen other bishops, couched in the most humble terms[4]—'that it would please your Highness, according to your accustomed benignity, to have gracious consideration of their humble suit ensuing'—urging the Queen to let the Bill go forward. But she firmly refused: no doubt the Commons must be taught the limitations of their province: matters of religion were not for them, but for the Queen and the bishops. She seems, however, to have been satisfied that the bishops were not to blame when she had their answer about their 'doings' on December 27, though once again Parker through illness was not able to be present at her meeting with the Archbishop of York.[5]

The other Bills about religion did not get more than a single reading in the Commons, but are of interest as showing what the agitators for further reform wanted. They were concerned with order of ministers (presumably age and qualifications), residence, avoidance of corrupt presentations, leases of benefices, pensions payable from benefices.[6] Doubtless they were attempts to deal with what would now be universally agreed were abuses. But there is no hint there that even the extremists were trying as yet to upset the episcopal government of the church.

Any hopes that such gentleness towards the Marian bishops on the one hand or the refusal to allow statutory sanction to the Articles on the other might lead to a lessening of tension soon

[1] *Correspondence*, p. 291.   [2] *Cal. S. P. Span.* i, 606.
[3] *Correspondence*, pp. 291–2.   [4] Ibid., p. 292–4.   [5] Ibid., p. 291, note.
                    [6] D'Ewes, pp. 132, 185.

proved to be illusory. During the next few years opposition to the settlement grew violently, both on the side of the Romans and of the extremer reformers. So far as the Romans were concerned, treatment was at first very gentle. Parker's wish that the Supremacy oath should not be asked for a second time (though it could still legally be demanded) was now fulfilled. Not even Bonner was attacked again—though he was kept in prison until his death in 1569: he was too dangerous to be set at large. Watson of Lincoln, too, had to be kept under surveillance or in prison till his death in 1584: he seems to have defeated by his intrigues any attempts to treat him generously. But Heath died at liberty, in his own house, in 1579. Thirlby was more or less free, though under the eye of the Archbishop, till his death in 1570—indeed Parker was rebuked by Cecil in 1567 for allowing him too much freedom![1] Others, too, were well treated, and some of them even managed to escape abroad.[2] Moreover, the Queen was obviously on extremely good terms with the Spanish ambassador, de Silva, and talked to him (apparently, at least) in great confidence, if his letters may be trusted. Even Parker, for all his tolerance, was upset by their intimacy; he feared that the Queen might be enchanted by him, and prayed that she might be enabled to 'understand all foreign sleights'.[3] Despite all this tolerance—possibly encouraged by it—the attitude of Roman non-conformity was alarmingly stiffening, especially in the northern counties, notably in Lancashire. Here the enthusiast William Allen, himself a Lancashire man, who had fled abroad in 1561 and was ultimately the founder of the College at Douai, was busy in 1562–6, bitterly attacking the growing habit of Catholics to save themselves by occasional attendance at church. He was also active near Oxford and in Norfolk where he had the protection of the Duke. But his chief work was in Lancashire, and it was probably due to his fiery zeal that recusancy became so strongly entrenched there. His work was backed in 1566 by

---

[1] *Cal. S. P. Span.* i, 682.   [2] Gee, *Elizabethan Clergy*, pp. 192–6.
[3] Strype, *Parker* i, 518, quoting a letter of July 17, 1567, not given in the *Correspondence*.

the mission of Laurence Vaux—also a Lancashire man—who firmly taught that any who attended the English services were not in a state of salvation. He was followed by other delegates, officially commissioned by the Pope to reconcile such Romans as had lapsed into occasional conformity.[1] For the new Pope, Pius V (1566), was not content to wait on events in England, but was determined to interfere. The result was that the extent of recusancy in Lancashire soon became notorious, and a cause of justifiable anxiety. As early as December 1567 certain of the gentry there had bound themselves by oath not to come to communion; in the following February the Queen issued a commission to the Earl of Derby, the Bishop of Chester and the Sheriff of Lancashire to attach persons who, under pretence of religion, were drawing gentry and others from their duty and allegiance, and in the same month there was a letter to the sheriff to arrest some deprived ministers, whose names were given (including Vaux and one of Bonner's chaplains), and another to the Bishop to enforce conformity in his diocese.[2] By March, the Spanish ambassador had heard that in Lancashire (where, he wrote, nearly all the people were Catholics) many folk of position had been arrested for refusing to take communion and for having mass celebrated in their houses; in April, he reported that three of them had been sent to London for trial by the Council.[3] It is true that in the following November the Bishop sent a reassuring report of his proceedings, and emphasized the conformity of the gentry among whom the preaching of the Dean of St. Pauls (Nowell, himself a Lancashire man) had been particularly effective[4]—he had gone there specially to deal with the situation. But Downman, the Bishop, was easy going and readily satisfied. Events were soon to show that recusancy was not effectively suppressed in Lancashire. In the following May (1569) the Spanish ambassador declared that 'All the North and Wales are, for the great part, Catholic'.[5] Of course, allowances

---

[1] Dixon, *History* vi, 217–22. [2] *Cal. S. P. Dom.*, pp. 305, 307.
[3] *Cal. S. P. Span.* ii, 12, 22. [4] *Cal. S. P. Dom.*, pp. 321–2.
[5] *Cal. S. P. Span.* ii, 147.

must be made; de Spes was a new ambassador and not always wise or well informed—he succeeded the subtle and cautious de Silva in 1568, and at once began to engage in plots. Many of his comments show how seriously he failed to understand the position in England; he was ridiculously optimistic about the chances of a successful Catholic rising. Still a report of the Bishop of Bangor to the Council in October 1567 suggests that he was right about at least parts of Wales, where was great use of images, altars, pilgrimages.[1] And in the north, where the arrival of Queen Mary of Scotland in May 1568 and her captivity provided a focus for the discontented, the uprising of the Northern Earls at the end of 1569 shows how wide-spread catholicism was among the gentry. Even after the rebellion had been crushed with considerable severity Grindal, when he became Archbishop of York, found the greater part of the gentry not well affected to 'godly religion', while there were many superstitious practices among the common people.[2] Both Pilkington and Grindal, in July 1570, told Bullinger how the people were longing for a fresh disturbance.[3]

There was trouble in London, too, centred on the Spanish and Portuguese embassies. In December 1567, while de Silva was still ambassador, some Englishmen who had attended mass at the embassy were brought before the commissioners, and six of them were put in prison for refusing the oath.[4] By January 1569 de Spes was so deeply suspect that he was under house arrest, his messengers and all who came to the embassy were spied upon[5]—not unnaturally, for he was deeply involved through Ridolfi in plotting on behalf of Mary of Scotland.[6] In May he reported that Catholics were being severely treated, that the prisons were full of them and that the house of a rich Spanish merchant had been entered by government officers who carried away many crucifixes and statues of the Virgin and saints which were greeted with jeers by the mob, and then publicly burned.[7] Similarly, in October 1568 there was interference with the

[1] *Cal. S. P. Dom.*, p. 301.   [2] Ibid., p. 390.   [3] *Zurich Letters*, i, 223, 225.
[4] *Cal. S. P. Span.* i, 686.   [5] Ibid., ii, 97, 113, 134.   [6] Ibid., ii, 164.
[7] Ibid., ii, 148.

Portuguese embassy. Agents of the Bishop of London actually entered the house to arrest Englishmen who were at service there, and a hostile crowd collected outside. The Bishop assured Cecil that his messengers had, in their zeal, exceeded his orders; they should not have entered. But the Mayor of London declared that he would rather help the bishop than discipline the mob.[1]

It is strange that de Spes, in view of such disturbances, should have regarded the cause of Catholicism as popular, for he did admit that the Queen's government was generally acceptable.[2] His mistake was that he over-estimated the number and the fervour of the English Catholics. None the less, there was sufficient support for papalism to force the authorities to act. The refusers sent up from Lancashire in the spring of 1568 were committed to ward, but by July had all been brought to submission, save Sir John Southworth who was sent to Parker and the commissioners. He refused, on grounds of conscience, to take the oath prescribed for him, though he was prepared to promise not to entertain in the future 'disordered persons'; but he would not attend his parish church nor receive communion.[3] He asked to be allowed to leave the country. He seems to have been released,[4] but in the next year was imprisoned again and was a great nuisance to Grindal and Nowell, who could do nothing with him—though the former urged in the end that he might be released for fear of 'prison sickness'.[5] In his determination to 'follow the faith of his fathers' and to 'die in the faith wherein he was baptized' his sheer conservatism was probably typical of many of the north country gentry; and it is plain that the government was very patient in its endeavours not to make a martyr of him. But he could not just be ignored, nor others like him. There were still, seemingly at the end of November (the date is uncertain), dealings of the commissioners with Lancashire recusants.[6] The Council in 1569 wrote round the whole country

---

[1] *Cal. S. P. Span.* ii, 80, and *Cal. S. P. Dom.*, p. 321.
[2] *Cal. S. P. Span.* ii, 157. [3] *Correspondence*, pp. 328–31.
[4] Strype, *Parker* i, 526. [5] Grindal, *Remains*, pp. 305, 306.
[6] *Cal. S. P. Dom.*, p. 321.

requiring J.P.s (on whom, after all, the local government of the country really depended) to take an oath to observe the Act of Uniformity, and from November onwards the State Papers are full of lists of those J.P.s who had agreed to do so. It was a serious attempt to check recusancy among influential local men all over the country just about the time of the Northern Rebellion.

Nor was Parker himself idle in the matter. As early as the beginning of 1568 he was demanding from the lawyers attached to the Court of Arches an oath to the Royal Supremacy—de Silva was quite sure that it was against the Queen's wishes, but felt that it would be unwise for him to try to interfere![1] The next year Parker was also concerned in the attempt to deal with the many recusant members of the Inns of Court, though here the chief agent seems to have been Grindal, urged on by the Council.[2]

On the other side, the measures of 1566—*Advertisements* and in Parliament—resulted in an outbreak of actual separatism. The best known case is that of the meeting in Plumbers' Hall in June 1567, the account of which from the Puritan side is still preserved.[3] The hall had been hired under pretence of a wedding, but had been used for a meeting which was attended by about a hundred folk. Fourteen or fifteen were sent to prison, and of these seven were brought to trial before the Lord Mayor, Grindal, the Dean of Westminster (Goodman) and other commissioners. If there is partiality in the account of the trial, it would obviously be on behalf of the prisoners rather than of Grindal, for it is a Puritan account. Even so, Grindal comes out rather well—he was patient, reasonable and, indeed, to some extent sympathetic. He admitted that he had in the past said mass and was sorry for it, and that even now he would rather minister at Paul's without cope or surplice, which he wore only 'for order's sake and obedience to the Prince'. But he had re-

---

[1] *Cal. S. P. Span.* ii, 4, 5, 6.

[2] Strype, *Parker* i, 567 sqq., and *Grindal*, pp. 203 sqq. According to Strype, some of the questions put in the interrogatories were in Parker's own hand.

[3] *Parte of a Register*, pp. 23 sqq.; reprinted in Grindal's *Remains*, pp. 201–216.

ceived letters from the Council that the dissidents were to 'leave off'. If possible they were to be brought to conformity by gentleness; else they were to lose their 'freedom of the city and abide that would follow'. The charges were that they had absented themselves from their parish churches, and that they had made assemblies 'using prayers and preachings, yea, and ministering the sacraments among yourselves'. He urged them to conformity on the grounds that the doctrines of the Church were truly reformed and that the habits were in themselves indifferent and the use of them legitimately ordered by authority.

The prisoners were difficult but Grindal, though much provoked, did not lose his temper. Of their sincerity there can be no doubt, but their enthusiasm was so excited that one or other of them kept bursting in when others were being questioned. They did not deny that they could still hear preachers of their choice—Sampson and Lever (though they had been deprived) and Coverdale (whom they surprisingly call 'Father Coverdale'), though they had difficulty in finding out where he was to preach as he dare not publish the places beforehand. What had really touched them off was the insistence on the habits which they were not prepared to tolerate even as an order of the state. But they had other grievances, too, of the sort now coming more to the front—the maintenance of 'the Pope's canon law', livings still held by those who had been papists, the use of wafer-bread, the functions of Godparents at baptism, the observance of Saints' days on which no work could be done, the absence of discipline as exercised in the best reformed churches. They maintained that 'we hold nothing that is not warranted by the word of God'. So, remembering that there had been secret assemblies under Queen Mary, they had broken away and had used the book of the English exiles at Geneva, approved by Calvin himself. Nothing would shake them in their conviction that the habits were contrary to Scripture, and therefore could not be legitimately ordered by the Prince—and they were sent back to prison.

Nor were they an isolated example. Stow says that about this time there were 'many congregations of the Anabaptists in

London, who called themselves Puritans or Unspotted Lambs of the Lord'.[1] They met in secret in varying places—one group in the Minories, then in a lighter in St. Catherine's Pool, then in a house—but only two, the preacher and the householder, were arrested. On another occasion seven were arrested in a minister's house in Pudding Lane. Later on (in March 1568) about sixty were taken in a house near the Savoy, but only three were sent to prison—and so on. Clearly, there were a good many of them—Stow gives other instances—but the authorities wished to stop them without wholesale imprisonments. Once Grindal, forewarned of a meeting, actually bade the constables to let them alone. De Silva, too, had a good deal to say about them. In February 1568, about 150 met in a house where the preacher 'used half a tub for a pulpit, and was girded with a white cloth'; in imitation of the early Christians, they divided money and food among the poorer members. But only six were arrested (possibly to be identified with the second incident above in Stow). There were said to be at least 5,000 of them in London. In March, orders were given to release those in prison on condition that within twenty days they either conformed or left the country. But again in June there were arrests (unless de Silva gives various accounts of what was really only one occasion: it is remarkable that three times he gives the number who were sent to prison as six). He regarded them as strict Calvinists, who would not go to parish churches or allow ceremonies or anything not contained in the letter of the Gospel. But he says that only few of them were arrested and 'no harm is done to them and, rather than try to escape imprisonment, they offer themselves for it'. He knew that they had powerful friends.[2]

Obviously, they were a tiresome problem. In March 1568, the Council ordered Grindal to suppress conventicles and devise proper measures for enforcing conformity,[3] but in April Grindal wrote to the Council suggesting that imprisonment did no good,

[1] *Memoranda (Three Fifteenth-Century Chronicles,* J. Gairdner, Camden Society), p. 143.
[2] *Cal. S. P. Span.* ii, 7, 11, 12, 43, 49.   [3] *Cal. S. P. Dom.,* p. 308.

and that those confined (whose 'friend' he declared himself to be) should be released with a warning that further punishment would follow if they behaved 'factiously or disorderly'.[1] His suggestions were accepted and on the Bishop's orders twenty-four were released. (It is odd that de Silva should put this in March—but so it is: Grindal definitely says April.) But clemency was in vain. They would not conform: they misrepresented what Grindal had said to them, and some of them were soon in prison again. They appealed to the Council, and Grindal in January 1569—obviously really provoked—suggested that they should be 'severely punished, to the example of others', and that the punishment should be inflicted by the Council to 'breed greater terror' and that they should be sent to prisons outside London where they would not find so much sympathy.[2] How serious a danger they presented to ecclesiastical stability it is hard to assess. Despite his wish to win them to obedience, Grindal did not think very highly of them. To Bullinger he described them as 'more zealous than they are either learned or gifted with pious discretion', 'London citizens of the lowest order ... remarkable neither for their judgment nor learning'. He gives their number as about 200, more women than men, but adds (what does not come out elsewhere) that they had 'ordained ministers elders and deacons' and practised excommunication. He also says that the Council, not himself, had committed some of the leaders to prison, and that Humphrey, Sampson and Lever would have nothing to do with them, and so were regarded by them as 'semi-papists'.[3] Nor did they get any support from foreign protestants, for as yet the idea of breaking away into independency was generally disliked. But their unease and obstinacy were symptomatic of the feelings which, in a few years, gave support to the much more dangerous movement to try to promote presbyters and 'the discipline' within the church—a movement which had much more reputable and learned backing. There is no evidence of such separatism outside London, and the burden

[1] Grindal, *Remains*, p. 317. [2] Ibid., pp. 316–19 and 216, note.
[3] *Zurich Letters*, i, 201–2.

of dealing with it fell chiefly on Grindal (and the vigilant Council). But Parker could not help being worried by it: Grindal says that he had had 'divers conferences' with him about their treatment.[1] But they were not eliminated. In August 1571, Horne wrote to Bullinger that there were some who 'call together conventicles, elect their own bishops, and holding synods one with another, frame and devise their own laws for themselves'.[2]

A further cause of anxiety was the large number of refugees from the Low Countries. As early as February 1560, the church of the Austin Friars was set apart for the use of strangers,[3] and many of the returned English exiles would, no doubt, extend a hearty welcome to them. But the government was vigilant to see that undesirable aliens did not take refuge here. Already in September 1560, there was a royal proclamation. Understanding that 'of late time sundry persons, being infected with certain dangerous and pernicious opinions in matters of religion, contrary to the faith of the church of Christ, as Anabaptists and such like' had arrived, the Queen ordered a strict search to be made in London. Any who held such 'heretical opinion' as the Anabaptists were to leave the country within twenty days if they would not conform or else to suffer fine and imprisonment; and all secret congregations or conventicles were forbidden.[4] (Presumably, services in Austin Friars under the eye of the Bishop were permitted.) Henceforward a strict check was kept on foreigners— for example there is a list of all of them resident in the city of London, Southwark and the suburbs in January 1563.[5] In 1567 the problem became much more difficult. The arrival of the Duke of Alba, fierce opponent of protestants, as Captain-General in the Netherlands caused a vast emigration, much of it directed to England. The State Papers in the late summer that year are full of requests from foreigners to be allowed to settle here and carry on their trade. Southampton and other places

[1] Grindal, Remains, p. 318.   [2] Zurich Letters, i, 249.
[3] Cal. S. P. Dom., p. 150.   [4] Grindal, Remains, pp. 297-8.
[5] Cal. S. P. Dom., p. 216.

were ready to receive them, and Bishop Horne was anxious that they should be allowed to come.[1] The vast majority was, of course, a most welcome addition to the population; they were skilled and honest craftsmen (though later on they did, like the English at Frankfort, give trouble by their religious squabbles among themselves). But some of them were active trouble makers, and by November, Bacon was complaining before the Council of rumours of the bringing in of seditious books to the danger of the established religion.[2] In November and December a search was made throughout London to find how many strangers there were, how long they had been there, their trade or occupation, which of them attended their parish churches or the churches appointed for them in London and which were 'vehemently suspected or defamed of any evil living, or to be setters forward or favourers of any naughty religion or sect'.[3] In July 1568 Cecil was demanding from the Lord Mayor of London a list of the names and professions of all strangers who had arrived since the last inquisition; by September, the list of all strangers resident in London was to be certified weekly.[4] In July also there was a proclamation against receiving 'rebels' from the Low Countries—though in it the Queen said she had not heard of any who had come save as merchants or for conscience sake. Naturally, in all this Parker was involved. The Queen wrote to him in May. Fearing that among the unusually large number of refugees who had come to live here 'with the satis-faction of their conscience in Christian living' there might be some with dangerous opinions such as Anabaptists and other sectaries or 'that be guilty of some other horrible crimes of rebellion, murder, robberies or such like' to whom she did not propose to offer refuge, she ordered him and the other bishops to hold 'special visitations and inquisitions'. The quality and condition of strangers were to be found out, the cause of their coming, how they lived and what churches they attended. Registers of them were to be made and continued, and those

---

[1] *Cal. S. P. Dom.*, pp. 292, 294, 299.   [2] *Cal. S. P. Dom.*, p. 302.
[3] Grindal, *Remains*, pp. 296–7.   [4] *Cal. S. P. Dom.*, pp. 312, 317.

either suspected of the foresaid crimes, or not conforming to the
laws of religion here (allowance being made for the places
specially set apart for their worship) were to be reported to the
lay authorities for trial.[1] Parker duly sent on the royal instructions to Grindal for his observance and for transmission to the
other bishops. But it would be grossly unfair to the Archbishop
to suppose that he was only interested in repressive measures.
There is also clear evidence that he was much concerned to
relieve distress among the foreigners who had fled to England
solely for religion's sake. In May 1568 Jewel wrote to him that,
according to his promise (presumably to Parker) he had sent
£3 6s. 8d. to the Bishop of London for poor exiles, to be used as
the Archbishop or Grindal should direct, and in 1569 the Chapter
of Canterbury assigned £6 13s. 4d. towards the relief of the
French church in London in response to the Archbishop's appeal.[2]

Though the main burden of dealing with Romanists in the
north or protestant extremists in London did not fall on Parker,
he was fully alive to the dangers which threatened the church from
both sides. He saw the difficulties which might be caused by the
flight of Mary of Scotland to England in 1568—our good Queen,
he thought, held a wolf by the ears.[3] In 1570 he was alarmed by
'more massing than hath been heard of this seven years'[4] and
suggested names for 'the new necessary commission' to deal with
it. Earlier in the year, he had sent for one Culpepper, brother-in-
law of Leonard Dacres, one of the leaders of the Northern
Rebellion, who was realizing his property and appeared to be
preparing to leave the country.[5] In November 1569, he had a
chiding letter from the Council accusing the bishops of neglecting
their duty with the result that 'no small number' of the Queen's
subjects 'partly for lack of diligent teaching and information,
partly for lack of correction and reformation, are entered either
into dangerous errors, or into a manner of life of contempt or
liberty, without use or exercise of any rites of the church, openly

---

[1] *Correspondence*, pp. 321-3.
[2] Jewel, *Defence of Apology*, p. 1,274; Strype, *Annals* I, ii, 290.
[3] *Correspondence*, p. 325.   [4] Ibid., pp. 369, 370-1.   [5] Ibid., p. 367.

forbearing to resort to their parish-churches'.[1] In view of this 'universal oversight and negligence (for less we cannot term it) of the bishops' the Council was writing to all of them, and so to Parker, seeking understanding of all the dioceses. As quietly as he could and without any proceeding likely to breed public offence, he was to find out particulars of those in his diocese who did not attend their parish churches or receive the sacrament. Further, the Council wished to be told what officers he had in his diocese to see that the laws were obeyed, what preachers there were, what was the staff of the cathedral and how many were resident there, what livings were vacant. A postscript added that he should report as soon as possible the names of the recusants without waiting till he had collected the other information. He was also to supply similar details for Chichester and Oxford dioceses which were vacant. The whole letter was written in the strongest terms of condemnation (though it was admitted that some dioceses and bishops were better than others) and was quite enough to cause serious anxiety to the Archbishop if he had been carelessly inactive, for the letter claimed to have behind it the authority of the Queen herself.[2]

In point of fact, he had not been idle. Quietly and without fuss, by routine procedure rather than extraordinary measures, he had been steadily working to see that parishes were properly served, that the clergy were of suitable character and education, and that abuses were checked. As early as 1567 he wrote to the Bishop for names and degrees of all the clergy of the cathedral and diocese of

---

[1] *Correspondence* pp. 355-7.

[2] Parker's reply is probably contained in Vol. LX, 71 of Domestic State Papers (*Cal. S. P. Dom.*, p. 357). It is true that this is calendered as an account of the 'visitation of the Province of Canterbury'—but there was none such this year, but only of the diocese. Moreover, though some of the information might well be the result of the visitation of 1569, the whole seems to be exactly arranged to answer the Council's questions and—as requested—there is also a full account of the diocese of Chichester (though it was not 'visited'). Dixon (op. cit., vi, 200 sq.) gives a full and interesting summary. Evidently Chichester was full of Papists—though also there were some Puritans; there was little preaching, many Marian clergy, and much evasion of the law. Obviously the diocese was a dangerous area of recusancy.

London; he wished to know how many were resident, how many were ministers or deacons and how many 'no priests or deacons' (a significant admission), how many were able and licensed to preach; how many kept suitable hospitality; what livings were vacant and who received the fruits of them.[1] In letters dimissory in 1568, he stated what he regarded as the requirements for an ordinand—good character, knowledge of Scripture and of Latin, and that he should not have been educated in 'illiberal arts'. He was steadily carrying on his campaign to see that livings were filled and that suitable clergy should be available.[2]

In June 1568 he issued a commission for the visitation of three parishes in Bucks which were exempt from normal episcopal visitation.[3] In May 1569, before he had the letter from the Council, he had set on foot a normal episcopal visitation of his own diocese of Canterbury[4] by the Bishop of Dover and others.

Most striking, however, was his metropolitan visitation of Norwich in 1567. The Bishop, Parkhurst, was notoriously favourable to the extreme reformers—as early as 1561 Cecil spoke of his remissness in ordering his clergy, and of his winking at schismatics and Anabaptists. The people did not like surplices, and the ministers 'follow the folly of the people'.[5] But Parker had now also heard that there was vast simony in the diocese and that many of the gentry, even knights, had accumulated four or five or even eight livings in their hands, 'somewhere setting boys and their serving-men to bear the names of such livings'.[6]

---

[1] *Correspondence*, p. 308.   [2] *Register*, pp. 497–8.   [3] Ibid., p. 498.
[4] Ibid., pp. 527–8. There is some obscurity about the articles of visitation. Wilkins (*Concilia* iv, 257) followed by Cardwell (*Documentary Annals* i, 320) gives some articles, and quotes as authority Parker's *Register* i, 302 (p. 623 in the printed edition). The articles there, however, are definitely the articles for the metropolitan visitation of 1560, not diocesan articles for 1569. But the articles given in Wilkins for 1569 are practically identical with the Norwich diocesan articles of 1567 (see p. 223), save for the addition at the end of one article enquiring whether parishioners have paid all the money they have been cessed at for the relief of the poor. Probably they represent a more or less standard form reached for Norwich in 1567 and used in 1569 too—but where Wilkins found them (or Cardwell) is not clear: certainly it was not in the passage in the *Register* they refer to.
[5] *Correspondence*, p. 149.   [6] Ibid., p. 311.

Parker felt he had to act. The list of his visitors was impressive, headed by Yale, the Vicar-General, and including the Dean of Canterbury and various legal members of the Archbishop's court, with Incent to act as registrar. It was a strong body, but did not include (as was common in such visitations) the Bishop of the diocese, who was indeed subject to the enquiry. A revised set of visitation articles for cathedrals was issued, based on those of 1560.[1] Most of the changes were merely verbal, but it was now insisted that members of the cathedral staff should communicate at least thrice a year, instead of once, as previously (the rubric in the Prayer Book said each Sunday!); and to the list of strange doctrines which might not be preached was added that 'any man may, or ought by his private authority' to alter rites or ceremonies, or encourage the use of beads. It was also made explicit that the 'outward calling' of ministers must be by 'the magistrates appointed'—no doubt to exclude the idea that the calling by a mere congregation was enough. For the diocese as a whole, too, there were new articles, based on those of 1560, and 1563.[2] Here again the changes, though slight, are interesting. Are the services said not only as set forth by law but also, it is added, as ordered by 'the Queen's Majesty's Injunctions and by the *Advertisements* set forth by public authority' (a significant description of them). Further additions concerned the decent covering of the communion table, insistence on the use of the font (not basins) which should be decently kept, on wafer-bread according to the Injunctions, on the use of a cup provided and kept for communion and not profane cups or bowls, nor even chalices previously used for the mass. Was reception standing, sitting, or kneeling? There was also a sweeping question whether Ordinaries, Chancellor, Officials and the like had themselves to their uttermost power obeyed the laws, statutes and Injunctions and also whether they had favoured or commended such as did not do so, or allowed them to go unpunished for 'money, gain, pleasure, friendship or other affectionate respect'. The visitors

[1] Printed in Strype, *Parker* iii, 155 sqq.
[2] W. H. Frere, *Visitation Articles and Injunctions*, iii, 197 sqq.

were instructed to reduce the clergy to one uniform order of ministration and preaching (again with a reference to the *Advertisements*), and to inform not only the clergy but also the churchwardens that no one was to be allowed to preach or minister until his licence under seal in due form had been produced. There was also a strict order that no unaccustomed dues were to be exacted, that a careful account of receipts of the visitors was to be kept and that any balance over the expenses was to be divided among such poor and needy clergy as were resident and kept hospitality. It was a moderate and sincere attempt to produce orderliness in a diocese notoriously lax, and in such a way as not to be financially oppressive.

The visitation lasted from June to October 1567, and is extensively documented in Parker's *Register*.[1] But trouble did not end when the Bishop's jurisdiction was restored to him on October 4. A commissioner was appointed by the Archbishop on October 6 to deal with the *detecta*; he was refused recognition by two of the proctors of the Norwich Consistory who were due to be dealt with, and by other proctors along with them. There was much acrimony about this. Moreover no fewer than sixty-one rectors or vicars absent from their parishes had to be cited, on October 2nd, to take up residence and duty within six months, or to appear before the Archbishop or his Vicar-General on the second day after Trinity Sunday in St. Paul's, to state their reasons for absence. In June 1568, thirty-two of them were deprived for contumacy in not so appearing; twenty-six more were sequestered and in November twenty of them also were deprived. Evidently of the original sixty-one absentees, only nine proved obedient and satisfactory. Even before the end of October 1567 several gentry of the diocese wrote to Parker requesting him to restore a regular preacher (not one of the above) who had been disturbed by the visitation![2] There was, they said, great lack of such. Evidently laity in the diocese as well as clergy were reluctant to be reformed.

Of conditions at the cathedral we have the account of one of the

[1] pp. 720–67.   [2] *Correspondence*, pp. 306–7.

prebendaries, George Garidner.[1] His main complaint was about the members of the Chapter. The Dean resided, but only two of the four archdeacons and three of the six prebendaries, of whom one was one of the archdeacons. Of the six prebendaries, Gardiner himself was the only one who preached, though one of the others did provide a substitute to preach in his turn. Three of them never came to the cathedral except to draw their money and two were described as not priests. The most surprising member of the Chapter was Wendon, Archdeacon and prebendary; he was no priest, never preached, lived at Louvain and, two years before, was seen dressed in a 'cloke with a Spanish cape and a rapier by his side'. But Gardiner did not seem to think that apart from the Chapter much else was amiss; services were properly carried out, save for the use of a 'chalice, contrary . . . to the *Advertisements* of the Queen'.[2] There was indeed no grammar school attached to the cathedral, but a private schoolmaster was paid to take such scholars as were sent to him. The accounts were properly kept—though the woods were much spoiled. Gardiner knew of no unlawful preaching nor of simony among the higher officials, though many of the servants (sextons, butlers, cooks etc.) were obviously hiring substitutes to do their work at a profit to themselves. One canon was suspected of immorality. But the cathedral was properly furnished and in better repair than for forty years. The only improvements he wished were the addition of more psalms at the beginning and end of the services, a cup in place of the chalice, and prebendaries who were both priests and resident.

It was a moderate indictment, but would not be acceptable to some of his fellow prebendaries. It is not surprising to find, therefore, that Gardiner himself was shortly on trial before Yale in the Consistory Court on all sorts of charges[3]—that for sixteen years he had been a trouble-maker, that he had betrayed pro-

[1] Strype, *Parker* iii, 159–61.

[2] This cannot refer to Parker's *Advertisements* which do not mention chalices, but possibly to some lost royal order. Frere (op. cit.) points out that there was a growing desire to get rid of chalices in favour of cups.

[3] *Register*, pp. 761–6.

testants under Queen Mary, that he had been expelled from his Fellowship at Cambridge for breach of statutes, and that he had been a real nuisance at Norwich, the cause of brawling, of intrigue, and of disorder. He was found guilty by Yale, but punishment was reserved for the Archbishop. It is significant that nothing seems to have happened to him; Parker must have assessed the situation with tact and discernment. So Gardiner stayed on at Norwich to become Archdeacon and ultimately Dean.[1] In 1572 Parkhurst even suggested his name to Parker for appointment as a commissioner.[2] It would thus seem likely that the accusations against him were largely due to his enemies in the Chapter, which was plainly not a harmonious or happy body. But Gardiner himself was not one who was easy to live with, as his later troubles with Parkhurst show.

The metropolitan visitation of Norwich was not a success; it did not at once put all things in order in the diocese,[3] for Parkhurst himself had to visit it again in 1569. Moreover, in that same year a royal commission, appointed at the request of Gardiner to consider disorders in the cathedral, reported that three of the statutory prebendaries were neither priests nor preachers, that there was no divinity lecture nor library for the help of students and (astonishingly) 'no statutes to govern the House withal'. There was great negligence in preaching and resorting to sermons, much wasting of money, plate, lead and timber. The register books were ill-kept and copies of leases either not received, or lost.[4] Evidently there had not been much

---

[1] Strype, *Annals* II, i, 443–9. Gardiner certainly showed himself very contentious in securing these posts, but he was a worthy Dean who served the cathedral well. Ibid., 450, 485.　　　　　　[2] Strype, *Parker* ii, 137.

[3] Later on, *Correspondence*, p. 473, Parker gave a very depressing account of the visitation. So far from there being a surplus of visitation fees for distribution, 'the visitors spoiled all; and I spent £20 of mine own purse, to have that diocese well visited, and yet no good done'. He suggests that there had even been bribery—no doubt of the under officials: it can hardly have been of the actual visitors themselves.

[4] Frere, *Visitation Articles and Injunctions*, iii, 217. The commissioners included Parkhurst and the Mayor of Norwich, Thomas Parker, the Archbishop's brother.

improvement. And in September 1570 the Queen had to order Parkhurst to enquire into innovations at the cathedral, where some of the prebendaries had broken down the organs and committed other outrages.[1] Probably other dioceses were not so much disordered as Norwich had become under Parkhurst, but the whole proceedings there show not only how many anxieties a man so conscientious as the Archbishop must have had, but also how well informed he was about conditions, though, of course, he had a special concern for Norwich.

He actually became personally involved over the visitation in a way which caused him real distress, as he explained at length in a letter to Lady Bacon.[2] The visitors had ordered that non-resident prebendaries should not have their stipends until they had satisfied Parker that they had good cause of absence. One of them—Smith—neither priest nor preacher, according to Gardiner —came to Parker for permission to receive his money. Parker found that he was no priest and that he did not wish to be so, though he had some profane learning. He therefore advised him to resign his prebend though reserving to himself a pension from it. Smith was willing to do so, especially as there was a preacher very popular in the city called Walker, who could thus be provided for and kept in the city. Parker therefore arranged with Gardiner that when he resigned his prebend, keeping a pension of £5 from it, he should receive the back stipend due to him. But the whole agreement was upset because Smith had undertaken to pay £5 a year from his emoluments to a nephew of the Lord Keeper's, who was studying at Cambridge. It was a clear case of simony, for Bacon had given him the prebend—but Bacon would not forgo the annual payment to his nephew! So the bargain fell through: in the end, Smith was deprived in 1570 for not being in Orders.

The incident led to a serious disagreement between Parker and Bacon. Presumably on the assumption that all was settled, Walker, the preacher, was sent to Bacon with a letter of recommendation from the Duke of Norfolk. He left the letter in the

[1] *Cal. S. P. Dom.*, p. 393.   [2] *Correspondence*, pp. 309–16.

morning and was to call for a reply in the afternoon. Meantime
he went to see Parker who at once wrote a private explanatory
letter to Bacon so that he might have it before he gave his reply.
Parker had been very cautious about the affair—he had not even
told his wife about it. But Bacon in a fury sent back an angry
answer, apparently verbal ('in word') by the messenger, whom
Parker had wished to be kept in ignorance of the whole matter.
Naturally the Archbishop was deeply hurt. He had always
spoken highly of the Keeper and been his friend, and had supposed that Matthew Parker might 'write privately to Nicholas
Bacon in matter of good friendship without offence'. Even the
Queen when she had rebuked him privately had yet in public
given him 'good looks' saying that 'she must needs countenance
mine authority before the people, to the credit of my service'.
He was obviously really angry at Bacon's lack of tact, but was
not to be put off doing his duty. He did not esteem either the
solemnity or commodity of his office—'I was sorry to be so
accumbered, but necessity drave me . . . I am grown now into a
better consideration by mine age, than to be afraid or dismayed
with such vain terriculaments of the world'. But it was not
merely that his feelings were hurt: he was dismayed by the
thought of the 'common slanderous speech' which the matter
would cause when it was known. He wished he had offered to
pay the £5 out of his own pocket! That even Bacon, firm friend
of reform, should have acted in such a way shows that Parker
was not merely querulous when he complained of the difficulties
and burdens of his office.

CHAPTER XIV

UNIVERSITY AND ROUTINE BUSINESS: THE BISHOPS' BIBLE

THE two colleges in Oxford of which Parker was visitor called for attention about this time. At All Souls there was still reserved certain plate of a 'superstitious fashion'—no doubt retained in case there should be a chance of reviving the old services. In March 1567, the Archbishop wrote to the Warden reminding him that he had previously ordered such plate to be defaced or melted down, and that he had not been told that this had been done. He now asked for a complete inventory of such plate and of all vestments etc. not in use. If any of the Fellows objected, their names and reasons were to be reported to him, and they were to be sent up to be examined by him.[1] The Archbishop had good reason to fear factiousness in the college; he had already been compelled to send a rebuke for ill attention to the statutes, and had twice had to nominate college officers, presumably because the Fellows, could not agree among themselves.[2] Once more he was not immediately obeyed, for three weeks later there was a letter to the college not simply from himself, but from the ecclesiastical commission ordering the dispatch 'immediately upon the next repair of any common carriage' of a number of old service books fully catalogued in a schedule.[3] The Warden also and two of the Fellows were ordered to present themselves before the commissioners. This was followed, about three weeks later, by another letter from the commissioners ordering in the Queen's Majesty's name four named Fellows immediately, 'all excuses and delays set apart', to appear before the commissioners

---

[1] *Correspondence*, p. 296.
[2] *Archives of All Souls* (ed. C. T. Martin, London, 1877), p. 303.
[3] *Correspondence*, pp. 297–8.

and not to depart again without special licence.[1] This, at last, was effective. Four days later, the Warden and four Fellows (though, even then, not exactly the ones named in the letter) presented themselves before the commissioners. They were ordered on their return to see that all the chapel plate (with certain specified exceptions, which did not include chalices) was defaced and broken up, and two books of the Epistles and Gospels sent to the commissioners. Any Fellows who objected were to appear before the commissioners within ten days. In August, Parker was able at last to report that the plate was 'turned whole and reserved as bullion among them',[2] and their church books 'turned out of the way', whatever that may mean. But it is to be observed that he had to obtain the backing of the commissioners: his authority as Visitor did not prove sufficient. Even so, some vestments seem still to have been kept. For in 1573 a new commission ordered the defacing of 'all copes, vestments, albs, mass books and crosses'—and even that order had to be repeated strongly before it was finally obeyed.[3]

At Merton conditions were even more serious. Man, the Warden imposed on the college by Parker, was away, sent by the Queen as ambassador to Spain. In his absence, party spirit broke out bitterly. In August 1567 the Archbishop had to interfere for 'the appeasing of certain controversies' over the calling of some of the B.A.s of the college to the degree of Master. He declared that two of them, called by the Vice-Warden and five seniors, had been lawfully and orderly promoted, but three others had not been properly promoted because, in the absence of Warden and Vice-Warden, a Fellow who was not the senior in residence had presided at the meeting. For the sake of peace, however, he ordered the college to confirm them in their Mastership, but imposed a fine on the disorderly Fellow who had presided out of turn. He also ordered the question of seniority among Fellows—an important matter in the absence of Warden and Vice-Warden—to be settled by a committee of three. Once

---

[1] *Correspondence*, p. 300, and note ad loc.   [2] Ibid., p. 304.
[3] *History of All Souls* (C. Grant Robertson, London, 1899), pp. 70–71.

more there seems to have been reluctance to obey, for in September the Vice-Warden was personally before Parker and was
strictly enjoined to see that the settlement was carried out, the
fine paid—and that, before the coming Easter, at least three of
the Fellows should take Orders.[1]

Shortly afterwards there was further trouble, now over one of
the Fellows, Ralph Latham, whom most (if not all) of his colleagues wished to deprive. Parker urged them not to do it, at
least on the grounds—apparently of immorality—they alleged,
though he would not interfere if it were proved that Latham was
guilty of perjury. He also saw Latham and impressed on him
that it would be better for him to resign than face the disgrace
of expulsion.[2] That was in December 1567. Once more, the
Visitor's views were opposed. Latham was expelled, and a
number of Fellows joined together, by oath, to 'wage war against
the Archbishop of Canterbury', to raise money on a college
estate to meet their expenses and to maintain the expulsion of
Latham. Parker was thus forced to fall back again on the ecclesiastical commissioners, who in March 1568 dealt with the
college. They had before them three of the conspirators, whom
they forbade to leave London throughout Lent. An oath renouncing the conspiracy was drawn up, and none of the conspirators was to receive any of his commons in college till he
had taken it. Some of them were more heavily punished—they
were to absent themselves from the college till midsummer—
one was finally deprived. But that was not all. There was a strict
ruling that at least three of the Fellows should be ordained—and
that in order of seniority, unless younger Fellows would take
their place. And there were also instructions to secure that the
college property was not misused, as the conspirators had
intended, either by alienation or fines for leases. The commission
carefully insisted that nothing they had done was to be regarded as
derogating from the Archbishop's rights and interest in the
college as Visitor.[3] They even ordered that their injunctions

---

[1] *Register*, pp. 473–6.   [2] *Correspondence*, pp. 308–9.
[3] *Register*, pp. 486–91.

should be authentically engrossed under his seal. For greater security, the careful Archbishop caused to be entered in his Register[1] a copy of an act of Parliament of Henry IV, showing that both under him and previously under Richard II the University of Oxford was not privileged to exemption from but was subject to visitation by the Archbishop. If so, no doubt it was even more certain that it was subject to royal visitation by the commissioners.

For the moment, at least, the Archbishop had won. Latham was restored—and the Archbishop was able to resist an appeal that he would not insist on three Fellows being in Orders.[2] 'If there be no preachers to maintain Christ's religion, to move the subjects' hearts in persuasion of obedience to the prince, and the tenants to their landlords, neither Westminster Hall will long continue nor outward force will rule the matter'. As always, he felt that order in Church and State were closely joined. And, if founders had bestowed their money for certain purposes, it was unreasonable to use the funds otherwise ('in idle pleasures'); in fact, by statute, all the Fellows should have taken Orders, he points out. His dealings with the colleges show not only his zeal for the promotion of learning in conditions of harmony, but also his impartiality. He was not prepared to countenance Romanistic tendencies in Oxford any more than protestant vagaries in Norfolk.

At Cambridge an even more dangerous crisis arose: the Vice-Chancellor denied the right of the ecclesiastical commissioners to have any authority over the University, claiming that it was exempt from outside control. To make matters worse for Parker, the occasion was disorders in Corpus. The Master, John Pory, was an old friend of Parker—they had been undergraduates of the college together, and Pory had been a Fellow of Stoke-by-Clare when Parker was Dean. But he was now old, and did not spend much time in Cambridge, for he was a great pluralist—canon of Westminster, rector of Landbeach and of Lambeth as well as Master of Corpus. The college was therefore ill supervised; and there were bitter factions, for George Withers

[1] *Register*, pp. 491 sq.   [2] *Correspondence*, pp. 325-6.

was there, and, on the other hand, there were some who were still loyal to the old religion. Despite his interest in the college, Parker had no legal authority to interfere personally, but towards the end of 1568 the ecclesiastical commissioners, having 'information' (doubtless supplied by Parker) of 'divers misdemeanours as well in manners as in doctrine', intervened. They sent their commission (an interesting case of delegation) to the Vice-Chancellor and some Heads to deal with the college. The Vice-Chancellor, in a letter to Cecil as Chancellor, at once questioned the power of the commissioners so to interfere. Cecil asked the commissioners for their views and accepted their ruling that their authority, by virtue of the words 'in places as well exempt as not exempt', did extend to the University, without prejudice to its liberties. But the Vice-Chancellor still was tardy to act—so the commissioners revoked their commission to him, and undertook the examination of the case themselves. Most of the Fellows concerned voluntarily appeared at Lambeth and submitted; but one who was principally concerned, Stallard, did not come. He was then formally summoned by the commission—but the Vice-Chancellor forbade him to go! He further withstood the officers sent by the commission to search for suspected books, and caused a door they had sealed to be undone for his own agents to remove the books. All this he did, as Parker informed the Chancellor of the University, on the ground that no 'extraordinary or foreign authority' had ever so interfered. Parker naturally expostulated, pointing out that the commission had already removed out of two Universities 'divers stubborn papists and head adversaries of God's true religion to the number of forty and more', and that the Vice-Chancellor's action discredited such acts of the commission and derogated from their authority committed to them by Parliament. He asked for Cecil's views before further action was taken.[1] However humble Parker was personally, he was always prepared to fight for the authority of his office.

'What further issue this business had, I find not' remarks Strype.[2] Probably the disagreement was not pressed to a final

---

[1] *Correspondence*, pp. 343–5.   [2] *Parker* i, 533.

issue. The Chancellor had accepted the view of the commissioners as to their powers, and there would soon be a new Vice-Chancellor. Parker at last persuaded Pory to resign at the beginning of 1569. He was succeeded by Thomas Aldrich, both at Corpus and Westminster, a man strongly approved by Parker at the time,[1] though he was later to cause much trouble. The commissioners may well have rested content with that. Certainly Stallard was not removed but continued to be a Fellow of Corpus until 1570, and went on to a successful career afterwards, becoming Archdeacon of Rochester in the end.

Strype connects these doings with widespread discontent at Cambridge over the use in colleges of a Latin version of the Prayer Book ordered by the Queen and imposed by authority.[2] Some declared that 'Latin service was the Pope's dregs' and said grace in English at the common table. On this matter, too, the Archbishop appealed to the Chancellor for help—with what result does not appear.[3] Further, he was shocked at the great 'infamy' because of 'unnatural filthiness . . . in this great liberty of marriage'.[4] From the very beginning of Elizabeth's reign, Parker had been horrified by the way in which the old laws concerning prohibited degrees were being neglected. He had written an Admonition on the subject and caused it to be set up in the churches, with a list of the prohibited degrees.[5] In Cambridge seemingly, it was not observed, and William Fulke, who had been expelled from St. John's because of the vestiarian controversy and then restored, was now 'under a great blot for it' and was, it seemed, likely to have his head 'stroken' and be made Master of the college![6] (In fact, Fulke was cleared of the charge, and was not in the end made Master.) The condition of religious study, too, was deplorable there. In December 1569, just about the time when Cartwright was elected to the Margaret Chair, Parker wrote to the Queen that 'in your University of Cambridge

[1] *Correspondence*, p. 358.   [2] *Parker* i, 534-5.
[3] Strype refers to the letter, but the present writer has not been able to discover it.
[4] *Correspondence*, p. 353.   [5] Strype, *Parker* i, 174.
[6] Strype, *Parker* i, 555. *Correspondence*, p. 353.

not two men in the whole able or willing to read the Lady Margaret's lecture'.[1] This was, unquestionably, unfair to Cartwright who was both willing and clearly able; but his views, of course, were not acceptable to the Archbishop. There was small comfort for him in the contemplation of his cherished University.

Apart from such major business as was caused by the Universities and the Norwich visitation, the *Register* and the *Correspondence* show Parker in these years to have been involved in an infinity of smaller, almost routine, matters which must have taken time and trouble. He had the help, of course, of numerous officials; and it is likely that they relieved him of all personal concerns in some cases, but not in all. Yale could, for example, issue dispensations for marriage without banns, and even delegate the power to do so.[2] But more serious matrimonial cases needed the Archbishop's personal attention.[3] There were times when he had to intervene actively and not merely formally. The visitors of 1560 had ordered a certain Justinian Grigby of Sutton and his wife Jane to live together again, and Justinian's mother not to disturb them.[4] But in 1567 they were still separated, and the Archbishop, stirred up by information sent to him, wrote a letter to try to get sworn statements about them (to save the parishioners the trouble and expense of going to Lambeth to give evidence) so that he might 'proceed accordingly'.[5] On another occasion, he described himself as 'occupied with all the wits I have' in trying to separate a man and his sister—german who were living as man and wife, and had already two children, with a third expected.[6] The affair had gone on for twelve years; six years ago he thought he had persuaded the man, but was disappointed. Now he had spent the whole afternoon with the sister, in vain. 'Before God, I know not what to do with them and how to deal.' More distressing still was the case of Dr. John Hardyman, who had 'misused my favour long borne to him'. He had clearly been well known to the Archbishop, who made him vicar of Lydd in 1560, to which was added Snargate in 1567. He had

---

[1] *Correspondence*, p. 374.   [2] *Register*, p. 573.   [3] Ibid., p. 583.
[4] Ibid., p. 648.   [5] *Correspondence*, p. 303.   [6] Ibid., p. 353.

been one of the original prebendaries of Westminster in 1560. In 1568, the parishioners of Lydd accused him of matrimonial irregularity, profligacy, and incontinence. Presumably, Parker forced his resignation, for there was a new vicar of Lydd in February 1569 and of Snargate in June. But Hardyman apparently still lingered in Lydd, so that Parker had to write in March to the bailiff to order him immediately to go away because of the scandal he caused. If he refused, he was to be arrested and brought before the Archbishop.[1] It was evidently no mere figure of speech when he spoke of himself as 'travelling here about divers disorders in my diocese, specially of those persons that live either incontinently or in fashion of a divorce assunder from their wives'.[2]

Some of the things Parker was called upon to do now seem incredibly trivial. There was the licensing of schoolmasters, of which the *Register* gives several examples, though on occasion Yale could act in this matter too without bringing in the Archbishop.[3] But the only case recorded of the licensing of a midwife required his personal attention.[4] The applicant appeared *coram reverendissimo* supported by eight witnesses to her efficiency—their names are carefully given. The Archbishop 'diligently' examined her and gave her leave to practise her office after she had sworn a long oath not to allow false paternity to be alleged, nor any substitution to take place, nor to use sorcery or incantation, nor to destroy or hurt any child born under her care; and to serve equally poor and rich. In case of need, she promised to baptize with the proper words and pure water. The terms of the oath show what opportunities a midwife might have, under pressure or bribery, of harmful conduct and how important it was that only reliable women should be admitted. But only the one admission is recorded and it must remain uncertain whether the Archbishop had personally to examine all applicants.

Dispensations to hold livings under age or unordained were normally issued by the Court of Faculties, usually to enable a young man to pursue his studies at a university, with the proviso

---

[1] *Correspondence*, p. 342; *Register*, pp. 771, 832, 348, 852.
[2] *Correspondence*, p. 366.　　[3] *Register*, p. 510.　　[4] Ibid., pp. 470–2.

that he should wear clerical dress and see that a curate was provided for the living at a stipend approved by the Ordinary.[1] Such dispensations required confirmation by royal letters patent. But here again the Archbishop had at times to intervene personally. In 1570, before Grindal succeeded to York, a prebend in the cathedral there was vacant. A rich Yorkshireman had secured the nomination and wished to put in his son, who was under age. Parker was applied to by 'a certain nobleman'[2] to give a dispensation. Grindal urged him not to do so, and was supported by the Dean of York who pointed out that the prebend was a wealthy one and would support a much-needed preacher, while the boy suggested was 'of tender age, and little learning and discretion'. Parker refused the dispensation, no doubt giving offence in powerful quarters. But, in writing to Cecil about it, he makes some suggestive remarks—that those who have obtained his dispensations should carefully examine them to see that the seal is not forged. 'For I know what I have done. And if I be sifted never so narrowly, yet shall it not be found that I have given dispensation of ecclesiastical livings to bishops' sons, neither six, nor three, to my remembrance.'[3] The implication is clear enough. Though dispensations were granted by the Court of Faculties, Parker himself kept a keen eye on what was going on there; and he did not regard forgery as impossible.[4] Anyhow, he very much disliked the whole proceedings of the Court of Faculties. 'I have a long time offered in convocation to my brethren' he added to Cecil, 'to procure the dispatchment of this offensive court. I have signified the same to your honours. For I have more grief thereby than gain, and I would it were wholly suppressed.'[5] A little later, he wrote that he was having trouble

[1] *Register*, p. 318 etc.   [2] Leicester, according to Strype, *Parker* ii, 13.

[3] *Correspondence*, p. 362.

[4] E.g. see Strype, *Annals* II, i, 145—the Archbishop's seal moved from one document to another: *Annals* II, i, 336 refers to a man who was skilful in forging seals. In March 1573 Parker had to warn Parkhurst about forged letters, *Correspondence*, p. 418.

[5] *Correspondence*, p. 363. Strype (*Parker* ii, 15) quotes from the archives of Canterbury wholesome rules laid down by Parker for the Faculty Court, to prevent fraud, extortion and undesirable dispensations. All faculties were to be

with some official who 'seemeth to discredit my office'.[1] No clear
details are given, but the occasion moved Parker to press for a
renewal of the ecclesiastical commission, so that his responsibility should be shared. His request was granted, for a few months
later he wrote to Cecil about it, to point out mistakes in the
actual deed of commission. A necessary clause had been acciden-
tally omitted, certain additions to the list of commissioners were
desirable; and it should be made plain that diocesan commissioners (apart from the general commissioners) were not to act
outside their own dioceses.[2]

Sometimes he was forced into action against one or other of his
diocesans. His visitors had sequestrated a vacant living in Cambridge; then the diocesan, the Bishop of Ely—or rather his Vicar-
General—had named other sequestrators. Parker had to insist
that those named by his visitors should be recognized and the
others present themselves for examination in his Consistory
Court.[3] In 1569 he had to sequester a prebend in Lincoln because the Bishop had failed to fill it; there was a similar case of
neglect at Chichester in 1571, where the Archbishop filled the
vacancy.[4] At Hereford a prebendary had been deposed by the
Bishop for non-payment of tithes, and his place filled by another.
The deprived prebendary appealed to the Archbishop, who
sequestered the prebend till the case was heard—he feared a
fight about it. In Hereford, too, he had to interfere about a living.
The Bishop had presented to it. A layman had taken the matter
to law, and had established that the right of presentation was his.
Thereupon the Archbishop had to order the Bishop's nominee to
depart, and the layman's nominee to be inducted.[5] In the general
disturbances of the times there were endless small cases for the
Primate.

Moreover, though Parker wrote to the Queen protesting
'myself and all I have to be at your commandment, to tarry or to

examined and assigned by himself or the master, fees were to be fixed, and a
careful register kept; certain dispensations were not to be given without his
personal assent.

[1] *Correspondence*, p. 368.   [2] Ibid., p. 370–1.   [3] *Register*, pp. 462–4.
[4] Ibid., p. 855, 882.   [5] Ibid., pp. 837; 847–51.

forego the vocation your Highness hath called me unto, better content for myself to live with the tenth part, than with the whole, if it be to the glory of God and to the honour and quiet governance of your realm',[1] he was yet always vigilant to maintain the dignity and rights of the Archbishop. When a bishop was appointed to Oxford, he wrote to remind Cecil that the royal assent alone was not enough: the new bishop must in person or by proctor present himself to the Archbishop to take the oath and be confirmed in his spiritual jurisdiction.[2] He strongly objected when Cecil maintained that the Queen had powers of dispensation equal to his own. He would not personally dispute the Queen's absolute power—but there were in fact 'parliament laws precisely determining causes of dispensation'; those allocated to the Archbishop were for him to decide.[3] He objected, too, to the Queen's attempt on one occasion to provide for her chaplains by prebends in Canterbury. They would not be in regular residence and yet would receive their full stipend—which would seriously hinder the hospitality due from the Chapter to important travellers.[4] Once she actually wrote to nominate to a canonry and prebend just vacant at Canterbury—if it was not in her gift but that of the Archbishop, he could have the next one which was hers![5] Her nominee was the Dean of Winchester—a not unusual sort of pluralism. Parker was saved from the embarrassment of refusal by the fact that he had acted with promptitude and already nominated some one else.[6]

Church property, too, urgently needed protection in an age when it had come to be regarded as an almost inexhaustible mine for those who wished to enrich themselves. A long letter to the Queen, despite its humble tone, is really an expostulation about the way he had himself been treated. After several years of quiet possession, he had suddenly been called on to justify his use of a wood, which his predecessors had enjoyed—though he was not selling the timber but improving it, and using the 'wood of the

[1] *Correspondence*, p. 373.   [2] Ibid., p. 306.   [3] Ibid., p. 351.
[4] Ibid., p. 319.   [5] Ibid., p. 341.   [6] *Register*, p. 844.

fall' for the benefit of the neighbourhood. It had now, apparently, been let to some one else at a higher rent. He had too, tried to renew a lease of a house at Charing, held by previous Archbishops, but the man he had asked to act as his supporter in the matter had, behind his back, secured the lease for himself—and so on.[1] Though in the exchanges of land with the Crown it might be said that there had been 'penny for penny' (though in fact there had not[2]), yet the Queen herself, he continued, had not had full benefit from it, and the exchange had certainly had the effect of lowering the status of the see of Canterbury, which would well suit the wishes of those who wished to abolish bishops. (This was in 1570: there had already been an attempt to sink Parker in the Thames by boring holes in his barge.[3]) But if 'this room should be either too low abased or quite abolished, I think your Highness' Council should have too much ado . . . in staying the unruliness of some part of the ministers of religion'. The ordinary clergy, too, were in 'wonderful impoverishment'— so much so that he refrained from exacting all his rights from them. He feared that 'Christ's holy religion . . . will fall to the ground among beggars which shall set their whole care and force of mind not to study but to live, which at this day experience showeth it'. It has sometimes been suggested that Parker did not escape the love of show and riches rampant in his day. But here at least there is no worldly motive: the clergy must be paid enough to keep the wolf from the door, and bishops able to maintain their dignity and status. In this latter wish he may have been mistaken —but it was not mere worldliness.

Possibly the attack on his wood was due to so-called 'concealers'—men who had a royal commission to search out land or goods which, having been used in the past for so-called purposes of superstition, should have been surrendered to the Crown but had been 'concealed'.[4] They were liberally rewarded out of what they found, and were a terror to ignorant incumbents. As early as 1561 there is evidence of their activity[5]; in 1567 there were

---

[1] *Correspondence*, pp. 371–4.   [2] Ibid., p. 102, note.   [3] Ibid., p. 364.
[4] Strype, *Annals* II, i, 309 sqq.   [5] *Cal. S. P. Dom.*, p. 155.

commissions for such searches in Southampton and Berkshire.[1] In 1571 Whitgift had trouble with them at Worcester, where they tried to deprive him of Hartlebury Castle, the episcopal residence.[2] So scandalous were their proceedings that in February 1572 there was a royal proclamation calling in all commissions for concealment. In some cases claims had even been made on the lead of churches and chapels, and on church bells! The commissions were thus publicly revoked by royal proclamation because the Queen feared that if any less open measures were taken, the concealers would not let them be known. Moreover, any who thought that they had been wrongly treated were given the right to appeal to the Justices of Assize at the next circuit, or to any two or three justices in the shire. Not that the Queen intended to abandon her claim on concealed property, but she would in future only commission such persons as could be trusted for their honesty.[3] In fact, such commissions continued to be granted intermittently: as early as December 1572 Parker warned Burghley against one who had had such a commission and was now seeking 'to be let loose' again.[4] In March the next year, the Bishop of Norwich (to whom, in January, Parker had written suggesting that a collection should be made to help clergy who had lately been victimized by 'certain extraordinary visitors'[5]) wrote that he had received a letter from the Archbishop urging him to advise his clergy to pay money to buy off the 'concealers'—which shows that even the royal proclamation had not become effectively known. Parker indignantly replied that his supposed letter was a forgery and reveals, incidentally, that some of the concealers had actually been brought to book for their extortions and imprisoned in the Fleet.[6]

It is significant that it was in 1567 that Parker had to write to Cecil about Canterbury cathedral 'of whom so great information was made'.[7] It looks as though concealers had been busy there

---

[1] *Cal. S. P. Dom.*, pp. 287, 290.   [2] Strype, *Whitgift* i, 171.

[3] Robert Steele, *Proclamation*, p. 72; and Strype, *Annals* II, i, 310.

[4] *Correspondence*, p. 413.   [5] Ibid., p. 415.   [6] Ibid., p. 418.

[7] Ibid., pp. 303–4.

too: it was said that plate of the value of £1,000 had been sold, and vestry ornaments, and the proceeds divided. Parker's comment to Cecil is revealing. He admits that at his coming to Canterbury there was not a tenth part of the plate that had been there when Wotton became Dean, after the dissolution of the monasteries (Wotton was the first dean, under Henry VIII, and remained so till his death early in 1567. He was also dean of York, and ambassador in France.) Under him, plate, instead of being surrendered, had been divided among the Chapter, and some of it was still in the possession of Wotton's family as his son could testify! But under the new Dean nothing of the sort had happened. There had been no share out; the proceeds of the sale of superfluous plate had been used for corporate purposes, or kept for such uses. 'As for the church stuff, nothing stirred, but such as it is, is rotting in their custody, of no great value.' Again, in 1570 he heard that Manchester College was in difficulties and that the Warden saw no chance of carrying on, 'except he betrayeth that College with giving over a lease of the best land it hath'. On this, his suggestion to Cecil was that its endowments should be transferred to some College in Cambridge—perhaps St. John's, Cecil's own College![1] He was much agitated by the suggestion in 1567 that the Queen should appoint commissioners to enquire into the matter of leases by the clergy of Church property—it was alleged that in some cases long leases were being given, to the long-term impoverishment of clerical incomes—no doubt in return for a substantial sum or fine paid down.[2] He had also, on one occasion, to resist—or at least postpone consideration of—a claim by Lord Abergavenny, suddenly advanced when he had been Archbishop for years, to be Steward of the Liberties of Canterbury.[3] The need for such constant vigilance to defeat spoliation was naturally an unpleasant burden.

In this connection, the issue of new statues for Eastbridge Hospital in 1569 must have given real satisfaction to the Archbishop. The hospital had been visited in 1561,[4] and presumably

[1] *Correspondence*, p. 365.   [2] Ibid., p. 305.   [3] Ibid., pp. 285–6.
[4] *Register*, p. 380.

passed muster, for no change was made. But in 1569 it was found that the statutes were unobserved and the property spoiled through the 'carelessness fraud or negligence' of Masters. Originally founded for poor travellers, of whom many would be pilgrims, it was no longer needed to fill its original purpose. Parker's new statutes were sensible and businesslike, adapting so far as possible the original purpose to contemporary needs, showing both care for the poor and a characteristic zeal for education.[1] Henceforward, the Master was to be a reputable person—either the Suffragan Bishop of the diocese, or the Archbishop's Commissary General—who was actually to reside in the hospital or one of the manors belonging to it. In peace time, on each Friday thirty pence were to be given to thirty poor persons of Canterbury. In war time—and for three months after—such distribution was to cease in favour of a payment of four pence a day to soldiers, wounded or whole, passing through the city, with provision for a night's lodgings—or more in the case of the sick. Twelve beds were to be provided for poor soldiers especially. Books were to be properly kept and yearly shown to the Archbishop. So much for the adaptation of the original idea. But besides, there was to be established a free school for twenty boys between the ages of seven and eighteen (though no boy was to enjoy it for more than four years), presided over by the Master or his nominee. And two scholarships at Corpus Christi Cambridge were also provided. (There is still an 'Eastbridge' exhibition at the college.)

Parker was no longer a young man, and there are constant references in his letters to ill-health, which at times prevented him from going to Court when he wished, or seeing Cecil in person. He was troubled with stone, and catarrh; on one occasion he was unable to write to Cecil as 'my head would not bear it'; he was prevented—it must have been a bitter disappointment— from personally presenting to the Queen a bound copy of the new translation of the Bible which he had so carefully overseen.[2]

[1] Given in Strype, *Parker* iii, 169–76, and summarized in *Register*, pp. 165–6. [2] *Correspondence*, pp. 325, 332, 334, 363.

The appointment of a Suffragan Bishop of Dover in 1569 must have brought some relief from routine duties, but the care of all vacant dioceses still fell on his shoulders. Oxford, for example, was vacant from the beginning of the reign till a bishop was appointed in 1567, but he died in the following year, and the diocese lacked a bishop for the next twenty years. That was, it is true, exceptional. But even York was vacant from June 1568 until 1570. Parker was consulted—and was clearly much concerned— about vacant sees, and the length of the vacancies.[1] He was anxious that Grindal should go to York—'a heady and stout people, witty, but yet able to be dealt with by good governance', and was worried at the delay in making an appointment. The filling of London presented great difficulties, and so did the vacancy in Oxford, where lack of an episcopal house made it desirable that the head of a college should be appointed!

Despite all his burdens—age, ill-health and the inevitable toils of his office (to which he was still not fully reconciled)—the Archbishop did not become merely a mechanical administrator. He retained his human sympathy, and was always ready if he could to consider and help a hard case. At the instigation of Leicester, he apparently interfered to protect against slander the good name of Lady St. Loe ('Bess of Hardwick'); he interceded on behalf of Thomas Keyes, who had been in disgrace for five years because he had married Lady Mary Grey, sister of Lady Jane. The Queen was furious—the marriage might have produced a claimant for the throne. The couple were kept apart, and Keyes actually imprisoned for a time. He appealed to the Archbishop who urgently asked Cecil to take up the case with the Queen, though it was not really any business of Parker's and might easily have provoked a royal outburst. Another of his letters to Cecil showed his concern with local affairs—it was an appeal to the Council to help, financially, in making navigable the river to Canterbury.[2] On a humbler level, he twice took the trouble to write to All Souls, pleading for the renewal of the lease of a

---

[1] *Correspondence*, pp. 305–6, 331, 350, 353, 359.
[2] Ibid., pp. 301–2, 367, 322.

college farm to a widow who was willing to pay generously for it[1]; and to Cecil to intercede to obtain for his steward the lease of a royal farm.[2]

Above all, he still kept his avid interest in antiquities and scholarship. A letter from Grafton the printer[3] shows that he was reading some of Grafton's 'copy' before it was in print—for Grafton wanted it back as his printers were waiting for it. But the letter also shows that Parker's interest was not perfunctory— he had asked for the loan of a Chronicle Grafton possessed, and had even queried some details of names in it. He was in correspondence, too, with Dr. Caius of Cambridge, urging him to answer a pamphlet which asserted the greater antiquity of Oxford University.[4] Caius sent him a copy of the rough draft of his answer, asking for Parker's views and corrections. From Caius' own account, the task set for Parker can hardly have been easy. Caius had not had time to compare the copy with his original and feared that there might be mistakes due to careless copying. He thought that the Archbishop might wish to add and to delete. It sounds as though the manuscript was rather a mess: many things were 'roughly left'. It is a testimony to the Archbishop's zeal in such matters that Caius obviously thought he would work through it and send his personal corrections—for he was anxious that no one else should see it yet, and especially not Joscelyn who might show it to everybody, and 'do little good in it himself'! Again, in July 1568 the Archbishop was successful in procuring a letter from the Privy Council giving to him 'special care and oversight' regarding 'ancient records and monuments' which had been in monasteries and were by then in private hands. His deputies, if authorized by him, were to be allowed to inspect such documents and, if need be, to borrow them, under guarantee of return, for closer inspection. The letter issued from the Council—but it was Parker who suggested it and, probably, drew it up.[5] The next year he wrote to Cecil for support for an English printer in the production of Latin

---

[1] *Correspondence*, pp. 320, 324.   [2] Ibid., p. 324.   [3] Ibid., pp. 295-6.
[4] Ibid., pp. 298-300.   [5] Ibid., pp. 327-8, and note.

texts—Terence, Virgil, Cicero; if he were 'privileged' Parker thought he could produce the books well, and cheaper than foreign imports. Besides, it 'were not amiss to set our own countrymen on work'.[1] At the same time, for his own purposes, he reiterated a request for the loan of Cecil's copy of Matthew Paris: he would only keep it for a week or two. He was now preparing his own edition of Matthew Paris.[2]

The most notable literary event of these years, however, was the publication of the so-called *Bishops' Bible*. To what extent the original impulse for this may have come, as has been suggested, from Cox rather than Parker himself cannot now be determined.[3] The former may have been the first to press for it—though Parker nowhere gives any hint to that effect. Certainly the main part of the arrangements fell on the Archbishop's shoulders. He allotted the portions among the translators, gave them instructions on the lines to be followed and saw to the editing of the whole. By October 1568 a copy was printed and bound, ready to be presented to the Queen. Parker was not well enough to offer it in person, and so, to prevent delay (characteristically, for the consideration of 'the poor printer' among other things), he sent it to Cecil with a covering letter to the Queen, asking him to present it to her.[4] He enclosed a list of those

[1] *Correspondence*, p. 353.

[2] Strype, *Parker* i, 552–3. Strype notes the careful collation of MSS.

[3] Cox had more than once suggested to Cecil that there should be a new translation of the Bible (Cooper, *Ath. Cant.* i. 440). Cox would be naturally suspicious of the Geneva Bible, largely the product of Whittingham with whom he had had grievous differences at Frankfort. Published in 1560, the Geneva version at once became popular: it was printed in verses, in legible Roman type not black letter, and in a manageable *quarto* form. Though it is sometimes said to be strongly Calvinistic in its notes, Westcott finds its 'marginal commentary' only 'slightly tinged with Calvinistic doctrine' (*History of the English Bible*, 1st edition, p. 125), and in 1565 Parker and Grindal had thought 'so well of the first impression, and review of those which have sithence travailed therein' that they urged that Bodley should be given a licence to print for twelve years. They had already in mind to publish a single edition for use in churches, but thought it might do good to have a 'diversity of translations' (*Correspondence*, p. 262). By 1568 the position was different. The *provenance* of the Geneva version made it suspect in view of the activities of the left-wing leaders.   [4] *Correspondence*, p. 334.

who had travailed in the work and what portions they had undertaken, and added that 'the letters of their names' had been
partly affixed to their books, 'to make them more diligent, as
answerable for their doings'. In fact, such initialling was not
strictly or universally observed in the printed Bible, but so far
as it was done it does in the main confirm the list of translators
sent to Cecil by Parker.[1] Strype declared that the Archbishop's
'province was not so much to translate, as to order, direct,
overlook, examine, and prepare and finish all'.[2] But if the
catalogue sent to Cecil is reliable, Parker himself did a very great
deal—the Books of Genesis and Exodus, the Gospels of St.
Matthew and St. Mark, the Pauline Epistles (save Romans and
1 Corinthians) and Hebrews, to say nothing of the Prefaces to
the Bible as a whole, and to the New Testament and to the
Psalms as well as the Sum of the Scripture and the Tables of
Christ's Line. Admittedly, the exact authorship of each translation is not ascertainable beyond any question. Still, it seems
unlikely that in writing to Cecil Parker would claim for himself
more than was his due.[3] It must have been a formidable task in
an already busy life.

The rules laid down for the translators are a testimony to
Parker's moderation, fairness and common sense.[4] The usual
familiar English translation was to be followed where it did not
manifestly differ from the Hebrew or Greek. There were to be
'no bitter notes upon any text', nor were they to 'set down any

[1] *Correspondence*, pp. 335-6; compare Strype, *Parker* ii, 222. Westcott
(p. 135) suggests that Lawrence was one of the translators and that his name
was omitted. He relies (p. 310) on a statement of Strype (*Parker* ii, 223).
But all Strype says is that he was one of those consulted by Parker about the
text and translation of the N.T., not that he was actually one of the translators. The Third and revised edition of Westcott (p. 237) notes this.

[2] *Parker* ii, 223.

[3] This seems to be confirmed by the fact, noted in the Third (revised)
edition of Westcott, p. 100, that the initials 'M. C.' appear not indeed at the
end, but under the initial letter, of each of the books attributed to Parker in
his letter to Cecil, save for St. Mark's Gospel. This would seem to suggest at
least a final personal revision by the Archbishop if not the actual full translation.   [4] *Correspondence*, p. 336.

determination in places of controversy'. Genealogies and 'places not edifying' were to be noted so that they could be omitted in public reading, and words likely to give 'offence of lightness or obscenity' were to be exchanged for 'more convenient terms and phrases'. And, very sensibly, the thickest paper was used for printing the New Testament 'because it shall be most occupied'. The aim was to produce a version acceptable (so far as possible) by its familiarity, inoffensive to contentious spirits, suitable for reading in church. Parker urged Cecil to obtain from the Queen permission that it alone should be licensed and ordered to be read in church 'to draw to one uniformity' (he evidently no longer thought a variety of translations desirable); and that 'Jugge only may have the preferment of this edition'. If it were pirated, he would lose much money.

In the covering letter for the Queen,[1] this last commercial point—the reverse of discreditable to Parker—was not included! It is a graceful letter asking her 'to accept in good part' the efforts of the translators, and asking that the result may have her 'gracious favour, licence and protection'. He does, however suggest that it should be ordered for reading in churches because in some of them there were in use 'translations which have not been laboured in your realm, having inspersed divers prejudiced notes, which might have been also well spared'.

The Bishops' Bible was a splendid volume, clearly printed and lavishly illustrated with wood-cuts, but it did not have so great an immediate success as Parker must have hoped. The Queen did not give it the sole authorization to be read in churches which was desired. The Constitutions and Canons Ecclesiastical of 1571 ordered, indeed, that every bishop should have a copy of it along with the Memorials of the Martyrs, and other similar books, placed in his hall or dining-room for the use of strangers and servants; that every cathedral should have a copy, and every church, along with Prayer Book and Homilies—so far as it could 'conveniently' be done.[2] And it does seem to have superseded for public use the *Great Bible*, of which there was no printing

---

[1] *Correspondence*, p. 337.   [2] Cardwell, *Synodalia* i, 115, 123.

after 1569. In a further edition of the *Bishops' Bible* in 1572 the Old Testament was in the main unchanged, but the New carefully revised. The chapters were now divided into verses, in the fashion of the *Geneva Bible*, divers tables and new explanatory notes were added, but some of the old notes were dropped. This revision must indeed have been a considerable task for which the main responsibility, if not the detailed work, again rested on the Archbishop. But it is significant that in this later edition the older version of the Psalms was re-printed from the *Great Bible* side by side with the Bishops' version: and in all subsequent editions, save one, was printed alone. Familiarity was too strong to be overcome. Nor, in fact, was the Genevan version put out of popular favour. It has been calculated that it was reprinted four times as often as the *Bishops' Bible*, and that it was the version with which educated Englishmen were brought up till the authorized version appeared. The *Bishops' Bible* was indeed an attempt to get a fair text unprejudiced by partisan interpretations. But its value lay ultimately not in any immediate wide acceptance but in its influence on the Authorized Version, of which the revised edition of 1572 formed the basis.[1]

[1] Westcott, op. cit., p. 316.

CHAPTER XV

VISITATION OF CANTERBURY CATHEDRAL; PARLIAMENT AND CONVOCATION OF 1571: ARTICLES AND CANONS

THE year 1570 marks a clear turning point in the religious history of Elizabeth's reign. Hitherto, opposition to the Settlement had been, on the whole, spasmodic and unorganized. There had been discontent, criticism, secret or even open disobedience; some Romanists had fled or been deprived; some protestants had been punished. From 1570 onwards both parties of opponents took up positions of clearer determination to upset—and to work for the deliberate upsetting of—the *via media*. Official opposition to both parties became therefore more active and rigid.

At the end of 1569 the Rebellion of the Northern Earls was easily crushed, and was punished with great severity[1]—though, as Grindal discovered, that did not eliminate Romanism in Durham and Yorkshire; and in Lancashire, which the rising had not touched, the old religion increasingly flourished. Parker was not himself directly affected, however anxious he may have been made by the rebellion. Certainly he recognized the duty of the Church to help the state. Earlier in 1569, when an invasion from the Low Countries was feared, he was ordered by the Queen and Council to provide a certificate of the armour etc. to be supplied by the clergy of his province according to the rate used in the time of Philip and Mary. He showed no resentment, but passed on the order to the Bishop of London to be signified to the other bishops of the province that all might send their returns to him

[1] Dixon, vi, 238.

at Lambeth.[1] He enclosed a schedule to show exactly how the clergy were to be assessed. A similar letter, with the schedule, was sent to the Dean and Chapter of York, the see being vacant; they were to report direct to the Council, not to Parker.[2] There was no attempt on his part to evade such responsibilities—it would not have been wise under the Elizabethan government. But he was anxious to protect the clergy from unjust claims. He was careful to point out to Cecil that it would be safest to depend on the official returns from the bishops rather than on an unofficial list which was 'in many respects imperfect' drawn up by one Godfrey.[3] He enclosed a table he had made for his own diocese to satisfy Cecil,[4] in which the liabilities of the Archbishop himself were very generously assessed. But there can be little doubt that he suspected that, if unofficial lists were used, the poorer clergy would be victimized. When the Northern Rebellion actually took place, the Archbishop must himself have sent some troops, for in a later letter to an anonymous lord he thanked him for 'the great favour and gentleness showed with my poor lances at York'.[5]

The first part of 1570 he spent at Lambeth dealing with normal routine, but worried about vacant sees and the delay in filling them.[6] Early in May he was at Canterbury where he remained till the latter part of July. Once more he was able to provide the lavish hospitality he so much enjoyed giving—and the *Matthaeus* so much enjoys retailing! On Ascension day he preached to clergy and people in the cathedral. On Whitsunday and the two following days he magnificently entertained the citizens of Canterbury and their wives. On Trinity Sunday there was another great feast attended by the newly appointed Archbishop of York, and the Bishops of Winchester, Rochester and Chichester, the last of whom, Curteys, formerly one of his chaplains, he had consecrated that morning, forgiving him the usual fees. Though this last also was a magnificent banquet it was more ecclesiastical

---

[1] *Correspondence*, p. 345.   [2] Ibid., p. 347.   [3] Ibid., p. 348.
[4] Strype, *Parker* i, 544–5.   [5] *Correspondence*, p. 388.
[6] Ibid., pp. 359, 360.

in character, attended not only by bishops, but by all connected with the cathedral, even servants and children, and by the poor of both sexes from the hospital of St. John of Harbledown. The whole proceedings were given a special note of thanksgiving in memory of King Henry VIII who had expelled the monks from Christ Church and reformed it. On the 11th of July there was another feast for the Judges of Assize and their company.[1]

But there was more serious business too. With his strong historic sense and his appreciation of the dignity of the position he held, it was obviously[2] grateful to him to perform in the metropolitan church of his province some of the most important duties which fell to his lot. Curteys was consecrated there; on the next day in the cathedral he confirmed Grindal as Archbishop of York, in the presence of Horne and Guest. Later in the month, he received there Sandys, entertained him kindly for two days and confirmed him as Bishop of London in succession to Grindal.

A less pleasant task was a visitation of the cathedral, which the Archbishop undertook in person. It was, presumably, a continuation of the visitation committed in the previous May to the Bishop of Dover and others.[3] Why it should now have been necessary for Parker to intervene in person does not appear, for the commissioners had then certainly been authorized to deal with the cathedral as well as the diocese, and in November the Dean had delivered to them certain writings belonging to the cathedral and had received the visitors' injunctions.[4] Possibly their authority had not proved sufficient to rectify all disorders. Be that as it may, on the 29th May 1570, Parker issued his citation for the Dean and all members of the cathedral to present themselves for his visitation on July 3. The proceedings are minutely recorded in the *Register*,[5] including the exact order for the opening ceremonies—the service in the cathedral to be over by eight in the morning, when the Dean, canons and preachers were to wait upon the Archbishop to conduct him to the cathedral,

[1] *Matthaeus* in Strype, *Parker* iii, 291–3.
[2] This is clear from the *Matthaeus*.　　　　　　[3] *Register*, pp. 527–8.
[4] M. R. James; Corpus Christi MSS, ii, 184 (Item 9 of 349).　　[5] pp. 531 sqq.

and so on. There follows the account of how this order of procedure was actually carried out, and the Royal Letters Patent of
the Foundation exhibited. The visitation continued almost daily
until July 22nd, and usually Parker appeared in person; if not,
Yale was deputed to act for him. In spite of the impressiveness of
the formalities, there is little evidence of serious shortcomings,
beyond a certain amount of bickering among the prebendaries,
and minor irregularities of discipline. Two of the prebendaries
were in dispute over houses and gardens—they signed a bond to
accept the award of arbitrators. On the complaint of some of the
prebendaries and preachers that they lacked stables, a small
committee was ordered to go into the matter and report what
stables and wood-houses were needed and what were available;
and to suggest improvement in the accommodation for the school
house and hall for the Grammarians. Other complaints of which
details are not given were presented to Yale on succeeding days,
but from the Injunctions he delivered in English it does not seem
that very much was wrong. An inventory was to be made of all
church plate and goods, certificates were to be presented of the
times of reception of communion by minor canons and others
over the last year, and such of them as were 'Suspected in Religion' were to be examined; so were the scholars in the grammar
school as to their progress, and the members of the choir as to
their skill. Such orders do not suggest the existence of any serious
scandal. Additional Injunctions issued by Yale, also in English,
do not go much further. The plan for convenient housing in the
Close was to be completed, church debts were to be more speedily
collected, the prebendaries were to preach more often. Residences
and the grammar school were to be repaired, and the gardens
cleaned. Steps were to be taken to stop the using of the church
and cloister as a 'high-way or passage' for market folks, and the
porters were to be more strict in closing the gates at the proper
time. Any who possessed deeds belonging to the church were to
hand them in, and Dean and prebendaries were to restore such
'goods and ornaments as they have of their private authority
taken away from the said Church'. The Archbishop himself laid

down the order for settling the quarrel of the two prebendaries, and for the allocation of certain dividends among prebendaries who had not kept continuous residence either because they were royal chaplains or for other causes. Finally, some Latin Injunctions of more permanent character were delivered, the reasons for them alleged by the Archbishop being simply that some of the statutes of the cathedral were neglected or not diligently observed, and that there were serious dissensions. But, once more, there is little to support the idea that much was wrong, save financial irregularities and some slackness. The statutes were to be observed; no important business was to be transacted without full and open discussion, especially in regard to property; accounts were to be carefully kept and examined; minor canons and officials were to be fined for non-attendance at services; there were for the present to be no more dividends of casual profits among the canons; the rules for election of scholars to the school were to be more strictly enforced; there was to be twice a week (save in August and September) a lecture on some portion of Scripture by a learned man which the Dean and prebendaries were to attend. In sum, it looks as though buildings and gardens were ill-kept, the Close insufficiently protected and enclosed, the school not as good as it might be—all matters which would give concern to the Archbishop. There was irregularity in attending services in the cathedral. But the worst fault of all was probably jealousy and quarrelling among the canons. All were defects which rightly called for the attention of the Archbishop. But it is difficult to suppose that the impressive character of the ceremonial and the personal attention of the Archbishop were solely caused by the enormity of the faults suspected. Parker in his metropolitan city was giving play to his sense of the dignity and duties of his office.

After the visitation, Parker returned to Lambeth, shortly to face a heavy loss. On the 17th of August, Mrs. Parker died of fever. They had been married more than twenty-six years and she had happily shared both the misfortunes of Mary's reign and the anxieties of great position under Elizabeth. She had been a good mother and had cheerfully and carefully looked after his house and undertaken the burden of his lavish entertaining.[1] The sole reference Parker made, in his extant correspondence, to his loss was in writing to Cecil a week later. 'It hath pleased Almighty God, whose will is always the best and must be obeyed, to offer unto me some matter of patience, and foolish frail nature troubleth me yet so, that I have much ado with myself to gather my wits and memory together.'[2] Perhaps a deeper light is thrown on what must have been his desolation by the revealing remark he made to Lady Bacon that he had treated a matter as so confidential that he had not mentioned it even to his wife. She was evidently his confidant and sympathizer in all his cares and troubles. Her death came at a time when the ageing Archbishop could ill spare her.

Early in 1570, probably at the end of February, after some sort of judicial process in Rome, the Pope issued his Bull of Excommunication *Regnans in excelcis*,[3] claiming full power over all races and kingdoms. He listed a long catalogue of the sins of the 'pretensed' Queen of England—her heresy and support of heretics, her suppression and removal of Catholics—and declared that she and all who supported her were anathematized, and herself deprived of all lordship, dignity and privilege. He absolved from their oath all who had sworn allegiance to her and forbade them to obey her orders and laws under pain of anathema.[4] The bull was the act of an austere zealot, not of a statesman. Doubtless he was influenced by English refugees in Rome, and misled by false information about conditions in England and especially about the extent of Romanist feeling against the Queen. In fact, the bull fell flat. The secular rulers in Europe were upset or even angered by it—the Emperor, the Kings of Spain and France, the Duke of Alva, all in various degrees disapproved.[5] It came too late to help the Northern Rebellion, and did not seriously shake the loyalty of the vast majority of Catholics in

[1] *Matthaeus* in Strype, *Parker* iii, 294.   [2] *Correspondence*, pp. 368-9.
[3] R. W. Dixon, *History* vi, 250 sqq., deals very fully with the whole matter.
[4] The Bull is in Cardwell, *Documentary Annals*, i, 328.
[5] Dixon, op. cit., vi, 267-8.

England though it no doubt did encourage the small minority who were already plotting the Queen's removal. It was never allowed to be officially published in England, though a copy was smuggled in and about the beginning of June posted on the gate of the Bishop of London in Paul's Yard. It only remained there for a night and Felton who had put it up suffered the full rigours for an act of high treason. But though not officially published in England, it was soon well known and was immediately answered[1] —by Jewel, and by Bullinger at the request of English bishops. Parker caused Bullinger's answer to be printed.[2] Indeed, by anticipation, the Queen had already answered it in 'A Declaration of the Queen's Proceedings since her Reign'. This is a manuscript in Cecil's writing with extensive and significant alterations and additions by the Queen herself.[3] It probably was written in January or February 1570, after the suppression of the Northern Rebellion. She claimed that by the authority committed to her, next under God, she was bound to direct all estates to live 'in the faith, the obedience and observation of Christian religion'. None the less she had not desired or allowed any of her subjects to be 'molested either by examination or inquisition in any matter' of faith, if they did not gainsay the authority of Scripture and the Creeds; or for ceremonies or other external matters if the said subjects were not 'manifestly repugnant and obstinate' to the laws established by the whole realm for resorting to their ordinary churches. Later, she assured all subjects obedient to her laws that they should not in future suffer any molestation by any person 'by way of examination or inquisition of their secret opinions in their consciences, for matters of faith'. If any 'potentate in Christendom, challenging any universal and sole superiority over the whole Church of Christ' denied her authority, she was willing 'in place and time convenient' to have the case tried—but not if the potentate so claiming was to be the judge in his own cause: 'other Christian monarchs, potentates, and

---

[1] Dixon, History vi, 274 sqq. [2] Strype, Parker ii, 78.
[3] Printed in W. E. Collins, Queen Elizabeth's Defence of her Proceedings in Church and State (S.P.C.K.: London, 1899), pp. 35 sqq.

princes' should be there, allowed to speak freely 'as in former better times'. Thus she was prepared to challenge the papal claims. Whether one is willing to accept her position in that respect or not, her statement of her own policy and wishes rings true, and deserves admiration. She really had not tried to search consciences, but had only punished Romanists for disobeying the laws of the realm.

Though, at the conclusion, the statement was ordered to be published and read out in parish churches, there is no evidence that it was ever printed in Elizabeth's day. But a statement drawn up by Cecil, stating the same scrupulous policy, was published in the Star Chamber by the Lord Keeper on June 15[1] (after the contents of the bull were known) to the effect that 'as long as they shall openly continue in the observation of her laws, and shall not wilfully and manifestly break them by their open actions, her majesty's meaning is, not to have any of them molested by any inquisition or examination of their consciences in causes of religion'. For the age, it was a most liberal policy, and it is remarkable that not even the bull was able to shake the Queen out of observing it. None the less, the bull did have serious consequences in England. It made it much more difficult for those who favoured the old religion but yet were loyal to the Queen to continue to compromise by occasional outward conformity. To that extent it made more rigid the position of the Romanists. And it made them all in the eyes of the Council (much more concerned, apparently, than the Queen herself about her personal safety) potential traitors and even regicides. If they really believed themselves to be freed from their oath of obedience and loyalty—indeed encouraged to break it—they were obviously a suspect and dangerous element in the country.

Meantime, a serious threat from the other side suddenly developed in Cambridge. Thomas Cartwright, elected to the Margaret Lectureship at the end of 1569, began to lecture on the Acts of the Apostles early in the next year.[2] In doing so, he

[1] Strype, *Annals* I, ii, 371.
[2] A. F. Scott Pearson, *Thomas Cartwright and Elizabethan Puritanism* (Cambridge, 1925), pp. 25 sqq., gives a clear and fully documented account.

contrasted vividly the sort of church organization he thought he found there with that existing in the Church of England. That, no doubt, might have been a legitimate academic exercise. But in Cartwright's case it was inspired by a deep belief not only in the absolute authority of Scripture (which none of his opponents would have denied) but also that the pattern displayed in the Acts was thereby laid down for all Churches and for all time. Inevitably, he seemed to be suggesting the need for the total reconstruction of English church polity. It was no longer, for him, a question of clerical dress, of unleavened bread and kneeling to receive at communion, of the signing with the cross and interrogatories at baptism, of the use of the ring at marriage, of the position of the holy table in church. It was not even a matter of serious defects such as pluralism, non-residence, ignorant clergy. All those things of which the Puritans complained could have been altered without affecting the fundamental ecclesiastical organization. But the clear implication of Cartwright's lectures was that the whole constitution of the Church, when tested by the inviolable rule of Scripture, was wrong—and should therefore be changed. Under pressure from the Vice-Chancellor he reduced the sum of his doctrine to six articles, which he signed.[1] The names and present offices of archbishop and bishop should be abolished, so should all non-New Testament officers such as chancellors, officials, archdeacons. Bishops might remain, but only with a spiritual function, and deacons should confine themselves to the care of the poor. Church government should rest solely with the minister and presbyters of the local church. A minister should be attached to a particular congregation, and should be elected by it and not by the authority of a bishop. Though not fully worked out, the whole picture is fundamentally that of a presbyterian organization: later on, Cartwright would not allow even to St. Peter a great authority than that of a 'leading speaker in the lower house'.[2]

Cartwright was a good scholar, but he was more than that. He was intensely sincere, of great eloquence, leading a life of

[1] Scott Pearson, pp. 28–29.   [2] Ibid., p. 26.

strictest discipline. He was exactly the sort of man to compel the enthusiasm and devotion of idealist youth; what he taught seemed to be purely Scriptural. (At this stage, he had not been abroad: he based his views on his reading of the Bible, not on what was done in Geneva.) He quickly had a large and eager body of supporters among the younger members of the University. But most of the Heads of Houses and the older men were strongly opposed to him. There were appeals to Cecil as Chancellor to put a stop to his teaching; he obtained from Cartwright a promise not to deal any further in such matters for the time being. But, with characteristic caution, Cecil refused himself to try to adjudicate in the matter—the authorities in Cambridge, he argued, were much more fitted to judge of such things than he—though he did later on say that he thought Cartwright had dealt with the topics concerned in an academic not a turbulent manner. But he made it clear that he would not interfere as Chancellor but would leave the University authorities on the spot to deal with the situation and would support them. This attitude he maintained despite more than one well-signed testimonial on Cartwright's behalf— and, on the other hand, a letter from Whitgift saying that he thought the Chancellor did not really understand Cartwright's position![1] In Cambridge, Cartwright was prevented by the authorities at the end of June from taking his Doctorate of Divinity; there was much commotion. In August he was inhibited from lecturing. In September, new statutes for the University were confirmed by the royal seal; they much increased the power of the Heads of Houses and correspondingly lessened that of the younger Masters of Arts. Under them, Cartwright was, in December, deprived of his chair, and went abroad. The real leader—the strong man—both in dealing with Cartwright and in procuring the new statutes to check the power of juniors in University business, was John Whitgift, Master of Trinity, of which College Cartwright was a Fellow.

A new stage was thus opened in the history of English

---

[1] *Works of Archbishop Whitgift* (J. Ayre, London, 1853, Parker Society), iii, 598.

Puritanism. There had been many—especially among the returned exiles—who had looked back with longing eyes to the church of Geneva. They had envied its enthusiasm, its preaching, its discipline. They had criticized all manner of points in the Prayer Book and customs of the English Church. But they had not worked openly for a fundamental re-casting of it, only for further amendment.[1] Henceforward, the aim of the keen young leaders of the Puritans was to introduce—gradually and without violence if possible—an effective presbyterian order, and strict discipline on Genevan lines. The old complaints about the church were still maintained (ignorant and non-preaching ministers, pluralism, non-residence, the church courts, the abuse of ex-communication as well as details in the Prayer Book) but in effect the movement was now differently orientated: its essence was the desire for presbyterian instead of episcopal control.

Increasingly as time passed the Archbishop was to be troubled about both papish recusants and presbyterianizers: initially he does not seem to have been deeply involved. Against the Romans the lead was taken by the Council: there were proclamations in July against those who brought into the country seditious books and bills, and in November against fugitives and rebels who spread traitorous books and speeches. All that Parker seems to have done (besides trying to prevent Culpepper from escaping) was to press for additions to the number of the ecclesiastical commission because of the increase in massing; for correction of faults in the commission when it was issued, and for the establishment of branches to act in various dioceses.[2] And it was Cecil rather than he who had to deal with the crisis in Cambridge, though Whitgift did suggest that the Chancellor if he were too busy to peruse the new University statutes might ask the Archbishop for his views.[3] But by the end of the year a letter to the

---

[1] Yet, as early as 1570 one Axton had argued with the Bishop of Lichfield that every minister of God was a bishop, and that calling and laying on of hands by the elders was a necessary part of a true ministry and that he had been so called though 'that was the least part of my calling', *Seconde Parte of a Register* (ed. A. Peel, Cambridge, 1915), i, 70–71.

[2] *Correspondence*, pp. 369, 371.   [3] Scott Pearson, op. cit., p. 39.

Queen showed that Parker was under no delusion as to what was happening and the dangers of it, for State as well as Church.[1] 'Some learned, some of other private respects' so dislike his position 'that they conclude plainly in doctrine and hold in affection, *quod archiepiscoporum nomina simul cum muneribus suis et officiis sunt abolenda*; which practice when they have brought about . . . that this room should be either too low abased or quite abolished, I think your Highness' Council should have too much ado, beside their other great affairs, in staying the unruliness of some part of the ministers for religion, and in some others of the laity for their insolent living.'

Even among such Puritans as did not actually seek the abolition of the episcopate, the bishops were violently attacked for their enforcement of clerical attire and the Prayer Book. They, not the Queen, got all the blame, and the language was unrestrained— 'Our bishops . . . being now fatted with promotion, honour and wealth, forgetting what they have been, and looking only to their present estate, are blinded with estimation of themselves, with desire to please those who are in high authority, and with careful carking, as well to keep that which they have, as also greedy to gather more to it.' They are blinded by 'wealth, honour and dignity'.[2] There is nothing in the tract—*A Comfortable Letter*— to suggest presbyterian ideas: it is chiefly about the apparel and other 'toys and trifles'. It is, indeed, anti-prelatical rather than anti-episcopal. But such views so violently expressed were not calculated to strengthen the episcopate against direct attack.

In 1571 both Parliament and Convocation met in April. Even before that Parker had good reason to know the turbulent mood of the discontented. In January he had found it necessary to write to Cecil concerning the kind of bread to be used at the communion service.[3] Apparently the latter did not know that ordinary table bread was even permissible, despite the rubric

---

[1] *Correspondence*, p. 373.

[2] *A Comfortable Epistle* in *Parte of a Register*, pp. 2-3, 5. Attributed to Percival Wyburn *c.* 1570 by Albert Peel in *Seconde Parte of a Register*, p. 30.   [3] *Correspondence*, p. 375.

in the Prayer Book that 'it shall suffice that the Bread be such as is used to be eaten; but the best and purest Wheat Bread that conveniently may be gotten'. The Royal Injunctions had, sub-sequently to the Uniformity Act, ordered the use of bread similar to the 'singing cakes, which served for the use of private Mass', though somewhat bigger. That was the rule generally followed—but it was, not unnaturally, objectionable to the Puritans and they were making trouble about it. Parker tried to set Cecil's mind at rest. The rubric in the Prayer Book was simply permissive —in order to avoid 'occasion of dissension or superstition' it would suffice if ordinary bread were used: there was nothing to suggest that any other sort of bread was illegitimate. The Queen's order in her Injunctions supplemented, but—according to Parker —did not contradict the rubric. He argued that the proviso at the end of the Act of Uniformity which enabled the Queen, on the advice of her commissioners or of the Metropolitan, to take further order concerning the ornaments of church and minister, in fact allowed her to 'ordain and publish such further cere-monies, or rites, as may be most for the reverence of Christ's holy mysteries and sacraments', and that therefore 'the injunction hath authority by the proviso of the statute'. That, no doubt, was ingenious—but it was not likely to satisfy contentious minds. The proviso only referred to ornaments, not to rites and cere-monies: and the communion bread was certainly not an orna-ment. No wonder there was what Parker calls 'great disquiet babbling' about it. A month after his first letter to Cecil, he sent him a sample of the form of bread approved by himself and the Bishop of London,[1] and urged him to try to pacify the opposition.

A little later he had to write to Cecil to re-assure him that the question '*an principibus sit potius resistendum quam obediendum in rebus adiaphoris*' had not been debated (presumably among Puritans) as Cecil had apparently been informed. But if that sort of thing should happen it might well be that Mr. Mullyns (the Archdeacon of London) should 'openly tell the precisians that her Highness' sword shall be compelled to cut off this

[1] *Correspondence*, p. 378.

stubborn multitude, which daily groweth'. It would be a great mistake if it should be 'slily with a flourish passed over'.[1]

There is also one small scrap of evidence that Parker was being personally abused. He had heard that a nobleman had imputed it to his doing that the cross was once more put up in the royal chapel.[2] He can only attribute it to 'envy' for in fact he knew nothing about it and did not think its restoration expedient.

In such a restless atmosphere, it was natural that the Council should regard the composition of the new House of Commons with apprehension. Consequently a letter was sent to the Archbishop and the Lord Warden of the Cinque Ports (and to others, it was said, of similar authority in other places) asking them to confer with sheriffs and leading men to see that those chosen to be members of Parliament should be 'qualified with knowledge, discretion, and modesty, and meet for those places'. For in the past some at least had been named for their private interests, or to avoid arrest! or 'to set forth private causes by sinister labour and frivolous talks and arguments'.[3] Such efforts of the Council to influence the personnel of the Commons did not, however, prevent the election of a strong Puritan element, led by William Strickland and Peter Wentworth, which was not only vocal but persistent in pressing for interference in ecclesiastical matters, even in the face of strong government disapproval.[4] Their tactics were made the easier by the failure of the Speaker to control them and by the absence from the Commons of Cecil, promoted to the Lords in February 1571 as Baron Burghley. An unofficial Bill was immediately introduced into the Commons concerning attendance at church. Its object was to enforce the provisions of the Uniformity Act by stiffer fines for non-attendance more effectively exacted. But it had a significant new feature—everyone of age to do so was to take communion once a year or pay a fine of 100 marks. That would indeed have been to force consciences, and there were protests against it on that ground in the

---

[1] *Correspondence*, p. 377.   [2] Ibid., p. 379.   [3] Ibid., p. 380-1.
[4] For a full account, see Sir John Neale, *Elizabeth and Her Parliaments 1559–81*, pp. 177–240.

Commons. Ultimately, however, with amendments, it passed both Houses; the conduct of Alva in the Low Countries, the Northern Rebellion, the Bull of Excommunication, the suspicion of Mary of Scotland, had combined to make the majority of both Houses thoroughly suspicious of Rome. It seems likely that some of the bishops and even Burghley were in favour of the Bill. It only failed to reach the Statute Book because the Queen, with brave consistency, refused her assent. More Bills followed, of a definitely Puritan flavour. Strickland wished the *Reformatio legum ecclesiasticarum*[1] to be considered; and on his suggestion a committee of the Commons was appointed to confer with the bishops about reform of the Church. Some of the 'alphabetical bills' of 1566 were revived, and a new one to forbid commutation of penance by a bishop without the consent of two J.P.s. Strickland even introduced a Bill for the reformation of the Prayer Book—to abolish copes and surplices, the confirmation of children, the interrogation of god-parents at baptism, the ring at marriage, kneeling at communion, and so on. That, at least, was going too far. He was promptly sequestered by the Council, though not for long. But his Bill was not proceeded with. The question of insistence on signing the *Articles* of 1563 led to long and tortuous proceedings—for the Puritans were not now ready to accept all of them. In the course of one interview with Parker, when he asked why they had not accepted them all, Wentworth declared that they had been so busy with other things that they had not had time to compare them with the Word of God. Parker suggested that in such a matter they should surely accept the views of the bishops; Wentworth replied 'we will pass nothing before we understand what it is, for that were but to make you Popes. Make you Popes who list, for we will make you none'.[2] Shortly afterwards, the Queen put an end to such wrangles; she firmly

[1] This was an attempt, begun under Cranmer, to produce a complete code of Canon Law for the English Church. Parker revived and amended the draft and had recently had it printed by Jn. Foxe. It never received any authority, and, indeed, contained many features to which the Puritans would have objected had it been considered again.

[2] Neale, op. cit., p. 205.

intimated that she would have such matters dealt with by the bishops, not in Parliament.

The practical outcome of all such fervour and agitation was small. Most of the 'alphabetical bills' disappeared either after a single reading in the Lords, or after the Lords had made in them amendments which the Commons would not accept. No doubt their fate was attributed—and probably with justice—to the action of the bishops. The Queen refused to accept the Bill for coming to church and taking communion yearly. The net result, so far as religion was concerned, was an important *Act to reform certain disorders touching ministers of the church,* an Act to limit the leasing of benefices not impropriated to cases in which there was a resident minister; and certain anti-Roman measures—against introducing or executing bulls, and depriving of their property Englishmen who had gone abroad without licence. The first Act of all was significant: it disabled from succession to the throne any person who claimed a right to it during the Queen's lifetime or refused to acknowledge her title; it was obviously aimed at Mary Queen of Scots.

The Act concerning disorders laid down that no one was to be admitted to a benefice unless at least twenty-three years of age and a deacon, and that none was to receive a living of the annual value of £30 or more unless a B.D. or a licensed preacher. There was also a clause which ordered that any minister who claimed to be so by any form of institution, consecrating or ordering other than that used in the Church of England under Edward VI and Elizabeth was to be deprived unless, before the coming Christmas, he declared his assent and subscribed to 'all the Articles of Religion which only concern the confession of the true Christian Faith and the Doctrine of the Sacraments', as contained in the Book of Articles of 1562 (i.e. 1563. The reference is definitely to the English, not the Latin version). The oath was also to be taken by all who were appointed to livings in the future, and all candidates for ordination. The clause was chiefly intended to catch the Marian clergy, but it would also affect those who had been 'called' in foreign protestant churches and not ordained in

England. It was for their sake that the words 'which only concern'
etc. were added. They were not intended as a general description
covering all the *Articles*, but as a limitation of the oath to certain
of them alone, meant to exclude such articles about rites and
ceremonies and so on, as the Puritans disliked. There is some
evidence that at first the oath was taken with those limitations,[1]
but soon they were forgotten, and the oath was required to all
the *Articles*—and not to those of 1563 as the Act demanded, but
to the *Articles* as slightly revised by Convocation in 1571.

It is to be observed that all the efforts of the Puritans in this
Parliament were aimed at giving effect to the changes they had
long worked for. There was as yet no suggestion of Presbyterianism. That they obtained so little—a very mild qualification of
the oath to the *Articles*—was no doubt due to the opposition of
the bishops, who were now weary of Puritan obstinacy and
evasion—and rudeness. Perhaps that was at least one reason why,
in the next year, the Puritan campaign took on a definitely anti-
episcopal character.

Concurrently with the meeting of Parliament was one of
Convocation.[2] The opening sermon was preached by Whitgift—
a choice presumably made by Parker, and highly significant in
view of his recent firm stand against Cartwright. It was an outspoken sermon, treating of the authority of synods, of the enemies
of the Church, 'to wit puritans and papists', of the use of vestments and ornaments, and of many things in need of reformation.
The meetings of the Convocation were first at St. Paul's, then at
Westminster (after the permission of the Dean and Chapter
had been duly received); and there was a meeting of the bishops
at Lambeth—Strype conjectures that this was because of the
ill-health of the Archbishop.[3] Its proceedings are very imperfectly
recorded, but it is clear that they were chiefly concerned with the

---

[1] E.g. by Goodman, Wyburn, Dering and Field in 1571. (*Seconde Parte of
a Register*, p. 82.) In Parker's *Register* (p. 613) there is a certificate, sealed with
Parker's seal, to testify that an incumbent had so subscribed in 1571. In a
similar certificate of the same month (p. 987) the saving clause is omitted.

[2] The proceedings are given in Cardwell, *Synodalia*, ii, 528–31.

[3] *Parker* ii, 53.

Articles, some Canons for discipline, and the case of Richard Cheyney, Bishop of Gloucester.

At the second session the Archbishop ordered all the members of the Lower House who had not already subscribed the *Articles* of 1563 to do so at once or else to be excluded. On May 4, after secret consideration, the Archbishop and his brethren unanimously agreed that 'when the book of articles touching doctrine shall be fully agreed upon' it was to be printed under the guidance of the Bishop of Salisbury and a price fixed for it; that each bishop should procure a convenient number for use in his diocese; and that it should then be read four times a year in each parish church.

Further consideration was given to the *Articles* by the bishops at Lambeth on May 11th, *'secrete semotis omnibus arbitris'.* They ultimately emerged in their present form, very little changed from those of 1563. The list of apocryphal books which might be read for 'instruction of manners' was extended. Article 29—'Of the wicked which do not eat of the body of Christ'—which was not in the previous printed versions though possibly it should have been[1]—now was finally included, as were the opening words of Article 20, concerning Rites and Ceremonies. Any other alterations from the 1563 version were merely verbal and of no real significance. The provision that the *Articles* should be officially edited by Jewel was highly necessary, for there had been all sorts of variations in both manuscript and printed versions, English and Latin, of the *Articles* of 1563.[2] There was now an official version to which (and not to the *Articles* of 1563) subscription was required by the bishops under the Act of Parliament. They had the 'assent and consent' of the Queen as well as the subscription of both Houses of Convocation.

The disciplinary Canons of 1571[3] were agreed and signed by the Archbishop and most of the bishops of the Southern Province, and were also signed, by proxy, by the Archbishop of

[1] Hardwick, *History of the Articles,* p. 315 note.
[2] e.g. Hardwick, op. cit., p. 145.   [3] Cardwell, *Synodalia* i, 111 sq.

York and by the Bishop of Durham. There seems to be no evidence that they were ever passed by the Lower House of Convocation. They are concerned with the duties of the officers of the Church, from bishops downwards, and with hardly any-thing else, and were an attempt to amend the daily working of the Church, not to change its constitution. Bishops themselves were to be diligent preachers; they were to take great care that the members of their household were suitable and caused no scandal in conduct or dress. They were not to ordain men who were not well educated or had no Latin or knowledge of Scrip-ture, or who had not adequate testimonials of character; nor were they to ordain anyone save to a definite title. In particular, they were to call in all preaching licences and cancel them, issuing new licences to those who on examination proved to be suitable and subscribed the *Articles of Religion*. Henceforward, readers who refused ordination were not to be allowed to func-tion in the Church. The bishops were to provide a copy of the *Bishops' Bible* and Foxe's *Martyrs* and other suitable books for the use of their households.

Deans and cathedral dignitaries were also to provide such books in their cathedrals and private houses for general use. They were to be diligent teachers not only in the cathedral but also in other churches, especially in those parishes from which their emoluments were drawn. The Dean should reside for at least a quarter of the year, and exercise hospitality. He and the resident prebendaries should see that the cathedral statutes were observed, and that minor canons and vicars did not pass their time in laziness but in study of the Scriptures. If any strange preacher uttered doctrine contrary to the word of God or the *Articles of Religion* he was to be reported to the bishop. Arch-deacons were to visit each year and in person, unless they speci-ally nominated a suitable agent. They were to prescribe to such clergy as were not Masters of Arts some portion of the New Testament to be learned by heart, to be repeated at the next visitation. Chancellors, Officials and commissaries were to sub-scribe to the *Articles of Religion*. They were not—and this, at least, seems to have been a concession to Puritan complaints—to excommunicate except in case of urgency, but to report to the bishop who alone should pronounce such a sentence, unless some one was specially nominated by him to do it. Nor was any one to be absolved from excommunication privately and as it were in a corner, but publicly in court. The Chancellor and Officials were to keep a general eye on the clergy to see that they followed exactly the Book of Common Prayer, neither adding nor omitting anything, and that they wore the dress laid down in the *Advertisements*.

Every minister was to sign the *Articles* before ordination. He was to report to the bishop each year the names of those of fourteen years and over who had not taken communion, and of those parents who had not sent their children to be catechized. On Sundays and feast days if there were no sermon they were to read one of the homilies provided. If they had no licence to preach, they were at least to teach the children to read and to know their Duty to God, parents and others. They were especially to stress the wrongfulness of marriage without consent of parents.

On churchwardens in particular heavy responsibilities were placed. They had not only to look after all church funds, and repairs to the fabric so that no one at a service should be subject to 'coeli injuriis'; they had also to keep order and report to the bishop or archdeacon all who behaved badly or disturbed the services by ringing of bells, walking about, talking or noise. They were to see that the churches and books were clean, and to provide, if convenient, a copy of the *Bishops' Bible*. They were to advise inn-keepers to close their premises during service time—and to report those who did not. Perhaps hardest of all, they were to admonish to repentance adulterers, fornicators, incestuous persons, drunkards, usurers or any guilty of 'impurity of life'; if they did not reform, the churchwardens were to report them to the vicar or rector for severer admonition, and they were to be forbidden communion if they did not reform. If that failed, the churchwardens were to report them at the visitation of the bishop or archdeacon. The churchwardens were also to see that Sunday

was observed (though not so strictly as the Puritans wished) and
to note who failed to come to church and to communion. They
were to supply the bishop with a list of all strange preachers.
They were to see that all things were observed which were
ordered in the Royal Injunctions or the book of *Advertisements*.
One cannot help wondering what would be the reaction of a
modern churchwarden to such a list of duties. It was the nearest
approach—though, even so, not very near—made in the Canons
to the sort of discipline the Puritans were always wanting.

Preachers, whose licences were to be invalid if dated before
30 April 1571, must subscribe the *Articles* and not preach
contrary to them: they must wear the dress laid down in the
Advertisements, and they must not demand pay beyond food
and a night's lodging. Ministers were urged to reside in their
parishes and provide hospitality, nor was any one to hold more
than two livings, which might not be more than twenty-six
miles apart. Schoolmasters were to be licensed by bishops, under
seal. They were especially to teach the Catechism, and see that
their pupils attended sermons—and to examine them to see if
they had listened. Each year they were to report to the bishop
such of their pupils as seemed most promising for service in
Church or State. As to patronage, if there were any proof of
simony or corruption, it was to be publicly proclaimed to the
disgrace of the patron, while the priest concerned was to be
disabled from all ministry. All marriages within the prohibited
degrees were to be dissolved.

No doubt the Canons fell far short of the complete revision
outlined in the *Reformatio*; they did not nearly approach the
kind of discipline used at Geneva and desired by the Puritans.
They were, seemingly, only the work of the bishops, not of the
whole Convocation, and they never received the Queen's
authorization. But they do represent a serious effort on the part
of the bishops to amend many of the more obvious blemishes in
current usage—non-residence, pluralism, simony, excessive use
of excommunication, irregular marriages, disobedience to Prayer
Book rubrics, failure to use the prescribed habits. Had the

bishops been strong enough to insist on them, a real reform would have been effected. But at least it may be said that their formulation showed that Parker and his fellows saw much of what was wrong and seriously tried to correct it.

The conduct of Richard Cheyney, Bishop of Gloucester, demanded the attention of Convocation. He was a man who did not run with the crowd, but had his own convictions and the courage of them. Under Queen Mary he had dared to argue in Convocation against the doctrine of transubstantiation—but still managed to stay in England, no doubt in obscurity. He had the friendship of Cecil and, at first, of Parker when Elizabeth came to the throne. He was one of the original canons of Westminster[1] in 1560. In 1562 he was made Bishop of Gloucester, and received also the see of Bristol 'in commendam' from the Queen, and was made guardian of the spiritualities of the see by Parker.[2] But his independence soon seems to have made Parker suspicious. Though he was present at the Convocation of 1563, his signature was not attached to the Articles—probably because he objected to the statement in Article 28 that reception at communion was 'only' in heavenly or spiritual manner. For he held firmly the Lutheran view of consubstantiation. It is difficult not to see in this the reason why, in May 1563, Parker appointed some one else to be the guardian of the spiritualities of Bristol,[3] though Cheyney continued to hold the see in commendam—for that he had received from the Queen, not from the Archbishop.[4] Later on, in October 1568, he got into trouble with the citizens of Bristol for his outright profession of belief in free-will and rejection of Calvinism,[5] and for his advocacy of the authority of the Fathers in the interpretation of Scripture. Even before that, Parker had evidently found him a difficulty. In August 1568 he wrote to Cecil urging that he should not be translated to the vacant see of Chichester[6]—'We learn by experience what rule

---

[1] *Register*, p. 348.   [2] Ibid., pp. 946-7.   [3] Ibid., p. 947.
[4] Ibid., pp. 952 sqq.
[5] *Cal. S. P. Dom.*, p. 320; Strype, *Annals* I, ii, 277 sqq.
[6] *Correspondence*, p. 332.

Gloucester maketh in his people.' He was seeking, suggested
Parker, to win them over to his views and having discovered that
he could not, pretended a wish to be discharged—'but he meaneth
another thing'; no doubt to be moved to another diocese. He was
too much of a conservative even for Parker, with his firm rejection of Calvin, and his belief in a substantial change in the
elements at communion: he is even said to have liked images and
pictures in churches. He did not tread the *via media*, and Parker
was not prepared to support him any more than he would support
those who erred on the other side. Cheyney did not come to the
Convocation of 1571, and that laid him open to attack. On April
27 he was solemnly excommunicated on the charge of 'contumacy
and contempt' for not attending nor appointing a procurator.[1]
Even so, he did not appear in person, but sent a proxy to plead
that he was ill. On the basis of that, he was excused attendance
until June 15, by which time, in fact the Convocation was dissolved. In the end the whole matter was allowed to drop, and
Cheyney continued as Bishop of Gloucester and commendator of
Bristol till his death in 1579. Whether he really was ill or whether
he was merely out of sympathy with his fellow bishops does not
appear. Obviously it was the latter which was suspected at the
time. He illustrates forcibly the difficulties Parker had to face in
trying to insist on uniformity of doctrine and discipline.

[1] Cardwell, *Synodalia*, pp. 530-1.

CHAPTER XVI

MILD REPRESSION: THE NORTHAMPTON MODEL AND THE PROPHESYINGS; ADMONITION TO THE PARLIAMENT, 1572

CONVOCATION was dissolved on May 30: its results were the *Articles* as they now are, and the Canons agreed by the bishops. On June 4, Parker wrote to Burghley about it all.[1] He maintained that a reference to St. Augustine in Article 29 was justified: the amazing Cecil had found time carefully to examine even that, and ask about it! Parker also pressed Cecil that the Queen might be pleased 'to grant our Book of Discipline'. If she would, he would have it printed—but he clearly had doubts. In the end, the Queen did not confirm it—but the Canons were printed, though it is more than doubtful if they were ever enforced in full. The Bishop of Ely, however, and presumably others, did call in licences to preach dated prior to April 30.[2] The ecclesiastical commission did what it could to help. In a letter of June 7 to all 'Churchwardens, sidesmen, swornmen, and others having any government or oversight for the time being' they willed and required and strictly charged and commanded them in the Queen's name that they should not suffer any services to be said save in accordance with the Book of Common Prayer and the laws; and that none should be allowed to 'teach, read or preach' either in churches, chapels or private houses unless they had licence from the Queen, the Archbishop, or the diocesan, dated after the first of May.[3] As the Queen had not confirmed the

---

[1] *Correspondence*, pp. 381-2.   [2] Strype, *Parker* ii, 61.
[3] *Correspondence*, p. 383.

Canons, it is a little difficult to see how the commissioners could claim her authority for the refusal to recognize preaching licences of earlier date. But they did it—and six bishops were among the signatories of the letter. So far as it was effective, it was a serious blow to Puritanism and its preachers.

In his letter to Burghley of June 4 Parker also says that he is about to spend the week examining some leading Puritans—Goodman, Lever, Sampson, Walker, Wiburn, Gough and others. He felt that it was important and wished for the support of other bishops who were of the commission—Winchester, Ely, Worcester, Chichester: Salisbury had promised to 'stand by me', but he doubted whether Sandys of London would agree to stern measures. Even now, he himself did not wish such measures if they were not needed: he preferred 'to work prudently, rather to edification than destruction'. We have no formal account of the proceedings, but what evidence there is does suggest gentle dealing at this time.

There survives 'A kind of agreement' offered to a bishop in 1571 by Goodman, Wiburn, Dering and Field.[1] They were ready to subscribe the Articles 'which only concern the confession of the true Christian faith and doctrine of the sacraments'; they found imperfections (more than the bishop admitted) in the Prayer Book, but were willing to subscribe that, too, 'for doctrine of the faith and administration of the sacraments'; the vestments they thought to be insufficiently authorized in the word of God, and dare not therefore use them; but they would not condemn others for using them, nor themselves break the unity of the Christian faith by withdrawing from their duty of preaching. It was a grudging agreement—but it was something: they were leniently treated. Goodman, a life-long friend of Knox, had at first not ventured to return to England because of his attack on the rule of women in his tract *How superior Powers ought to be*

---

[1] *Seconde Parte of a Register*, i, 82. The 'bishop' is presumably of London. In that case, the document would refer not to Parker's dealings, but to some sort of effort by Sandys to induce conformity. He did make one, early in 1571 (Strype, *Annals* II, i, 40).

obeyed, published in Geneva. By 1570 he had a living in Durham and was Archdeacon of Richmond. In April 1571 at Lambeth before the Archbishop and five other bishops he had fully protested his obedience to Elizabeth.[1] Now 'beaten with three rods' as he said (subscription to Prayer Book, Apparel and *Articles*), he was only forbidden to preach but was allowed to keep his living. There is no evidence that the other three signatories of the agreement were in any way punished at this time. Of the rest whom Parker said he was to examine, Sampson, long allowed to preach without surplice, retained his Mastership of Wigston's Hospital at Leicester until he died there in 1573; Lever continued as Archdeacon of Coventry, though he, too, refused the surplice; Walker (the man for whom Parker had tried to get a prebend in Norwich[2]) even received further promotion, becoming Archdeacon of Essex in July 1571. Possibly they gave the commission satisfactory assurances, rather on the same lines as the 'agreement'. This seems to be confirmed by the case of Robert Johnson, another who was examined by the commission though Parker does not mention him. He was a man of some position—canon of Peterborough and Norwich, prebendary of Rochester as well as chaplain to Bacon and sometime Fellow of King's College, Cambridge. None the less, when he refused subscription on July 4 he was suspended despite his position and powerful friends. On August 14 he wrote a submission accepting the Prayer Book, though hoping for its improvement, admitting that the apparel was not wicked, though it was neither expedient nor edifying, and accepting the *Articles* so far as they concerned faith and sacraments.[3] On that basis, he was restored, and added a canonry of Windsor to his offices in 1571. (Hence Parker's reference to him in 1573 as 'cocking abroad, with his four several prebends'.[4]) He was one who soon showed the futility of gentle treatment. Before the Bishop of Lincoln he maintained all the usual Puritan points; in February 1574 in a most abusive letter

[1] Strype, *Annals* II, i, 141.   [2] Supra, p. 227.   [3] Strype, *Parker* ii, 70–71.
[4] *Correspondence*, 450. He did, however, use some of his wealth to found Oakham and Uppingham Schools.

to Sandys (whom he addresses as 'superintendent of popish corruptions in the diocese of London') he showed that he had now moved on to the advocacy of presbyterianism. In the same month he was condemned by the commissioners to a year's imprisonment for specific breaches of Prayer Book orders. His letters are a sad example of really foul-mouthed abuse.[1] Bishops are like 'wilful and fat-fed belwethers which can be content to feed in the pastures, but in no wise will be penned in the fold'. He died 'at the gate' before his year's sentence was ended, despite a request from the Council in May that he might be released on bail to go home.[2] Even such a man was gently treated in 1571, and there is no evidence of any drastic measures taken by the commission in that year. But at least they demonstated that they were prepared to act even against the most eminent of the Puritans, and that with effect. When the Duchess of Suffolk tried to protect her chaplain, one Brown, possibly later the founder of the sect, from the attention of the commissioners, she was very firmly rebuked.[3] There is little evidence of smaller men being troubled, but some were deprived for not subscribing the *Articles*.[4]

Impartially, on June 17, Parker wrote to Burghley to complain that the measures taken to suppress Romanists in the Inns of Court were now being neglected; he suggested that the Council should strengthen the position of the ecclesiastical commission by ordering it to see that the measures were duly enforced—and even sent a draft of the sort of letter he would like.[5] Whether it was ever signed and sent does not appear, though the Council would be likely to react favourably to any anti-Roman measure. But in August, Parker did have strong support in a letter from the Queen.[6] She had heard that, with the help of the Bishops of Winchester and Ely, he had 'well entered into some convenient reformation of things disordered'. But the Bishop of Ely (Cox,

---

[1] *Parte of a Register*, p. 103; *Seconde Parte*, p. 124, shows how much he disobeyed the Prayer Book.

[2] *Privy Council Acts* viii, 212.   [3] *Correspondence*, p. 390.

[4] Strype, *Annals* II, i, 277.   [5] *Correspondence*, pp. 384-5.

[6] Ibid., p. 386.

a very firm and steady supporter of Parker) had now on her command departed to his diocese. She, therefore, wishing for 'a
perfect reformation of all abuses', empowered Parker in her
name to require the Bishops of London and Sarum to help him
between then and October in correcting abuses. If any of the
said bishops or others whose aid he needed not did help satisfactorily, he was to inform her—'We mean not that any persons,
having credit by their vocation to aid you, should for any respect
forbear'. One wonders whether Parker had asked for this letter,
too; the Queen's exact knowledge of the details of what was
happening suggests it. It is clear, too, from a letter of Grindal's[1]
of August 28, that Parker (with Winton and Ely) had been stir-
ring up the northern Archbishop to action. But Grindal still was
very cautious. He had summoned Whittingham, the difficult
Dean of Durham, to appear, and hoped to get from him some
sort of conformity; but he refused to act against Gilby, another
prominent Puritan, because he was 'nearer to London than to
York'. He also said that he liked the book of Discipline (i.e. the
Canons) but doubted if it really had the force of law unless confirmed by the Queen in writing or by Act of Parliament. It would
seem that he was still unwilling to give Parker the firm support
that was needed.[2] But Parker obviously was trying to carry out
the rules of the Canons—in such a way as not to create hardship
or trouble if it could be helped. There is a highly significant
sentence in a letter from him to Parkhurst in the following
January[3]—'It is not intended by our canons that everything should
be so precisely kept, but for the most part, and as occasion of
edification should require.' Parkhurst was finding difficulty in
providing enough satisfactory preachers, and evidently asked
whether he might license some who did not conform. The Archbishop was against that on the whole, but did not absolutely
forbid it, for he had sympathy with parishioners who did not

---

[1] Grindal, *Remains*, pp. 326–7.
[2] His Injunctions for York (Cardwell, *Documentary Annals*, i, 334) are
remarkable for the omission to insist on points which would offend the
Puritans—kneeling at communion, and clerical apparel inside and outside
church.   [3] *Correspondence*, p. 389.

wish to have to go to a neighbouring church. Parkhurst, he suggested, must use his discretion.

Neither the Archbishop nor other commissioners seem as yet to have taken notice of what was soon to prove one of the most significant and effective developments of Puritanism—the emergence of 'exercises' or 'prophesyings'. Strype says that these 'were much used now throughout most of the dioceses[1]—though most of the evidence suggests a rather later date. But the well-known Northampton Model of which he gives full details[2] was set up in 1571. It was an attempt, without serious disloyalty to the Prayer Book, to establish some sort of discipline on continental lines. It had the consent of the Bishop of Peterborough, and of the Mayor of the town and various Justices of the Peace. The Prayer Book was used, but the place of organs and elaborate singing was taken by frequent singing of psalms. On every Sunday and holy day there was a sermon in the chief church, and services in other churches were to be over by nine o'clock so that all could attend it. Every Sunday and holy day evening the youth were to be catechized—significantly, with Calvin's Catechism—in the presence of their elders. There was to be a lecture of Scripture of an hour in the chief church each Tuesday and Thursday. In every parish church there was to be a general communion once a quarter, after four weeks' notice. The minister with the churchwardens was to examine all communicants beforehand as to 'the state of their lives', and to report discords to the Mayor and his brethren for settlement—or, failing it, for exclusion from communion. After the communion, the minister was to enquire into the cases of those who had not partaken and certify to the Mayor. Simplicity was aimed at. Common prayer was 'brought down into the body of the church', and the communion table brought there for the service. The ringing of bells was restrained. Each week, too, after the Thursday lecture, 'the mayor and his brethren, assisted with the preacher, minister and other gentlemen appointed to them by the bishop' met to deal with discords, and 'notorious blasphemy, whoredom,

---

[1] *Annals* II, i, 133.   [2] Ibid., pp. 133–40; *Cal. S. P. Dom.*, p. 414.

drunkenness, railing against religion, or preachers thereof, scolds, ribalds or such like'. It was a vigorous attempt to control the lives of the parishioners with regulations which were to be enforced by the civil powers; and to spread instruction.

Even more striking was the effort to bring together, educate and control the ministers themselves. Once a quarter, after due notice, all ministers of the shire were to assemble and, after a sermon, to withdraw 'to confer among themselves of their manners and lives'. Those who were found to be at fault were to be rebuked, and, if there were then no improvement after three such rebukes, to be reported to the bishop. So much for discipline—designed to allow the ministers to deal among themselves and only bringing in the bishop as a last resort. Such meetings of ministers for self-correction were an important part of the Geneva system. But the most striking feature was a meeting of the ministers every Saturday for two hours to deal with the interpretation of Scripture—at first openly among the people and at the conclusion privately among themselves. Careful rules were laid down for set speakers, to see that the discussions were orderly and, so far as possible, scholarly, avoiding 'any commonplace, further than the meaning of the said Scripture'. Those who took part had to sign a confession insisting on the sufficiency of Scripture and its authority far exceeding all other authority, but also condemning 'whatsoever men have set up of their own inventions' including not only the supremacy of Rome, the mass, transubstantiation and the like but also (Calvinistically) free will and justification by works, and 'distinction of meats apparel and days'.

The whole 'model' tended towards Geneva. Later on the similar meetings of ministers elsewhere, known as 'prophesyings', became dangerous centres of subversive talk and of presbyterian zeal. That, clearly, was not at first foreseen. The Bishop of Peterborough approved. Later on other bishops did the same for the 'exercises' or prophesyings—Parkhurst of Norwich for Bury St. Edmunds in February 1573,[1] and the Bishop of Lincoln

---

[1] Strype, *Annals* II, i, 325 and ii, 494.

for Hertfordshire in 1574.[1] Parkhurst declared that such exercises, evidently well established elsewhere in his diocese, brought 'no small benefit and furtherance to the church of Christ'; both bishops actually ordered their clergy to attend. But both showed some sign that they were by then aware of possible dangers. The presiding officers were not to be appointed locally but by the bishop, and the Bishop of Lincoln in particular insisted that no stranger was to be allowed to speak 'to the defaming of the present state of the church of England'. But in 1571 the Northampton Model was encouraged as likely to raise the standard of conduct and knowledge in the laity, and the exercises as helping to correct the clerical ignorance which the bishops deplored as much as the Puritans.

The unveiling of the Ridolfi Plot in September 1571 led to a political rather than a religious crisis, and Parker was not immediately involved, though no doubt the underlying motive of the plot was religious. Its effect on public opinion was shattering. The dislike and fear of Rome—and of English recusants—and of Mary of Scotland, became a dominant feature of the background of the rest of Parker's life. There was, too, on the other hand, suspicion of the increasing numbers of protestant refugees in the country: a close eye had to be kept on them. The State Papers show lists of how many there were, their nationality and so on, not only in London and Southwark, but in other places too—Harwich, Colchester, Lynn, Dover.[2] The Bishop of Norwich had difficulties with the quarrels of the Dutch church there.[3]

Despite all such alarms, Parker was not diverted from his normal interests. It was in this year that he completed and gave to the University of Cambridge the path, paved and walled, from St. Mary's to the Schools in Cambridge[4], and began to renovate and beautify Lambeth Palace, recovering the great hall and introducing a fresh water supply for the gardens and household, to which the next year he added a new and more effective

[1] Strype, *Annals* II, i, 472 sqq.   [2] *Cal. S. P. Dom.*, pp. 412, 413.
[3] Strype, *Parker* ii, 82, 84.   [4] Strype, *Parker* iii, 296.

system of drainage.[1] The flow of his other benefactions to Cambridge did not slacken. He paid for the inner library and the room for Bible Clerks at Corpus and gave the College £100 to provide for a fire in the hall; and plate was given to that College and to Caius and Trinity Hall.[2] It was in this year, too, that he had the satisfaction of seeing the production, after much work and comparison of manuscripts, of his edition of Matthew Paris.[3]

There is, in the *Register*, an interesting document dated November 7[4]—a consent from the Archbishop for the marriage of a priest. It declares that the bride has the approval of the Ordinary and of others as required in the royal Injunctions, and that she and the priest could therefore enter into '*matrimonium legitimum ut dicitur*'. The form of words is interesting. The marriage of the clergy was not allowed by law in the reign of Elizabeth; but the royal Injunctions laid down conditions for such marriages! Hence the qualifying phrase '*ut dicitur*'.

The mildness shown to Puritans did not conciliate them. They were, besides, thoroughly alarmed by the failure of the government to deal sternly with the late plot against the Queen. It is true that the Spanish ambassador was expelled for his part in it, but Norfolk, though in the Tower, was still alive, and Mary of Scots was unharmed. Thus when a new Parliament met on 8 May 1572, a vigorous Puritan element was determined to press for strong measures both to further reformation and to suppress Romanism. In his opening speech Lord Bacon laid great stress on religious matters, recognizing that all was not well[5]— danger of faction, non-attendance at church, shortage and inadequacy of ministers, rites and ceremonies neglected, simony rife and so on. He urged the bishops to take firmer measures about such things, and to ask Parliament for 'temporal acts' if they needed more power to deal with them. But the Puritans were not to be appeased by such suggestions. Lords and Commons united in pressing for the death of Norfolk and for a Bill to declare Mary guilty of high treason, the Commons showing even

---

[1] Strype, *Parker*, pp. 296-7.   [2] Ibid., pp. 351-3.   [3] Ibid., pp. ii, 98.
[4] *Register*, p. 615.   [5] D'Ewes, op. cit., pp. 192-3.

more zeal than the Lords. But the Queen was difficult. After some delay, Norfolk was executed on June 2; but she refused, for personal reasons to confirm the Bill about Mary, though she admitted that probably the advice of Parliament was for the best.

Even bolder was the action of the Commons over religion, despite their previous rebuffs. A quite amazing Bill was produced and was read twice. Its Preamble was practically a manifesto. It starkly declared that though the Prayer Book was sound in doctrine, yet 'divers orders of rites, Ceremonies and observations' had been retained in it because of the great weakness of the people still blinded by superstition at the time of the Act of Uniformity. But now further advance had been made. There were 'a great number of learned pastors and zealous ministers' who had (with 'favourable permission of some godly Bishops and Ordinaries') started 'godly exercises' for the instruction and edifying of their congregations. In favour of this, they had omitted the 'straight observation' of the form and order of the Prayer Book and some of its rites and ceremonies and had conformed themselves more nearly to the imitation of the ancient apostolical church and 'the best reformed churches in Europe'. But their proceedings had been opposed by a 'number of malicious adversaries of the truth' who insisted on exact obedience to the Book, and had taken legal measures against those who departed from it, so that 'the course of the Gospel is greatly hindered, many godly preachers restrained from their godly exercises, to the great dishonour of God, grief of the godly and triumph of the enemy'. The Bill thereafter went on to propose that the Uniformity Act should continue to be in force only against such as 'do or shall use any manner of papistical service, rites or Ceremonies by the same Act abolished, or do or shall use the same form so prescribed more superstitiously than the same Act doth authorize and allow'. Furthermore any vicar or minister, being a preacher with charge of a congregation, should be allowed, with the consent of the bishop, to omit any part of the Prayer Book service as and when he thought expedient in order to preach the word of God 'or to use any other godly exercise' for the instruction of his congregation. And it should be lawful, with the same consent, to use such form of prayer and ministration of the sacraments 'and other godly exercises of religion' as were printed for the use of the French and Dutch churches in London.

The second reading of the Bill was on May 19; on the 20th there was opposition to it, and it was sent to a committee which produced a much milder form, omitting a great deal of the Preamble (about superstitious rites in the Prayer Book and the bishops' support of the godly exercises), but still complaining that the slightest deviation from the Prayer Book—even an omission, or reading one chapter for another—led to heavy punishment. The new form of the Bill still ordered that the Uniformity Act should be enforced only against papistical uses, and that any preacher with charge of a congregation should be allowed to omit, but now with the consent of 'the most part of Bishops of this Realm', such parts of the Prayer Book service as he thought fit in order to preach or use any other godly exercises. The suggestion that the Dutch or French book in use in London should be legalized was omitted, as was the reference in the Preamble to 'the best reformed churches in Europe'.[1] In its revised form, the Bill was obviously much less offensive. The Preamble, instead of being a Puritan battle cry, seemed to be only a complaint that slight deviations from the Book were so heavily punished. But still, if the Bill were enacted its effect would be to allow (with the consent of the bishops) any sort of omissions from or additions to the Prayer Book services by Puritans, though Romanists would not be allowed similar concessions.

But the authorities were not asleep. On May 19, the day on which the Bill had its second reading, Parker wrote a plaintive letter to Burghley.[2] He was alarmed and depressed that no steps had been taken against the Duke of Norfolk; he deplored the 'Machiavel government' under which the papist was favoured as much as the 'true protestant'. Though he was not a man of

---

[1] The two forms of the bill are given in W. H. Frere and C. E. Douglas, *Puritan Manifestoes* (London, 1907), pp. 149–51.

[2] *Correspondence*, p. 391.

blood, he was sure there would be no peace and quiet till the *homo peccati* had his just reward. He had heard that even Burghley in some of his private letters had professed to be at his wits' end, and urged him if he had such feelings to conceal them by a good countenance so that the world should know nothing of it. There is no explicit reference to what was going forward in Parliament, but it was surely in his mind, as well as the delay in dealing with Norfolk, when he declared that had he not expected to be dead before this, they would have had to send for him from Cambridge more than twice. 'Ye see and have seen for a long time what they seek . . . Think you not that it is perceived that when her Majesty hath truly determined and spoken, ye over-throw not what is purposed?' For himself he does not care— 'Let us be quite out of estimation, and of no credit, and let us . . . be objected to envy, be put to peril, yea, cast away.' For himself he would be happier to live with one man only than with forty. But 'Think you, that this way you among yourself shall escape?' It was, as always, Parker's conviction that revolt against the bishops, if not checked, would spread into a challenge to all the recognized powers of State.

Burghley, too, whatever his depression, was keeping an eye on the Commons—he had written to the Speaker who sent him in reply an account of the proceedings on May 20 when the Bill was again discussed.[1] There had been long debate in which the Speaker thought that the chief grievance to emerge was that ministers were brought to court for reading chapters not appointed by the Prayer Book and 'divers such like things.' He plainly did not realize how much the Bill would have annoyed the Queen nor how far-reaching were the changes it suggested. But he added that it was now to be submitted to a conference so as to 'provide for this inconvenience' while preserving general uniformity. He admitted that in its present form the Bill was not liked by all and that it would not take effect.

The result of the conference was the revised Bill, with its modified Preamble, which had its first reading on May 21. But

[1] *Puritan Manifestoes*, p. 152.

now the Queen herself stepped in. On May 22 the Speaker informed the House of her will that no bills about religion be proposed or received in the House unless they had first been considered and liked by the clergy.[1] She asked to see the two bills which had been before them. On the next day a message was brought that she utterly disliked the first Bill and that, as to the second, if protestants were unnecessarily prosecuted over trifles, she must be told and would protect them. And there, so far as Parliament was concerned, the matter ended. On June 30 it was prorogued.

In the Convocation which met at the same time as Parliament, no important business was transacted. Parker did, however, make a Latin speech in which he urged that resort should be made to antiquity to correct faults in the Church: he plainly knew that much was still wrong. But the mood of the Lower House was not for extremes of reform, as was clearly shown when they elected as their Prolocutor John Whitgift, now Dean of Lincoln as well as Master of Trinity, well known for his opposition to Cartwright's views. He was charged by the bishops, along with others of the Lower House, to prepare in writing a list of what reforms were still needed.[2] Their report was the basis of the Canons of 1576, which sought to raise clerical standards and to provide instruction for the laity, but which fell far short of what the extremer Puritans were by then demanding.

Some little time before the prorogation of Parliament and Convocation in 1572 there appeared a tract which marked an epoch—the secretly printed *Admonition to the Parliament*.[3] Whereas the two Bills suppressed by the Queen had sought mainly to gain liberty for ministers to depart from the Prayer Book, this was a plea for the entire reformation of the Church on the lines suggested by Cartwright's lectures. In one passage, indeed, it is allowed that bishops may still be employed, but only 'to such ends as they were in the old church appointed for'. But there is no hint what that function was: on the contrary,

[1] D'Ewes, op. cit., p. 213.   [2] Cardwell, *Synodalia* ii, 537-8.
[3] Printed in *Puritan Manifestoes*, with full preface, notes and appendices.

in one place it is said that 'instead of an Archbishop or Lord bishop you must make equality of ministers', which seems to put an end to them. In fact the whole existing machinery of Church government was roundly condemned. The preface sets out the main thesis beyond possibility of doubt. Of 'Lordly Lords, Archbishops, Bishops, Suffragans, Deans, Doctors, Archdeacons, Chancellors and the rest of that proud generation' it is said that their 'Kingdom must down, hold they never so hard; because their tyrranous Lordship cannot stand with Christ's Kingdom'. After the preface there are two sections—'*An Admonition to the Parliament*' and '*A view of Popish abuses yet remaining in the English Church, for the which Godly Ministers have refused to subscribe*' to Prayer Book, Apparel and the *Articles*, as required by the commissioners. The criterion throughout is 'that nothing be done in this or any other thing, but that for which you have the express warrant of God's word for'.

The *Admonition* was written with complete sincerity and great indignation. It is concise, its case is put with clarity and abundance of Scriptural references (though they are not always strictly relevant) and without any of the personal abuse which later on spoiled so much of Puritan polemics. Its very simplicity made it immensely effective, the more so as it could not be answered without elaborate argument. It is so packed with brief, pithy points that it cannot fairly be analysed. But the underlying argument is clear—that the Church had not been fully reformed because the Scriptural model had not been exactly followed, and much of traditional Roman custom and ceremony had been retained. The chief blemish was that there were no elders. These should be the main strength and authority of the local church. 'You have to plant in every congregation a lawful and godly seignory.' To 'the Ministers, seniors and deacons is the whole regiment of the church to be committed'. To the lack of elders or seniors were traced practically all the shortcomings of the Church. The clergy were unsatisfactory because they were ordained by the bishops alone, without examination, and without the laying on of hands and calling by the elders of the local church. Elders should choose their ministers and so provide against pluralism, non-residence, simony, non-preaching clergy—they would 'look that they preach, not quarterly or monthly, but continually: not for filthy lucre sake, but of a ready mind'. They would see that the ministers were able to teach, not needing, like children, to learn a catechism, and not restricted to reading homilies nor constricted in their prayers to the letter of a book. The elders, too, should deal with all matters of discipline; for 'their office was to govern the church with the rest of the ministers, to consult, to admonish, to correct, and to order all things appertaining to the state of the congregation'. So the whole company of 'Chancellors, Archdeacons, Officials, Commissaries, Proctors, Doctors, Summoners, Churchwardens and the like' could be swept away. Discipline could then be administered on primitive lines, penance not commuted privately for money and without repentance, nor excommunication pronounced for the most trivial acts of disobedience—at present 'because it is a money matter, no whit at all esteemed'.

The catalogue of 'Popish abuses' is arranged under the headings of objections to the threefold subscription to Prayer Book, Apparel and *Articles* required by the commissioners. All the regular Puritan complaints re-appear—'private Communion, private baptism, baptism ministered by women, holy-days ascribed to saints, prescript services for them, kneeling at communion, wafer cakes for their bread when they minister it, surplice and cope to do it in'. The blessing of the water at baptism, the signing with the cross, the questions to godparents; the ring at marriage; confirmation; the burial service, and that for the churching of women; the manner of saying the psalms; the Ordinal—all meet with the usual condemnation. In fact, the Prayer Book is 'culled and picked out of that popish dunghill, the Mass book full of all abominations'. The cathedrals are 'dens . . . of all loitering lubbers'; the ecclesiastical courts are all wrong and only have authority from 'this petty pope, metropolitan and primate of all England'; the clerical clothes are 'as the garments of Balamites, of popish priests, enemies to God and all Christians'. So far as the *Articles* are concerned with doctrine 'using a godly interpretation in a point or two . . . we were and are ready according to duty to subscribe unto them'.

An epilogue apologized for the anonymity of the work, and urged that, in case of doubt, 'the judgement of the best churches' should be sought. There were added (explicitly as a counterblast to the publication of the letters of Bullinger, Bucer and Martyr in 1566[1]) a letter from Gualter to Parkhurst and one from Beza to Grindal, showing that leading continental reformers though they might, under pressure, allow the habits rather than countenance desertion of a flock, were yet opposed to other rites and ceremonies ordered in the Prayer Book. Beza's letter, in particular, is long and carefully argued. He admits that the Apostles had to develop organization step by step, but they were in part subject to the conditions of their day, so that even 'all that hath been done by the Apostles in case of ceremonies, is not by and by, nor without exception to be followed for a rule'.[2] Certainly later additions by the Fathers should be abolished. 'If authority be required: Christ is the foundation, the Apostles are the master builders, and the shepherds and teachers are bound to build gold and silver upon that foundation. Therefore let the gold and silver abide still: and as for the hay and chaff, seeing that the day of the Lord hath discovered them, why I pray you do we build them up again?' There is nothing there to suggest that he would have accepted Jewel's criterion of the first six hundred years.

Though the *Admonition* was not, in fact, formally presented to Parliament, its effect was immediate and sensational. The blemishes it denounced were not, indeed, new. Unlearned clergy, pluralism, non-residence, simony were widely admitted to exist and to be wrong; the best bishops were trying to remedy them. Most of the so-called faults in the Prayer Book and services, too, were not now for the first time attacked: there had been growing discontent among Puritans spreading far beyond the original dislike of clerical apparel. What was new was the conciseness

[1] Supra, p. 201.   [2] *Puritan Manifestoes*, p. 46.

and vigour of the attack, its apparently firm basis on a Biblical foundation, its simple directness which everyone could understand, and, above all, its suggestion that the only remedy was to reconstruct the Church on a presbyterian basis. It speedily gained notoriety and popularity. Before Parliament was prorogued, Bishop Cooper of Lincoln preached against it at Paul's Cross on June 27, though admitting some of the faults it criticized.[1] In August, Parker wrote to Burghley that 'we' (presumably the commissioners or the bishops) had written to the Mayor and some aldermen of London to 'lay in wait for the charects, printer and corrector, but I fear they deceive us. They are not willing to disclose this matter.'[2] Since the first printing there had by then been two reprints, now with additions. Meanwhile, John Field and Thomas Wilcox had been arrested in July on the charge of being its authors—which they admitted in September.[3] In October, they were condemned to a year's imprisonment for offending against the Act of Uniformity.[4] Despite their captivity, fresh tracts appeared, showing that they had active and courageous supporters—two 'Exhortations' to the bishops, one to 'deal brotherly with their brethren', dated September 30, and one asking for an answer to the Admonition. Towards the end of the year appeared 'A Second Admonition to the Parliament',[5] generally though not universally thought to be by Thomas Cartwright. It lacks the force and freshness of the original Admonition, nor is it always clear in its meaning. But it was important as sketching out a more or less complete plan for a full presbyterian system which had not been done by the original writers, who judged themselves not 'so exactly to have set out the state of a church reformed, as that nothing more could be added or a more perfect form and order drawn: for that were great presumption, to arrogate so much to ourselves'.[6] This lack the Second Admonition set out to supply. Each local church was

---

[1] Strype, *Annals* II, i, 287 quotes a very violent answer to the sermon.
[2] *Correspondence*, p. 397.   [3] *Seconde Parte of a Register*, i, 88.
[4] *Puritan Manifestoes*, p. xv.
[5] All three are printed in *Puritan Manifestoes*.
[6] *Puritan Manifestoes*, p. 19.

to have a consistory composed of the ministers and assistants (presumably the elders) appointed with the consent of the parish and certified by laying on of hands. Above that was to be a conference, made up of representatives of neighbouring consistories: above that, provincial and, in case of need, national synods. If a parish needed a minister—pastor or teacher—the conference should be told. It would select a man and send him to the parish for a trial period. If the parish consistory approved him, then a minister would be sent by the conference to join with the local officers in laying hands on him to signify that he was 'lawfully called' to that parish. He might not be dismissed on the mere verdict of the consistory, but had a right of appeal to the conference or even to a provincial or national synod. Thus the suggested system was not simply congregational. But there was to be a great deal of local independence. The local consistory should deal with all matters of discipline, even to excommunication (though that sentence and its removal were to need the assent of the whole congregation); it was to examine ceremonies and reject such as were disordered, and was even to have the power to introduce other ceremonies in their place. But the conference was to be empowered to consider the affairs of the whole circuit and, if found necessary, to criticize the 'demeanour' of local ministers.

In such a scheme there was no place for bishops, but neither Field and Wilcox[1] nor Cartwright proposed to break away from the English Church to form a separatist movement. They wished by lawful means to re-model the Church according to their plan. Actually, it is possible that some such local remodelling was attempted as early as November 1572 at Wandsworth, where it is said that eleven elders were appointed, their names being given.[2]

[1] Seconde Parte of a Register, i, 86.

[2] Puritan Manifestoes, p. xvi. The only evidence for the date is Bancroft's Dangerous Positions (1593), p. 43. As Frere points out, it seems very early for such a development, and he is doubtful if the date can be correct. But it is to be noted that Bancroft, too, was astonished to find the movement 'so far gone' so early. Moreover, he was a careful writer depending on a great deal of written evidence he had unearthed. It is extremely unlikely that he would

If so, it seems that it was kept so secret that the authorities did not know of it or take any steps. What is certain is that henceforward there was an advanced party among the Puritans who were demanding not merely improvements in episcopal administration, nor changes in services and apparel but some form of presbyterianism. They did not carry with them the whole of the old guard; Humphrey and Sampson, for example, did not agree with them.[1] Moreover, some of the bishops who had sympathized with some of the early Puritan complaints were now hardened in opposition—Cox, and even Pilkington and Grindal.[2] None the less, the movement spread among the younger Puritans and soon gathered great force, for it had a good deal of support from influential laymen.

use a forged document in his bitter attack on Puritanism: he was much too clever to do that. It seems, therefore, fairly safe to accept Bancroft's statement. The fact that he says that the 'Order' was signed by Field on November 20 need not cause any difficulty. Field was by then in prison—but it is quite clear that he was not completely cut off from communication with the outside world.

[1] *Zurich Letters* i, 292.   [2] Ibid., 280–1; 285; 288; 292.

PARKER STRIVES FOR ORDER; HIS DIFFICULTIES; SPREAD OF PRESBYTERIAN VIEWS

PARKER was, of course, aware of the dangers of the new movement, though he possibly underestimated them. In November he wrote to Cecil, in reply to an enquiry about what he was doing, complaining that the Puritans 'slander us with infamous books and libels, lying they care not how deep'.[1] But he does not as yet seem to draw any line between the old complaints and the new programme; he merely complains that for the last seven years the situation had been mishandled—'Our bearing and suffering, our winking and dissembling, have such effects as now we may see everywhere to be fallen out.' He did what he could—but it was little. He failed in his attempt to call in copies of the *Admonition* or to find the secret press. Probably his most important move was to set Whitgift on the task of answering the pamphlet, thus leading to one of the major literary debates of the period. A better defender of the established order could hardly have been found: Whitgift was learned and able, and he had at Cambridge close acquaintance with the new movement. It was perhaps unfortunate that it was he who had been largely responsible for depriving Cartwright of his Professorship and, more recently, of his Fellowship at Trinity. This last was done nominally for breach of College statutes, because he had not taken Orders in the time prescribed; really, no doubt, because he was being a nuisance in the College where affairs were 'marvellous troublesome and contentious, which I can ascribe to no cause so much, as to Mr. Cartwright's presence here'.[2] There

[1] *Correspondence*, p. 410. [2] Strype, *Whitgift* i, 96.

was thus personal antagonism between the disputants which at times added acrimony to their arguments. But in the main these were carried on in a scholarly way through Whitgift's *Answer to the Admonition*, Cartwright's *Reply to the Answer* and Whitgift's *Defence of the Answer*—a veritably enormous tome which appeared in 1574. The first part of the *Answer* was finished and had been read by the Bishop of Lincoln (Cooper) and Perne, Master of Peterhouse, by the end of September 1572, though the whole work was not published till the following February.[1]

There was little more that Parker could do as Archbishop; if offences had been committed they were against the law of the land (the Act of Uniformity) by attacks on the Prayer Book rather than against any definite ecclesiastical laws. Anyhow, so far as his extant letters show, he was still much more alarmed by papists than by the Puritans. In August, a Spaniard, being led to execution, had produced a 'popish bull' on the strength of which he had been emboldened in his crime, whatever that was.[2] In September, after the massacre of St. Bartholomew, Parker was even more disturbed. He had, as requested, returned to the Council a list of recusants so far as he could, but 'to certify the names and qualities throughout the realm of all such papists as do not like the religion, it were an infinite matter. I marvel what it mean that they grow so fast; whether it be of private maintenance, or for that they be exasperated by the disordered preachings and writings of some puritans, who will be never at a point, I know not; but cunningly they be encouraged of some persons that pretend otherwise.'[3] The only way in which the papists' daily expectations could be vanquished was by the removal of 'that only desperate person'—presumably the Queen of Scots. True, such of them as he saw expressed dislike of 'those cruel and viperous murders, but I learn by other inferiors how they triumph' concerning St. Bartholomew's day in France. He had seen Catholic books full of the spirit of persecution. 'They be full of spite and secret malice. Their imps be marvellous bold, and

[1] *Works of Archbishop Whitgift*, Parker Society (ed. J. Ayre, Cambridge, 1851), iii, 600–2.   [2] *Correspondence*, p. 397.   [3] Ibid., p. 398.

flock together in their talking places, as I am informed, rejoicing much at this unnatural and unprincely cruelty and murder.' In October he wrote again to Burghley in a way apologizing for what he had written in bitterness of heart,[1] but claiming that it was his devotion to the Queen which had prompted him. He added a rumour of a man who had spread shocking stories about the Queen, and had boasted that in Calais it was hoped that in the winter there would be 'so many throats cut here in England as be reported to be in France', and that within a year Elizabeth's bones should be openly burned at Smithfield. Yet, on trial, 'this party is yet delivered, and sent home to London again, to the rejoice of his friends. Sir, if this be true, God be merciful to us; I can say no more.' In the same month he and other commissioners urged Parkhurst of Norwich to take steps against a suspected papist, Cotton, residing within six miles of Norwich—to search his house for unlawful books and to take sureties for his presenting himself before the commissioners.[2] Parkhurst did what he could—collected the books and sent them to Parker, but had to be content with Cotton's own security for appearing before the commission, as there was no one else who could or would provide it. In November, Parker wrote to acknowledge 'two books and the lewd book of prophesies'. He took the opportunity to urge on Parkhurst against 'unordered persons papistically set', but charges against them 'must not be proved by surmises, but by their deeds, words or letters'. He was, however, surprised that Cotton had not yet come in person (apparently he never did: he simply disappeared[3]).

Parker was active, too, in the examination of papist writings—letters from abroad were submitted by the Council to him and the Bishop of London. 'We have examined divers parties and find no great matter', he wrote: but he had been impressed by the ability of Campion's History of Ireland and thought that if its writer could be 'reclaimed or recovered . . . he were worthy to be made of'.[4] On the other hand he thought much less highly of the 'De

[1] *Correspondence*, p. 400.   [2] Ibid., pp. 401–2–3.
[3] Ibid., p. 415.   [4] Ibid., p. 407.

Visibili Monarchia Ecclesiae' of Nicholas Sanders, an English secular priest who was one of the chief leaders among the Catholic refugees abroad. It was a 'babbling book' which few could answer, not because it was invincible but because it was so huge! Parker thought Jewel's work should be sufficient for Englishmen.[1] None the less, the Archbishop saw that Sanders ought to be dealt with. He had got hold of some half dozen copies of his book through an order by the Commissioners to book-sellers, who had to submit inventories of all books before they sold them. One copy he had sent to Cox of Ely who had managed to plough through it all, divide it into various sections and suggest writers to reply to them. Parker had therefore delivered a few quires to Edward Dering—'the greatest learned man (so thought) in England'—to answer, but the result had been a confutation in which 'too much childishness appeared'. Thus he wrote to Burghley who was evidently worried about the book and asked Parker what steps he was taking about it. (At first it might seem that Parker was, for once, indulging in sarcasm in his reference to Dering's learning; more probably, he was being apologetic. Dering had sent a rude, violent and offensively sanctimonious letter to Burghley concerning the new statutes for Cambridge approved by him as Chancellor.[2] Parker was no doubt explaining why, despite that, he had used him.) Later on, when Burghley expressed a wish that the book should be answered Parker replied that he had taken care thereof and engaged certain men who had the leisure 'to do somewhat'.[3] In particular he had entrusted to Dr. Clerk that part which concerned 'the honour and state of the realm, the dignity and legitimation of our prince, with just defence of King Henry's honour, Queen Anne's and partly your own', and had given him a room in the Arches for his work. He had, too, arranged with Day the printer to cast a new type for printing it (and, incidentally, urged that Day should be allowed to open a shop in Paul's

---

[1] *Correspondence*, pp. 409–10. But when he suggested to Parkhurst that copies of this should be provided for the diocese of Norwich, Parkhurst objected that it would be dangerous since it contained also the papist views which Jewel was answering. *Correspondence*, p. 417, note.

[2] Strype, *Parker* iii, 219 sqq.   [3] *Correspondence*, p. 411.

Churchyard for the sale of his stocks of books, at present prevented by 'envious booksellers'—a typical instance of Parker's
benevolent concern for those who worked for him). About a week
later, he sent part of Clerk's answer to Burghley for his views
and, when the latter guessed that 'the writer's pen was holden
by my hand', he refused credit for it.[1] He admitted that he was
ready to give such help as he could, but 'the writer is a pithy
man, and apt to deal in such a cause'. (Parker shortly after made
him Dean of Arches.) He thought Clerk had dealt well with the
matter of Henry's divorce, but added that 'One time her Majesty
secretly told me of a pope's bull wherein King Henry's marriage
with Queen Anne was confirmed. She willed me to seek it out.'
He had not been able to find it though he had tried. If Burghley
had it, it would 'serve well to amplify the falsehood of the pope,
and disprove this loving writer, Saunders'.[2]

It is thus quite clear that Parker was awake to the recusant
danger and needed no spurring on from Burghley. But he did not
even so lose his fairmindedness. At the time of the discovery of
the Ridolfi plot Norfolk's brother Henry Howard was committed to his custody as a suspected person. He was honourably
treated,[3] though he complained of the strictness of his captivity.[4]
Evidently satisfied of his innocence, after Norfolk had been put
to death, Parker wrote to Burghley to intercede with the Queen
for him to be set at liberty.[5]

In other ways, too, Parker's zeal for legality and orderliness
showed itself. Dering's hasty and rude protest to Burghley
against the new statutes for Cambridge in 1570 was followed by a

[1] *Correspondence*, pp. 412–13–14.

[2] Parker, in March 1573, did tell Burghley that he had 'found matter of that
bull of the King's marriage', but gives no details (*Correspondence*, p. 420).
But it seems highly doubtful if such a Bull was ever confirmed, even privately,
by the Pope, though it does appear to have been considered. Its chief purpose
was to allow Henry, if his marriage to Katharine was declared legally null,
to marry Anne despite the legal ban caused by his relationship with her elder
sister. It was not a Bull to declare his marriage with Katharine void. (Cf.
J. Gairdner, *English Church from Henry VIII to Mary*, London, 1902, p. 87.)

[3] Strype, *Parker* iii, 300.   [4] *Cal. S. P. Dom.*, p. 441.

[5] *Correspondence*, p. 394.

formal complaint[1]—'of the young men against their elders' as Parker described it; no doubt supporters of Cartwright, for it was largely troubles centred on him which had caused Whitgift to obtain the new statutes. Burghley submitted the complaints to Parker along with Grindal, Sandys and Cox for their judgement. At the end of May their comments were sent to him.[2] They were well satisfied that the new statutes should stand, and that the younger men had been 'far overseen to seek their pretended reformation by disordered means'. Again, a few days later, Parker wrote to Burghley on another matter of order. 'At the last, with much diligence of conference and long debating, we have finished the book of statutes as may concern the cathedral churches newly erected.' He urged that Burghley, or some one else appointed by the Queen, should go through the statutes and suggest any desirable changes so that the statutes for each cathedral could be fairly engrossed for the Queen's subscription and for sealing.[3] Nothing, however, seems to have come of this attempt to produce symmetry in the new foundations.

Shortly afterwards, as Visitor of All Souls College, Parker became involved in an apparently trivial matter which none the less involved principles on which he would not give way. A Fellow named Wood wished to be excused from his statutory duty of taking Orders that he might devote himself to the study of physic. Strype[4] says that he obtained from the Queen a dispensation and a letter to the College to continue him in his Fellowship. Under the leadership of a new, vigorous young Warden, Hovenden, the College refused to accept this decision and protested both to the Queen and to Burghley. Strype does not give his authority for his account, but it would fit in well with a letter from Parker to Burghley.[5] Therein he quite plainly shows that Wood had lied in what he had said to Burghley, who seems to have thought well of him—he had not, in fact, approached Parker personally as he claimed to have done. Moreover, he was

---

[1] *Cal. S. P. Dom.*, p. 444.   [2] *Correspondence*, p. 393.   [3] Ibid., p. 395.
[4] *Parker* ii, 105.   [5] *Correspondence*, p. 396.

perjured in a double breach of College statutes both in not
taking Orders and in applying for a dispensation from the statutes.
Parker plainly did not approve of Wood, and urged that his
request should not be allowed. Out of forty Fellows, only two
were ordained—'whether this be a good example to the University
for men to run in open perjuries, and whether it be good to the
governance that so few priests and preachers (specially in the
University) should be, I leave that to her Majesty's consideration
and your wisdom. If her Majesty will take it upon her conscience
to break such ordinance, I refer it to her Majesty'.[1] He added
'for myself, I cannot bear it in reason'. A few days later, he
wrote to Burghley a commendation of 'this honest young man,
the Warden of All Souls College'[2] (whom he knew as one of his
chaplains). It is not unreasonable to suppose that Hovenden was
seeing Burghley about the business of Wood. Whatever the issue
of the dispute (unknown to Strype but elsewhere said to have
been a compromise[3]), Parker, as Visitor of the College, stood up
against both the Queen and Burghley in defence not only of the
Founder's intention but of what he himself thought right and
honourable.

Another trouble this year which must have distressed the
Archbishop was an unseemly dispute between the Bishop of
Lincoln, Cooper, and his archdeacon, Aylmer. It concerned the
jurisdiction of their respective courts, the underlying cause being,
doubtless, the question of fees and who should receive them.
Probably chief blame rested on the law officers of the two sides,
but it is not impossible that the Bishop and the archdeacon had
also some personal financial interest; anyhow both of them were
later set in a very unfavourable light by Marprelate. In the end,
they submitted their dispute to the arbitration of the Archbishop and the Bishop of Winchester, who issued a most
elaborate and detailed award,[4] very carefully dividing the spoils
and arranging for any further disagreement to be submitted to

[1] *Correspondence*, p. 396.   [2] Ibid., p. 398.
[3] *History of All Souls*, C. Grant Robertson, p. 74.
[4] *Register*, pp. 1040 sqq.

arbitration. Parker was himself critical of the unsatisfactoriness of the ecclesiastical courts and their charges. But to have a diocesan and his archdeacon so quarrelling was clearly scandalous.

There were other causes, too, which gave him trouble, not so much because he was in doubt about the proper judgements to make as because they involved him against powerful antagonists. The Queen herself as well as Leicester and Burghley were all concerned in the case of a Dr. Willoughby, incumbent of Aldborough in Suffolk.[1] He was not at best a very satisfactory person—he was so old as to be 'childish', and at the Archbishop's visitation more complaint was made of him than of any other cleric in the Norwich diocese; the chancel of the church down and the vicar's house almost decayed. He had got into trouble, too, for not signing the *Articles* as the Act of 1571 ordered, and had been therefore treated as deprived. But he had been physician to Queen Anne and so was known to Elizabeth, who re-presented him to his living. Meantime, the Bishop had filled a second living he had held in plurality, that of Snoring. Willoughby complained to the Queen, and she to the Bishop of Norwich for so treating one whom she obviously regarded as a sort of personal retainer. The situation was further complicated by the fact that Willoughby had farmed out his benefices—that of Aldborough to one Levers. Willoughby now claimed that his deprivation had ended the bargain, and that Levers had no claim to the income when he was re-presented to the living. Parker was given by the Queen the task of clearing up the complicated matter. He allowed Levers to have one year's rent and a pension of ten pounds for two years; confirmed the new vicar of Snoring, 'a good preacher', but arranged that he should pay fourteen pounds a year to Willoughby. He also made other provision for the old man. Thereupon Levers complained to Burghley that Parker had been unfair, suggesting that it was because Willoughby was his kinsman. Hence Parker's letter to Burghley, declaring that Willoughby was no more his kinsman than 'the man in the moon', and justifying all he had done—though he had expressly in his

[1] Strype, *Parker* ii, 156–60. *Correspondence*, p. 404.

award referred the whole matter to the Queen's confirmation. The whole incident shows the kind of detail with which the Archbishop might be pestered, the care he had to take not to offend 'interested' parties, the kindness of heart which cared for even an unsatisfactory incumbent, combined with a strong desire that real fairness should prevail.

A second case, though in itself much clearer, was also difficult because of those who were induced to take part in it.[1] A man called Stowell had been reported by the Bishop of Bath and Wells for co-habiting with a gentlewoman while his wife was still alive. He was therefore called before the commission, where he refused to answer the question whether he was married to the woman with whom he was living, because that might prejudice him in the Arches Court where his wife was claiming restitution and where, too, he had refused to answer the questions. He was sent to prison by the commission. But Stowell was wealthy and had influential friends. He claimed to have letters of comfort even from the Bishop of Wells; he offered £100 or £200 to members of Parker's household to 'mollify me', and got Burghley and Leicester to write to Parker on his behalf. Parker wrote to the two lords explaining the exact state of the case, for he was sure that Stowell had misinformed them. He also, later, took full responsibility for what had been done by the commission—some had said that he was 'carried' by Yale; but 'the truth is not so; for when I know and can resolve the matter myself, I take none of his coat to be my counsellors, but I will follow the counsel of them that fear God' (a shrewd comment on what he thought of lawyers!). None the less, out of consideration for Burghley he proposed to delay the case both in the Arches Court and before the commissioners for a time. What the ultimate outcome was does not appear. But at least the Archbishop was not brow-beaten by the two lords—there is no suggestion that Stowell was to be released from prison, but only that the hearings should be delayed. What is significant is the pressure to which he was put. He feared that Leicester would be angry, and he did not wish

[1] *Correspondence*, p. 405–8. Strype, *Parker* ii, 160–3.

to quarrel with those in the Queen's favour. He wrote specially
to placate him, and asked Burghley to 'pacify him if he be offended'. How well his fears were justified was shown by Leicester's receipt of his letter—he refused to read it; though he was
at leisure, he just thrust it in his pocket!

Such incidents—and doubtless there were others of which we
do not know—serve to underline the difficulties of the Archbishop's life, when he was no longer a young man and was
constantly unwell.[1] He was, too, grievously worried about the
poverty of the clergy, and unjust exactions from them—'sums
and arrearages twice and thrice discharged'; and now sought
out to be victims again of concealers.[2] Even so, his passion for
building held. He completed the improvements at Lambeth this
year. It was also in this year that the revised edition of the
Bishops' Bible was published.

The imprisonment of Field and Wilcox did not silence their
cause. It was not only that the *Admonition* was reprinted[3]—
with additions, one dated September 30, another containing a
reference to the writers of the *Admonition* as 'in the place of
thieves and murderers'[4]. There was also the '*Second Admonition*'
before the end of the year. Moreover, the prisoners had influential protectors. Though Burghley was always in public a
supporter of legality and continued to be a loyal friend of
Parker, he was suspicious of anything like unfairness or persecution; possibly he had himself some private inclination to
Puritan views. At any rate, the Puritans confidently appealed to
him. Leicester, too, was thought to be their friend, it is generally
supposed from less admirable motives; he was an enemy of
Parker and possibly wanted to weaken his authority. There was
thus no likelihood that the prisoners would languish, forgotten.
Even before their actual condemnation, they addressed a defence
to Burghley.[5] By 20 March 1573 their friends had so far prevailed
that the Privy Council wrote to the Bishop of London to try to

[1] *Correspondence*, pp. 408, 412.   [2] Ibid., p. 413.
[3] Ibid., p. 397.   [4] *Puritan Manifestoes*, pp. xiv; 61, 69.
[5] Strype, *Annals* II, ii, 482.

bring them to conformity and then to show them more favour.[1]
On March 30, the Council wrote to the Bishop that, in view of
his report of their good conformity, they might now be put out of
prison into the keeping of Archdeacon Mullins and so remain
privately till they could receive the Queen's pardon.[2] Encouraged
by such support, they continued to be a cause of anxiety. On
2 July 1573, the Bishop of London wrote to Burghley hoping that
he would 'remember Mr. Mullins who of long time hath been
burdened with unthankful guests'.[3] In August, he complained
that there was a conspiracy breeding in London of certain men
'to procure hands for Mr. Cartwright's book and (to) promise to
stand in defence thereof unto death . . . The City will never be
quiet, until these authors of sedition, who are now esteemed as
gods, as Field, Wilcox, Cartwright and others, be far removed
from the city. The people resort unto them, as in Popery they
were wont to run on pilgrimage.' If only they were removed,
he shrewdly remarked, 'their honour would fall into dust'.[4]
Later in the same month, he says that the civil authority must
intervene. 'The new Masters authors of these troubles live in
great jollity having great access unto them boasting themselves
spitefully railing not only against particular men but also against
the whole state. If they were set at liberty they could do less
harm.'[5] Evidently they were acquiring almost the halo of
martyrdom. By the end of the year they were at full liberty,
unrepentantly eager to campaign again for their views.

In Cambridge, too, the presbyterian movement was still
growing. After losing his Professorship, Cartwright visited
Geneva, where he found confirmation of his views, but after a
stay of less than a year returned to Cambridge and became a
centre of agitation. Before the end of September 1572 he lost his
Fellowship at Trinity.[6] But in December, Chark of Peterhouse
preached a sermon *ad clerum* in which he maintained that the

[1] *Privy Council Acts*, viii, 90. No doubt this was the result of their petitions
to Leicester and the Privy Council, *Seconde Parte of a Register*, i, 91.
[2] *Privy Council Acts*, viii, 93.   [3] *Puritan Manifestoes*, pp. 154–5.
[4] Strype, *Whitgift* iii, 33.   [5] *Puritan Manifestoes*, p. 155.
[6] Strype, *Whitgift* i, 96.

status of bishop, archbishop, metropolitan, patriarch and pope
had been introduced into the Church by Satan and that among
ministers of the Church none should be superior to others. When
he refused to withdraw, he was pronounced to be excluded
from his college and expelled from the University.[1] Chark at
once appealed in person to the Chancellor of the University,
Burghley, who was at first drawn to him and sought to protect
him.[2] It needed a long letter from the Vice-Chancellor and other
Heads[3] to persuade him that Chark was not being persecuted.
Having been informed of Chark's 'fancies' he agreed that only a
recantation could suffice.[4] The incident shows how open was
Burghley's ear to protestant complaint—and how fair-minded
he was. About the same time, Nicholas Browne of Trinity was
summoned before the Heads of Houses for having apparently
criticized the manner of 'creating and electing ministers'; but
before he was punished, his case also was referred to the Chancellor before whom he made a full retraction in July.[5]

Naturally, Parker was agitated, nor was his anxiety soothed
by a letter from Cox of Ely. Cox had been at Frankfort when the
troubles took place in 1555 and had been the leader in driving
John Knox away. He was therefore fully awake to the dangers from
the left wing—his summary of their aims sent in the following
February to Zurich is masterly both in clearness and brevity.[6]
On Christmas Day 1572, Parker had from him a letter urging
vigilance 'that these godless schismatics overrun not the realm,
ne deface the religion of our godly and well reformed Church . . .
They are bent against us *toto*.'[7] The Archbishop at once sent on
the letter to Burghley without 'gloss', referring it to his prudence.[8]
There was little else he could do at the moment, but he obviously
felt that Burghley should be warned. Later, on 12 March 1573,
he wrote again asking that Burghley should reassure the Queen
that no new dispensation for the Puritans was contemplated by

[1] Strype, *Whitgift* i, 88–91.   [2] Strype, *Annals* ii, i, 280.
[3] Strype, *Whitgift* iii, 24 sqq.   [4] Strype, *Annals* ii, i, 279.
[5] Strype, *Parker* ii, 198–9.   [6] *Zurich Letters* i, 279–81.
[7] Strype, *Parker* ii, 193.   [8] *Correspondence*, p. 415.

him, and urging action against them.[1] 'Words may not now be used, but doings. It is (by too much sufferance) past my reach and my brethren. The comfort that these puritans have, and their continuance, is marvellous; and therefore if her Highness with her Council (I mean some of them) step not to it, I see the likelihood of a pitiful commonwealth to follow.' Is it rash to guess that Parker knew of the efforts just then being made in the Council on behalf of Field and Wilcox and was trying to forestall them? If so, his efforts failed: it was only a week later that the Council intervened on their behalf. None the less, Parker continued his campaign. On May 9 he wrote once more to Burghley[2] that the Queen was 'justly offended' by 'dissolute writing' and intended a reformation 'which if it be not earnestly laboured on your parties which be supreme judges . . . I fear ye shall feel Muncer's commonwealth attempted shortly. It must needs follow . . . if the law of the land be rejected, if the Queen's Majesty's injunctions, if her chapel, if her authority be so neglected, if our book of service be so abominable, and such paradoxes applauded to.' A few weeks later, in June, he wrote again to Burghley[3] 'I trust ye will proceed . . . If ye give over, ye shall hinder her Majesty's governance more than ye be aware, and much abase the estimation of your authorities.' Again, one wonders if Parker was aware of what was going on in the Council and was trying to influence it. Anyhow, on June 11 there appeared at last a royal proclamation[4] against those who did not attend church services but 'did use, of their own devices, other rites and ceremonies than were by the laws of the land received and used', threatening them with the Queen's indignation and the pains comprised in the Act of Uniformity. The proclamation also ordered the surrender within 20 days to a bishop or member of the Privy Council of 'The Admonition and all other books made for the defence of it, or agreeable therewith' by 'every printer, stationer, bookbinder, merchant and all other men' who had in their 'custody' any of the said books. Doubtless, the

[1] *Correspondence*, p. 418.   [2] Ibid., p. 426.   [3] Ibid., p. 427.
[4] Strype, *Parker* ii, 256.

proclamation was such as would please Parker, but it was not really effective.

As early as June 27, the Council took a remarkable step. Edward Dering, a Fellow of Christ's, Cambridge, who had been at one time favoured by Parker and even asked to write against Sanders, had now fallen into trouble. Though he later on maintained that he had always worn the prescribed habits and attended Prayer Book services, nor even spoken against them,[1] he had none the less become a violent partisan of Cartwright's views of the proper ministry for the Church, and even wrote to Burghley urging that Cartwright should be restored to his Professorship.[2] For various views he expressed, he was inhibited from preaching as a canon of St. Paul's round about the end of 1572—but on 27 June 1573, just after the royal proclamation, the Council wrote to him removing the restraint and allowing him to preach.[3] It was plainly, as the event proved, an impulsive and ill-considered decision. Before the end of July the inhibition had to be re-imposed.[4] For Dering was sincere and courageous as well as able and eloquent, as he showed in his long trial in the Star Chamber before the end of the year.[5] That the Council should have favoured such a man shows clearly how strong a bias there was to the Puritan side; they did not even trouble to consult the ecclesiastical authorities before acting. Parker and Sandys were obviously very much upset. On July 6 they wrote to an unnamed correspondent[6] enclosing a copy of the questions put to Dering and his answers and of the Council's letter 'to restore him to his former reading and preaching, his answer notwithstanding, our advices never required thereto. These proceedings puff them up with pride, make the people hate us, and magnify them with great triumphing, that her Majesty and the privy council have good liking of this new building . . . framed upon suppositions, full of absurdities and impossibilities, in the air.' The danger of such men was fully appreciated

---

[1] *Parte of a Register*, p. 84.   [2] Strype, *Annals* II, ii, 484.
[3] *Privy Council Acts* viii, 120.   [4] Ibid., p. 133.
[5] *Parte of a Register*, pp. 73–85.   [6] *Correspondence*, p. 434–5.

by the bishops. They 'seek the ruin and subversion both of learning and religion . . . Their colour is sincerity, under the countenance of simplicity, but in very truth they are ambitious spirits, and can abide no superiority.' They were a threat to civil policy as well as religious.

On July 18, Parker once again wrote to stiffen Burghley, who had received an abusive letter:[1] 'If this fond faction be applauded to, or borne with, it will fall out to a popularity, and as wise men think, it will be the overthrow of all nobility . . . We have to do with such as neither be conformable in religion, nor in life will practise the same. Both papists and precisians have one mark to shoot at, plain disobedience; some of simplicity, some of wiliness and stubbornness.' It was two days later that the council renewed the inhibition of Dering, which may have been some consolation to Parker.

But he was by now much concerned about another Cambridge man whose promotion he had favoured in the past. Thomas Aldrich, whom Parker described in 1570 as 'an honest young man, learned in all the tongues, and also in French and Italian . . . like to do service in the realm hereafter',[2] had been made Master of Corpus, Cambridge and a canon of Westminster largely through Parker's influence. By 1573, however, he, too, had become a supporter of Cartwright's views and (apparently in consequence of this) refused 'as an head precisian' to take the degree of Bachelor of Divinity as the College statutes required him to do. There was consequently dissension in the College. In February Aldrich resigned his canonry of Westminster (Parker, who had 'laboured' for it, was much ashamed of his negligence there),[3] and himself, 'with all the fellows' sup-scriptions' referred the College matter to Parker, apparently in a private capacity as 'most fit to decide this controversy'.[4] Whether Parker gave a formal decision is not clear, but he did advise Aldrich to depart quietly. Whereon Aldrich, it was said, decided to approach the Queen, to whom Parker therefore

[1] *Correspondence*, p. 437.   [2] Ibid., pp. 358, 427.
[3] Ibid., p. 439.   [4] Ibid., p. 438.

wrote in June[1] about this 'troublous precisian'. 'Now he saith he will stand utterly against me, and some of his friends be come up to sue your Majesty for letters of dispensation; and they say in jest that I am pope of Lambeth and of Benet College, and that I am out of all credit and of no reputation . . If your Majesty knew this whole matter as it is, I trust ye will not suffer such a scholar or his friends to triumph over your chaplain, to the confounding of your governance.' Whether there actually was such an appeal to the Queen is not clear, but the next move was a tactful letter from Parker and other members of the commission on July 5 to the Vice-Chancellor of Cambridge commanding him to take sureties for Aldrich to make his personal appearance at Lambeth before the commission.[2] Parker had no doubt that the authority of the commission covered Cambridge, for its authorization included places exempt as well as not exempt. But the letter, Parker explains, was sent to the Vice-Chancellor instead of direct to Aldrich so that the privileges of the University should not seem to be flouted. Such consideration, however, was wasted. On July 15 Parker wrote to Burghley[3] that he understood that the matter had been referred to him as Chancellor by the Vice-Chancellor. Parker much regretted such a step. It would have been better for the College that the case should have been quietly settled by the commission, whereas such an appeal to the Chancellor might lead to the 'utter undoing of that poor College'. 'Surely, Sir, his insolency is too great. The childish maliciousness for his vain tales, and his with his brother's ingratitude to me, besides their manifest precisianship, is too intolerable.' He quoted other instances where the commission had acted in the Universities. But Burghley evidently still hesitated, and sent on to Parker the Vice-Chancellor's appeal, which Parker found 'childish'.[4] He did not challenge Burghley's right to take over the case if he wished, but did suggest who should be present if the case was heard—himself, the Vice-Chancellor and others. Five days later he returned

[1] *Correspondence*, p. 429.   [2] Ibid., p. 433.   [3] Ibid., p. 436.
[4] Ibid., p. 438.

to the attack when Burghley had expressed his doubts whether such a case could properly be heard by the ecclesiastical commissioners.[1] 'I would be glad to attend upon you, if no prejudice or hurt to our commission might grow, in yielding to them of the University more than is needful; whose privileges yet I would be as glad to maintain as any of them.' There is no evidence that the case came to a hearing; in August Aldrich resigned[2]—presumably he knew that he would not win. Technically, the charge was of breaking College statutes; but the real trouble was his presbyterian views.

It is seldom that Parker shows himself so emotionally roused as he was about Aldrich. Insistence that the dignity of his position and the authority of the commission should be preserved were only normal. But for once in a way personal feelings were allowed to intrude—for he felt that his own beloved College was involved, and that he was to blame for putting Aldrich there— 'I do not care who hath the hearing of the controversy, so the College be saved, and lewd and monstrous governance escape not away unreformed'.[3] Nor can a better instance be found of the sort of difficulties which might be put in his way by the scrupulous determination of Burghley to be fair, and by the obstinacy and ingenuity of the precisians.

Though it took up so much of Parker's thoughts, the case of Aldrich was only one skirmish in the campaign. In the very month of Aldrich's resignation Sandys wrote to Burghley[4] that 'Her Majesty's proclamation took none effect: not one book brought in'. Besides the popularity of Field and Wilcox in prison, Cartwright was now lying hid in London 'with great resort to him'. There had been trouble, too, with preachers at Paul's Cross. One Crick, chaplain to the Bishop of Norwich, had confirmed Cartwright's book and had got away though both Sandys and the Archbishop had tried to apprehend him. Another, Wake of Christ Church, Oxford, despite a full warning, had preached to the same effect and then escaped to Oxford

[1] *Correspondence*, p. 440.   [2] Ibid., p. 443.
[3] Ibid., p. 438, cf. p. 428.   [4] Strype, *Whitgift* iii, 33–34.

where he was protected by the privileges of the University. 'You can hardly believe', Sandys complains, 'what parts are made, what mischief is minded. For my part I will do what I can; not in respect of mine own state, whereof I am very weary; but in respect of the Church of Christ, which is most dear unto me. But I am too weak. Yea, if all of my calling were joined together, we are too weak. Our estimation is little; our authority is less. So that we are become contemptible in the eyes of the basest sort of people.'

Things did not improve. In September, Burghley sent to Parker a book to show how even he and Bacon were 'bitten with a viperous generation of traitors, papists and I fear of some domestic hidden scorpions'—the last presumably Puritans.[1] Parker thought it outrageous, but not worth answering: silence was better than a stir. In October there was another royal proclamation,[2] angrily complaining of 'contentions, sects and disquietness . . . diversity of rites and ceremonies, disputations and contentions, schisms and divisions'. The cause the Queen did 'plainly understand to be the negligence of the Bishops and other magistrates'. They were ordered (both bishops and magistrates) to put in execution the Act of Uniformity. Anyone preaching or writing or speaking against the Book of Common Prayer was to be imprisoned. Those who refused to attend the services or receive the sacraments of the Church were to be punished with more care and diligence than heretofore. (The Queen can hardly have meant the part about the sacraments to be more than a threat, in view of her consistent policy not to force consciences.) Those who either in private houses or in public made assemblies and used therein other rites of common prayer and sacrament were to be punished with all severity. At the end, the proclamation returned once more to the scolding of the bishops and deans and a threat that, if they did not take action, they would suffer her 'high displeasure for their negligence, and deprivation from their dignities and benefices; and other censures to follow, according to their demerits'. Parker and Sandys, at any rate,

[1] *Correspondence*, p. 444.   [2] Cardwell, *Documentary Annals*, i, 348.

while they welcomed the substance of the proclamation, must have felt that they, at least, did not deserve such chiding; indeed, in November Parker wrote to Burghley to say that he did not know whether to smile or lament at the latter's protestation of his care for 'the state ecclesiastical'.[1] In the same month, he had to report to Burghley that a printer of Cartwright's book, who had been released after examination, had taken service under Day the printer and plotted to kill him because 'the spirit moved' him.[2]

Towards the end of November, Parker wrote to Sandys, and asked him to convey to the other bishops of the province an order from the Queen, to press on with the duty of enforcing the Uniformity Act and the late royal proclamation, and to report to him before Christmas; saying that he had been moved thereto by a letter from the Council sent at the Queen's command.[3] The Council's letter,[4] dated November 7, was hectoring: it accused the bishops of using their powers of visitation only to obtain money and not to secure obedience and uniformity. It ordered a strict visitation to see that there was no 'difformity' from the prescribed orders; those who disobeyed were to be punished. The whole trouble, it was said, arose because the bishops 'did wink at and dissemble' irregularities. As if to add injury to insult, the Council also appointed in each shire commissioners to see to the carrying out of the royal proclamation and to report, as though the bishops could not be trusted alone, though they were indeed among the commissioners appointed.[5] There seems to have been some justification for the Council's interference, despite its tone: both Parker to Burghley and Cox to Parker expressed dissatisfaction with the normal ecclesiastical commission: Parker thought it much abused and in need of

[1] *Correspondence*, p. 445.   [2] Ibid., p. 449.

[3] *Correspondence*, p. 451; *Privy Council Acts*, viii, 140.

[4] Cardwell, *Documentary Annals* i, 352.

[5] Strype, *Annals* ii, i, 384–5. The letter was strengthened by a long speech to the new commissioners in the Star Chamber from Burghley on 28 November, expressing the Queen's determination to secure conformity, and once more blaming the bishops and clergy—Strype, *Parker* ii, 350.

reformation; Cox feared that many of the 'physicians' were sick.[1] No doubt it was in pursuance of the same policy that the Council enquired of Parker what he and the other commissioners had done to deal with disorders and complaints in the city of Canterbury.[2] About now, too, was the trial of Dering—it is dated 26 Dec. 1573[3]—insisting that he should subscribe to the *Articles*, the Royal Supremacy, the Prayer Book and the ministration of the sacraments. Others, too, were being examined —there exists a subscription dated December 9 to those same four points.[4] The Council, it appears, had at last awakened to the dangers from the Puritans. And yet the bishops had still to be careful. In December, Parker was in trouble with the Council because sufficient commissioners had not appeared on one occasion to try a case, and the accused, it was alleged, was therefore unduly kept without a trial.[5]

No wonder Parker complained, in November, that he had been shamefully deceived not only by younger but also by older men.[6] He was having a difficult time with the Council blowing now hot, now cold, trying to use him but also very ready to find fault. In April, they sent to him one Banister, a disputer in religion, that the Archbishop should examine a book he had written and take suitable measures.[7] In the same month, Lord Stourton, a Catholic who had been prevented from flight overseas, was put in his keeping for instruction and reformation.[8] At first he was very stiff in his views, but gradually he was persuaded by Parker's patience and tact to attend the household services and listen to the sermons.[9] The Council then ordered the Archbishop to produce him before the Council, and he was released under sureties[10] in December. To one who was already burdened with anxieties about the general situation it must have been irksome to have to perform such tasks as it were under the supervision of the Council. And he was not well—there are

[1] *Correspondence*, p. 450; and Strype, *Parker* ii, 349.
[2] *Privy Council Acts* viii, 145.   [3] *Parte of a Register*, p. 85.
[4] *Seconde Parte of a Register*, p. 92.   [5] *Privy Council Acts* viii, 157.
[6] *Correspondence*, p. 450.   [7] *Privy Council Acts* viii, 95.   [8] Ibid., p. 96.
[9] *Correspondence*, pp. 422–3, 448.   [10] *Privy Council Acts* viii, 168–9.

once again constant references to illness in his letters. Even
Grindal, now at York, wrote to sympathize. He had not been a
very helpful collaborator when he was Bishop of London, but
he was now firmly opposed to the presbyterianizers and law-
breakers, though still sympathetic to such Puritans as kept within
the law. In December, he told Parker[1] that 'the late proclamation
and the council's late letters seem to lay a very heavy burden
upon your shoulders, and that generally and equally, without
respect of differences, whereas indeed there is not like occasion
of offence given of all'. He was sorry for Sandys too—'the bishop
of London is always to be pitied'. He knew even where Cartwright was lodging in London, and expressed astonishment that
certain prominent dissenters were still allowed to retain their
preferments—'they are content to take livings of the English
church, and yet affirm it to be no church'. From Grindal, of all
people, such a letter showed surprising understanding and
sympathy for Parker's trying position.

At last, on December 11, the ecclesiastical commissioners took
a firm step. They ordered all mayors, sheriffs or others who
could do so to arrest Cartwright and bring him before the commission.[2] He was not, in fact, arrested; he escaped to Germany.
But at least he was no longer a personal trouble to Parker for the
rest of his life. All the same, if the letter is rightly placed in his
Correspondence—there is no date—he did this year have to defend
himself to Burghley for not answering Cartwright's 'Reply' to
Whitgift's Answer.[3] He felt that he was not a suitable person to
write such an answer as he was one of those principally attacked,
together with all bishops. He left it to 'your own considerations,
whether her Majesty and you will have any archbishops or
bishops, or how you will have them ordered'. He himself would
be as happy to be a parish clerk as a parish priest. But, obviously
touched by a charge of show and extravagance, he did add a
list of his non-personal expenses for hospitals and charity, for
the support of scholars and payment of officers, for repairs to

---

[1] Grindal's *Remains*, p. 347.   [2] Strype, *Annals* II, i, 418.
[3] *Correspondence*, pp. 453–5.

chancels and to his houses, for gifts to Cambridge, for wages and household expenses. 'If other men could do better, I am pleased to be private.' He obviously did live in considerable 'style' as he confessed elsewhere[1]—'I have within my house in wages, drawers and cutters, painters, limners, writers and book-binders.' But he would have been bitterly attacked for meanness if he had lived simply: nor could he have entertained those whom the Council or the Queen constantly sent to him for care and supervision—Tunstall, Thirlby, Boxall and so on. He also drew up a defence of the powers of his Faculty Court to issue dis-pensations, with a list of its charges.[2] He did not like the court—but it was established by Parliament, and, he maintained, it did not abuse its power so grossly as its critics suggested. But he was anxious to prevent extortion, and laid down careful orders to prevent unreasonable charges by the apparitors of his Preroga-tive Court.[3] He also, in May 1573, issued regulations for the Court of Arches to prevent pluralism, to secure disinterested justice and to insist on the examination of witnesses and liti-gants without delay or corruption.[4]

No doubt such measures were the result not only of the Arch-bishop's conscientious desire for reform of abuses, which was very real, but also of the criticisms of the *Admonition* and its supporters. There is, however, little to show that he took any serious steps to deal with the problem of the real separatists. They did exist, and were now binding themselves by oath not to take part in the church services at all.[5] Moreover, Parker knew about them, as is clear from his endorsement of one of their *Protestations*.[6] The Queen's Proclamation of October also referred to those who held services apart. Their existence therefore was not concealed. But as yet, they were a much less threatening phenomenon than those learned and respected leaders who were striving to change the whole organization of the Church without cutting themselves off from it.

<hr />

[1] *Correspondence*, p. 426. [2] Strype, *Parker* ii, 259 sqq.
[3] *Register*, p. 1061. [4] Wilkins, *Concillia* (London, 1737), iv, 273.
[5] *Seconde Parte of a Register*, pp. 55, 57. [6] Strype, *Parker* ii, 285.

CHAPTER XVIII

PARKER AND THE QUEEN:
HER VISIT TO CANTERBURY;
THE 'DE ANTIQUITATE';
NORWICH MATTERS AND
PROPHESYINGS

PARKER'S letters in 1573 are revealing as to his relations both with the Queen and with Burghley. He had (as usual) a building plan in mind: he wished to 'remove some part of an old decayed wasteful, unwholesome and desolate house at Ford to enlarge the little house I have at Bekesborne . . . and to repair my palace with some better lodging'. All three buildings were archiepiscopal. Even so, he evidently dared not make the changes without the Queen's consent. Further, he felt that though the alterations would not cost her anything either in honour or in purse, yet 'I am so unlucky and unfortunate to win anything for myself or my friends that I will hereafter crave little'. He therefore had recourse to Burghley. He mentioned the matter to him, without pressing it, in December 1572; in the following March he put it more clearly, saying that he would leave enough houses at Ford for those who had to tend the grounds, and that he would be prepared to make a deed of gift of the house to the Queen so that she might grant it again to him and his successors. He showed no desire to question the Queen's authority, but committed the matter to 'her Majesty and to your discretion'. In April he referred to the matter again, and in November he was still hoping that 'your lordship would comfort me with her Majesty's grant' so that he might begin the work; six days later he returned to the subject.[1]

[1] *Correspondence*, pp. 414, 419, 424, 446, 448.

Whether Burghley ever applied to the Queen is not clear; it looks as though his 'discretion' thought it wiser not to raise the question. But Parker's letters give a glimpse of intimacy between him and Burghley which does not always appear in their official dealings. It peeps out again in December in a note of consolation from Parker to him on the occasion of some illness.[1] Whether Parker was indeed out of favour with the Queen as he seems to suggest, and, if so, why; or whether he was merely being very sensitive and touchy is again not clear. Undoubtedly he had enemies at Court, led by Leicester, who would wish to thwart him and lessen his authority in any way they were able: possibly they made the Queen look askance at any request from the Archbishop, particularly if it affected property. For one who felt that he stood in a special relationship to her because of her mother, any such estrangement must have been painful.

But it did not prevent his opposing her when he felt it right— and, astonishingly, opposing her with success. In May 1573, Yale resigned his position as Official Principal and Dean of the Arches Court. Parker appointed as his successor Batholomew Clerk.[2] He was a man who had high testimonials from Cambridge (signed by Whitgift among others) and had already done distinguished work,[3] including a partial reply to Sanders, *De Monarchia*. The Queen objected very strongly and said he must be dismissed as he was too young for the post—obviously a mere excuse. It is hard to see any reason for her action other than Strype's conjecture that she was moved either by papists (who would not like his work against Sanders) or by Puritans (who had Leicester's ear and would not like a friend of Whitgift). It was a highly arbitrary action on the Queen's part, for the appointment lay entirely within the Archbishop's control. But 'the Archbishop took care to manage himself with the greatest wariness and discretion, and seeming compliance with the Queen'.[4] He wrote to her to say that he had 'willed' Dr. Clerk to remove himself, and told her of his reaction—he would as soon

[1] *Correspondence*, p. 453.   [2] *Register*, p. 1058.
[3] Strype, *Annals* II, i, 351; *Parker* ii, 184.   [4] Strype, *Parker* ii, 185.

forego life itself as resign, and he was no younger than Dr. Yale and Dr. Weston when they were appointed. Parker took the precaution of sending a copy to Burghley of this letter to the Queen on June 15.[1] Four days later he had to write to the Queen again, more fully.[2] Once more he stated Clerk's position—and it was a strong one. If he lost his post he would be so discredited that he would be ruined; he was by law and by Parker's word fully entitled to it; his work against Sanders deserved reward; he was ready to face public trial of his sufficiency both in learning and ability. To Clerk's arguments Parker now added a strong personal plea. Not only would dismissal ruin Clerk, but even such a public trial as he was willing to face would be a novel procedure in the case of a man entrusted by the Archbishop with such high office. Then, emphatically, he urged that 'your Majesty will have some respect and consideration of me, and of that place whereunto your Highness hath placed me'. If he were reproved in the choice of his own officers, his credit would be shaken and his opponents encouraged. If, in spite of all, the Queen was determined that Clerk should go, he asks that at least he might not himself have to dismiss him but that the Queen should choose some one else to do it. It was as near to a flat refusal to carry out her wishes, however tactfully worded, as Parker could have made. She returned to the charge in December, for Strype quotes a letter then from Clerk to Burghley[3] asking for his support in retaining his post. In the event, he was not deprived: a notable and very rare instance of Parker not boldly, perhaps, but firmly standing up to the Queen.

However much he may have felt such disagreements, they were not unusual for those who had dealings with the Queen. Nor were they allowed to interfere with the seemliness of their outward relations when the Queen in her 'progress' visited Kent in the autumn of 1573. Despite—or perhaps because of—them Parker was elated to have the chance of playing host to her and took immense trouble to make the visit a success. No detail

---

[1] *Correspondence*, pp. 427, 428. [2] Ibid., pp. 429–32.
[3] *Parker*, ii, 189.

was left to chance. He had in May privately sent to Burghley,
for his comments, an advance copy of Lambard's *Perambulation
of Kent*.[1] When in July he heard of the Queen's plan, he at
once sent him a book on Dover and other books about the county;
a few days later he sent on, again privately, the proposed *Preface*
to Lambard.[2] It was important, he thought, that Burghley
should be equipped as a well-informed guide. Such care was
typical of all the Archbishop's arrangements.

The Queen left Greenwich on July 14;[3] though she did not
actually reach Canterbury till September, already on July 15
the Archbishop was preparing to go to Kent 'to make my houses
ready against her Majesty's coming'.[4] Three days later, he was
alarmed: there was measles and the pox at Canterbury and the
plague at Sandwich. He did not know what to do. His wine,
beer and provision had been already sent, but he would wish to
'stay the cost of my carriage' if she were not really going to Kent;
for 'as in fifteen years it should rejoice me to see her Majesty at
my house at Cantuary (for I weigh not so much the cost) so
would I be loth to have her person put in fear or danger'.[5]

The Queen, however, went on. She spent a week in the Archbishop's house at Croydon,[6] but there is, strangely, no indication
that Parker was there to receive her. Presumably her stay there
was unofficial, a mere matter of convenience. By August 17,
the Archbishop was at Bekesbourne, anxiously writing to
Burghley about the arrangements to be made at Canterbury, for
his only guidance was research as to 'what service my predecessors have been wont to do'.[7] He wanted to know whether the
Queen would stay with him or in her own palace, and offered
various places for the entertainment of Burghley and others. He
made suggestions for the Queen's reception at the cathedral on

---

[1] *Correspondence*, p. 424.   [2] Ibid., pp. 436, 441.
[3] There is a Latin account of this Progress in Strype's *Annals* II, ii, 539–44.
It was apparently intended for the *Matthaeus* but only appeared in a few
copies. No doubt it was kept back for modesty during the Archbishop's
life time (*Annals* II, i, 467).
[4] *Correspondence*, p. 436.   [5] Ibid., p. 437.
[6] Latin narrative, *ut supra*.   [7] *Correspondence*, p. 441.

her arrival and subsequently, urging that it would be a good example if she were to receive communion on the first Sunday of the month. He wished, too, to provide horses for the more important of her train. And he hoped Burghley would not be offended—but he was also consulting the Lord Chamberlain, Sussex, about it all, to make quite sure!

Besides the Latin account of the visit, Parker described it in March 1575 to Grindal[1] who had asked about it. (He thought the Queen was likely to visit the Northern Province, and he wanted to know what he should do.) The two accounts give the impression of a splendid occasion. The Archbishop with his train first met her when she reached Folkestone 'to show my duty to her and mine affection to the county'. He accompanied her to the outskirts of Dover, and then withdrew to Bekesbourne. On September 3 she arrived at Canterbury where Parker with the Bishops of Lincoln and Rochester met her at the West door of the cathedral. After an address in Latin from a boy of the grammar school, the Queen and congregation knelt for prayers. She then walked under a canopy carried by four knights up the cathedral, with Dean and prebendaries and choir on either side, to her traverse near the altar where she heard evening prayer. She then returned to her own palace where she stayed. Parker took several of the Council and Court home to an elaborate supper.

The Queen remained in Canterbury for a fortnight, and on each of the Sundays went to the cathedral to hear sermons, one from the Dean and one from the Bishop of Lincoln: it is not stated whether she received communion. But the climax of her visit was a magnificent banquet given by the Archbishop on her birthday, September 7: she was forty years old. Even as his guest, the Queen maintained a certain aloof dignity. Her table as she faced down the hall was shared only by two French ambassadors (who had met her at Canterbury with a train of a hundred gentry) and four high-born ladies who faced her. She and they were waited on by nobles and her own pensioners. The Archbishop did not sit with her, but at a lower table. At one

[1] *Correspondence*, pp. 475–6.

stage she ordered the centre of the hall to be cleared of standing spectators, so that she could see better, and after the meal she consulted with the French ambassadors while the rest of the guests were entertained by music. Afterwards she withdrew for private talk with the Frenchman till nightfall. It does not sound very gracious, but in the end she sent for the Archbishop and told him how welcome and honourable the feast had been. It was, in fact, the kind of extravagant pageantry she enjoyed. The hall was full of guests—three tables of nobles, men and women, the most eminent of the French embassage, the Mayor of Canterbury and leading Kentishmen.

Throughout her stay the Archbishop kept open house for important visitors in his great hall, and for their dependants in his smaller hall. When she left Canterbury, he used what was left of the ample provision he had made in entertaining guests from Canterbury and the neighbourhood and in providing for the poor. Moreover, he presented the Queen with a gold and jewelled salt, containing gold coins to the value of over 200 English marks, and a horse she had admired when he met her at Folkestone. He also gave horses to some of her train, and copies of Clerk's answer to Sanders to others, and elegantly bound books to the ladies. From the account, it is clear that Parker was immensely pleased with it all—but it is not surprising that he told Grindal that he did not think he need take it as an example as he was yet paying his first-fruits and had only his yearly revenue to depend on! It must have cost a very great deal; but he declared that 'her Highness did very lovingly accept my service'. He was evidently more than satisfied.

On the very day of the Queen's departure Parker turned to business and issued a mandate to the Dean and Chapter of the cathedral to present themselves for an ordinary and metropolitical visitation on September 23. The proceedings are fully recorded in the *Register*.[1] Parker himself conducted them, though the examination of legal documents was naturally committed to the Dean of Arches, Clerk, and George Acworth another lawyer. Those summoned who did not present them-

[1] pp. 905-36.

selves were pronounced contumacious and suspended, though the sentence was annulled on their later submission: Parker personally examined the Dean and canons concerning certain 'objections' against them. They admitted that some of the prebendaries had not been present at any sermon or lecture since the last visitation, that some of the church's stock was in private hands, and that some of it was decayed; that repairs had not been properly carried out, and that the keys to the Close were not kept as they should be. One canon admitted to a slander against the Archbishop. The Dean complained of lack of obedience to himself, which the others denied. He also defended himself against charges of financial irregularity and declared that the stock of the church was actually in better condition now than when he came to it. But he did admit that he had applied to the Justices of the Peace for protection against prebendary Bullen, who had threatened to nail him to the wall with his sword! (Bullen was he who had slandered the Archbishop: on examination he confessed that he had sworn 'upon provocation', and that on various occasions he had struck people: evidently a difficult and hot-tempered man). Minor canons, the organist, and others were examined. Days were fixed for minor canons and lay clerks to declare publicly their assent to the *Articles*. A dispute between Dean and Chapter over certain revenues of the church assigned to the use of the Dean in Wotton's time was referred to the Archbishop for settlement after legal advice had been obtained. The Archbishop appointed a divinity lecturer and fixed his stipend and gave orders as to who should attend his lectures; he ordered better accommodation for the use of the grammar school. On the seventh of October, he delivered, duly sealed, sixteen Injunctions. Very largely they were concerned with finance— important leases were only to be granted in General Chapter, 'fines' were not to be divided among the members of the Chapter but to be paid into the common funds of the church, quarterly accounts were to be presented, and all leases granted since the end of May were to be annulled. But other reforms also were suggested. The Founder's statutes were to be observed so far as they were not repugnant to the Word of God or the statutes of the realm (for there had been changes in the latter since the days of Henry VIII); nor was any one to seek to be dispensed from the statutes. Fines were prescribed for those not attending common prayers; each scholar in the grammar school was to have one of the prebendaries as tutor or curator, and every quarter two of the prebendaries were to inspect the scholars in their studies and general well being (a typical Parker concern). All entries save the two common gates into the precincts were to be closed—even doors and windows from private houses. Chapter servants—seneschal, cooks and so on—were not to appoint substitutes for their work. Dean, canons and the rest were assessed to pay fixed sums, together with ten pounds from the common chest, to the poor of Canterbury and neighbourhood. There was to be a divinity lecturer appointed each year.

Some of the Injunctions were obviously meant to correct admitted irregularities, others to promote novel improvements in the general tone of the chapter or the condition of the school. But it is clear that the Archbishop was not sure of obedience. After giving them out, he 'continued' (i.e. postponed further action in) the visitation until the 2nd of May. By November 3, he was back at Lambeth, writing to Burghley[1] that when he was in Canterbury 'I saw high time by injunctions to prevent evil, I saw high time for her Majesty to procure the safety of such foundations by sending to them statutes under her seal'. He had long had suitable statutes ready, if only she would confirm them —a plea which again produced no result. But he took what action he could. On November 9 he commissioned Bartholomew Clerk to inquire into the observation of the Injunctions, and ordered the Dean and Chapter to attend on December 9 to answer his enquiries. The outcome is not known. But there is in the Register[2] a certificate of the Dean and Chapter giving their

[1] *Correspondence*, p. 446.
[2] *Register*, pp. 942-5; it is dated 3 July 1573, which must be wrong; the Injunctions had not then been issued. Possibly it was the answer to Clerk's enquiries.

reactions to the Injunctions. On the whole, it is declared that they are being carried out, but objection is made to some of them. They cannot call in leases granted since the end of May which have been lawfully signed and sealed—which seems reasonable enough. To fix fines for non-attendance at services is 'not convenient' because it is contrary to the statutes; tutors could not be appointed for the scholars because few or none of the prebendaries or preachers were willing to act. Nor could they close all private doors and windows into the Close—they assume that the Archbishop could not really have meant that! Evidently they were prepared to try to put an end to financial irregularities —but not to take on extra duties for the school nor to sacrifice such privileges as they had. No doubt that was why Parker wanted new royal statutes.

Strype[1] says that while Parker was in Canterbury he also visited Eastbridge Hospital, but the *Register* does not say so. However, he did send to the Barons of the Exchequer in November a certificate[2] giving the terms of the original foundation by Becket, of its amendment under Archbishop Stratford, and of his own statutes of 1569, with an assurance that they were properly carried out. This was in reply to a demand for such information by the Queen on April 17, to make sure that charitable funds were properly used, for if not she would have had a claim on them for tithes and first-fruits. His answer was a complete vindication of the hospital—but he did not send it until November 9, though it had been required within a fortnight of Trinity Sunday.

Parker's interest in antiquities still had a strong hold, despite other concerns. When in May he sent to Burghley Lambard's *Perambulations* for comment, he also sent a copy he had caused to be made for the purpose of a treatise of Gervase of Tilbury[3] (whose *Otia Imperialia* is still in the Corpus library, with notes made by Parker) and also a copy of his own *De Antiquitate Britannicae Ecclesiae*. This was evidently already in print but apparently not generally bound—the copy he sent to Burghley

[1] *Parker* ii, 306.   [2] *Register*, p. 1065.   [3] *Correspondence*, pp. 424-5.

was 'bound by my man'. Parker meant to keep it by him while he lived, so that he could add or amend as occasion served, and he had not issued copies to four men in the realm, though he knew that 'some men, smelling of the printing it, seem to be very desirous cravers of the same'. His reason for composing it was that as neither his health nor his quiet allowed him to be a common preacher, he thought it 'not unfit for me to be otherwise occupied in some points of religion'. It was his aim to trace the course of religion from Augustine 'until the days of King Henry VIIIth, when religion began to grow better, and more agreeable to the Gospel'. The copy he sent to Burghley was for comment. It contained elaborate coloured 'church arms' (one of Parker's vanities) which could easily be detached and cast into the fire—as indeed could the whole book 'without great grief to me' if Burghley thought fit. It was meant to cover the privileges of the church of Canterbury as well as the history of the seventy Archbishops—himself being the seventieth.

It is generally supposed that Joscelyn, who was an antiquary, was mainly responsible for the notes on the various archbishops, relying on the ancient chronicles which Parker collected so assiduously, and doubtless subject to Parker's editing. The copy sent to Burghley can hardly have had the section about the 70th Archbishop—Parker himself—which does not appear in the earliest editions known. But it was written in the main before his death, again presumably under his correction, and appeared in some later editions.[1] Even so, as usually printed, there is a gap of nearly two pages where the account of the Queen's visit to Canterbury would appropriately fit and where indeed it is found in some rare editions. No doubt Parker's modesty kept the *Matthaeus* from publication in his own life-time. But that it existed is shown by a very free translation of it in 1574 by one who described himself as 'a household witness'—on the whole not unfriendly to Parker, but very critical of episcopacy and hoping that he would be the last archbishop 'as the number of seventy is so complete a number as it is a great pity there should

[1] It is printed in Strype, *Parker* iii, 269 sqq.—the *Matthaeus*.

be one more'. Such various stages of publication would perfectly agree with Parker's declared intention to keep it by him to alter and amend.

The long introductory section is, to the modern reader, the most striking, its purpose to express Parker's views of the planting of Christianity in England independently of Rome, and to show the primacy and rights of the see of Canterbury. That there was Christianity in the island before the coming of Augustine is shown by quotations from Origen and Tertullian, and by other evidence. But few would now accept the view that the Apostle Philip converted France and in A.D. 63 sent over to England twelve men to convert the country, headed by Joseph of Arimathea who stayed here till his death in A.D. 76, when he was buried at Glastonbury. That, however, was Parker's thesis, which would satisfactorily establish what he wished to prove—an original independence of the see of Rome. The fact that, later, Popes nominated the Archbishops as their legates was simply an attempt to make it seem that they had from Rome the authority which really was theirs *jure suo*. Even after the coming of Augustine, it is maintained that until the Norman conquest the English Christians rejected transubstantiation, insisted on communion in both kinds and on the saying in the mother tongue of the Lord's Prayer, the Creed and the Commandments.

More impressive than such views is the account of the prime historic importance of the Archbishop's position and of his continuing rights. He was supreme over all the diocesans of his province and had the sole right to confirm and consecrate bishops elect—even the Archbishop of York had to come to him for confirmation. Consecrations had to be at Canterbury, unless the Dean and Chapter agreed that they should be elsewhere, and were marked by expensive gifts (now much reduced, it is pointed out) to the Archbishop, his chaplains and household, and to the cathedral. When a bishop died, the Archbishop was entitled to his seals and second best ring and, in the case of Bangor and Asaph, to a horse fully equipped with saddle and, of Rochester, a silver cup and hunting dogs! The Bishop of London was his Dean of the Province to circulate his orders and to summon Convocation; Lincoln his Vice-Chancellor, Salisbury his precentor, Worcester his chaplain, Rochester his cross-bearer. The Archbishop's primacy among the bishops could hardly have been more strikingly emphasized than by such usages, still on the whole maintained in Parker's day.

Equal insistence was laid on the Archbishop's rights of administration and jurisdiction. He had the right to visit the whole province, the Universities of Oxford and Cambridge being specifically included. He could hold synods and councils, supply neglects and defects of inferiors, hear and reply to appeals, issue indulgences and dispensations. He had the right to try any ecclesiastical cases in his province, even if there were no appeal to him; he could inhibit all action, in case of appeal, in any lower court. The Archbishop's Court was an alternative to the diocesan—established after long opposition from the bishops' officials—for the proving of wills and the administration of intestate estates. There is included an account of the various archiepiscopal courts—Consistory (Arches), Audience, Prerogative, Faculty—in which such vast legal work was carried on. The whole section is an authoritative account of the working of the ecclesiastical system in Parker's day, and is the most important part, now, of the De Antiquitate.

Parker's visitation of the diocese of Norwich in 1567 did not effect the improvement he had hoped,[1] and he was still much concerned about the condition of his native county. When the Deanery fell vacant, in September 1573, he pressed Burghley to 'look well' when he appointed into 'that poor decayed room',[2] and, a few days later,[3] 'The church is miserable and hath but six prebendaries, and but one of them at home, both needy and poor; of which, some of those six I know to be puritans' (one was Johnson 'cocking abroad' with his four prebends; another a man who had been displaced by the Bishop of Lincoln). 'An hungry, scraping and covetous man should not do well in that so decayed a church.' Parker suggested a name, but in the end George

[1] *Correspondence*, p. 473.   [2] Ibid., p. 446.   [3] Ibid., p. 450.

Gardiner, the prebendary who had been a centre of trouble in 1567, was appointed. No doubt he, too, was a Puritan—he had the backing of Leicester and through him of the Queen, who made him one of her chaplains[1]—but he was now reconciled to Parkhurst and proved to be an active and useful Dean.

Parker concerned himself also in the appointment of a master of the school at Aylsham.[2] He wrote to Parkhurst to warn him against the appointment of one Harrison who was strongly supported by local influence. Parkhurst, too, was suspicious of the man who was a critic of the Prayer Book, but in the end gave way with certain conditions—he was not to be contentious with his pastor or neighbours, nor to have strange opinions and 'defend them obstinately in prophesying or any other conference'. Very soon, Harrison broke the conditions and was dismissed. The episode is illuminating: despite his known non-conforming views, Harrison had the support of the Mayor and some aldermen of Norwich. Parkhurst, though favourable on the whole to Puritanism, evidently was hesitant; even he wished to draw the line somewhere, though in the end he gave way. Most interesting of all is Parker's concern about a small local appointment in Norfolk and his informed and correct assessment of Harrison.

There were other proofs, too, that all was not well in the diocese. Parker's suspicions of extreme Puritanism there were aroused by complaints to him of the destruction of a rood loft in a parish church in Norwich. Parkhurst adequately defended the action by showing that the loft really was of Roman fashion.[3] A visitation of the diocese by the Bishop at the end of the year[4] showed that many of the clergy were refusing to wear the surplice (though some of them now promised to conform), that many churches had no surplices at all, that in places the Prayer Book was attacked. But Parkhurst (always hopeful) thought that there would not be 'much ado' with the clergy of his diocese, though 'I fear rather the laity will be more busy'. But even he was much upset by the insistence in the royal Injunctions on the

---

[1] Strype, *Annals* II, i, 448.   [2] Strype, *Parker* ii, 335–7.
[3] Strype, *Parker* ii, 338–9.   [4] Ibid., pp. 340–2.

use of wafer instead of plain bread, and asked Parker about it. The Archbishop evidently told him how he managed in his own diocese 'for peace sake and quietness', but Parkhurst returned to the charge to ask if the Archbishop would 'warrant' him either loaf or wafer bread. Presumably he did not merely wish to know how, quietly, the Archbishop dealt with the difficulty, but to obtain an authoritative ruling which would allow him free choice. Parker did not fall into that trap—'you know the Queen's pleasure. You have her injunctions and you have also the service book' he wrote on May 17, 1574.[1] Presumably Parkhurst then worked out some compromise—but even so his arrangements did not quiet the argument with the dissidents. For in June Parker wrote again[2] 'if the order you have taken will not suffice them, they may fortune hereafter to wish they had been more conformable; although I trust that you mean not universally in your diocese to command or wink at the loaf-bread, but, for peace and quietness, here and there to be contented therewith'— a not very satisfactory compromise. But Parker was in a difficult position. Himself he did not care what sort of bread was used,[3] but he could not openly reject the royal orders in the Injunctions. He could only hope that some slight concessions might avert an outburst of Puritanism.

The most difficult matter, however, that he had to deal with in the Norwich diocese was the prophesyings. In February 1573, Parkhurst answered a request from 'sundry godly and well learned persons, as well of the clergy as otherwise' that prophesyings might be set up at Bury St. Edmunds.[4] His reply shows that already there were such exercises in the diocese; he says they brought 'no small benefit and furtherance to the church of Christ'. He therefore appointed three men to be in charge at Bury with authority to order the clergy to attend when and where they directed and to report those who disobeyed. The three were given surprising latitude—'Whatsoever shall seem unto you . . . to order and decree, for the better execution of the

[1] *Correspondence*, p. 458.   [2] Ibid., p. 460.
[3] Ibid., p. 478.   [4] Strype, *Annals* II, ii, 494.

premisses, I do by these premisses promise to ratify, confirm and allow', though they were to keep within the law of the realm. Strype[1] says that the three were 'of the gravest ministers', but there is no statement to that effect in Parkhurst's letter, though the name of one of them, Thomas Fowle, is also the name of a canon of Norwich in 1575.[2] It seems likely, therefore, that one at least of the controllers was a cleric; but even that is not certain. Nor would the presence of a prebendary of Norwich at that time be a very strong guarantee of strict conformity!

Evidently, then, in 1573, the exercise of prophesying was well established in the diocese. Parkhurst strongly backed it; he even allowed some of the ministers who had been sequestered for disobedience to the Prayer Book to take part in it as well as in catechizing in the churches,[3] though aware of the risk of the spread of subversive views—as he had shown in the promise he exacted from Harrison. But the Queen herself, who must have heard what was going on, was less complacent than the Bishop. In 1574 she 'willed' the Archbishop to put an end to 'those vain prophesyings'. He therefore had to act, but it is a little difficult to discover from his correspondence with Parkhurst exactly what took place.[4] Parker definitely says that the Queen had willed him to send her command to all his brethren in the province; if so, he would naturally have done it through the Bishop of London, Dean of the Province. Such evidence as there is suggests that nothing of the sort was done, though it is astonishing to think that Parker should have failed to obey an explicit royal order. Certainly, what he did in the first instance was to write to one of the clergy in the Norwich diocese to tell the Bishop that 'in the Queen's name' he ordered the immediate cessation of the 'vain prophesyings'—surely a very unofficial course to take. Parkhurst answered by enquiring whether it was only 'the abuse of some vain speeches used' in some of them that he was to suppress, or the whole procedure generally, which he thought was very beneficial. A few weeks later he had a letter from the

---

[1] *Annals*, ii, i, 326.   [2] *Register*, p. 1,166.   [3] Strype, *Annals* II, i, 387–8.
[4] *Correspondence*, pp. 456–60, and notes ad loc.

Bishop of London (of all people) and three Privy Councillors (all Puritans) who had heard that 'some, not well minded towards true religion' had attacked the prophesyings, and urging him to support them so long as there was no seditious, heretical or schismatic doctrine taught or maintained. They could hardly have used such language had they known that the Queen and the Archbishop were the critics. Parker must have got wind of their letter, for in his reply to Parkhurst's enquiry he asked what was the 'warrant' of those who urged the continuance of the exercises, against the Queen's command; he treated the point as to whether all should be suppressed or only 'such as your discretion should count vain' as a quibble: the Queen's command was clear. Parkhurst was now in a real difficulty, and wrote to Sandys of London to ask how he should satisfy both his Metropolitan and the Privy Councillors! He also wrote for advice to the Bishop of Rochester, Freake (who, as it happened, was to succeed him at Norwich). He replied that he had heard of no such commandment for his own diocese, nor for London, nor elsewhere, though he did add that he and Sandys and others took precautions to see that matters of controversy were not raised. Otherwise, he thought the exercises were 'to the comfort of God's church and increase of knowledge in the ministry without offence'. Before Parkhurst received this letter, however, he had made his submission to Parker: the men of 'good peace and great credit' who had written to him had done so, he said, not by way of warrant but only as giving advice; but he had now arranged to have the prophesyings suppressed throughout his diocese. Parker acknowledged the letter, and warned him not to be led by 'fantastical folk', and not to take counsel with young men who 'when they have endangered you, they cannot bring you out of trouble'. Parker particularly warned him not to be worried about a Mr. William Heydon. He was actually one of Parkhurst's commissioners and had wished to allow the dispossessed ministers to continue to preach, prophesy and catechize. For Parkhurst wrote to him, almost apologetically, that they must be silenced—'the matter is of importance and toucheth me so near,

as less than this I cannot do, if I will avoid extreme danger'.[1] He
evidently was really alarmed about the line Parker was taking.
It had taken about two and a half months to settle the issue.
Perhaps Parker did not wish to resort to strong and open
measures, but to deal gently and yet firmly with prophesyings
where they were becoming notorious. There is no trace of any
official attempt to suppress them elsewhere, as can be seen from
the letters of Sandys and Freake, though already by April 1573
the Bishop of Peterborough was appealing to Burghley for help
in dealing with disorders arising from the Northampton Model
which he had so recently supported.[2] Nor did Parkhurst's action
kill the desire for prophesyings in the diocese, for on his death an
attempt was made to restart them in Norwich itself[3] while the see
was vacant in 1575. Actually the Bishop of Lincoln's orders for
prophesyings are dated in October 1574,[4] so far from being king-
dom-wide was the attempt in 1573 to suppress them. What
happened in Norwich must be regarded as exceptional, and due
to the excesses encouraged by Parkhurst's slackness, or even
favour. Parker did not, though he had the Queen's support,
take public action, but did insist privately and had his way.

[1] Strype, *Annals* II, i, 390.

[2] *Puritan Manifestoes*, p. xvii. (The deprivations of Northampton ministers
mentioned in the *Seconde Parte of a Register* (pp. 121-3), seem, however,
to have been for refusing to subscribe to the Prayer Book, not for prophesyings.)

[3] *Seconde Parte of a Register*, i, 133.   [4] Strype, *Annals* II, i, 476.

CHAPTER XIX

PURITAN VIGOUR: UNHAPPY
CLOSING MONTHS

THE background of the Archbishop's last months was restless, threatening and unhappy. Both Romans and precisians were increasingly bold and vigorous and though the Council showed itself alert, vigilant and well-informed, it is not easy to see that it followed any firm or consistent policy. On April 4 (Palm Sunday) 1574, acting on information received, magistrates in London made a search, and found mass being said, or prepared, in four separate places; fifty-three persons were arrested—'the most part were ladies, gentlewomen and gentlemen' says a contemporary account.[1] The priests actually boasted that there were 'five hundred masses in England said that day'. The Council ordered the sheriff of London to keep the priests under close arrest, but the congregation were to be released under bond to present themselves to answer the law.[2] But there does not appear to be evidence of further action against them. About now, too, the Council seems to have taken pity on some of the prominent Romans who had been in prison since the early days of the reign. Dr. Cole, who had been Dean of St. Paul's, was ordered in April, with the Queen's approval, to be released from the Fleet because of his great years, to live in a house, to be approved by the Archbishop, within thirty miles of London if he provided sufficient sureties that he would not interfere in religion.[3] Similarly, in July, Watson, the sometime troublesome Bishop of Lincoln, was released from the Marshalsea to live with his brother,[4] under similar sureties (a policy, in his case, mistaken: he subsequently

---

[1] Strype, *Annals* II, i, 497.　　　[2] *Privy Council Acts* viii, 218.
[3] Ibid.　　　[4] Ibid., p. 264.

had to be put under the charge of Bishop Horne).[1] At the same time, the late Abbot of Westminster, Feckenham, was similarly released, and in August several more, including the two Harpsfields, who were to be allowed to go to Bath till the end of October for their health, and thereafter to present themselves regularly before the Privy Council[2]—their daily appearances after their return are duly noted in the Council minutes. In the same month the Council ordered the release of three of the priests arrested for saying mass in Lent.[3] Yet, on the other hand, the Council wrote in June to the Earl of Derby and the Bishop of Chester to deal with disorders in Lancashire (which must have been papist disorders); in July they sent their thanks to Derby for what he had done in Lancashire 'the very sink of Popery'; in November they wrote again to him and the bishop urging vigorous action against the papists.[4] The only reasonable explanation would seem to be that the Council was afraid of wide-spread subversive action in Lancashire, but did not fear the same in London, and wished to avoid any appearance of making martyrs of elderly recusants. But it was what was done in London rather than in Lancashire which caught the eye, and there was thus an impression that things were being made easier for papists. Sampson wrote a long letter of protest to Burghley,[5] and in the north Grindal had to be firm with papists who were now demanding lenient treatment.[6] General alarm among protestants was increased by the flood of Romanist literature which was coming into the country,[7] and by the numbers of English Romans who were being supported in Spain.[8]

On the other hand, the Puritans also were very active. It is true that a conspiracy which Parker thought he had discovered was found in the end to be largely a mare's nest; but his alarm and despondency show how deeply he felt the menace.[9] Exact details of what happened are obscure, for Strype says that the

---

[1] Gee, *Elizabethan Clergy*, p. 196.   [2] *Privy Council Acts* viii, 269, 383.
[3] Ibid., p. 287.   [4] Ibid., p. 258, 277, 317.
[5] Strype, *Annals* II, i, 490 sqq.   [6] Ibid., p. 489.
[7] Strype, *Parker* ii, 392.   [8] Strype, *Annals* II, i, 494–5.
[9] Strype, *Parker* ii, 368–71; *Correspondence*, pp. 461–4.

chief actor, Undertree, tried to bribe Parker's steward into
joining the plot, in which case it was the steward, presumably,
who told Parker of it, whereas Parker himself says that he 'never
yet saw' the detector. What is clear is that Undertree produced
documents with forged signatures of, among others, Bonham
and Stonden, and that Parker's steward led him on with the
Archbishop's approval, and sought to lay traps for him. The
purpose of the 'conspiracy' was to murder Burghley and Parker,
and perhaps others, and it was of Puritan character. Already by
May Bonham and Stonden were under arrest (presumably
because of the documents forged in their names), for in that
month the Council wrote to the Archbishop and commissioners
complaining that they had been under arrest without trial for
too long, and ordering that action should be taken.[1] But in June
Parker still believed there was a conspiracy and was trying to lay
hands on Undertree, with Burghley's backing. By the end of the
month, the fraud was laid bare, and the Council wrote to the
Archbishop that it was the Queen's pleasure that Bonham and
Stonden should be released, with a warning to conform to the
law.[2] The documents which seemed to incriminate them had
been proved to be forgeries. If there was any conspiracy—and it is
difficult to suppose that Undertree invented the whole thing for
fun—it was at least of small importance and did not involve
leading persons or real dangers. From the *Correspondence* it is
clear that, as this gradually emerged, Burghley was irritated
that he had been bothered with the matter at all. But Parker had
been really afraid. 'This deep, devilish, traitorous dissimulation,
this horrible conspiracy, hath so astonied me, that my wit, my
memory be quite gone. I would I were dead before I see with my
corporal eyes that which is now brought to a full ripeness.' Even
when all was cleared up, he still thought the Earl of Bedford
was involved; as for Undertree, 'if this varlet be hanged . . .
I think it would be well'. All through he makes it clear that he was
concerned for Burghley and the common weal, not merely for
his own safety. But nothing could show more clearly his fears

[1] *Privy Council Acts* viii, 235.   [2] Ibid., p. 259.

of Puritan excesses than the violence of his reaction to the conspiracy.

And, truly, the Puritans were almost brazen in their attacks.
In 1574 there was printed at Zurich *A Full and Plain Declaration of Ecclesiastical Discipline,* an English translation, probably
by Cartwright, of Travers' *Disciplina Ecclesiae Sacra ex Dei
Verbo descripta.* It was more direct and succinct than Cartwright's *Second Admonition,* and at once became the text book
of those who wished to insist on presbyterianism. Both Archbishops saw its dangers. In March 1575, Grindal wrote to
Parker suggesting the names of various scholars who might be
asked to reply to it, including Aylmer and Nowell.[1] In his reply
Parker showed that he was already on the alert.[2] He had invited
Aylmer to undertake the task, and had received a refusal; but he
had procured an answer to it, though he was not going to put it
out until he was able to 'use more judgment'. (It is doubtful if
the reply ever appeared.) In 1574 or 1575 there was published the
account of the *Troubles at Frankfort,* probably by William
Whittingham who had been there and was now Dean of Durham
though he had never received Anglican Orders. It was a pamphlet, probably also printed at Zurich, which shed an unpleasant
light on many who were now in high office in the English
Church; it suggested that they had behaved tyrannously and
unfairly, and that certainly at Frankfort they had been very
willing to dispense with some of the things on which they now
insisted, such as episcopacy and full obedience to the Prayer
Book. In particular, Cox of Ely, Parker's old friend and firm ally,
comes out very badly. Possibly it did not appear before Parker's
death, but it was symptomatic of the Puritan offensive.

Grindal in his letter also asked Parker about the general
position in London,[3] for there was already in York 'a great
talk . . . of new sects and heresies sprung about London, of
Judaism, Arianism, etc. I would be glad to understand the truth.'
Parker, fully aware of what was going on, was able to reassure

---

[1] Grindal, *Remains,* p. 353.   [2] *Correspondence,* p. 477.
[3] *Remains,* p. 353.

him.[1] There had been trouble in the Temple caused by the preaching of the Reader there, a Spaniard Corranus, who affirmed free will and spoke unwisely of predestination, and was not sound about Arianism. (His fault seems to have been that he did not accept the full Calvinistic teaching to which many of the lawyers were addicted: in the end, he cleared himself.[2]) But apart from him Parker knew of no sects in London 'saving for the common precisianship'. But there had been a violent attack on Cox in a sermon at the Cross by Chatterton of Cambridge. Cox as Bishop of Ely was accused of tolerating sects in Cambridge—in fact, the last thing he would have been likely to do. But Parker had been into that matter too, and found that Chatterton was really anxious to succeed Cox at Ely, and had even promised, if he did, to surrender one of the episcopal houses to which Cox clung; his attack was merely personal, to discredit Cox and secure his removal from Ely. But that Cox, the staunch opponent of the Puritans, should be so boldly attacked was significant. And Parker had also been told that Chatterton had reported 'very ill words of me spoken to him by your successor' (i.e. Sandys).

The *Correspondence* affords other evidence of Puritan effrontery. A minister in the north who had exercised his function unordained for fifteen years, was at last about to seek a faculty to put him right! Warned by Grindal, Parker promised that he should not be so helped.[3] In February 1575[4] he wrote to Burghley that he heard 'the earl' (no doubt Leicester) 'is unquiet and conferreth by the help of some of the examiners to use the counsel of some precisians I fear, and purposeth to undo me'. He points out to Burghley that this was but a beginning, an attempt 'to go over the stile where it is lowest'. But if it is not defeated 'there will be few in authority to care greatly for your danger, and for such others'. For himself Parker did not care, but for Burghley and religion. That was why he had tried to appease Leicester not by an apology (for he had done no wrong) but by

---

[1] *Correspondence*, pp. 474–6.   [2] Strype, *Parker* ii, 404.
[3] *Correspondence*, p. 474.   [4] Ibid., p. 472.

an appeal to conscience. He was frightened of the growing power of the Puritans, and felt thwarted—'I may not work against precisians and puritans, though the laws be against them. Know one and know all.'

It was his fear of giving the Puritans a handle against him which guided his treatment of Cartwright's brother[1]—'a vain young stripling'. He was obviously mad, claiming that he was the 'rightful heir of the lands of this realm'. Instead of having him executed for such treasonous talk, Parker put him in the Gate-house in the hope that his friends would provide for his keep at Bridewell or Bedlam 'till his wits come again'. This he did that 'his brother and such precisians should not think that we deal hardly with this young man . . . for his brother's sake, whose opinions have so troubled the state of the realm'.

Parker in fact was full of fears. No doubt it was partly the result of age and tiredness. But there was more than that. He was constantly ill with stone,[2] and feared other illness; the last two letters in the *Correspondence* were dictated from bed.[3] More-over, though he was satisfied of the Queen's firm opposition to the precisians—'I see her in constancy almost alone to be offended with the puritans'[4] and although she consulted him about the filling of vacant sees,[5] yet for all his loyalty and devotion he seems to have felt himself cut off from Court—probably because of Leicester, 'Because her Majesty is come secretly to my Lord of Leicester, I know not whether I might offer myself to her Highness.'[6] It is 'of some policy that I neither write nor often come to the court'.[7] When he was perplexed to know whether he should, as he felt duty demanded, present himself at Court on her return from her 'journey' in October 1574, or refrain because there was plague at Lambeth, he put the matter to the Lord Chamberlain, the Earl of Sussex, and acknowledged his reply in terms which seem almost abject, even when allowance is made for the literary conventions of the day[8]—'I have great cause to

---

[1] *Correspondence*, p. 470. [2] Ibid., pp. 464, 477. [3] Ibid., pp. 477, 479.
[4] Ibid., p. 478. [5] Ibid., p. 476. [6] Ibid., p. 468.
[7] Ibid., p. 473. [8] Ibid., p. 467.

acknowledge my bounden duty of thanks and readiness of service to her Highness for her Majesty's special favour so to consider of me her poor chaplain. And furthermore I have to give your good lordship my hearty thanks, for your friendly declaration to her Majesty of my letters, in such good sort as I perceive your honour hath done.'

He was, in fact, thoroughly down and anxious to be done with it all[1]—'I toy out my time, partly with copying of books, partly in devising ordinances for scholars to help the ministry, partly in genealogies and so forth; for I have little help (if ye knew all) where I thought to have had most. And thus, till Almighty God cometh, I repose myself in patience.' The last letter included in the *Correspondence*,[2] of 11 April 1575, is really moving. He hopes it will be one of his last letters; he sees and feels that 'divers of my brethren partly are gone from me, partly working secretly against me'. The Queen, provoked by Leicester (so at least Parker thought) had attacked him for carrying out a visitation of the Winchester diocese, much though it was needed. How could he govern 'cumbered with such subtlety'? 'For cap, tippet, surplice or wafer bread or any such' he cared not at all. But he did object to contempt of law and authority. The Queen's 'princely prerogative in temporal matters . . . called into question of base subjects', and she does not proceed against them. It is a most depressed—and depressing—letter, but is clear evidence that to the very end his mind was clear, his purpose firm. He knew what was afoot, he knew the dangers and could only warn Burghley of them from his bed. He died five weeks later, on May 17; his letters make it quite clear that he was eager to go.

Still, to the end he had conscientiously fulfilled his duties and continued with pleasure his patronage of learning. When Parkhurst died early in 1575, Parker issued a commission to Dr. Yale and Nicholas Stuard (or Steward) to exercise spiritual jurisdiction in the Norwich diocese.[3] At once there was trouble.

---

[1] *Correspondence*, p. 474.   [2] Ibid., pp. 477–9.
[3] *Register*, p. 1017.

The Dean (the pugnacious Gardiner) and Chapter claimed that they should have the jurisdiction. Parker regarded this as a challenge to archiepiscopal rights, and personally took the matter up. On March 17, he wrote to Grindal[1] that he had been at Court 'to answer the Dean of Norwich and his chapter upon a rotten composition'. This composition agreed that in a visitation, the Dean and Chapter should be allowed to nominate one of their number as one of three visitors, but apparently admitted that when the see was vacant all the normal episcopal jurisdiction should pass to the Metropolitan. Parker would not surrender any of his rights, especially in such a disordered see. But the position cannot have been as clear as his letter suggests, for the dispute continued after his death, the Dean and Chapter of Norwich refusing to recognize the guardians appointed by the Dean and Chapter of Canterbury, on whom during the vacancy of the see of Canterbury the Archbishop's authority devolved.[2]

About the same time Parker also had trouble over the Winchester diocese. Much disobedience was there, apparently both of papists and Puritans, and Horne invited him to hold a visitation.[3] The interrogatories suggest a very thorough and exhaustive enquiry,[4] indicating that much was wrong in the diocese. Parker himself thought great good had been done by the visitation, and was taken aback when the Queen 'when I was at Richmond at her commandment, suddenly charged me for my visitation'. He obviously suspected that Leicester had been attacking him to the Queen for overgreat severity. The result was that already 'the Isle of Wight and other places of that diocese be now gone again from their obedience'. Small wonder that he complained 'If this be good policy, secretly to work overthwartly against the Queen's religion stablished by law and Injunction, I will not be partaker of it.'

Even Burghley worried him on the ground that he was not

---

[1] *Correspondence*, p. 476.   [2] *Register*, pp. 1185, 1187–91.
[3] *Correspondence*, p. 478.
[4] Kennedy, *Parker*, p. 279; W. H. Frere, *Visitation Articles and Injunctions*, iii, 374 sqq.

doing all he should for protestants from abroad.[1] Parker suggested that Burghley suffered from 'lack of information', and claimed that he sought to his 'uttermost ability' to help strangers, but that he had done it quietly and without show. Out of his own purse he had given a large portion to French ministers, he had given free entertainment to others. 'I am no gatherer, nor will be, whatsoever they prate abroad . . . I am compelled to borrow every half year before my money cometh in, for my own expenses. Excepting a little money that I have to bury me, I have no superfluity.' Though Parker does not say so, it is evident from the case of Citolini, an Italian, that the refugees were very demanding and easily dissatisfied. The Archbishop had entertained him 'friendly and gently', had given him money and offered to provide him with lodging and necessities of life. 'My Lord of Bedford and himself refused it, as not convenient.' Parker then obtained for him the offer of a prebend in Ely, and invited him, meantime, to go with himself to Kent, but 'he made no grant thereto, but would first commune with you or my lord of Bedford'. Plainly he was a tiresome customer who had won Burghley's ear—though Burghley himself did nothing save grumble at what Parker did! He would not agree to Parker's suggestion of a prebend at Canterbury, and did not send on the advowson of the prebend at Ely,[2] but had to be asked for it. Of course, it all was a trifling business compared with the greater issues at stake: but trifles can be worrying to a sick man, as Parker was at the time.

But the old zeal for learning and education was unabated. He was much concerned that Whitgift should not be interrupted in 1573 in the writing of his *Defence of the Answer*;[3] it duly appeared in 1574. In the same year he had printed by Day Asser's *Life of Alfred* in type specially set out at the Archbishop's expense to

[1] *Correspondence*, pp. 420–1. The letter is assigned to 1573 in the *Correspondence*. But it is endorsed by Burghley as 1575 (Sir H. Ellis, *Original Letters*. Third Series, London 1846, iv, 20).

[2] *Correspondence*, p. 470. Again (as on p. 104 above) 'advowson' is the word used: it should probably be the right to present for a turn.

[3] Ibid., p. 439.

represent the Anglo-Saxon of the original.[1] His benevolence to Cambridge still flowed generously. He presented to the University Library a valuable collection of a hundred books, and Strype records handsome letters of thanks both from the Vice-Chancellor and the University.[2] He was also urgent in securing gifts of books from others, including the Chancellor himself, Burghley.[3] It was in this year, too, that he finally handed over to the University the new approach to the Schools duly walled.[4] There were also further lavish gifts to Corpus, of land left over from the building of the street, and of £500, in return for which they were to be responsible for the upkeep of the new walls, and for the repair of the books given to the University Library.[5] Such practical and businesslike provisions testify no less to the Archbishop's love of his old University than to his unfailing grasp, even to the end, of administrative details despite his failing health and oppressive cares. Perhaps he might have been able to do even more for foreign refugees if he had been less generous in his gifts. But at least they prove the justice of his claim that he was 'no gatherer'.

He died on May 17, 1575, and was buried on June 6th. The funeral, of which Strype gives a full record[6] was of great pomp. Parker had himself prepared the orders for it, according to the *Matthaeus*:[7] that it should have been magnificent was only what he would have thought due to his office. By his own order, his bowels were buried in an urn in the Duke's Chapel in Lambeth church, near his wife; his body in the private chapel at Lambeth. But—again typically—the monument he had prepared for himself was a plain black slab with an inscription by his old friend Walter Haddon.[8]

Parker did not die a poor man. Though in his will he wished his funeral to be 'without pomp or worldly noise and splendour', he yet estimated that the arrangements he outlined for it would

---

[1] *Correspondence*, p. 468. [2] Strype, *Parker* ii, 407–12. [3] *Correspondence*, p. 468.
[4] Strype, *Parker* ii, 406: iii, 327: the actual date of the transfer was 25 January, 1575.
[5] Ibid., ii, 413; cf. iii, 327.   [6] *Parker* ii, 432–4.
[7] Ibid., iii, 307: ibid. 340–1.   [8] Ibid., ii, 434–5.

cost £1,000—in fact, they cost rather more.[1] And there was a great number of legacies—to the Queen an 'ivory tablet of Christ's life and his twelve Apostles' together with such other of his possessions as she desired (no doubt a wise insurance against the upsetting of his will); there were gifts to his successor, to the Archbishop of York and some other bishops; to Cecil and to Bacon and to various friends; to the city of Norwich, to the city of Canterbury for charity, to the poor of Lambeth; to Benet College and Caius and Trinity Hall. Most of these were of plate or other valuables, but there were also legacies of money (besides those to charity or to the colleges) to his son John, to god-children, a grandson and other relatives, to his servants. The total money value of legacies, debts and funeral expenses was over £4,000, apart from his gift to the Queen and one or two other items, and the plate and magnificent collection of manu-scripts and books to Corpus Christi. Of that collection it is impossible here to give an account[2] or to estimate its present value; it is, literally, priceless. Suffice it to say that it consisted of 457 volumes (though, according to his son John, some of them could not even then be found), including not only the highly important *Synodalia* but manuscripts of the Fathers and of mediaeval historians—Matthew Paris and others—and of Saxon writers, Gildas, Asser and the like. All this was additional to his gift to the University in 1574 of twenty-five volumes of manu-scripts, twenty-five volumes printed on vellum and fifty volumes of commentaries on the books of the Bible. His library at its best must have been stupendous. The purchase of the various items and the staff maintained to look after the collection and publish some of it—translators, illustrators, binders—cannot but have been a very heavy annual charge. It was, it would seem, his most treasured possession, and he laid down extremely business-like conditions to see that his books were not dispersed or

[1] His will, directions for his funeral, the value of his legacies etc., are printed by Strype, *Parker* iii, 333–45.
[2] There is a full statement in M. R. James, *The Manuscripts of Corpus Christi College, Cambridge.*

alienated. Once each year the books at Corpus were to be inspected by the Masters of Corpus, Caius and Trinity Hall. Fines were to be paid by the College for each leaf of a manuscript found missing, or for a printed volume. But if six manuscripts, or eight quarto volumes or twelve lesser ones were missing, the whole collection was to be transferred to Caius, on the same conditions, with Trinity Hall as the third beneficiary. Possibly it was these careful conditions laid down by the Archbishop which account for the remarkable preservation of the collection.

There is no evidence that Parker left any large accumulations of money or landed estate; or showed any desire to 'establish' a family. Indeed, of his four sons two had died young, a third died in 1574 and only John survived his father. He was already provided for. Before Mrs. Parker's death, the Archbishop had bought for her, in case she survived him, the Duke's House at Lambeth, and a house at Bekesbourne and one in Cambridge.[1] These, on her death and that of his brother, all passed to John. He was married to a daughter of Cox of Ely—a wealthy and careful bishop—and was the possessor of various estates either by purchase or by way of dowry.[2] He also held various offices, legal and other, connected with the see of Canterbury.[3] As both the succeeding Archbishops continued him in such offices or others, it looks as though he was adequate to them and not just a scandalous case of nepotism. He prospered and was knighted in 1603. But his legacy from his father was small—a mere £150. So also were the few other family legacies. In fact, all the details of his estate support Parker's claim[4] that he was no 'gatherer', and that every half year he had to borrow for his expenses before his money came in. In other words, he lived up to his income instead of hoarding money. But he was not selfish in his spending. Vast sums went on building and repairs at Lambeth and Canterbury; his gifts to Corpus and other colleges, and to the University of Cambridge, were continuous and generous; his

[1] Strype, *Parker* ii, 461.   [2] Ibid., pp. 467–8, 470–2.
[3] Ibid., ii, 468–9.   [4] *Correspondence*, p. 421.

expenditure on his books and their care was great. Such expenses were not for personal comfort or aggrandisement, but for education, learning, or the long-term interests of the see of Canterbury.

His household expenses must also have been heavy, for he lived graciously: the amount of plate and furniture he left is evidence of that. It is shown, too, in the charming account in the *Matthaeus* of his household.[1] It was large and well-ordered and included well-born as well as humble youths, all of whom were trained in some sort of learning or skill. Twice a day all were expected to attend prayers in chapel and were punished if they did not. His chaplains, carefully selected, saw to their instruction. In hall the tables for meals were orderly arranged, and the sitting was such that rank was duly observed. Food was adequate but not excessive: conversation though easy was seemly: any who spoke too loud, or improperly, was instantly ordered to be silent. His own speech was cheerful and witty, and if any were quiet, he tried to draw them out. If the talk turned to the consideration of Scripture or serious topics, he waited till each who wished to do so had contributed his part before giving his own views. It was more like a private academy than a private home. Both by his talk and his own example of moderation and temper, he was engaged even at home in the business he so much loved of training and educating youth. Besides them, he had constantly to entertain those given into his charge by the Council—Romans or others—that he might reason with them.[2] Of his chaplains many gained eminent positions in later life.[3] Such a household, of course, demanded a large staff of servants who were paid, says the *Matthaeus*, better than by any previous Archbishop; and Parker often increased the pay of the more needy or of those who showed special keenness. No wonder that he left little money though there was ample plate and furniture. As the *Matthaeus* points out,[4] his income would not have sufficed for all he did and gave away had there not always been, combined with liberality, caution and carefulness to supply the treasures of his bounty.

[1] Strype, *Parker* iii, 286–7; 300–2.   [2] Ibid., iii, 297–300.
[3] Ibid., ii, 457–60.   [4] Ibid., iii, 300.

Had his own wish for the Mastership of Benet College rather than the Archbishopric been granted, his life would probably have been happier. His love of learning, his passion for education, his administrative powers and orderliness and his businesslike interest in the care of buildings and estates would all have found scope in the Headship of a college. He would, too, have avoided the anxieties and frictions which tormented him—for he was very sensitive. He had, indeed, real grounds for complaint. The Queen was imperious but often failed to give him support when he was carrying out her wishes; Leicester was an open and unscrupulous enemy; even Bacon and, at times, Cecil did not give him the co-operation he had a right to expect; the Puritans were out-rageous in their attacks. All that he would have escaped had he been sent back to Cambridge—and he felt it very deeply. But it was, perhaps, that very sensitiveness, one side of his gentle nature, which above all fitted him for the office which was forced on him.

There can be little doubt that Bacon, Cecil and the Queen were supremely right in their insistence that he should be Archbishop. The model they had in view was a Church Catholic but reformed, its historic roots unsevered, avoiding the errors of Rome (as they thought them) and the excesses of protestantism. But it was, in its day, a novel idea which made little appeal at first to the majority of the nation. If it were really to be brought to fruition, it needed most careful tending. Parker was exactly right for the task, as no other contemporary ecclesiastic was, so far as we can judge. A weak Archbishop would have let things slide into confusion, as Grindal tended to do; one who was too unbending would have hopelessly alienated both Romanists and protestants from the start. The Church would have had no chance to win the support and affection of the nation. But Parker was just right. He really believed, quite passionately, in the sort of Church which was envisaged—dignified, preserving continuity with the past, maintaining all that seemed essential to Catholicity while shedding mediaeval accretions. He was gentle and conciliatory in dealing with critics either on the right hand

or the left. He laboured all he could to correct abuses and to
raise the standard of the clergy. And he was eminently one whose
character commanded respect—without guile or duplicity, humble
and without self-seeking or love of money; mild and conciliatory
yet unyielding where he thought principles were concerned,
even to standing up against Bacon or the Queen herself; honest
and dominated by a real love of justice; the trouble he often took
to secure fair dealing for quite lowly folk is striking. It is not easy
to imagine a man better suited to nurse the Elizabethan Church
in its early and perilous days. He deserves from all Anglicans a
greater measure of gratitude than he sometimes receives.

INDEX

Admonition to the Parliament, An, 285–9, 301, 304, 308.

Advertisements, The, 166–8, 184–90, 223.

Aldrich, Thomas, Master of Corpus, Cambridge, 234, 306–8.

Allen, William, 210–11.

Alley, William, Bishop of Exeter, 87, 134.

Anabaptists, 100, 103, 132, 133, 215, 218, 219, 222.

Andrewes, Lancelot, 109.

Answer for the time being to the Examination, An, 199.

Answer to the Admonition, 293.

Apology, The, Jewel's 96, 121.

Arthur, Thomas, Principal of St. Mary's Hostel, Cambridge, 9, 12.

Articles for Government and Order in the Church, 139.

Articles, The Eleven, 105–6, 107, 130, 167.

Articles, The *Thirty-nine,* 130–6, 141, 167, 208–9, 264–5 (limited subscription), 267, 274, 275, 276.

Articles, Latin, (1560–1) 103.

Augsburg Confession, The, 96.

Aylmer, John, Archdeacon of Lincoln, 110, 298–9.

Bacon, Lady, translation of Jewel's *Apologia,* 152–3.

Bacon, Nicholas, Lord Keeper, 49, 52, 60, 65–66, 67, 68, 170, 227–8, 257, 281, 341.

Bale, John, Bishop of Ossory, 53, 84, 150, 154.

Baptism, 132, 134–5, 137, 138, 190, 223.

Barlow, William, Bishop of Chichester, 76, 84–85, 87.

Barnes, Richard, 9, 10, 11, 12.

Bentham, Thomas, Bishop of Lichfield and Coventry, 58, 87.

Berkeley, Gilbert, Bishop of Bath and Wells, 87.

Best, John, Bishop of Carlisle, 88, 122.

Beza, Theodore, consulted by Sampson and Humphrey, 201, 203–4, 288.

Bible, The Bishops', 179–80, 246–9, 268, 269.

Bible, Geneva, 121, 179, 246 n., 249.

Bible, The Great, 121, 248.

Bill, Dr William, Master of Trinity, Cambridge, 50.

Bilney, Thomas, 6–9, 12.

Bodley, John, 179, 246 n.

Bonham, William, 333.

Bonner, Edmund, Bishop of London, 69–70, 95, 147–8, 157–8, 206, 210.

Book of Common Prayer, (of 1549), 45–46; (of 1559), 62–63, 132; Puritan attitude to, 202, 264, 274, 276, 282–3, 287. See under *The Ordinal.*

Bourne, Gilbert, Bishop of Bath and Wells, 95.

Boxall, Dr John, 75, 147–8.

Brief Discourse against the Outward Apparel and Ministring Garments of the Popish Church, A, 196–7.

Brief examination for the time of a certain Declaration, A, 197–8.

Browne, Nicholas, Fellow of Trinity, Cambridge, 303.

Bucer, Martin, 42–48, 50, 170, 198, 201.

Bullinger, Henry, 44, 98, 172, 178; letter to Sampson and Humphrey published, 200–1; 204; answers, bull of excommunication, 256.

Bullingham, Nicholas, Bishop of Lincoln and, later, of Worcester, 87, 90, 166, 238.

Caius, Dr John, Master of Caius College, 245.

Calvin, John, 44, 97, 278, 335.

Cambridge; reform movement, 5–11; Gardiner as Chancellor, 29–31, 32–34; royal visitation, 40; Queens' College, 67; further royal visitation, 75; disorders, 172–7; Corpus Christi College, 232–4; general condition, 234; Cartwright's lectures, 257–9; disturbances and new statutes, 259–60, 297; Presbyterian movement, 302–3; Aldrich and the ecclesiastical commission, 306–8; Parker's gifts, 280, 340, 341 and legacies, 341.

Campion, Edmund, 294.

Canons of 1571, The, 267–71, 273, 277.

Canterbury: visitation, 92, 94; palace repaired, 142–3; cathedral usage, 165, and plate, 241–2; Parker's visitations, 252–4 and, in person, 319–22; Eastbridge Hospital, 243, 322; Parker's legacy for poor, 341.

Cartwright, Thomas, Fellow of Trinity and Margaret Lecturer at Cambridge, 234–5; his lectures and their effect, 257–9; 289, 290, 292–3, 297, 302, 308, 312, 334, 336.

Catechism, The, by Nowell, 136–7.

Cecil, William, later Lord Burghley; Secretary of State and Chancellor of Cambridge, 49, 65–66, 67, 81, 109, 117–18, 146, 153, 158, 159, 162, 166, 169, 172, 175, 176, 179, 185, 192, 203, 233–4, 241, 256, 259–60, 261–2, 263, (Lord Burghley), 273, 284, 295, 297, 300, 301, 303, 307, 309, 314–16, 317, 322–3, 330, 335, 337, 338–9, 339, 341.

Ceremonies, 132, 134, 135, 282–3.

Chancels to be clearly separated, 119.

Chark, William Fellow of Peterhouse, 302–3.

Chatterton, William, Fellow of Queens' College, Cambridge, attacks Cox, 335.

Cheke, Sir John, 32, 49.

Cheyne, Richard, Bishop of Gloucester, 87, 271–2.

Christopherson, John, Bishop of Chichester, 57.

Citolini, Alexander, an awkward foreign refugee, 339.

Clergy, at beginning of Elizabeth's reign, 88–89; 92–93; 101–2; 117; London clergy, 185–6; Parker tries to improve standards, 221–2, 223–4, 268; Norwich clergy, 224; three Fellows of Merton to be in Orders, 232; Act to control holding of benefices and for subscription to the *Articles,* 265; the Canons of 1571, 267–72.

Clerical courts, 112–14, 237, 300–1.

Clerical habits, 63, 73, 98, 136, 138, 139, 167–8, 170, 173, 174, 183,

189, 190, 194-5, 196, 200, 261, 270, 287.

Clerical matrimony, 52-54, 83, 117-19, 131, 142, 281.

Clerical privilege, 112.

Clerk, Dr Bartholomew, 295-6, 315-16, 319, 321.

Cole, Dr Henry, Dean of St Paul's, 331.

Commission, the ecclesiastical, 64, 74, 102, 125, 126, 220, 229-30, 231, 232, 233-4, 238, 260, 273, 300, 307-8, 310-11, 312.

Communion, 137, 140, 167, 170; rules about reception, 188, 189, 223, 269; kneeling for reception, 137, 189; as a test 261-3; Parker's views about communion bread, 261-2, 327.

'Concealers', 240-1.

Consultation, The, of Hermann, 45.

Convocation:
1559—strenuously Roman, 59;
1563—Thirty-Nine Articles; discipline matters; extreme proposals defeated, 129-41;
1571—revision of the Articles; Canons, 266-72;
1572—committee to suggest needed reforms, 285.

Cook, Sir Anthony, 117.

Cooper, Thomas, Bishop of Lincoln, 279, 289, 293, 298-9, 301-2, 318, 330.

Corpus Christi College (Benet Hall), Cambridge, 2-4, 12, 13, 23-27, 36, 40, 130, 173, 232-4, 281, 306-8, 341-2.

Corranus, Anthony, 335.

Cotton —, An absconding papist, 294.

Council, The, tries to suppress illicit books, 199; examines Lancashire

Romanists, 211, 213; requires J.P.s to take an oath to observe the Uniformity Act, 213-14; orders suppression of conventicles, 216; chides the bishops, 220-1; 245; suspicious of Romanists, 257, 260; tries to control elections to Parliament, 263; acts in favour to Field and Wilcox, 301-2, 304; 305-6; orders bishops to enforce Act of Uniformity, 310-11; intervenes frequently, but on no clear principles, 331-3.

Coverdale, Miles, sometime Bishop of Exeter, 84-85, 99, 201, 215.

Cox, Richard, Bishop of Ely, 76, 79, 80, 87, 101, 108, 118, 161, 166, 179, 197, 238, 246 and n., 273, 277, 291, 295, 297, 303, 311, 334, 335.

Cranmer, Thomas, Archbishop, 37-38, 42, 43, 48, 49, 60, 150, 198, 201.

Crowley, Robert, 191, 193, 194, 196.

Culpepper —, a suspected Romanist, 220.

Curteys, Richard, Bishop of Chichester, 251, 252.

Davys, Richard, Bishop of St Asaph, and later St Davids, 87, 179, 180.

Day, John, printer, 296, 310, 330.

Day, William, Provost of Eton, 136.

De Antiquitate Britannicae Ecclesiae, 322-5.

Declaration of Doctrine offered and exhibited by the protestants to the Queen, 130.

Declaration of the Queen's Proceedings since her Reign, 256-7.

Defence of the Answer, 293.

Derby, Earl of, 332.

Dering, Edward, 274, 295-6, 305-6, 311.

De Visibili Monarchia Ecclesiae, 295–6.

Disciplina Ecclesiae Sacra ex Dei Verbo descripta, 334.

Discipline, 136; 138 (of laity); suggestions in 1563, 140; 141.

Disorders in 1565, 164–6.

Disputation, the, of 1559, 60–61, 67.

Downham, William, Bishop of Chester, 88, 332.

Durham, 250.

Elizabeth, Queen, attitude to Mrs Parker, 37; her popularity, 55; religious conservatism, 58–59; financial concession to the church, 77; her attitude to the bishops, 81, 87; deals with neglect of churches, 101; dines with Parker, 115; acts for re-building of St Paul's, 115–17; angry at clerical inadequacy, 117; forbids women and children in cathedral and college precincts, 118; order about chancels and fonts, 119; entertainment of French Ambassador, 114; strong letter about disorders, 162–4, but refuses to sign corrective orders drawn up by the bishops, 168; snubs Nowell, 166; urges action against disorders but refuses open support, 183–4, 186; irritation with Parliament of 1566, 206; vetoes bills about religion and blames the bishops, 208–9; unsuitable use of patronage, 239; Excommunication, 256; her *Declaration* of policy, 256–7, refusing to examine consciences; rejects bill to enforce communion, 264; quashes Puritan efforts in Parliament, 264–5; strong letter to Parker about disorders, 276–7; crushes attack on *Prayer Book,* 285; Romanist hostility, 294; the case of Aldrich, 307; orders bishops to enforce the Uniformity Act, 310; relations with the archbishop, and the matter of Clerk, 315–16; visit to Canterbury, 316–19; Orders suppression of prophesyings, 328; firm against Puritans, 336; seems hostile to Parker, 336–7; Parker's legacy, 341.

Erasmus, New Testament, 5, 6; *Praise of Folly,* 8.

Eton College, visited, 117.

Excommunication, Bull of, publication and effect, 255–6, 264.

Exeter, troubles at, 110–11.

Exhortation to the Bishops to answer a little book, 289.

Exhortation to the Bishops to deal brotherly with their brethren, 289.

Feckenham, John, Abbot of Westminster, 332.

Field, John, 274, 289, 290, 301–2.

Fonts to be kept and used, 119.

Foxe, John, 121, 182, 248, 268.

Frankfort, Troubles at, 334.

Frankfort, usages of English refugees at, 195.

Freake, Edmund, Bishop of Rochester, later of Norwich, 318, 329.

Fulke, William, 234.

Full and Plain Declaration of Ecclesiastical Discipline, 334.

Gardiner, George, 225–6, 325–6.

Gardiner, Stephen, Bishop of Winchester and Chancellor of Cambridge, 28–31, 34, 52, 53, 109.

German protestants, relations with, 96–97.

Gilby, Anthony, 277.

Goodman, Christopher, 274, 275.

Goodman, Gabriel, Dean of Westminster, 161.

Grafton, Richard, printer, 245.

Greek, study of in Cambridge and Oxford, 5; pronunciation of, 29.

Grey, Lady Catherine, 120–1.

Grey, Lady Mary, 244.

Grindal, Edmund, Bishop to London and Archbishop of York, 76, 79, 87, 90, 91, 98, 108, 112, 117, 120, 136, 146–7, 158, 159, 161, 166, 168–9, 170, 179, 183–4; 186, (non-co-operative), 192: begins to support Parker, 194, 199; 200; deals with London separatists, 214–18; 252 (Archbishop of York), 277, 291, 297, 312, 318, 319, 332, 334, 335, 338.

Guest, Richard, Bishop of Rochester, 87, 161.

Haddon, Dr Walter, Master of Trinity Hall Cambridge and President of Magdalen, Oxford; Master of Requests to Queen Elizabeth, 17, 49, 340.

Hardyman, Dr John, 235–6.

Harrison, Robert, a dissenting schoolmaster, 326.

Heath, Nicholas, Archbishop of York, 59, 60, 95, 105, 210.

Henry VIII, breach with Rome, 14; his conservative policy, 20; his care for learning, 33–34.

Heydon, William, 330.

Hodgkin, John, Suffragan Bishop of Bedford, 84–85.

Horne, Robert, Bishop of Winchester, 72, 87, 117, 122, 158, 159, 161, 166, 171, 177, 218, 219, 298, 332, 338.

Hovenden, Robert, Warden of All Souls, 297–8.

How Superior Powers ought to be obeyed, 274–5.

Howard, Henry, 296.

Humphrey, Lawrence, President of Magdalen, Oxford, 122, 159–62, 170–2; consults Bullinger, 200, and Beza, 201; replies to Bullinger, 201–2, 217, 291.

Hutton, Matthew, Archbishop of York, 175.

Incent, John, Archbishop's Registrar, 86, 92.

Injunctions, the Royal, 1559, 72–74, 262.

Interpretations and Further Considerations, 102–5, 106, 107, 167–8.

Jewel, John, Bishop of Salisbury, 51, 60, 72, 79, 87, 92, 95; Challenge Sermon and Apology, 95–96, 121, 295; 98, 108, 134, 152, 159, 171, 220, 256, 267, 277.

Johnson, Robert, a stubborn Puritan, 275–6.

Joscelyn, John, secretary to the Archbishop, 2 n. 245, 323.

Kett's rebellion, 38–40.

Keyes, Thomas, married to Lady Mary Grey, 244.

Kitchin, Anthony, Bishop of Llandaff, 69, 84.

Knollys, Sir Francis, Vice-Chamberlain of the Royal Household, 78.

Lancashire, 210–11, 250.

Latimer, Hugh, Bishop of Worcester, 9–10, 11, 20.

Leicester, Robert Dudley, Earl of, 169, 170, 178, 181, 244, 300–1, 301, 315, 335, 336.

Lever, Thomas, Master of St Johns', Cambridge, 50, 99, 215, 217, 274.

Life of Alfred, Asser's, 339.

Luther, Martin, 5–6, 10, 44, 131.

Man, John, Warden of Merton College, 230.

Manchester College, 242.

Martyr, Peter, 43–44, 79–80, 97, 98, 170, 198, 201.

Mary, Queen of Scots, 220, 264, 265, 280, 281, 293.

May, Dr John, Dean of St Paul's, 40, 88.

Melanchthon, Philip, 44, 201.

Meyrick, Edmund, Bishop of Bangor, 87.

Mullins, John, Archdeacon of London, 262, 302.

Nevinson, Stephen, 149.

Norfolk, Parker's loyalty to, 26–27; his concern for, 325, 327–30.

Norfolk, Duke of, 182, 210, 281, 282.

Northampton Model, The, 278–90, 330.

Northern Rebellion, The, 250, 251, 264.

Nowell, Alexander, Dean of St. Paul's, 130, 136, 137, 162, 169, 182.

Norwich, the Chapel in the Fields, 4; Norwich Scholars, 26; 341.

Norwich Diocese, abuses in, 109, 117; Parker's visitation in 1567, 222–7; state of the cathedral, 225–7, 325; irregularities and discontent, 326–7; prophesying, 327–30; Parker has trouble with the Dean and Chapter, 338.

Offendicle, The, 78–80, 115, 263.

Order of Communion, The, 45.

Ordinal, The, 81–84, 158, 206–8.

Ornaments Rubric, 62–63, 77, 79–80, 262.

Oxford, New College, 71; Merton, 123–4, 230–2; All Souls, 124, 229–30; Sampson and Humphrey, 170–2; disloyalty and unrest, 122; long vacancy of see, 244.

Pammachius, The, 28–31.

Parker, John, Son of Matthew, 342.

Parker, Margaret, wife of Matthew, 36–37, 254–5.

Parker, Matthew, Archbishop.

Birth and ancestry, 1; early education, 1–2; student life at Cambridge and ordination, 2–5; his relations with reformers, 12; and with Anne Boleyn, 15; rapid promotion, and Dean of Stoke-by-Clare, 16–22; unfairly attacked, 19; Master of Corpus, Cambridge, 23–28; Vice-Chancellor of Cambridge and trouble with Gardiner, 28–31; his care for the University, 32–34; his preferments, 34; deprived of Stoke-by-Clare, but made prebendary and Dean of Lincoln, 36.

Marriage and family, 36–37; Kett's Rebellion, 38–40; University business, 40–41; friendship with Bucer, 42, 47–48; used by the Council, 47–48; his eminent friends, 48–49.

Obscurity under Mary, 51–52; a translation of the Psalms and a defence of clerical matrimony, 52–54;

Under Elizabeth, sought to avoid

Parker, Matthew, Archbishop.—*cont.*
high office, 65–66, 68; nominated and elected Archbishop, 68; dealings with Tunstall, 70–71, and with recusants, 75; visitor of Cambridge and Eton, 74–75; protest against the *Offendicle*, 78–80; Consecration, 81–86.

Concern for the Northern Province, 88; early ordinations, 89–90; metropolitan visitation and articles, 91–94; attitude to foreign protestants, 97; attempts to impress order—*Interpretations and Further Considerations*; *Resolutions and orders*, 100–8; troubles at Exeter, 100–1, with Sandys, 111–12, with clerical courts, 114.

Urges the Queen to marry, 115; much upset by her exclusion of women and children from cathedrals and colleges, 118–19; trial of Lady Catherine Grey, 120–1; visits Merton and All Souls, 123–4; care for hospitals, 126; checks harsh use of Supremacy oath, 129.

Thirty-Nine Articles, 130–5; his views of fellow bishops, 135; suggestions for discipline, 136.

Repairs palace at Canterbury and entertains, 142–3; his household, 143; visit of French Ambassador and the *Via Media*, 144; visits his diocese, 145, and is alarmed at the state of the country, 146, 149; his views on special services, 146–7; put in charge of Romanists, 147–8, but refuses a disputation, 153–4.

Matrimonial cases, 155; Humphrey and Sampson, 160–2; a sharp letter from the Queen, 162–4; first draft of the *Advertisements*, 166–8; royal support not given, 168–9; Humphrey and Sampson, 170–2, George Withers, 172–4, restlessness at Cambridge, 174–7; Parker's difficulties, 178.

Plans the *Bishops' Bible*, 179; the Welsh dioceses, 180–1; protestant refugees, 181–2.

Pressed by the Queen who will not openly support, 183; with Grindal, reviews the London clergy, 184–6; the *Advertisements*, 187–90; disturbances in London, 191–5; answers Puritan pamphlet, 197–8, and urges the Council to act, 199.

Fears Queen's friendliness with Romanists 210; tries to deal with Romanist lawyers, 214, alarmed by Romanist troubles, 220, but blamed by the Council, 220–1; ordered to keep an eye on foreign refugees, 219.

Aims at improvement of clerical standards, 221–2; the Norwich visitation, 222–7 and quarrel with Bacon, 227–8; Merton and All Souls again, 229–32, and Corpus, Cambridge, 232–4; concerned about condition of Cambridge, 234–6.

Licensing of schoolmasters and midwives, 236; dispensations 236–7; Court of Faculties, 237, and risk of forgeries, 237, 241; wants a new ecclesiastical commission, 238.

Difficulties with bishops, 238; protects the rights of his see, 239; Eastbridge Hospital, 242;

Parker, Matthew, Archbishop.—*cont.*
care for vacant dioceses, 244.
The *Bishops' Bible*, 246-9; lavish
entertaining at Canterbury, 251-
2; visits his cathedral, 252-4;
death of Mr Parker, 254-5.
Alarmed by massing, 260; warns
the Queen against Presbyteri-
ans, 261; justifies use of wafer-
bread, 261-2; warns Cecil against
precisians, 262-3; is unjustly
attacked, 263; dispute with
Wentworth, 264; Cheney, 271.
Refusal of royal assent to the
Canons, 273; trials of Puritans,
274-6; seeks action against
Romanists in Inns of Court,
276.
The Queen strongly backs Parker
against disorders, 276-7; he
presses Grindal, 277, and tries
to enforce the *Canons* reasonably,
277; advises Parkhurst, 277-8.
Parker's distress, 284; action
against the *Admonition* fails,
289, 292; sets Whitgift to
answer it, 292; alarmed about
papists, urges Parkhurst to deal
with one, examines their writings, 293-6.
Approves new statutes for Cambridge, 297, prepares statutes
for new cathedrals, 297, opposes
breach of statutes at All
Souls, 297-8; arbitrates between the Bishop of Lincoln and
the Archdeacon, 298-9, and in
the case of Dr Willoughby, 299-
300; a difficult matrimonial
case and disagreement with
Leicester, 300-1.
Alarmed by growth of Puritanism
and urges Burghley to act, 303-
5; upset that Council acts without consulting bishops, and
urges Burghley again, 305-6;
the case of Aldrich, 306-8;
doubts about Burghley's policy,
310; orders the bishops to enforce conformity, 310; troubles
with the Council, 311; rebuts
charges of show and extravagance, and lists his expenses,
312-13; defends Faculty Court
and regulates Arches, 313.
Intimacy with Burghley but feels
estranged from the Queen, 315;
opposes her about Dr Clerk,
315-16; her visit to Canterbury
and his hospitality, 316-19; he
visits his cathedral, 319-22;
vindicates Eastbridge Hospital,
322.
The *De Antiquitate* and Parker's
view of the origin of the English
Church, and of the status and
rights of the Archbishop, 321-5;
Concern for Norwich and Norfolk, 325-6; dealings with Parkhurst, 326-30; prophesyings in
Norfolk, 327-30; alarmed by a
supposed plot, 352-3; Travers'
Ecclesiastical Discipline, 334;
re-assures Grindal about state of
London, 334-5, and defends
Cox, 335.
Alarmed by Puritan activity, 335-
6; depressed and estranged from
the Queen, 336-7; dispute with
Norwich chapter, 338; visits
Winchester diocese, 338; rejects accusation of greed, 339;
death and burial, 340-1; his
legacies and library, 341-2; his
household, 343, and character,
343-5.

Parker, Matthew, Archbishop.—cont.
    Interest in Antiquities, 141 n., 149–
        50, 154, 180, 245, 321–5,
        340.
    Concern about church property, 50,
        76–77, 108–10, 140, 239–42, 301.
    Love of building, 18, 24–25, 142–
        3, 280–1, 314–15.
    Generosity, 23–28, 220, 280, 316–
        19, 339, 340–1.
    Kindliness, 245–7, 294–6, 299–
        300.
    Poor health, 193, 208, 243, 246,
        266, 301, 311–12, 323, 336.
    Preaching, 15, 18, 38, 323.
        See also 'Schools'.
Parkhurst, John, Bishop of Norwich,
    80, 87, 108, 117, 125, 134, 179,
    181–2, 222, 226, 241, 277–8, 280,
    294, 295 n., 308, 326–7; Norwich
    prophesyings, 327–30.
Parliament:
    1559–58–65, 83;
    1563—concern for Queen's au-
        thority and marriage, 127–9,
        and for clerical incomes, 136;
    1566—the Ordinal, bills about re-
        ligion, royal interference, 206–9;
    1571—strong Puritan element; bill
        to enforce church attendance
        and annual reception of com-
        munion, which the Queen re-
        jected; Puritan attempts quash-
        ed by the Queen; Acts to con-
        trol Succession to the Throne,
        to control abuses of leases of
        benefices, for signature of the
        Articles in limited form; and
        anti-Roman measures, 263–6.
    1572—Attack on Uniformity Act
        crushed by the Queen, 282–5.
    Uniformity Act (1559), 61–63.
    Supremacy Act (1559), 64.

    For exchange of episcopal pro-
        perty, 64.
    For assurance of the Queen's
        Power (1563), 128.
    For Maintenance of the Navy
        (1563), 128.
    Confirming the Ordinal (1566),
        206–8.
    To reform disorders in the Min-
        istry and for signing the Articles
        (1571), 265–6.
    To control succession to the
        Throne (1571) 265.
Pates, Richard, Bishop of Worcester,
    95.
Paul's Cross, sermons at 57, 98, 170;
    Presbyterian preachers at, 308–9.
Pearson, Andrew, 154.
Pembroke, Earl of, 181.
Penance, 135.
Perambulation of Kent, by William
    Lambard, 317, 322.
Perne, Andrew, Master of Peter-
    house, 293.
Pilkington, James, Bishop of Durham,
    87, 88, 151, 160, 169, 291.
Pius V, Pope, 211; Bull of Ex-
    communication, 255–6.
Poole, David, Bishop of
    Peterborough, 95.
Pory, John, Master of Corpus
    Christi, Cambridge, 232, 234.
Preaching Licences, 102, 167, 173–
    4, 189, 268, 273.
Presbyterian Movement, The, Cart-
    wright's lead in Cambridge, 257–
    9; relation to older Puritanism,
    260; An Admonition to the Parlia-
    ment, 285–9; 291; growing in
    Cambridge, 302–3; Dering, 305;
    Aldrich, 306–8; preachers at the
    Cross, 308–9; Travers' Ecclesi-
    astical Discipline, 334.

Presence, the Real, 43–44, 62–63, 97, 131–2, 133, 134, 141 n.

Proclamations:
Forbidding preaching (1558), 58.
Communion in both kinds (1559), 59.
against defacing images, 100.
against Anabaptists, 100.
against excess of lay apparel, 183.
for Uniformity, 183.
against heretical refugees, 218.
against rebels from the Low Countries, 219.
against 'concealers' 241.
against seditious books, 260.
against traitorous books and speeches, 260.
against absentees from church, 304.
for enforcement of the Act of Uniformity, 309.

Prophesyings, 278, 279–80, 326; in Norwich diocese, 327–30.

Protestants—secret meetings under Queen Mary, 58; excesses in London, 71, 77–78; discontent, 98, 137–9, 159; open disobedience, 185–6, 191–4; bills in Parliament of 1566, 208–9.

Protestant refugees, 181–2, 218–20, 280.

Psalm singing, 110–11, 137, 278.

Puritan Movement, The, pamphleteering, 196–9; points of dissatisfaction, 201–3; many in London, 215–16; alarmed by Ridolfi Plot, 281, 291; influential friends, 301, great activity 332, and literary output, 334; the Queen firmly against, 336.

Readers, 90–91, 102, 168.

Reformatio legum ecclesiasticarum, 135, 264.

Reply to the Answer, 293.

Resolutions and Orders of the Bishops (1561), 106–8, 115, 167–8.

Rich, Richard, 109.

Ridley, Nicholas, Bishop of London, 28, 34, 37, 38, 48.

Ridolfi Plot, The, 280, 296.

Robinson, Nicholas, Bishop of Bangor, 181.

Rochdale, rectory and school, 151–2.

Rochester, Visitation of, 92, 94–95.

Romanist bishops, 69–71, 95–96, 124, 210, 331–2.

Romanists, many in Bath and Wells, 95; trouble with, 121–2, 124–6; in Lancashire, Wales, York, London, 210–14; suspect after Bull of Excommunication, 257; increasing boldness, 293–4, 331, 332.

Sacraments, The, 131, 134, 189–90.

St Bartholomew, Massacre of, 293.

St Paul's Cathedral, burning of, 115–17; order for seemly behaviour there, and in other churches, 119.

Sampson, Thomas, Dean of Christ Church, Oxford, 98, 122, 136, 159–62, 170–2; consults Bullinger, 200, and Beza, 201; replies to Bullinger, 201–2; 215, 217, 274, 275, 291, 332.

Sanders, Nicholas, 295.

Sandwich, 145, School at, 150.

Sandys, Edwin, Bishop of Worcester and of London, 50, 63, 67, 72, 79, 87, 111–12, 122, 134, 159, 179, 252, (Bishop of London), 274, 277, 297, 305, 308–9, 329.

Scambler, Edmund, Bishop of Peterborough, 58, 87, 278, 330.

Schools, Parker's concern for, 18, 93; at Sandwich, 150; at Tunbridge, 150–1; at Rochdale, 151–2; at Eastbridge Hospital, 243; at Canterbury, 321; at Aylsham, 326.
Scory, John, Bishop of Hereford, 76, 84–85, 87, 90, 91, 95, 121–2, 238.
Scott, William, Bishop of Chester, 148.

Second Admonition to the Parliament, A, 289–90, 301, 302.
Separatism, Plumbers' Hall and other meetings, 214–18, 313.
Simony, 108–9, 135, 136, 222, 227, 270.
Smith, Thomas, 32.
Smyth, Dr, Reader of Divinity at Oxford, 75.
Southworth, Sir John, 213.
Sowode (or Soud), William, Master of Benet Hall, 9, 12.
Stafford, George, 9–10, 12.
Stonden, –, 333.
Strickland, William, 263, 264.
Stoke-by-Clare, College of St John the Baptist, 16–18, 21, 35–36.
Supremacy oath, The, refusals to take, 71; administered by the ecclesiastical commission, 74; 168; administered by the bishops, 207–8.

Testimony of Antiquity, A, 141 n.
Thirlby, Thomas, Bishop of Ely, 38, 49, 95, 147–8, 210.
Tonbridge School, 150–1.
Travers, Walter, 334.
Tunstall, Cuthbert, Bishop of Durham, 59, 70.
Turberville, James, Bishop of Exeter, 95.

Undertree, –, a supposed conspirator, 333.

Varieties in the service and administration used, 165–6.
Vaux, Laurence, 211.
View of Popish abuses yet remaining in the English Church, A, 286, 287–8.
Visitation Articles, 92–94, 145–6.
Visitation, the Royal, 1559, 71–74, 102.

Waad, Armagil, on state of England, 56.
Wake, Arthur, Canon of Christ Church, Oxford, 308–9.
Walker, –, a Puritan preacher at Norwich, 227, 274, 275.
Wandsworth Presbytery, 290–1.
Warner, John, Warden of All Souls, 123–4.
Watson, Thomas, Bishop of Lincoln, 61, 95, 148, 158, 210, 331–2.
Wentworth, Peter, 263, 264.
Westcott, B. F., 246 n., 247 n., 249 n.
Whether it be mortal sin to transgress civil laws which be the command of civil magistrates, 201.
White, John, Bishop of Winchester, 57, 61.
Whitgift, John, Master of Trinity, Cambridge, later Archbishop of Canterbury, 175, 259, 260, 266, 285, 292–3, 297, 315, 339.
Winchester College, 182.
Whittingham, William, Dean of Durham, 160, 246 n., 277, 334.
Wilcox, Thomas, 289, 290, 301–2.
Willoughby, Doctor, 299–300.

Withers, George, 172–4, 232.
Wood, Henry, Fellow of All Souls, Oxford, 297–8.
Wyburn, Percival, 261 n., 274.

Yale, Thomas, Vicar-General to the Archbishop, 300.

Yorkshire, 250.
Young, Thomas, Bishop of St David's 87; Archbishop of York, 88, 105.

Zwingli, Ulric, 44, 132.